A HISTORY OF
THE BRICK PRESBYTERIAN CHURCH
IN THE CITY OF NEW YORK

THE BRICK CHURCH ON BEEKMAN STREET
From an oil painting in the possession of the church

A HISTORY

OF THE

BRICK PRESBYTERIAN CHURCH

IN THE CITY OF NEW YORK

BY

SHEPHERD KNAPP

"Inquire, I pray thee, of the former age, and prepare thyself to the search of their fathers. . . . Shall not they teach thee and tell thee, and utter words out of their heart?"—Job 8 : 8, 10.

"The Brick Presbyterian Church has, from its origin, occupied a position sufficienty prominent to justify, even in the eyes of the men of the world, some historical notices, which may perhaps be viewed with interest by others as well as ourselves." —Gardiner Spring, 1856, *Brick Church Memorial*, p. 7.

NEW YORK
PUBLISHED BY THE TRUSTEES OF
THE BRICK PRESBYTERIAN CHURCH
1909

To

MY MOTHER AND FATHER,

TO WHOM I OWE

MY HERITAGE IN THE OLD BRICK CHURCH,

AND ALL MY LARGEST OPPORTUNITIES

AND WORTHIEST AMBITIONS,

IN LOVING MEMORY

I DEDICATE

THIS BOOK.

PREFACE

THIS history has been prepared, at the request of the trustees of the Brick Church, in the hope that it will interest the large number of people who are bound to the church by ties of the past or of the present, and those, also, whose interest in the history of the Christian Church at large will incline them to an examination of any important chapter of it.

The author wishes, especially, that the volume might come into the hands of some of the young men who are about to choose among the various professions for their life-work, for it seems to him that a history like that of the Brick Church sets forth in an emphatic way the great opportunity which the Christian ministry offers in our time. The author has himself been so much impressed, as the facts of the history have unfolded before him, by the variety of interests with which he has been called upon to deal, the breadth of scope which the history has presented, and the close relation which it has disclosed, especially in the record of later years, between the specific work of the minister and some of the problems which most perplex our time and whose solution will most profoundly affect the future of our country and of the world, that he cannot doubt but others will be impressed in the same way.

A word should be said by way of explaining the

vii

very brief account, given in the following pages, of
the early years of Presbyterianism in New York
City. Although technically the Brick Church represents, not an offshoot from the original Presbyterian
Church of New York, but an integral part of it as it
existed until the division in 1809, so that the whole
history from 1706, in full detail, might without im-
propriety be included in the present work, it has
seemed proper to take as a beginning the building of
the first "Brick Church," and to leave the history of
the earlier years to be recorded more fully by some
future historian of "The Old First Church," which,
at the division, was created out of the congregation
worshipping in the older edifice on Wall Street.

It will be noticed by the reader as he proceeds,
that there are many quotations for which no references are given. These are drawn from the manuscript minutes of the church, and it has seemed unnecessary to burden the pages with references to
sources not accessible to the public, especially as the
date of the event or declaration will serve to mark its
place in the records almost as well as would an indication of the volume and the page.

A key to the abbreviated titles of the works most
frequently quoted in the notes will be found at the
beginning of the Bibliography.* A Chronology is
given in an Appendix.† The personal records of
the church from 1809 to the present, including
marriages, baptisms, members, etc.—some ten thousand entries in all—are published in alphabetical
order in a companion volume.

* Page 497.
† Appendix A, p. 513.

The author is glad of this opportunity to acknowledge the invariable kindness of the persons to whom he has turned for help in the preparation of this volume, and especially of Mr. Charles H. Olmstead, clerk of session of the Old First Church, for courteous permission to use the ancient records in his custody; of Mr. Daniel Parish, Jr., the Rev. G. McPherson Hunter, the Rev. Theo. F. Burnham and Mr. Austin B. Keep, all of whom have opened to the author valuable sources of information; of the officers of the New York Historical Society for permission to copy documents and pictures; of the Rev. George S. Webster, D.D., for placing at the author's disposal a large amount of material collected during many years, relating to the old and new churches of the Covenant; of Mrs. Samuel B. Jones, whose love for the Brick Church has led her to save for many years every allusion to it in the magazines and the daily press, and whose kindness in giving her whole collection to be incorporated into the Brick Church Historical Scrap-book has provided many important side-lights upon the events of the last three pastorates; and of the present clerk of the session, Mr. Hamilton Odell, who placed in the author's hands the notes made some years ago with a view to preparing a historical sketch of the church, and whose monumental service in keeping, with the utmost accuracy, and in his own exquisite hand, the session records for almost forty-five years, places not only the present author but the whole church under a great obligation. Nor ought gratitude to remain unexpressed for the services performed by those who now rest from their labors. Among the men who, in the past, have patiently kept those records, without which no detailed history of the Brick Church could have been written, ought to be mentioned Mr. Daniel J. Holden, who acted as clerk of the trustees for nearly twenty years, and Mr. Thomas Egleston, who served in the same capacity for full that time, while old Mr. Horace Holden, faithful in all he undertook, was clerk of session for almost twice as long.

The author takes a peculiar pleasure in recording that his mother, who lived to read only the first few pages of this history, collected for him some of the most interesting material included in the two chapters which deal with the period immediately before and during the Revolutionary War.

SHEPHERD KNAPP.

NEW YORK, *March* 16*th*, 1908.

TABLE OF CONTENTS

PART ONE: IN THE OLDEN TIME

xi

CONTENTS

CONTENTS

PART TWO: THE LONG PASTORATE

CONTENTS

CONTENTS

CONTENTS

PART THREE: THE MODERN PERIOD

CONTENTS

CONTENTS

LIST OF ILLUSTRATIONS

PART I

IN THE OLDEN TIME

CHAPTER I

THE PRESBYTERIANS ON WALL STREET: 1706–1765

"And from thence [we came] to Philippi, which is the chief city of that part of Macedonia, and a colony: and we were in that city abiding certain days."—*The Acts* 16 : 12.

"When we came to York,* we had not the least intention or design of preaching, but stopped at York purely to pay our respects to the Governor, which we did; but being afterward called and invited to preach, as I am a minister of the gospel I durst not deny preaching, nor I hope I never shall, where it is wanting and desired." —Rev. Francis Makemie,† 1707, "Memoirs of John Rodgers," p. 139, note.

ON a Sunday morning toward the end of the year 1765, George III. being King of England, and Sir Henry Moore being Governor of His Majesty's Province of New York, the people of the First Presbyterian Church in New York City were assembled as usual in their place of worship on Wall Street, waiting for the service to begin. Their new minister, the Rev. John Rodgers, had now been with them for some weeks, so that the first curiosity regarding him was beginning to subside, and on this occasion no one was expecting that anything of special interest would occur, except that the new minister's sermons were found to be always interesting. But Mr. Rodgers had barely entered the church when attention was riveted upon him, for instead of proceeding to the clerk's desk below the

* New York.

† The first minister to conduct an English Presbyterian service in New York City.

3

pulpit, and there offering the introductory prayer, reading the Scriptures, and giving out the first Psalm, as had been the custom until this time, the minister was seen to mount to his pulpit at once and begin the service there.

In spite of the severe decorum which prevailed in the congregations of that period, some slight commotion was evident—silk dresses faintly rustled, glances were swiftly exchanged,—for this matter of the proper place in which to open the service was one that had long been a subject of dispute. The majority of the congregation clung firmly to the old way, but some others had for many years urged this very change, which Mr. Rodgers, without consulting a single person, whether member or officer, had now suddenly introduced.

Was it possible that in a state of absent-mindedness he had unintentionally reverted to a custom made familiar to him in his former parish? No, the firmness and composure with which he met the evident surprise of the congregation at once dispelled that theory. It was plain that what he had done he had fully intended to do, and it is safe to assume that during the rest of that service not a few of the people were guilty of a certain inattention, through reflecting upon the probable consequences of Mr. Rodgers' action. Would the majority of the members, or the session whose wishes in the matter had not even been asked, require a return to the old custom, and gently but firmly counsel the minister to act in a less headstrong manner in the future? Such a result seemed not unlikely.

But as a matter of fact, nothing of the sort happened. The subject was not even broached in session meeting, and the majority in the congregation could find no one inclined to voice their protest. Mr. Rodgers, in short, had correctly read the situation. Regarding with distinct disapproval the conducting of the service from two places (probably because this savored of conformity to the Church of England usage), but perceiving at the same time that to stir up a church quarrel on such a matter of detail would be almost unpardonable, he decided that the bold method was the safest, and cut the Gordian knot at a stroke. His plan succeeded. There was dissatisfaction, of course. Some leading members privately expressed with considerable emphasis their disapproval of what Mr. Rodgers had presumed to do, "but such were the popularity and success of his ministrations," says the narrator of this incident, "and such his influence among the people, that the unpleasant feelings expressed on this occasion by these individuals were but little regarded by the body of the congregation, and soon entirely ceased to be manifested."*

The somewhat picturesque glimpse which this anecdote gives us of the Wall Street minister at the beginning of his New York pastorate, introduces us in an appropriate way to the history of what is now known as "The Brick Church," for the origin of that church was directly connected with the settlement of Mr. Rodgers over the Wall Street congregation. We have but to follow through a few months more his work among the New York Presbyterians, in order to reach the definite beginning of the history which is

* "Rodgers Mem.," p. 179 f.

to be related in this volume. But in order to understand what is to follow, we must first glance backward for a moment at the earlier history of the Presbyterian Church in New York City and of John Rodgers, the minister who was to guide its destinies for nearly half a century.

Presbyterianism in New York began in 1706 with the gathering in private houses of a few persons who desired to worship in the Presbyterian manner. In January of the following year the Rev. Francis Makemie passed through the city on his way from Virginia to Boston, and at the request of the few Presbyterians preached at the house of one William Jackson on Pearl Street. Lord Cornbury, the Governor, a bigoted High-churchman, endeavored by the use of force to put an end to this activity of dissenters, and Mr. Makemie was arrested and sent to jail. On the morrow he was examined, the following being a portion of the proceedings:

"Lord Cornbury. How dare you take upon you to preach in my government without license?

"Mr. Makemie. We have liberty from an act of Parliament, made the first year of the reign of William and Mary, which gave us liberty, with which law we complied.

"Lord C. None shall preach in my government without my license.

"Mr. M. If the law of liberty, my lord, had directed us to any particular persons in authority for license, we would readily have obtained the same; but we cannot find any directions in said act of Parliament, therefore we could not take any notice thereof.

"Lord C. That law does not extend to the American plantations, but only to England.

"Mr. M. My lord, I humbly conceive it is not a limited or local act; and am well assured it extends to other plantations, which is evident from certificates of record of Virginia and Maryland, certifying we have complied with said law.

"Lord C. The courts which have qualified these men are in error, and I will check them for it. *You shall not spread your pernicious doctrines here.*"*

Mr. Makemie, who was kept in jail for nearly two months, was at length tried by jury, and, to the chagrin of the authorities, acquitted. Such was the beginning of New York Presbyterianism, uncomfortable, but on the whole, not inauspicious.

After this there was, for a while, no settled pastor, but from time to time the ministrations of some travelling Presbyterian clergyman were enjoyed, and occasionally services were held in the Dutch church on Garden Street (now Exchange Place); but there was little enough of outward permanence about the movement until 1716, when the Presbyterians called the Rev. James Anderson to settle permanently among them.

A letter written by Mr. Anderson to Principal Sterling of Glasgow, on December 3d, 1717, gives us an interesting view of the situation at that time. "This place, the city of New York, where I now am," he says, "is a place of considerable moment, and very populous, consisting, as I am informed, of about three thousand families or householders. It is a place of as great trade or business (if not more now)

* Quoted in "The Presbyterian Magazine" for January, 1851, p. 30.

as any in America. In it are two ministers of the Church of England, two Dutch ministers, one French minister, a Lutheran minister, an Anabaptist, and also a Quaker meeting. . . . Endeavors were used again and again by the famous Mr. Francis Makemie, Mr. McNish, and others toward the settlement of a Scots church in this city, but by the arbitrary management and influence of a wicked high-flying governor, who preceded his excellency Brigadier Hunter, our present governor (may the Lord bless and long preserve him), that business has been hitherto impeded, and could never be brought in a likely way to bear.

"The last summer, I, being providentially here, and being obliged to stay here about business the matter of a month, at the desire of a few, especially Scots people, preached each Sabbath. Though there were pretty many hearers, yet these were not able and willing to do anything toward the setting forward such a work. A few there were willing to do their utmost, but so few that I had small grounds to suppose that anything effectual could be done. Some time before our last Synod, this small handful, with some few others that had joined them, came to the Presbytery of Newcastle [Delaware], desiring a transportation of me from Newcastle to New York, which the Presbytery referred to the Synod, then soon to meet. The Synod . . . transported me hither.

"The people here who are favorers of our Church and persuasion, as I've told you, are but few, and none of the richest, yet for all I am not without hopes that with God's blessing they shall in a little time increase. Some are already come to live in the city, and more are expected, whose language would not allow them to join with the Dutch or French churches, and whose conscience would not allow them to join in the service of the English Church. The chief thing now wanting, in all appearance, with God's blessing, is a large convenient church to congregate in." *

After two or three years, during which the Presbyterians worshipped in the City Hall on the corner of Wall and Nassau streets, they succeeded in erecting a church building for themselves on the north side of Wall Street between Nassau and Broadway.

The second pastor was the Rev. Ebenezer Pemberton. † During his term the celebrated George Whitefield visited New York, and we read of his preaching in the Presbyterian church on Sunday evening, having in the afternoon preached "in the fields." This visit quickened and increased the congregation. They found it necessary to enlarge their church; and in 1750 they called a second minister, Mr. Alexander Cummings, to be colleague of Mr. Pemberton.

The way of progress, however, was by no means altogether easy. Soon after this an obstinate dispute arose on the question of psalmody: Should Watts's imitation of the Psalms ‡ be substituted for Rouse's, or, as it was commonly called, the "Old Scotch,"

---

* This letter was first printed in "The Presbyterian Magazine" for October, 1851 (pp. 480 ff.), having been copied from the original, preserved among the Wodson Manuscripts in the Advocates' Library, Edinburgh.

† He served from 1727 till 1754.

‡ Some desired the version of Tate and Brady. See "Rodgers Mem.," p. 149.

Version? *   Before this burning question was settled, in the affirmative, both pastors had resigned,
the church had spent two years in a vain attempt to
find successors for them, and a part of the membership had seceded to form a separate church on Cedar
Street.†   Under the Rev. David Bostwick ‡ peace
and quiet were gradually restored.   A few years later
the Rev. Joseph Treat was made associate minister,§
and after the death of Mr. Bostwick he continued to
serve the church as colleague of the new pastor, who
was the Rev. Mr. Rodgers, named at the beginning
of this chapter.

The generally auspicious outlook for the church
at this time is described in one of the letters written in connection with Mr. Rodgers' call.   "This

* As late as 1789 some Presbyterians continued to be greatly exercised
on this matter.   In that year a Mr. Adam Rankin, of the Presbytery of
Transylvania, addressed to the General Assembly a "Quere" whether it
had not been "a great and pernicious error for the late Synod of New
York and Philadelphia to permit the disuse of Rouse's Version and the
substitution of that of Watts."   The comment of the Assembly was as
follows: "The General Assembly, having heard Mr. Rankin at great length,
and endeavored to relieve his mind from the difficulty he appears to labor
under, are sorry to find that all their efforts have been in vain; and therefore only recommend to him that exercise of Christian charity toward
those who differ from him in their views of this matter, which is exercised
toward himself; and that he be carefully guarded against disturbing the
peace of the Church on this head."   ("Assembly Digest," p. 209.)

† The Scotch Presbyterian Church now at Central Park West and
Ninety-sixth Street.

‡ Installed in 1755; died in 1764.

§ The following information is contained in Sprague's "Annals"
(Vol. III, p. 132, note): "Joseph Treat was graduated at the College of
New Jersey in 1757; was a tutor in the college from 1758 to 1760; was
licensed to preach by the Presbytery of New Brunswick in 1760; and
retained his connection as pastor with the Presbyterian Church in New
York till 1784, when, in pursuance of an application by the congregation,
it was dissolved.   In 1785 the Presbytery of New York report that they
had, during the preceding year, dismissed Mr. Treat to the Presbytery of
New Brunswick; but I find no further trace of him."

From "Harper's Magazine," Copyright, 1908, Harper & Brothers

THE OLD WALL STREET CHURCH

church," the session writes, "from small and despised beginnings has mightily increased in a few years by the kindness of God, and [is] now in the happiest union, though the members thereof are a collection from Scotland, Ireland, and many places in America, people of various education and circumstances." The writers go on to express the fear that any disappointment of their desire to secure Mr. Rodgers might endanger this hard-won prosperity.*

The man upon whom so much was thought to depend was at this time thirty-eight years of age.† His parents had in 1721 come from Londonderry, in Ireland, to Boston, where he was born, but when he was but a little over a year old they had again moved, to Philadelphia, and he was reared in that city. He appears to have been by nature a precocious child and was early concerned with the matter of religion. The rather sombre and ponderous narrative in which this part of his experience is described by his pious biographer would be oppressive to modern readers, but in it an anecdote has been preserved which more pleasantly, and yet quite as truly, reveals the boy's early religious development.

It appears that, like the church which he was later to serve, he had come under the strong influence of George Whitefield. Many times, when this moving preacher spoke in Philadelphia, little John Rodgers was among his hearers and greatly impressed by the message that he heard. On one occasion, when

* For period 1706–1765, see "Manuscript Hist.," pp. 1 *ff*; "Presb. N. Y.," pp. 3 *ff.*; "Br. Ch. Mem.," p. 8; "Handbook of N. Y. Presbytery," 1903–1904, pp. 13 *f.*; "Disosway," pp. 131 *ff.*

† He was born August 5th, 1727. For the facts of his life, see "Rodgers Mem."

Whitefield was preaching, as he often did, from the Court House steps in Market Street, the boy, in his eagerness to hear, had pressed his way through the crowd until he stood directly beside the speaker, and as it happened was entrusted with the holding of a lantern for Mr. Whitefield's accommodation. "Soon after the sermon began," says the story, "he became so absorbed in the subject, and at length so deeply impressed and strongly agitated, that he was scarcely able to stand; the lantern fell from his hand and was dashed in pieces; and that part of the audience in the immediate vicinity of the speaker's station were not a little interested, and for a few moments discomposed by the occurrence." *

It was not long after this time, we are told, and when he was but a little more than twelve years of age, that he came, as he hoped, to "a saving knowledge and acceptance of Jesus Christ," and entered upon the Master's service with devotion. He very early formed the purpose of entering the Christian ministry and set about the definite task of preparing himself for that work. He prosecuted his studies under various masters with great diligence, and in October, 1747, in his twentieth year, he took his examinations for licensure, which he passed with more than usual approbation.

Not until over a year later was he ordained and

* "Rodgers Mem.," p. 14. Sprague, in his "Annals of the American Pulpit" (Vol. III, p. 154), adds: "Some time after he was settled in the ministry, Whitefield being on a visit to his house, Mr. Rodgers alluded to this incident and asked him if he recollected it. 'Oh, yes,' replied Whitefield, 'I remember it well, and have often thought I would give almost anything in my power to know who that little boy was and what had become of him.' Mr. Rodgers replied with a smile, 'I am that little boy.'"

settled in a church, but that year was by no means a barren one. Obstacles which he experienced in Virginia, due to the intolerance of the established clergy there, served only to increase his determination, while a few months spent in Maryland, which might have been passed in idle waiting, he turned to such good account that he afterward referred to these months as perhaps the most useful of his life. One incident at this time may serve to illustrate his strength of will and the determination with which he had entered upon his work. He was preaching one Sunday to a large congregation in the open air, when in the midst of the sermon he suddenly swooned, apparently without any warning, and fell lifeless to the ground. Whatever the cause of this alarming experience, it was more than an ordinary fainting-turn, for his friends, when they had gathered around him, supposed him to be dead, and were amazed, when, after some time, he returned to consciousness. "He arose with a little assistance," says his biographer, "walked into an adjoining wood, and in about half an hour returned and finished his discourse, resuming it, as his audience remarked, with the very word which was on his lips when he fell." His conduct is the more remarkable in that on the following Sunday the same thing happened and was met by him with the same indomitable spirit. Strangely enough, and most happily, the second occurrence was also the last.*

On March 16th, 1749, he was ordained and installed pastor of the Presbyterian Church at St. George's, Delaware. He had received calls from

* "Rodgers Mem.," pp. 62–64.

four different churches. The one at St. George's was the smallest and feeblest, but having been assured that its very existence depended on his coming, he determined to make that church his choice. His ministry there, which lasted sixteen years, was blessed in every possible way. The church began at once to increase in membership and soon the building required to be enlarged. At a later time the people of the neighborhood so crowded to hear him that the church of another denomination was literally deserted.

He was not only admired as a preacher, but respected and beloved as a pastor. When we read the description of his annual calls upon the families of his church, we cannot but admire the thoroughness of his method, and still more their patience in submitting to it. There are times when one is content, it must be confessed, to live in a less heroic age. On these occasions, we are told, "he called upon every member of the family to repeat a part of the Assembly's Catechism; asked them a number of extempore questions on doctrinal and practical subjects in religion; prayed with them; and gave a warm and pathetic exhortation." *

His own people were not the only ones who valued him. He soon won the confidence and esteem of his brother clergymen round about, and was more and more sought to give counsel and to aid in the performance of important tasks. It was no wonder that, when in 1765 the Presbyterian Church of New York was seeking a colleague for Mr. Treat, the name of Mr. Rodgers should be mentioned. Indeed, ten years before this they had sought to bring him to

* "Rodgers Mem.," pp. 88 ff.

New York without success. This time their call was more effective, though for a while the result was in doubt. The people of St. George's were most reluctant to part with him. He himself was deeply attached to them and to his work in that place. His Presbytery, before whom the call was laid, refused to decide, and referred the question to the Synod of New York and Philadelphia. It was only "after a full and patient hearing of all parties for near three days"* that a conclusion was reached by the Synod in favor of Mr. Rodgers' acceptance of the call to New York.†

He and his family ‡ were settled in their new home by July, 1765, and he was installed as pas-

---

* "Rodgers Mem," p. 120.

† Sprague, in his "Annals of the American Pulpit" (Vol. III, p. 157), says of Mr. Rodgers: "In the early part of the year 1765, he received two calls, one from the congregation in New York, then just vacated by the death of the Rev. David Bostwick, and another from a large and important Congregational Church in Charlestown, S. C. Mr. Whitefield, who happened to visit him about that time, gave it as his decided opinion that the indications of Providence were in favor of his removal, but was doubtful in which direction he ought to go. The question . . . was finally referred to the Synod. . . . His installation as pastor of the church in New York took place in September following. The installation sermon was preached by the Rev. James Caldwell of Elizabethtown."

‡ He married September 19th, 1752, Elizabeth Bayard, who died January 20th, 1763. On August 15th, 1764, he married Mrs. Mary Grant, a widow. Interesting evidence of the manner in which he had made provision for his wife, in the event of his own death, is provided by a document still in existence, having been handed down in his family to his great-grandson, Mr. Robertson Rodgers, who presented it to the author of this volume. This is a bond given by John Rodgers to the "Corporation for the Relief of Poor and Distressed Presbyterian Ministers, and of the Poor and Distressed Widows and Children of Presbyterian Ministers," for the annual payment of seven pounds sterling during his natural life, in return for which his widow or surviving children were to receive "an annuity of thirty-five pounds current money." One of the conditions agreed to by him was, "That on the second marriage of the said John Rodgers and on every subsequent marriage of the said John Rodgers, he shall or will pay. . . the sum of seven pounds over and above the annual rate." To the bond are

tor * on September 4th following. He was cordially received by the Presbyterians of New York City and was soon hard at work with an ardor and devotion which began at once to show good results. Not many months had passed after his installation when a decided revival of religious interest was apparent. The church was crowded with worshippers; many were making serious inquiry about their religious obligations; and it could not be doubted that the Spirit of God was at work in the hearts of the people. As we now look back at that time from a distance of nearly a hundred and fifty years, we can know but little of what took place in the experience of the individuals who were then led into the ways of the Christian life—their very names are now unknown to us,—but that revival has left behind it one tangible memorial which in itself has proved to be not the least of the spiritual blessings of the city of New York. The thronging congregations which were gathered by Mr. Rodgers' ministry, were soon too large by far to be accommodated in the church on Wall Street. At the same time the enthusiasm that had increased the numbers of the Presbyterians had also increased their courage and their readiness to assume enlarged responsibilities. They determined that they must at once build a new church.

attached receipts from the treasurer, the earliest of which is for the year 1775; and at the end of the document are a number of notes in Dr. Rodgers' own hand, of which the following are the earliest: "N. B. May 22d, 1793, I, this day paid my annual subscription to the Widow's fund as appears by the Treasurer's Rect and the Entry in his Books. John Rodgers." —"This I have done yearly & every year since the Year 1763 when I became a Contributor—and I also paid the sum of Seven Pounds extraordinary on my marriage to my present Wife. John Rodgers."

* See Appendix B, p. 516.

CHAPTER II

THE NEW CHURCH : 1765–1767

"And Araunah said, Wherefore is my lord the king come to his servant? And David said, To buy the threshingfloor of thee, to build an altar unto the Lord."— 2 *Samuel* 24 : 21.

"A decent Edifice Erected on this Spot, properly Enclosed in a pail fence, will be a Great Ornament to the Green."—OFFICERS OF THE BRICK CHURCH, "Minutes of the Common Council of the City of New York," Vol. VII, p. 11.

IN providing the new place of worship the first problem that presented itself was the securing of a suitable plot of ground. The Presbyterian Church owned no land that could be used for this purpose, and it would doubtless have been very difficult to raise sufficient money for the purchase of a site, but it was hoped that, if properly approached, the city authorities would come to the rescue. Accordingly on February 19th, 1766, a petition* was drawn up, which plays so important a part in this history that it must be given in full.

"TO THE WORSHIPFUL THE MAYOR, ALDERMEN AND COMMONALTY OF THE CITY OF NEW YORK, IN COMMON COUNCIL CONVENED:

"The petition of the ministers, elders, deacons, trustees, communicants and other members of the English Presbyterian Church of the City of New York, according to the Westminster Confession of Faith, Catechism, and Directory, and agreeable to the

* See "Document No. 37," pp. 564–566.

17

present Established Church of Scotland, humbly
sheweth:

"That while the church to which your petitioners
belong has not unmeritedly been esteemed for the
purity of her doctrines, her members, we would pre-
sume to hope, have approved themselves good subjects and useful members of society; that by the
blessing of Almighty God your petitioners have so
increased in numbers, as at this day to constitute
a very considerable part of the freemen, freeholders,
and inhabitants of this flourishing city; that although
your petitioners are already possessed of a spacious
and convenient edifice for the public service of Almighty God, and the administration of divine ordinances according to their wholesome and approved
form of discipline and worship, yet, by their great
and continual growth, that building is rendered altogether incapable of containing their congregation,
and the cemetery too small for decent interment of
their dead; that, urged by these necessities, your petitioners have lately cast their eyes around them in
search of a convenient spot of ground for the erection
of another church, and for supplying it with a cemetery; that in this survey the known and approved
benevolence of the Honorable Board toward every
Protestant denomination in this city, and its abilities
to relieve the present necessities of our congregation
could not fail to command its attention; nor will the
distinguished generosity by which our brethren of
Trinity Church were supplied with a large and convenient burying-ground, of the free gift of this Honorable Board, nor the late grant of a number of lots
to the Reformed Protestant Dutch Church in this

city, upon a reasonable rent, permit us to doubt of
the success of this our application; that, though your
petitioners would not be thought to prescribe, yet
upon the view of the several lots belonging to this
Honorable Board, within the compass of the improved
parts of this city, the angular lot adjoining to the
ground lately called the Vineyard * and to the
Green † appeals to your petitioners to command the
preference, not only with a view to convenience, but
what will doubtless ever merit the attention of this
Honorable Board, the public ornament; that influenced by the latter, as a first motive, your petitioners
beg leave to observe, that it will be necessary to keep
open a cross street ‡ between this piece of ground
and the Vineyard, by which the angle being short-
ened at its base, will be so much diminished as to
contain of about six lots only, which your petitioners
humbly conceive will be a compass too small, especially if its disadvantageous form be considered, to
contain a decent edifice and a suitable cemetery;
that therefore, should this Honorable Board conde-
scend to relieve the wants of your petitioners, they
would beg leave to suggest the necessity of an additional piece of ground, with such convenience in
point of situation and quantity, for the use of a cemetery, as to this Honorable Board shall seem meet, for
which, as well as the angular lot above mentioned,
your petitioners are freely willing to render to this
Honorable Board a rent suitable to the circumstances of their church, and to erect such an edifice,

* "North-eastward of the Vineyard," is the fuller description given
elsewhere. "Common Council," Vol. VII, p. 9.

† The present City Hall Park.

‡ This was the later Beekman Street.

as will contribute to public ornament. Your petitioners, therefore, humbly pray this Honorable Board
to take their extreme necessities into your serious
consideration, and to grant to them the aforesaid
angle of ground for the erection of a new church,
with an additional lot, suitable for a cemetery, subject to such an annual rent to be rendered forever to
the Honorable Board, as they, in their great wisdom
and justice, shall think reasonable; and your peti-
tioner shall ever pray, etc." *

When it is realized that the "angular lot" so
boldly, though respectfully, asked for is approxi-
mately the land bounded to-day by Nassau and Beekman streets and Park Row, one is inclined to regard
with admiration and even with amazement the te-
merity of the petitioners. But in truth their request
was not so extraordinary as it sounds to us. In the
first place, the relation of the authorities to the individual citizens and their personal interests was at that
time much more paternal than at present, a condition
that had its advantages as well as its drawbacks; and in
the second place, the property in question had in 1765
comparatively little value. It must be borne in mind
that New York City at the time covered but a small
area at the southern end of Manhattan Island. On
the west side the region of houses had passed into the
region of fields not far north of what is now City Hall
Park. On the east, which was then the more pros-

---

* The names of the petitioners were: Ministers; John Rodgers and
Joseph Treat: Elders; William Smith, Garret Noel, Nathaniel McKinley,
Peter Van Brugh Livingston, John Smith, and Thomas Jackson: Deacons;
John Stevens and Peter Riker: Trustees; Thomas Smith, Peter R. Liv-
ingston, Joseph Hallett, John Lashor [Lasher ?], Jr., William Smith, Jr.,
John Dunlap and John Morin Scott.

References

	1 Fort George in Lat. 40° 41' 58"	19 The College
	2 Trinity Church	20 Free Eng! Sch!
	3 St. Pauls Ch.	21 Secretarys Off!
	4 St. Georges Chap!	22 City Hall
	5 Old Dutch Ch.	23 The Prison
	6 New Eng! Dh. Ch.	24 Poor House
	7 New Dutch Cals. "	25 Exchange
	8 Presbyt!? Meet?	26 Barracks
	9 New do. do.	27 Fish Market
	10 French Church	28 Old Slip do.
	11 Lutheran do.	29 Fly do.
	12 New Luth! "	30 Peck's do.
	13 Calvinist "	31 Oswego do.
	14 Moravian Meet?	32 Powder House
	15 Anabaptist "	33 Jews'Bury? Gr?
	16 New Scots "	34 Wind Mill
	17 Quaker "	35 Tan Yard
	18 Jews Synagogue	36 Theatre
		37 Arsenal

JAS. S. KEMP.

Courtesy of Harper Brothers.

NEW YORK IN 1767

From Thomas A. Janvier's "In Old New York"

perous portion of the city and the more fashionable, the houses extended somewhat farther, but in a north-easterly direction. Standing on the ground that was wanted for the new church and looking northward across the Green, one would have seen the poor-house (on the site of the present City Hall) and the City Prison (in later years the Record Office). Back of these he might have caught a glimpse of the barracks, but, except for these buildings, as far as the eye could reach was open country. In fact, the land desired was on the extreme northern edge of the city.

At the same time it was sufficiently accessible, and what was more, the petitioners believed that there was a good chance of getting it. In this they were not disappointed. A committee of five was directed by the Common Council to confer with the representatives of the church and to report,* and there seems from the beginning to have been a dis-position to grant the request in substance, only the details being matter for further discussion; for in the next communication from the church the petitioners say expressly that they "take very kindly the Speedy Attention Given by the Corporation to their Request."

There was at first some doubt whether, instead of

* For this and the following statements see "Common Council," Vol. VII, pp. 5 *ff*. Some items from the minutes of the Board of Aldermen, for the meeting at which the Presbyterian petition was received, and the one held the next week after, relating to the ferries on the East and North rivers, point out in an interesting way the primitive conditions of that time. We learn that there was but one ferry to Nassau (now Long) Island, a petition for a second one being rejected. It was ordered that after ad-vertising "in all the publick or weakly Gazzetees," the existing ferry should be farmed out "by Public Outcry to the highest Bidder." As to the means of reaching New Jersey, we learn that an exclusive grant of the right of ferriage across the Hudson from New York was given to one man, who agreed to keep in use three large boats and two small ones.

the lot petitioned for, another piece of land, described as "opposite the Old Wind Mill Spot," might not be made to serve the church's purpose. This the petitioners vigorously opposed, and some of their arguments are interesting, not only in themselves, but in the light they throw upon the conditions of life in New York at that time. They urged that the land proposed as an alternative, and which lay near the juncture of the present Elizabeth and Hester streets, was "too remote," that the streets leading to it were inconveniently narrow and would "probably not be paved for many years to come," and that there would be danger to the proposed church from the small wooden buildings of that neighborhood. They therefore renewed their request for the lots adjoining the Vineyard, on the ground that this land was "nearer the Inhabited Part of the City," and "more convenient to the Petitioners, as it will admit of an Easy Access at all times of the Yeare," and also because it was the choice most likely to improve the appearance of the city, "whereas," say they, "it is at Present Entirely Useless, or Rather a Nuisance, as it is now a Receptacle for all the Dirt and Filth of the Neighborhood." * They add, moreover, that an accurate measurement having shown the plot to contain the equivalent, not of six, but of nearly nine city lots, twenty-five by a hundred feet each,† it will be unnecessary to provide extra land elsewhere for a "Cymetery"; and finally they make an offer of forty pounds sterling ground-rent per annum.

* "Common Council," Vol. VII, p. 11.

† The property measured on its south-west side (Beekman Street), 152 feet, on the south-east side, 200 feet, on the north-east side, 62 feet, and on the north-west side (toward the "Green"), 214 feet.

The committee of the Common Council reported favorably upon the request of the petitioners in its entirety, and on February 25th, 1766, the Board conveyed the "Vineyard lot" * to the ministers, elders, deacons, and trustees of the Presbyterian Church and to their heirs and assigns forever ("in consideration of the pious and laudable designs of the said parties") on condition that within a reasonable time they should "enclose the same within a good and sufficient fence, and either erect an edifice or church thereon, or on a part thereof, for the worship of Almighty God, or use the same, or a part thereof, for a cemetery or church-yard, for the burial or interment of the dead, and shall not appropriate, apply, nor convert the same at any time, forever thereafter, to private, secular uses," and also upon further condition of the payment of an annual ground-rent of forty pounds sterling.

Several clauses in this grant were destined to create more or less discussion and even controversy in later years. The right of burial here given was made the basis of a claim upon the city in the next century; the meaning of the phrase "private, secular uses," proved, as we shall see hereafter, to be not as clear as was at first supposed, and especially the matter of the ground-rent demanded readjustment from time to time.

The land for the new church was now provided, but the church itself was still a thing of the future. Mr. Rodgers set about the raising of the money for this purpose and soon proved that in this practical

* Loosely so described, though the lots merely adjoined the "Vineyard." See above, page 19.

department of his work he was as energetic and successful as in his spiritual ministry. For several months he went from door to door, literally collecting with his own hands the money needed for this purpose.* In after years he is said to have narrated many anecdotes of those days, describing sometimes the unexpected repulses and sometimes the agreeable surprises that he encountered. One incident of the latter sort has come down to us and is worth repeating, for it makes us realize that the building of the church on Beekman Street was no mere business enterprise, but a labor of love. Mr. Rodgers with an officer of the church, in the course of his money-raising, called one morning at the house of a certain widow who had recently lost by death a dearly loved daughter, and who was known to be in very narrow circumstances. Little or nothing was expected from her, and indeed the two callers were loath to ask her for anything. Their reason for coming to her at all was that they would not hurt her feelings by seeming to overlook her, or to despise her little gift. They were, accordingly, amazed when, after she learned their errand, she brought and put into their hands a sum which for her was very large indeed. She could well spare it, she assured them, when they expressed reluctance to take so much. It was money saved in former years; in truth, laid by to be her daughter's marriage portion. We need not be told that the good minister and his companion went out from that humble house with renewed courage for their difficult task. The other anecdotes of that soliciting tour have been forgotten, but when the

* "Rodgers Mem.," pp. 181 *ff.*

story of the Brick Church is retold from time to time the gift of this woman shall still "be spoken of for a memorial of her."

Of the appearance of the new church on its completion at the end of 1767,* we have very little direct knowledge, but there is no reason to doubt that, so far as the exterior was concerned, the main features were much the same as in pictures and descriptions that come down to us from about 1800.† Without attempting at this time to describe the details of the building, we may with certainty say that, though much plainer and in many points less attractive, it

* There is to-day, set into the outer wall of the present Brick Church, immediately south of the north entrance, a piece of brownstone, bevelled, with this inscription:

P. V. B. Livingsto
1767

The author has been unable to gain any direct information in regard to it, but the date suggests, of course, that it was in some way connected with the building of the church on Beekman Street. Is it, perhaps, a fragment of the original corner-stone? A newspaper report of an address by Dr. Spring at his fiftieth anniversary in 1860, quotes him as saying that the original corner-stone was laid by Dr. Rodgers' "own hands, with those of Livingston." The conclusion to be drawn would appear certain, were it not that Dr. Spring has also stated ("Br. Ch. Mem.," p. 8), that this corner-stone was laid in the fall of 1766. But what was his authority for this statement? Most probably the words of Dr. Miller ("Rodgers Mem.," p. 181), "the foundation of the new church was laid in the autumn of the same year," that is, 1766. "Foundation," it will be noticed, is the word used in this older record, not "corner-stone." Doubtless Dr. Spring made an erroneous, though natural, inference, and we may assume that the stone is a part of the original corner-stone laid by Dr. Rodgers and Peter Van Brugh Livingston in 1767.

† Except that, apparently, the steeple was not added till a later time, Noah Webster, in 1788, describes the church as "a genteel brick building, . . . with a steeple not finished." The following extract from the diary of Dr. Alexander Anderson, preserved in the New York Historical Society, suggests a possible date for the steeple's completion. "Jany 11th, 1794. Saturday Evening We had an alarm of 'Fire.' I believe it arose from trying the new Bell in the Brick Meeting, which gave an alarm to the other bells."

was built in the same style as the present St. Paul's
Chapel, which had been erected about two years
before, and stood but a short distance away. The
front was on what is now Beekman Street, so that
the church almost had its back to the Green—looked
at it over its right shoulder, as it were—a fact which,
were it still standing to-day, when almost the whole
city lies to the north of City Hall Park, would give it
a singular appearance. The northern end of the
church, however, was by no means neglected. The
large colonial window in that wall was in excellent
taste, and indeed in general it is evident that the
promise to build a church which should be an ornament to the city, as set forth in the petition for the
land, was by no means forgotten. The church,
while it stood, was one of the truly admirable speci-
mens of the city's architecture.

One feature of the structure must be mentioned
even if all others should be disregarded: it was built
of brick. It has been assumed by some that on account of this fact, and because the old church on
Wall Street was of stone, the new structure was at
once called the "Brick Church." This does not
appear to be exactly the history of the name's origin.
For a number of years after the church was built, in
fact, till 1799, the session records speak of it consistently as the "New Church." There is evidence, it is
true, that in popular usage the name Brick Church
or Brick Meeting-House had been commonly employed at an earlier time, but it certainly had no
official standing until about the date that has been
mentioned. At that time a third church had been
completed, so that to call the building on Beekman

THE BRICK CHURCH FROM THE NORTH-EAST IN 1800

Showing St. Paul's Chapel on the right

VIEW FROM THE SAME POINT IN 1908

Steeple of St. Paul's in the centre

Street "new" was no longer appropriate. In England, where the spirit of conservatism is strong, this difficulty would not have been regarded; the church would have continued to be called the "New Church" till the end of time, after the manner of New College, Oxford, which was founded in the year 1379, or the New Inn at Gloucester, which claims to be the oldest in the Kingdom. But it is interesting to observe that even as early as the end of the eighteenth century Americans were moved by the desire to keep up to date. The name "New" was surrendered to the younger organization on Rutgers Street, and the Brick Church assumed its present title. This, however, took place as has been said, more than thirty years after the erection of the building, to which event we must return.

The possession of the new land, and the investment of a considerable amount of money in the building erected upon it, brought to the front once more a difficulty that had already existed for many years, and had caused the officers of the church no little concern. According to the law of the Province no charter of incorporation could be obtained by a Presbyterian organization, a fact which made it extremely difficult to hold property or to secure the payment of legacies. Attempts had been made as early as 1720 and repeatedly in the half century that followed* to secure these very necessary privileges, but without success, owing largely to the determined opposition of the vestry of old Trinity, who were reluctant to share with others the privileges enjoyed by the Established Church.

* See "Rodgers Mem.," pp. 135 *ff.*, 140 *ff.*, 166.

In 1730, fearing that those who were moved by this unfriendly spirit might take further advantage of their position, the Presbyterians determined to make their property safe by putting it into the hands of a body outside the jurisdiction of the colony. Accordingly, they conveyed it to a committee of the General Assembly of the Church of Scotland. The practical management, however, of the church's temporal affairs was, at this period, by common consent, entrusted almost entirely to Dr. John Nicoll, a physician of New York, whose devoted service to the church deserves to be gratefully remembered. After his death in 1743 the congregation appointed for this task a self-perpetuating committee of eight * gentlemen, who were called trustees, but whose obligation to the church rested, of course, on a moral, not a legal, basis. The trust, which was thus by necessity reposed in the faithfulness of individuals, was so far from being abused in any way that when, in 1762, the church acquired possession of a "parsonage-house," the cumbersome method of applying to Scotland was not resorted to, and the property was vested in private persons, members or officers of the church.

This was the method by which it was proposed to hold the New Church on Beekman Street. It could not but be evident, however, that this plan was open to very grave objections as applied to such large interests as were now at stake, and spurred on by their increased necessity the church authorities made a new attempt to secure a charter. It was discovered that the Governor of the Province, Sir Henry Moore,

* Increased to twelve in 1771. ("Manuscript Hist.," p. 16.)

was favorable to their desire, but some doubt was raised as to his power to act in the premises, and a reference of the question to the Provincial Council, constituted as it then was, did not seem at all likely to help the matter.

The officers of the church, therefore, in March, 1766, addressed a petition to King George. The Privy Council, before whom it was laid by His Majesty, referred it in turn to the Board of Trade, whose President, Lord Dartmouth, the patron of Dartmouth College in New Hampshire, showed himself a sincere friend to the petitioners and their cause. In spite of delays and discouragements, the request might have been granted at this time, had not the Bishop of London declared himself its enemy, appearing twice before the board in opposition to it. The report to the King was unfavorable and the petition was rejected.

It will be perhaps as well to trace at this time the further history of this matter. In 1774, when still another request for a charter was made, the concurrence of the King, the Governor, and the Council was actually obtained, but the obstinacy of the King's Attorney in New York, who pigeonholed it, delayed action until the imminence of the conflict with Great Britain turned the minds of men in other directions. It was finally in 1784, when the War of Independence had been won, that the Legislature of New York passed an act to incorporate the churches af all religious denominations, allowing each of them to hold an estate of twelve hundred pounds sterling per annum gross revenue. The Presbyterians at once availed themselves of this law, appointing nine trus-

tees, and taking the name "The Corporation of the
First Presbyterian Church in the City of New York."
To this corporation the lands and buildings of the
church were conveyed by the individuals, who had
until that time faithfully held and managed the
property.*

It will have been observed that in the building of
the New Church no steps were taken toward creating
a separate ecclesiastical organization. The so-called
collegiate arrangement by which such a separation
was made unnecessary, and which continued for
forty years, should be clearly understood. The two
congregations, on Wall Street and on Beekman
Street, respectively, constituted one undivided church.
The ministers belonged equally to them both, and
preached alternately in the two churches on Sunday
mornings. The second Sunday service was held in
one church one Sunday, in the other the next. All
the elders, deacons, and trustees were officers of the
united congregations. The number of these officers
was increased soon after the New Church was built,
in order to enable them to cover the more extended
field, but even then there was no such person as an
elder of the Wall Street Church, or a deacon of the
New Church: all belonged to both. From the very
beginning, moreover, there was not, so far as the
records show, the slightest indication that one of the
congregations was in any way inferior or subordinate
to the other, nor did there ever come between them,
in any marked degree, the spirit of envy or of the
selfish desire for power. The causes which finally
ended the union lay, not in any failure of Christian

* "Manuscript Hist.," pp. 17-20.

charity, but in the inherent faults of the system. It
was throughout a noble and truly Christian relationship, and it set up an ideal which, as one observes
with interest, the Brick Church of later years has
striven once more to realize, not without success.*

The strong feeling of unity and equality which
existed, was no doubt produced at the beginning by
the fact that the congregation of the New Church
was taken bodily out of the Wall Street congregation.
There existed no little nucleus of people who had
been already worshipping separately in some sort
of makeshift quarters at the north end of the town,
and for whom the good people of the Wall Street
district provided a decent place of worship. The
good people of Wall Street themselves were the ones
who lacked adequate quarters, and they provided the
New Church for those of their own number who
found it convenient to worship there, or who for any
other reason were willing to make the change.

At the same time it must be admitted that even
from the start there was a certain observable difference between the two congregations. For one thing,
tested by the record of the charitable offerings made
from year to year, the Wall Street congregation was
the wealthier. This is in part explained by the
probability that the younger rather than the older
portion of the congregation moved to the New
Church, both because they had not so deeply rooted
an affection for the very walls and pews of the old
building, and also because the young people probably lived further uptown, in the region where the
New Church stood. But there was another differ-

* In its relation to its two affiliated churches.

ence also which was even more important than that
of wealth or that of age. Either by accident or, more
probably, by the drawing together of congenial persons, the strong Scotch and Irish element of the
Presbyterian membership remained for the most
part in the older church, while the New England
element was largely transferred to Beekman Street.*

It is not to be supposed that this difference of
origin amounted to a sharp demarcation or that the
diverse characteristics of these two classes, the conservatism of the Scotch-Irish and the more democratic spirit of the New Englanders, were obtrusively
displayed by the respective congregations, but the
difference existed and was bound to play its part in
the subsequent history.

* See "Br. Ch. Mem.," p. 153.

CHAPTER III

IN COLONIAL DAYS : 1768-1774

"The pews were all immediately taken, and it soon became abundantly evident that the erection of an additional church was neither unnecessary nor premature."— "Memoirs of John Rodgers," p. 182.

"As we have therefore opportunity, let us do good unto all men, especially unto them who are of the household of faith."—*Galatians* 6 : 10.

O N New Year's Day, 1768, the congregation assembled in the New Church for the first time and dedicated it to the service of God. Even the very imperfect picture of the scene that, by the help of the records, rises to our view is well worth looking upon. Members of all the representative Presbyterian families are in the pews—Livingstons, Broomes, McDougals, Ogilvies, Quackenbosses. The clerk is in his desk and Mr. Rodgers, in gown and bands, with his full, curled wig upon his head, has ascended into his lofty pulpit. There he offers the introductory prayer, reads from the Scriptures and gives out the Psalm, not improbably the one hundred and twenty-second as being most appropriate for this occasion.

"How did my heart rejoice to hear
My friends devoutly say,
'In Zion let us all appear,
And keep the solemn day.'"

Though we must guess at the Psalm, we have precise information about the text of the sermon. It

33

was taken from Haggai 2 : 7, "I will fill this house with glory, saith the Lord of hosts." The theme and spirit of the discourse, thus introduced, cannot well be mistaken. Although both minister and people had themselves given so freely and worked so faithfully to build the church, they were not permitted on that day to think of their own powers or their own success. The house belonged to God and its only real value must come through His blessing it and using it. The occasion was in itself impressive, and Mr. Rodgers was a preacher thoroughly capable of putting it to its best use. We are assured by those who listened to him through many years that his sermons were remarkable for their effect upon his hearers. He had the power to stir the emotions as well as convince the mind, and commonly, before he had concluded, both preacher and congregation were literally moved to tears.*

But while we may well believe that on that day such a preacher drove home to the hearts of the people his message of the divine presence and power, we may believe, also, that as the congregation dispersed after the service they were by no means unmindful of the leading part that had been played in the creation of this New Church by Mr. Rodgers himself. They must have felt, too, that its future success would, under God, depend in no small measure upon his continued energy and devotion. And we, also, if we are to understand the history of the church, must recognize at the outset the power of leadership in the pastor.

We have already seen what manner of man he was

* "Rodgers Mem.," p. 88.

at the time of his call, endowed with a strong personality, one who might be confidently expected to take a commanding position in all the affairs in which he was concerned, and to lead them to a successful conclusion. During his early years in New York he had continued to display these same qualities. His prompt settlement of the difference regarding the manner of opening divine worship, whether at clerk's desk or pulpit, has already been described, but another anecdote may be added which reveals in a still more entertaining manner the forcefulness with which he exercised his authority.

It seems that at one of the services a stranger had entered the church and had walked nearly the length of the aisle without being invited to a seat by any of those who occupied the pews. Mr. Rodgers, "from his pulpit watch-tower," as the narrator describes it, saw clearly what had happened and chose an unexpected way to remedy it. His house-servant, a negro, was at that time the sexton also. To him Mr. Rodgers called out in a loud voice, "Frank, show the gentleman to *my* seat." We are told that this broad hint to the congregation had an instantaneous effect, and that so many pew doors flew open as to make the stranger's choice among them almost embarrassing. The noteworthy thing about such incidents as these is not that they should have occurred, but that the minister who ventured to make his points in such a direct and unconventional manner, carried his congregation with him, as Mr. Rodgers indisputably did. A weak man, acting so, would soon have been disliked as a meddler, but in Mr. Rodgers the strength of genuine leadership was recognized by everybody, and his bold strokes, whether in great or in small matters, were justified by their success.

Even at this early date his reputation was by no means local only. On December 20th, 1768, he received from the University of Edinburgh the degree of Doctor of Divinity,* at that time a most extraordinary honor for an American clergyman, and rendered doubly significant in his case by the fact that Dr. Benjamin Franklin had been sufficiently interested to write from London the commendatory letter which led to the granting of it. Dr. Rodgers was at this time only forty-one years of age.

But we must return to the history of the New Church itself. The pews, we are told, were all immediately taken, showing that the forming of a second congregation had been no mistake. The list of pew-holders must, however, have included a considerable number who were not communicants, for we learn from a list of the united congregations, drawn up at this time, that there were in all three hundred and ninety-one members, allowing only about two hundred to each church.

It would appear that the part which the Christian laymen of those days were expected to take in the church activities was very limited, a striking contrast to the ideal of the present time. Besides living Christian lives, their duty was practically confined to attending public worship and contributing to the church collections. None of the societies, which to-day form a natural part of the machinery of every

* The diploma conferring this degree is now in the possession of the Brick Church, having been presented by Dr. Rodgers' great-grandson, Mr. Robertson Rodgers.

BRICK CHURCH RELICS

1. Diploma from Edinburgh University conferring degree of D.D on John Rodgers. 2. Pocket calendar of Dr. Rodgers, with entries of marriage fees. 3. Dr. Spring's sand-box (old-time substitute for blotting paper). 4. Brick from the Brick Church on Beekman Street. 5. Breastpin made from wood of the Beekman Street steeple. 6. Manuscript of sermon preached by Dr. Rodgers at close of Revolutionary War. 7. Sermon-case of Dr. Rodgers, worked in colored crewels. 8. Printed form of sermon shown in No. 6.

church, had then been conceived of, and it is especially noteworthy that the women had not begun any active or organized work, such as in later times has so greatly added to the church's usefulness.

In a word, the work of the church was carried on by its officers. The ministers, of course, conducted the public worship and administered the sacraments; and theirs for the most part, was the work of visiting the families of the parish; the session busied itself especially with the matter of church discipline; and to the deacons was committed the administration of the benevolences. We may examine the work of the New Church, during the first seven or eight years of its existence, under this threefold division.

The public services of the church were not many in those days, little more than half as many as at the present time, but it is to be presumed that they were a good deal longer, and that in them a much larger proportion of time was devoted to the sermon or the lecture. The congregation on Beekman Street assembled every Sunday morning and on alternate Sunday afternoons. Four times in the year the Sacrament of the Lord's Supper was administered, apparently on the first Sundays of March, June, September and December. It is indicative of the close personal oversight given to individual members in those days, that in order to partake of the Communion it was always necessary to obtain in advance a sort of certificate of good standing. To those members who were deemed worthy of it—and the judgment was a strict one—this certificate was given in the form of a "token," evidently either a metal voucher or a ticket. These, we know, were applied for in person at a fixed time in advance, for in the session records we read of being "directed to attend for receiving a token for admission to the Lord's Supper." Only those who presented tokens were allowed to receive the sacrament.

We are not informed whether at first there were week-day meetings held at the New Church. We know that among the Presbyterians at this time there was a weekly class for the instruction of children in the shorter catechism, and a public lecture on the catechism on Thursday evenings,* at which the doctrinal exposition was followed by an earnest practical application. There were also private associations for prayer established in different localities. But it is uncertain whether any of these week-day meetings was at the beginning actually held in the New Church. We must remember in this connection that Beekman Street is but a short distance from Wall Street.

By Dr. Rodgers the work of visiting the people of the congregation was most thoroughly and persistently performed. We know already the methods he had employed in his former parish, and these he continued in New York.

The work of the minister and elders meeting as the session of the church is very fully preserved in the minutes of that body, so that we are able to say

* This was started by Dr. Rodgers soon after coming to New York, and was originally intended for the older children. It was open, however, to all who chose to attend, and the room was usually filled to overflowing by people of all ages. Dr. Rodgers frequently, in later years, expressed his belief that these Thursday evening lectures had been more signally blessed to the spiritual benefit of his people than any other part of his ministrations. ("Rodgers Mem.," p. 176.)

with certainty what the nature of it was and how
thoroughly it was done. They regularly passed upon
the worthiness of all persons who desired to be admitted to church membership, and once a year they
received and examined the financial report of the
deacons; but the distinctive occupation of the session at this time was the uncongenial work of church
discipline, for, to an extent, now utterly unheard of,
the private morals of the individual members of the
church were then investigated, corrected, and controlled. Delinquents, or suspected persons, or persons accused of wrong-doing by other members, were
summoned by formal citation to appear at session
meeting, and there their conduct was thoroughly
sifted. At times the examination was so extended as
to amount to a formal trial, witnesses being examined at great length, and the full testimony being reduced to writing. Not only was judgment pronounced upon offenders whose wrong-doing had
already become a public scandal, but the attempt
was made to discover and check, before it was too
late, every sort of evil in the conduct of the members
of the church. Not infrequently, on the other hand,
the investigation ended in a complete acquittal, and
it is apparent that in at least some of these cases the
accused person had been most forward to bring the
case before the session, as a means of silencing unjust or malicious attacks, without resorting to law.

During the period with which we are at present
occupied the session, it must be remembered, belonged not to the New Church alone, but to the two
united congregations, and we have no means of
ascertaining when the recorded acts of discipline

had reference to New Church people. It will, therefore, be best to defer the more full and serious discussion of this part of the church's life till we come to the time when the New Church had a session of its own. A passing reference may, however, be made to the curious and sometimes (in spite of the serious occasion) amusing passages which the subject of discipline has introduced into the records of this reverend body. It is certainly odd to turn over page after page in which is discussed the fate of a red-and-white handkerchief supposed to have been stolen, or of "a pair of speckled silk stockings of a bluish cast," that had similarly disappeared. You may read, in the handwriting of the session clerk, the momentous history of a certain blue cloth cloak, and how the material of it was afterward identified with great certainty, although transformed into a "surtout and a pair of trousers." Or you may even learn at the mouth of an apparently friendly witness that Mrs. —— "loved a little Small Beer dashed with Rum every Day to refresh Nature whenever she had Money to buy it." And, by the way, the verdict of the session in this particular case is interesting for its very moderate severity. They did not decide in so many words that the accused had been guilty of intemperance, but only went so far as to affirm that she had "given too much grounds to suspect her of too great a fondness for Strong Liquor."

Upon the shoulders of the deacons rested the whole work of caring for the poor of the church. And this is the same thing as saying that they administered the whole of the church's benevolences, for in those days no collections were taken and no money was given through the church for any other benevolent purpose than to supply the needs of the parish poor. The Church of Christ had not yet awakened to her duty and her power as the organizer and supporter of every sort of religious and philanthropic enterprise.

The money which the deacons distributed in alms was received in the offering made at each Communion Service, known as "table money," and also in a special offering taken in connection with an annual "Charity Sermon," which in the New Church was preached usually on the second Sunday afternoon in December. In this special offering from twenty to thirty pounds sterling was given annually, and about an equal amount was received from the four communion offerings together.* The entire sum was annually divided among the deacons, who attended personally to the distribution of it, and reported upon their work to the session at the end of the year.

One is impressed, in this brief review of the first years of the New Church, by the air of maturity to which it almost immediately attained. Sharing as it did from the beginning the whole history and experience, and all the methods, customs, and traditions of the older church of which it was an integral part, it seems almost to have had no youth. As soon as the stir which accompanied the provision of land and building had passed, the church life appeared to settle at once into a placid middle age of routine use-

---

* On one occasion at least (in 1773), the deacons endeavored to increase their ability to aid the poor by investing in two lottery tickets, showing that the moral objections to the lottery were not felt by them in that period.

fulness; and, so far as its own internal affairs were concerned, it might have so continued indefinitely. But there were outside factors to be reckoned with, through which the second period of the New Church's history, beginning in 1775, was destined to be anything but serene and uneventful. Political affairs, even during the seven years studied in this chapter, were clearly moving toward a crisis, in which the church would inevitably be involved, and we must now turn back to study these contemporary events.

CHAPTER IV

"THE PRESBYTERIAN JUNTO": 1752-1775

"The early and just alarm our country took at the measures pursued by the British Court towards us strongly points us to the watchful care of a kind Providence over us."—JOHN RODGERS, "The Divine Goodness Displayed in the American Revolution," p. 12.

"When the centurion heard that, he went and told the chief captain, saying, Take heed what thou doest: for this man is a Roman. Then the chief captain came, and said unto him, Tell me, art thou a Roman? And he said, Yea. And the chief captain answered, With a great sum obtained I this freedom. And Paul said, But I was free born."—*Acts* 22 : 26-28.

THAT little or nothing should have been said until now about the affairs of the country at large, at the time when the New Church was founded or during the first years of its existence, must appear strange and perhaps neglectful; for the period was, of course, a momentous one. The episode of the Stamp Act was still fresh in men's minds when the church on Beekman Street was projected, and throughout the succeeding years the clouds of threatened conflict with the mother country were becoming more and more ominous. Indeed, so absorbing were the political questions of the period that one can but wonder how men at the same time found energy for starting and maintaining a new church. It can be explained only on the assumption that those colonial Presbyterians did really seek first the kingdom of God.

Why, then, it will be asked, since political questions were at the time of such absorbing interest, has

43

no mention of them been made until we have almost reached the outbreak of the Revolution? This question may, perhaps, be best answered by asking another, Why is it that the church's own records maintain an almost unbroken silence in regard to the momentous events of the years before the war? For such a silence they do indeed maintain. Between 1768 and 1775 the minutes of the session contain but two important references to current politics. In October, 1770, when Lord Dunmore arrived from England to take the office of Governor of the Province, and again in July, 1771, when Governor Tryon succeeded him, the officers of the church presented addresses of welcome; and in both of them, it is noticeable, loyalty to King George was most unequivocally expressed.* Beyond these two allusions the records have nothing to say about current events.

This silence, however, was very far from indicating that the members of the church were indifferent to the problems and conflicts of the time. Abundant evidence will presently be adduced to show that they were not only intensely interested but highly influential in the events that led to the Revolution. The silence means rather that the church itself, as an institution, took no formal part in the conflict.

It was neither necessary nor proper that it should do so. The principles of religion were not involved, and there were, of course, good Christians on both

---

* For this they have, by Tory sympathizers, been accused of insincerity, for many of these very men were ardent and active patriots, pledged to resist every encroachment upon their liberties. But at this time they refused to believe that insistence upon their rights would end in a break with England. On the contrary, they conceived themselves more loyal to the true England than were the so-called loyalists.

sides. Even within the Presbyterian Church of New York, although the large majority of its members were of the patriotic party, there were also a number who, by sympathy and conviction, belonged to the other side. Indeed, it was one of the melancholy reflections of the time that in the event of a resort to arms, the very men who had joyfully united in building the New Church and who, under its roof, had together received the Sacrament of the Lord's Supper, might soon be fighting in opposite armies. There was every reason, therefore, why the church, as a church, should not take active part in the conflict, and why its records should make little reference to the events which were dividing men into two opposing camps.

At the same time it was, of course, impossible that a church, which after all was but a collection of individuals, should preserve an actual and absolute neutrality. Even though the majority made no attempt to commit the church officially to the political views which they themselves held as individuals, there was no disguising the fact that the majority was decisive, or that when a Presbyterian congregation assembled—in the New Church, for instance— it was likely to include leading spirits among the New York patriots. It was well known that if war came, and if the British occupied New York, as they would certainly try to do, the New Church would be closed for want of a congregation. When we add to this that Dr. Rodgers, whose sermons and prayers from Sunday to Sunday could hardly have been quite colorless, was "an early and decided friend to American independence," * it becomes

* "Rodgers Mem.," p. 206.

evident that, to say the least, the Tories who attended a Presbyterian service must have felt somewhat lonely. There is on record at least one Tory protest * against petitions offered by Dr. Rodgers in public worship in which, with great distinctness, he asked a blessing upon the cause of American liberty. He continued to pray loyally for the King also,† but that did not affect his views, or the views of the congregation, on the subject of American rights. In short, that the New Church, as a whole, belonged distinctly to the party whose first, and controlling determination was to uphold and maintain American liberties—by peaceable methods, if possible, but by force, if at last no other way were found—there was, and could be, no real doubt.

Our immediate concern, however, is not with the church as a whole, but with the individual Presbyterians of whom the church was composed. Our present object is to ascertain what was the relation of these individual church members to the thoughts and doings of the time, first during the years that led up to the Revolution, and afterward (in the next chapter), during the Revolution itself. For while the personal affairs of individual members would commonly lie beyond the scope of this history, there are special reasons why an exception should be made in regard to the service rendered by the officers and members of the Presbyterian Church in New York during the Revolutionary period.‡

* Jones "N. Y. in Rev.," Vol. II, p. 4.
† "Rivington's Gazette," January 12th, 1775.
‡ It should be noted that in what follows no separation is attempted between members of the Wall Street and members of the New Church congregations. We possess, in fact, no means of distinguishing between

In the first place, although, as we shall see, the institutional life of the church completely ceased soon after the war began, public worship being perforce discontinued and the whole machinery of the church's work coming to a stand-still—even the building being soon in the hands of the enemy—nevertheless the church life did not come to an end. It was interrupted only. It was immediately renewed as soon as the opportunity arrived. And the continuity between the new and the old was preserved by the fact that the old members took up again the new work. In them the church had remained alive. In them the spirit, which animated the church both before and after, lived through the war; and we cannot properly understand the church's history, its interruption or its renewal, unless we are more or less familiar with the record of the men whose hearts were her tabernacle in the period of exile.

But there is a still clearer reason for regarding their personal conduct in the war as a part of the church's history. Their contemporaries very generally believed that there was a direct and vital connection between their Presbyterian faith and their republican politics. In New York, in those days, if a man was known to hold to the one, it was assumed, almost as a matter of course, that he held to the other also. In the literature of the day, and especially

them, for no separate lists are in existence. We must rest content, therefore, with the assumption that a fair proportion of those whose service is mentioned in the text belonged to the New Church. Mr. Daniel Lord, indeed (in the "Br. Ch. Mem.," p. 153,), claims that in the Revolution the New Church was the more democratic and "patriotic," the Wall Street Church the more Tory and "conservative," but we possess no contemporary evidence to prove this.

among the Tories, you will frequently find the word Presbyterian used almost as though it had a distinctly political significance.

Of course, this means chiefly that in practical experience Presbyterian patriots were found to be noticeably common, and also, on the other hand, that at least in New York City, the loyalists were observed to be most often members of the English Church. For this there may have been some merely superficial reason, or it may be that the representative form of government, which is characteristic of Presbyterianism, had exerted a direct influence upon the political views of its members. But whatever the cause, the fact is that Presbyterians had come to be closely identified with outspoken devotion to colonial liberty.

As early as 1752, a club had been formed in New York called the Whig Club, in which we may discern the beginnings of an organized resistance to British aggression, and in it the three most prominent members, William Livingston, William Smith, the younger, and John Morin Scott,—"the Triumvirate," as they were called,—besides others less active, were closely identified with the Presbyterian Church. Livingston was a member, while Smith and Scott, though not on the list of communicants, were trustees. Judge Jones, indeed, the loyalist historian, states incorrectly that they were all Presbyterians by profession and uses that statement to explain their activities on the side of "anarchy and confusion."

These three men were all of good family. The name of Livingston was one of the most highly honored in the province. William Smith was the son of a prominent member of the New York bar.* John M. Scott was a descendant of the baronial family of the Scotts of Ancram, Scotland.† They were all lawyers, and had been educated at Yale College, another cause of their perversity, thinks the loyalist, who describes the New Haven institution as "a college remarkable for its persecuting spirit, its republican principles, its intolerance in religion, and its utter aversion to Bishops and all earthly Kings." "A nursery of sedition, of faction, and of republicanism," he calls it elsewhere.‡

These three able men had early devoted themselves to the cause of liberty, and had already won a certain position as leaders, when the Stamp Act, in 1765, at length aroused the people to decisive action. Livingston, Smith and Scott were then the organizers in New York of the "Sons of Liberty," that patriotic society which sprang up everywhere, to

* Fiske in "The Dutch and Quaker Colonies in America" (Vol. II, p. 285), says: "This William Smith, son of the accomplished lawyer in the Zenger case, was himself one of the few literary men of the province, the author of a 'History of New York to the Year 1732,' which is sturdy and racy, but so full of partisan bitterness that Smith himself admits it 'deserves not the name of history.' As literature, however, it has decided merits."

† The following is from the diary of John Adams, afterward second President of the United States. The date is Monday, August 22d, 1774:

"This morning we took Mr. McDougal into our coach and rode three miles out of town to Mr. Morin Scott's to breakfast. Mr. Scott has an elegant seat there, with Hudson's River just behind his house and a rural prospect all around him. Mr. Scott, his lady and daughter, and her husband, Mr. Litchfield, were dressed to receive us. We sat in a fine, airy entry till called into a front room to breakfast. A more elegant breakfast I never saw,—rich plate, a very large silver coffee-pot, a very large silver teapot, napkins of the very finest materials, toast and bread and butter in great perfection. After breakfast a plate of beautiful peaches, another of pears, and another of plums, and a muskmelon were placed on the table." ("Works of John Adams," Vol. II, p. 349.)

‡ See Jones "N. Y. in Rev.," pp. 3, 5.

voice the instantaneous opposition of the colonists to the hated tax. So largely were the Presbyterians represented in this organization that in New York it was known, we are told, as "The Presbyterian Junto." *

In the opinion of their opponents, the Sons of Liberty were a group of hot-headed rebels, eager, on the slightest provocation, to sever connections with the mother country. As a matter of fact, the idea of separation was, at this time, repugnant to all of them, and was destined, as it gradually came to the front, to find them by no means of one opinion. The strikingly divergent careers of the three leaders, for instance, in whom as Presbyterians we are especially interested, well illustrates this.

Livingston, together with his ardent love of liberty, showed a strong conservative tendency. No one was more staunch than he in his insistence upon the rights of Americans, but he most decidedly desired to maintain those rights by such means as would avoid anything bordering upon revolution. As events developed, we find him one of those who with reluctance perceived that loyalty to America and loyalty to England were incompatible; one of those, therefore, whose leadership, when in the crisis he did come out strongly on the patriot side, was felt to be peculiarly trustworthy, free as it was from the influence of hasty passion. His honorable career in New Jersey, whither he moved in 1773, and where he held the offices, first of General of Militia and afterward of Governor, was proof of the confidence he inspired.

* Bancroft's "Hist. of the U. S.," Vol. IV, p. 326.

William Smith was also a conservative. To him, too, the break with England, toward which the advancing patriotic sentiment gradually pointed, was a thing by all means to be avoided. From a choice between the two allegiances he most decidedly shrank. But in his case the result of this attitude was a state of uncertainty and vacillation at the crucial moment which left him in an unenviable position. Up to a certain point, all had gone well with him. When Washington took command in New York in April, 1776, Mr. Smith put his house at the General's disposal, and after the occupation of the city by the British he was found among the patriots at some distance up the Hudson. But he could not remain in hearty sympathy with those who were now entering into open conflict with England. When called upon to take the new oath of loyalty, by which he would cease to be a British subject, he declared himself unable to do so. He was therefore ordered to leave the patriot territory and returned to New York, "forced out of his inglorious neutrality," as the patriots expressed it.* In their view, it was no time for a nice balancing of opinions. Though suspected in much the same way by some of the loyalists, he was received by the British authorities and was later made Chief Justice of New York, and after the war he held the same office in Canada. Yet at the beginning of the agitation and, indeed, down to the actual outbreak of the war, the cause of liberty found in him a strong and able supporter. So long as the opposition was to the British ministry, but not to Great Britain herself, he was a willing leader in it.

* "Pennsylvania Packet," September 15th.

John Morin Scott, on the other hand, was naturally of a bolder and more aggressive temperament than either Smith or Livingston, and, as the history proceeds, is found to ride ever upon the crest of the advancing wave, his eloquent tongue putting courage into many who were waiting only for a determined summons. We shall hear much more of him as we proceed.

From the period of the Stamp Act, Scott was ably supported, and, indeed, at length surpassed in energy, by another man of the same type—Alexander McDougal. He, also, was a Presbyterian, not only an attendant like Scott, but a communicant; the men of three generations in his family were members of the Presbyterian Church. In his case we have a man of poor and obscure origin, one whose sympathies were by experience, as well as from conviction, with the people. We are told that he had followed the sea in his youth, starting as a boy before the mast and ending his nautical career as captain of a vessel. At a later period he had built up a good business as merchant in New York. In short, he was a man of parts, and when the occasion called, he soon rose to the top.*

There were among the Sons of Liberty, and at first influential among them, men still more radical, such as Isaac Sears; but none of these having been

---

* Of both Scott and McDougal John Adams, in his journal for the year 1774, gives an estimate. Of the ability of both he speaks in high terms; "sensible," he calls them, by which, no doubt, he means that their political views coincided more or less closely with his own. Personally he found McDougal the more acceptable, speaking especially of his openness: "he has none of the mean cunning which disgraces so many of my countrymen." Of Scott he says, bluntly, that he was "not very polite." (John Adams "Works," Vol. II, pp. 345-347.)

Presbyterians, we are not concerned to follow their fortunes. Scott and McDougal, who did represent the Presbyterian congregations among the more ardent patriots, were, moreover, of more importance in the final issue. Though they, also, were certainly passionate in their love of liberty, impatient of the counsels of prudence and compromise and often suspicious of those who offered them, inclined to violent utterance, and clamorous for decisive action, they did not, like Sears, for instance, get completely out of touch with the moderates. When at length the issue was clearly defined, they and the moderates were found acting again together as they had at the very outset. Meantime these more radical patriots played a part whose importance can hardly be overestimated. It is not too much to say that except for their constant and spirited agitation, and especially their organizing of the common people and voicing of the popular demands, the strong loyalist element in New York might easily have gained control of the situation. The conservatives, even when they rejected the definite proposals of "the Presbyterians," were themselves supported and emboldened by the popular enthusiasm which "the Presbyterians" had aroused.

The Stamp Act went into effect on October 31st, 1765. The next day the inhabitants of New York, at the call of the Sons of Liberty, came together in indignant meeting on the Common. During the preceding years, and still more in the stirring years that were to follow, the Common * was New York's rec-

* It will be remembered that this open space then included not only the present City Hall Park but the site of the post-office.

ognized place of popular meeting. When there was need of giving expression either to great indignation or to great rejoicing, the Common was invariably the scene of the demonstration. It was on the Common that, at critical junctures, the will of the people was made known in no uncertain tones to obstinate governors or timid committees. In short, this open space at the north end of the city was, as has been well said, the Faneuil Hall of New York.

Now, directly adjoining the Common, it will be remembered, was the land which, in February, 1766, was secured for that New Church whose history we are tracing. The same men who, out there on the Common, were making American history, were here, on the "Vineyard lot," building their Presbyterian Church. It is agreeable to know that the same staunch qualities were going into both enterprises, and to be thus reminded that the patriots owed much to their Presbyterianism and the Presbyterians much to their patriotism. The walls of the New Church, rising while the American nation was coming into existence across the way, and her windows, looking quietly,—one might say approvingly,—at the momentous events which there ushered in the Revolution, may be taken as fitting symbols of the part which the church, as a living force in the hearts of her members, played in the events of those memorable years.

One might almost tell the rest of the story of this period under the title "What the New Church Saw from the Edge of the Green." First, there were the battles about the Liberty Pole, a flag-staff originally erected at the great rejoicing over the Stamp Act's repeal, and designed to carry a flag inscribed "The King, Pitt, and Liberty." That was in June, 1766. Every few weeks, from that time on, the pole would be cut down by the soldiers, who acted as agents of the alarmed and outraged loyalists, and immediately restored by the indomitable Sons of Liberty. The fourth pole was standing when the New Church was dedicated. Its life was longer than that of its predecessors, but when it finally fell in January, 1770, the church witnessed a great commotion: three thousand angry and determined citizens assembled on the Common to devise means of overwhelming the pestilent soldiery and the still more hated power behind them.

In all these doings the Presbyterians, McDougal and Scott, had been leaders. In February, 1770, a very foolish attempt was made by the exasperated authorities to rid themselves of McDougal, by charging him with the authorship of certain alleged libels that had recently appeared. As might have been expected, his popularity increased vastly with persecution. While imprisoned in the New Gaol (on the Common), he was so besieged by callers that he was forced, or humorously gave out that he was forced, to set an hour for visits, namely, "from three o'clock in the afternoon till six." A notice to this effect was inserted in the newspapers.

Because of a similarity to the case of John Wilkes, in England, among whose followers the number "45" was used as a sort of watchword, the press accounts of McDougal's prison life were given in such arithmetical form as the following: "Yesterday, the 45th day of the year, 45 gentlemen . . . cordial

friends to Captain McDougal and the glorious cause
of American liberty, went in decent procession to the
New Gaol, and dined with him on 45 pounds of
beefsteak, cut from a bullock 45 months old,* and
with a number of other friends, who joined them in
the afternoon, drank a number of toasts expressive,
not only of the most undissembled loyalty, but of the
warmest attachment to liberty, its renowned advocates in Great Britain and America, and the freedom
of the press." † The prisoner was indicted and
tried, but finally, for lack of evidence, was discharged
after an imprisonment of several months.

In 1774, when the conflict was rapidly nearing,
McDougal still held his place among the mass of the
people as hero and leader, but many of the more conservative patriots were beginning to fear the effects of
his headlong enthusiasm. The question had plainly
arisen whether he and others like him should seize
the entire control of the movement, or should rather
play the part of inspirers and energizers, while the
helm was held by more cautious hands.

A committee of fifty (afterward fifty-one), chosen
by the inhabitants of New York on May 16th, 1774,
in response to certain proposals from Boston on the
subject of the importation tax, included men of all
types, and in it the contest between conservatives and
radicals began at once. The conservatives, as it
proved, were in the majority. When, in July, John
M. Scott and Alexander McDougal were nominated
as delegates to the General Congress, they were de-

---

* Judge Jones, in his account of this episode, gives, among the donations
to the prisoner, "From the two Presbyterian Parsons, Rodgers and Treat,
45 lbs. of candles."

† "N. Y. Journal," February 15th, 1770.

feated, and the committee chose instead a group of moderates and loyalists.

The people were greatly dissatisfied with this, and with other acts of their representatives. On July 6th they met in great numbers on the Common, "the Great Meeting in the Fields," it was afterward called. Alexander McDougal presided and the action taken was an emphatic rebuke to the committee of fifty-one. For several days the contest raged, but without a decisive issue at that time. The chosen delegates, having made a solemn profession in writing of their devotion to liberty, were finally accepted by the people; but the real differences, which the incident revealed, remained as a problem of the future.* It was no doubt wise that a moderate policy should, at that juncture, prevail, though the protestors were right, as events proved, in their suspicion that many of the moderates were men who, in the last division, would choose the side of Great Britain against the Colony. At the same time, the best men in the moderate party, and happily those who gained and held control in it, were true patriots, seeking in their more cautious way the same great ends to which Scott and McDougal and their comrades were devoting themselves with noble and unselfish enthusiasm.

* Among the Presbyterians who, at this time, were active in urging and voicing the popular protests were McDougal, Scott, Joseph Hallet, P. V. B. Livingston, and John Broome. Mr. Livingston is described by John Adams, in 1774, as "a sensible man and a gentleman. He has been in trade, is rich, and now lives upon his income." ("Works," Vol. II, p. 351.)

CHAPTER V

IN THE REVOLUTION: 1775–1783

"Little did we think of such an event as this, when we began the struggle for our invaded privileges. The growing injustice of the British Administration—their accumulated injuries—opened it upon us, and forced us into the measure, as the only alternative to save our oppressed land. It was this or the most abject slavery. A dread alternative, indeed, . . . but which an all-governing Providence has wisely overruled for our salvation."—JOHN RODGERS, "The Divine Goodness Displayed in the American Revolution," p. 11.

"If thy people go out to battle against their enemy, whithersoever thou shalt send them, and shall pray unto the Lord, toward the city which thou hast chosen, and toward the house which I have built for thy name; then hear thou in heaven their prayer and their supplication, and maintain their cause."—1 *Kings* 8 : 44 *f*.

ON Sunday, April 23d, 1775, when the stirring news from Lexington reached the city, the inadequacy of the conservative policy became suddenly evident and, for a time, the sway of the ardent patriots again increased. A party of them under the leadership, we are told, of Peter R. Livingston, a Presbyterian, seized at once upon a sloop loaded with lumber for the barracks in Boston and threw the cargo into the harbor, the people at the same time being urged to arm themselves by an attack upon the arsenal. In the meeting of His Majesty's Council at the house of the Lieutenant Governor, that afternoon, William Smith, of whom we read in the last chapter, took the position that the excitement then prevailing was general throughout the city, and that it was not without due cause in the obstinate injustice of the British Ministry. He opposed strongly the purpose of the extreme loyalists to call out the militia and read the riot act.

The most definite evidence, however, of the renewed influence of the more pronounced patriots, is found in the abandonment of the old "Committee of Fifty-one" at this time, and the selection by the inhabitants, on May 1st, of a new committee of one hundred. The conservative element was still strongly represented in it, but the proportions of influence had been somewhat changed. The committee declared its resolve, in the most explicit manner, to stand or fall with the liberty of the Colonies, and at its first meeting, held without delay, a motion, offered by Scott and seconded by McDougal, was passed, providing for an association which should engage, by all the ties of religion, honor, and love of country, to submit to the Colonial Congress, to withdraw support from British troops, and at risk of lives and fortunes to repel every attempt at enforcing taxation by Parliament.

Nine at least of the Committee of One Hundred were Presbyterians,* and five of these † were among the twenty-two delegates selected to meet deputies of the other counties in the Provincial Congress on May 22d. The contemporary loyalist historian,‡ describing the reception tendered at this time to the delegates sent from New England to the second Continental Congress, as they passed through New York on their way to Philadelphia, speaks in the bitterest terms of "the Presbyterian faction" who

---

* P. V. B. Livingston, McDougal, Scott, Joseph Hallet, Thomas Smith, John Broome, Samuel Broome, John Lasher, John White.

† The first five in the above list.

‡ Judge Jones. See Jones "N. Y. in Rev,"

took the lead in the matter. He gives a list of them, which includes their two ministers, Rodgers and Treat, besides most of the others with whom we are now familiar. He tells us that the escorting company of grenadiers was commanded by John Lasher, the Presbyterian shoemaker ("of the lowest extraction," he adds) and he ends by classing all these persons with "other fomenters and demagogues of rebellion." Yet in spite of these uncomplimentary remarks, it is certain that these men were now taking more and more a position of command in New York.

In June, John Morin Scott appeared in a picturesque incident not without significance.* The British soldiers, whose position in New York after Lexington was anything but comfortable, were leaving the city by permission of the Committee of One Hundred, when it was observed that they were taking with them a cartload of extra arms. Marinus Willett, a patriot, endeavored to stop them, on the ground that the committee had not authorized this act, but he found a strong supporter of the soldiers in another bystander, no less a person than Mr. Gouverneur Morris. At this point, Scott happened to make his appearance, himself "an influential member of the committee," says Willett, in his narrative of the event, and one "whose reputation for talents was as great as any in the city." Taking in the situation at a glance, he exclaimed in a loud voice, "You are right, Willett; the committee have not given them permission to carry off any spare arms," and in spite of Mr. Morris, the wagon was turned into a

* "New York in the Revolution," p. 63.

side street, while the soldiers proceeded without it to the wharf.

It was a time of curious confusion in which these New Yorkers were then living. Regiments of soldiers were being raised by the colonists for a purpose that could not be disguised, while the very men active in this work claimed, and with perfect sincerity, that they were loyal subjects of King George.

No clearer evidence of this could be desired than the Pastoral Letter which was issued by the Presbyterian General Assembly, sitting at New York about a month after the battle of Lexington. It deserves the more a place in this history because Dr. Rodgers served on the committee of two ministers and four laymen who prepared it. After a long opening exhortation, it proceeds to "offer a few advices to the societies under our charge, as to their public and general conduct."

"First. In carrying on this important struggle, let every opportunity be taken to express your attachment and respect to our sovereign, King George, and to the revolution principles by which his august family was seated on the British throne. We recommend, indeed, not only allegiance to him from duty and principle, as the first magistrate of the empire, but esteem and reverence for the person of the prince who has merited well of his subjects on many accounts, and who has probably been misled into the late and present measures by those about him; neither have we any doubt that they themselves have been in a great degree deceived by false information from interested persons residing in America. It gives us the greatest pleasure to say, from our own certain knowledge of all belonging to our communion, and from the best means of information of the far greatest part of all denominations in the country, that the present opposition to the measures of administration does not in the least arise from disaffection to the King or a desire of separation from the parent state. . . . We exhort you, therefore, to continue in the same disposition, and not to suffer oppression, or injury itself, easily to provoke you to anything which may seem to betray contrary sentiments. Let it ever appear that you only desire the preservation and security of those rights which belong to you as freemen and Britons, and that reconciliation upon these terms is your most ardent desire."

The rest of this document, also, is so clear an exposition of the attitude of Presbyterians at the beginning of the war that the quotation may properly be extended. The letter proceeds as follows:

"Secondly. Be careful to maintain the union which at present subsists through all the Colonies. Nothing can be more manifest than that the success of every measure depends on its being inviolably preserved, and therefore we hope that you will leave nothing undone which can promote that end. In particular, as the Continental Congress, now sitting at Philadelphia, consists of delegates chosen in the most free and unbiased manner by the body of the people, let them not only be treated with respect and encouraged in their difficult service,—not only let your prayers be offered up to God for his direction in their proceedings,—but adhere firmly to their resolutions; and let it be seen that they are able to bring out the whole strength of this vast country to carry them into execution. . . .

"Thirdly. We do earnestly exhort and beseech the societies under our care to be strict and vigilant in their private government, and to watch over the morals of their several members. It is with the utmost pleasure we remind you that the last Continental Congress determined to discourage luxury in living, public diversions, and gaming of all kinds, which have so fatal an influence on the morals of the people. . . . As it has been observed by many eminent writers that the censorial power, which had for its object the manners of the public in the ancient free states, was absolutely necessary to their continuance, we cannot help being of opinion that the only thing which we have now to supply the place of this is the religious discipline of the several sects with respect to their own members; so that the denomination or profession which shall take the most effectual care of the instruction of its members, and maintain its discipline in the fullest vigor, will do the most essential service to the whole body. . . .

"Fourthly. We cannot but recommend and urge in the warmest manner a regard to order and the public peace; and, as in many places during the confusions that prevail, legal proceedings have become difficult, it is hoped that all persons will conscientiously pay their just debts, and to the utmost of their power serve one another, so that the evils inseparable from a civil war may not be augmented by wantonness and irregularity.

"Fifthly. We think it of importance at this time to recommend to all of every rank, but especially to those who may be called to action, a spirit of humanity and mercy. Every battle of the warrior is with confused noise and garments rolled in blood. It is impossible to appeal to the sword without being exposed to many scenes of cruelty and slaughter; but it is often observed that civil wars are carried on with a rancor and spirit of revenge much greater than those between independent states. The injuries received, or supposed, in civil wars, wound more deeply than those of foreign enemies. It is therefore the more necessary to guard against this abuse and recommend that meekness and gentleness of spirit which is the noblest attendant upon true valor. That man will fight most bravely who never fights till it is necessary, and who ceases to fight as soon as the necessity is over. . . .

"We conclude with our most earnest prayer that the God of heaven may bless you in your temporal and spiritual concerns, and that the present unnatural dispute may be speedily terminated by an equitable and lasting settlement on constitutional principles." * This noble letter was dated May 22d, a Monday. Six days later, we may be sure, it was read from the pulpit of the New Church.

During the summer of 1775 military operations, we learn, continued to be active. McDougal was now Colonel of a regiment. "Colonel" Lasher was another Presbyterian who had been promoted. His battalion was reviewed by Major-General Schuyler on July 3d, "in the presence of a very respectable number of principal gentlemen and ladies." It was remarked that "they went through the exercises and

* "Assembly Digest," pp. 480–482.

evolutions with the greatest order, alertness and decorum." * Toward the end of August some shots were exchanged between His Majesty's ship *Asia* and this same battalion of Colonel Lasher's. On November 15th, John Morin Scott writes: "All business stagnated; the city half deserted for fear of a bombardment. . . . Nothing from t'other side of the water but a fearful looking for of wrath. Our continental petition most probably contemned; the bulk of the nation, it is said, against us; and a bloody campaign next summer. But let us be prepared for the worst,—who can prize life without liberty? It is a bauble only fit to be thrown away." †

It is not surprising that the regular ongoing of the church life was, by this time, greatly interrupted. Even in the session records, usually reticent in regard to contemporary events, the state of turmoil now becomes evident. The omission of one of the stated meetings of the session, for instance, is attributed to "the confusion our city was then in, by reason of our public trouble." On the morning of the last Thursday in November (the day, as it happens, which we now celebrate as our day of national Thanksgiving) the people assembled in the New Church to observe a day of prayer and fasting "on account of the melancholy situation of our public affairs." A few lines beyond this entry the records stop short, not to be resumed for eight long years.

For a few weeks or months, however, the church life in a measure continued. Dr. Rodgers, toward the end of February, 1776, removed his family to

* Gaines's Mercury," July 17th.
† "New York City during the American Revolution."

a place of safety near the city, but he himself went in and out as his duties required. In April he waited on General Washington, then in New York to prepare for its defence, and was received with great consideration. The General, we are told, "followed him to the door, and observed that his name had been mentioned to him in Philadelphia . . . as a gentleman whose fidelity to the interest and liberties of the country might be relied on, and who might be capable of giving him important information; and added, 'May I take the liberty, Sir, to apply to you, with this view, whenever circumstances may render it desirable?'"

A city preparing for a siege was, of course, no place for women and children, and within a few weeks after this conversation a general exodus had begun. Before long, none of Dr. Rodgers' congregation remained save the men who were on duty in the patriot ranks, and those who had determined to remain loyal to Great Britain, the latter constituting a very small minority.* Dr. Rodgers, however, was not left without an occupation. In April he was appointed chaplain to General Heath's Brigade, stationed near Greenwich Village, on Manhattan Island. His service continued through the summer and autumn and was prosecuted with his usual energy. After a brief interval spent in Georgia on private business, he was again claimed for public service as chaplain of the Convention of the State of New York (April, 1777). Later he held the same

---

* Among Presbyterian loyalists were Andrew Elliot, Collector of the Port, and later (1778) Superintendent of Police; Samuel Bayard, Deputy Secretary of the Province; and James Jauncey (a pewholder).

office in the Council of Safety and in the first Legislature of the State.*

But in valuable service to the American cause the minister was outdone by many of his parishioners. Alexander McDougal, who had been Colonel of the first troops raised in New York, was Brigadier-General in 1776, and Major-General in 1777. He took part in the battles of Long Island, White Plains, and Germantown, and served in the New Jersey Campaign. Later he had command of important posts on the Hudson. Washington spoke of him as "a brave soldier and a disinterested patriot." † John Morin Scott, who had been, perhaps, the most influential member of the Committee of One Hundred,

---

* During the latter part of the war, Dr. Rodgers, having no public duty to perform, spent his time in such temporary pastoral work as offered itself. After a brief service in Sharon, Conn., he in 1778 took up his residence in Amenia, N. Y., where he continued as minister of the church for about two years (see "Early History of Amenia," by Newton Reed, p. 41). We learn from the records of "The Society in Amenia Precinct" that Dr. Rodgers received at first fifteen dollars a Sunday for his services, his parishioners agreeing "to pay the money to him, or lay it out for Provisions for him either of which Doct. Rogers Chuses." Several months later it was voted "that this Society give to Doct. Roges 10 dollars per Sabbath during the continuance of the State Act," while a committee of two was appointed to collect provisions and "other necessaries" for him. Still later we find one man directed to "provide Forage for Doct. Rogers for the ensuing year," six men together are to supply some one hundred pounds of butter, while three other individuals provide "1 pig about 100 lbs," "1 do. and a Beef" and "600wt pork." In a historical paper read in Amenia in 1876 by Newton Reed, Esq., the following reference to Dr. Rodgers appears: "He was very courteous and winning in his manners. . . . As an evidence that this courtly gentleman had the good sense to accommodate himself to the simplicity of his rural parish, it was told of him that he made an afternoon's visit with his wife and daughters, to the family of one of his parishioners, riding in an ox-cart." During the last years of the war Dr. Rodgers performed pastoral duties in Danbury, Conn., and Lamington, N. J.

† "Writings of Washington," Vol. IX, p. 186.

was equally prominent in the Provincial Congress
and rendered important service in drawing up the
state constitution. He was appointed one of the first
Brigadier-Generals in June, 1776, and was with the
army until he became Secretary of State (1777–
1779). It is gratifying to see that when the time of
action came, these two men, noted at first for an enthusiasm which seemed sheer recklessness to the
timid, had in reserve the wisdom and strength req-
uisite for real leadership. No doubt, moreover, they
had themselves developed under experience. The
historian Bancroft, speaking of the policy of caution
which New York followed even in the period immediately preceding active hostilities, and pointing out
its wisdom from a strategic point of view, affirms
that this policy was then "maintained alike by the
prudent and the bold; by Livingston and Jay, by
John Morin Scott and McDougal."

Some of the Presbyterians rendered most distinguished service as civil officers of the new government. Peter V. B. Livingston was, in 1775, President
of the Provincial Congress, and later Treasurer of
the State. In the former office he was followed by
his kinsman and fellow-church-member, Peter R.
Livingston, who was also Colonel of Militia from
1775 to 1780. Ebenezer Hazard, who had been
Postmaster for the district of New York in 1775,
served as Surveyor-General of Post Offices of the
United States from 1777 to 1782 and was afterward
Postmaster-General.

But to return to the military branch of the public
service: Colonel Lasher we already know, (the shoemaker "of the lowest extraction"). John Broome

was Lieutenant-Colonel of Militia. Nicholas Berrian, Prentice Bowen, John Quackenbos, and Jeremiah Wool were Presbyterians who rose to the rank of Captain. Peter Vergereau was a Lieutenant. And to these must be added the long list of men who served in the ranks,* many of them men of the highest standing, like Peter V. B. Livingston and Ebenezer Hazard, whose civil offices have been enumerated above.

It would be unnecessary, even if practicable, to follow the fortunes of these individual Presbyterians through the whole war. After the British had taken possession of New York, these men were, of course, scattered as the exigencies of the war demanded. Many of them were never to see again the home or the church which they had abandoned for freedom's sake.

The church building, meantime, rooted on Manhattan Island, was unwillingly rendering service to the enemy. It had escaped the disastrous fire which raged through the city a few nights after the British took possession and which destroyed the parsonage, but, as was to have been expected, it had been put to secular uses by the invaders, and soon began to

* The following list includes only those soldiers whose identification as New York Presbyterians seems practically certain. Positive knowledge in such a matter can hardly be obtained. The list would be twice as long had less rigid tests been applied: Alexander Anderson, William Barber, Samuel Broome, David Campbell, William Frazier, William Gordon, Thomas Graham, Joseph Hallet, Robert Harpur, Joseph Hawkins, Ebenezer Hazard, William Inglis, Thomas Jackson, John King, James Lamb, Peter V. B. Livingston, John McDougal, John Michael, Robert Nesbit, John North, Alexander Patterson, Joseph Pierson, Philip Pelton, Isaac Slover, Benjamin Smith, Gilbert Smith, Melancthon Smith, Robert Stewart, William Todd, Daniel Turner, Abraham Van Gelder, Nathaniel Weekes.

show the effects of rough treatment. For a time, we are told, it was made to serve as a prison, but afterward, and through the greater part of the war, it was used as a hospital for the prisoners. In this way the church, though in the hands of the enemy, did, in a measure, serve the patriot cause, but the measure was, after all, but scant, for the hospital, as described by one who had experience of it, must have seemed to provide little more than a roof to die under.

The description comes to us from one Levi Hanford, who had been taken sick in late December, 1777, on one of the prison ships in the river. "We were taken," he says, "to the Hospital in Dr. Rodgers' Brick Meeting House (afterward Dr. Spring's), near the foot of the Park. From the yard I carried one end of a bunk, from which some person had just died, into the church, and got into it, exhausted and overcome. Wine and some other things were sent in by our Government for the sick; the British furnished nothing. . . . [The doctor] was an American surgeon and a prisoner,—had been taken out of prison to serve in the hospital. . . . Of all places, that was the last to be coveted; disease and death reigned there in all their terrors. I have had men die by the side of me in the night, and have seen fifteen dead bodies sewed up in their blankets and laid in the corner of the yard at one time, the product of one twenty-four hours. Every morning at eight o'clock the dead-cart came, the bodies were put in, the men drew their rum, and the cart was driven off to the trenches." *

* Disosway, p. 145.

One attempt was made during the war to restore the church to its religious uses. In the fall of 1780 the two Presbyterian loyalists, Elliot, then Lieutenant-Governor, and Smith, the Chief Justice, started a movement to this effect, and proposed that Dr. Rodgers be invited to return to the city and conduct services in the restored church. Governor Robertson promised his coöperation in this somewhat surprising plan. That Dr. Rodgers would have acquiesced in it is impossible. We are not surprised that to most of the loyalists the proposal seemed as absurd as it was objectionable. They, on their part, considered the Presbyterian minister "to be a person of rigid republican principle, a rebellious, seditious preacher, a man who had given more encouragement to rebellion by his treasonable harangues from the pulpit than any other republican preacher, perhaps, on the continent." Smith and Elliot knew, of course, that these ferocious opinions were exaggerated by hatred, and their own proposal is a tribute to the old relation of confidence and esteem between pastor and people, but they were, as might have been expected, unable to carry their point. The most practical difficulty was met in the veto of Dr. Booth, the British Superintendent of Hospitals, who said that he could not surrender the church unless provided with its equivalent elsewhere.*

It is asserted that the British Government paid a rental for those churches in New York which were seized and used during the English occupation, but it is also admitted that the money went no further than to the barrack-masters. Certainly no com-

* Jones "N. Y. in Rev.," Vol. II, p. 2.

pensation was received by the Presbyterians for the use of the New Church or for the damage done to it; and at the end of the war little more than the shell was left. Within, it was completely dismantled.

CHAPTER VI

RESTORATION AND PROGRESS: 1783–1808

"The Lord doth build up Jerusalem; he gathereth together the outcasts of Israel. He healeth the broken in heart, and bindeth up their wounds."—*Psalm* 147 : 2 *f.*

"Their numbers greatly reduced by death and by permanent removals to the country, the pecuniary resources of all of them impaired and of many of them exhausted, both their houses of worship in a state little short of complete ruin, their parsonage burnt, and a considerable debt accumulated in consequence of their long exclusion from the city—it may be supposed that nothing but Christian faith could have preserved them from total discouragement."—SAMUEL MILLER "Memoirs of John Rodgers," p. 243.

O N November 13th, 1783, nearly two weeks before New York City was finally evacuated by the British, the following notice appeared in "The New York Packet and the American Advertiser:" * "The Members of the Presbyterian Congregation are requested, at the desire of some of the late Trustees, to meet at the New Brick Church, This Afternoon at Four o'Clock, to provide means for putting their Church in order for Public Worship."

The New Church had suffered less than the building on Wall Street,† and it was, accordingly, chosen as the one to be immediately repaired. The need became increasingly urgent after the British evacuation, when large numbers of Presbyterians

* A semi-weekly sheet printed by "Samuel Loudon, No. 5, Water-Street, between the Coffee-House and the Old Slip."

† The latter building had been used as a barrack by the enemy.

73

returned to the city, so that Dr. Rodgers soon found himself surrounded by a considerable congregation for whom no place of worship was yet provided.

At this juncture an unexpected and most welcome offer was made by the vestry of Trinity Church. It was proposed, in a spirit of Christian courtesy, that St. George's and St. Paul's chapels should be used alternately by the Presbyterians until their own place of worship had been restored. The offer was accepted and this arrangement continued from November, 1783, until the following June.

Thus is explained the unusual fact that the sermon, whose manuscript is still in existence, preached by Dr. Rodgers on the day of Thanksgiving and Prayer, recommended by Congress and observed throughout the United States on December 11th, 1783, was delivered in an Episcopal church, St. George's, corner of Beekman and Cliff Streets.* The text was taken from Psalm 126 : 3, "The Lord hath done great things for us, whereof we are glad," and the sermon is a faithful ascription of praise to God for all the providences and mercies of the war.

It is always interesting to see events through the eyes of a contemporary, when he is as well qualified to describe and estimate them as Dr. Rodgers was. The special evidences of the favor of God which he enumerates are certainly well chosen. First, he mentions "that union which proved our strength in the day of trial," and which was so difficult of attainment that men might readily ascribe it to the benev-

---

* It was repeated by Dr. Henry van Dyke in the present Brick Church on the one hundredth anniversary of "Evacuation Day," November 25th, 1883.

olent intervention of God.   He continues by pointing
out that the first attack of the enemy was providentially made "upon a place where our greatest strength
lay," that throughout the war, and in spite of war's
ravages, there was abundance of provisions of every
kind, and that the general health, both in the country
at large and in the army, had, on the whole, been
astonishingly good.   The choice of the commander-
in-chief is singled out as an event peculiarly indicative of the divine guidance, "for," says Dr. Rodgers,
"by his commanding address, exemplary patience,
and invincible fortitude, he encouraged and taught
our soldiers to endure the greatest hardships, and
prepared our army for disbanding, when no other
man could have done it." *   Finally, the preacher
ascribes to the Lord of hosts "the success of our
arms," and in a brief survey of the war he points out
the many instances in which a power greater than
man's might be clearly discerned.   As he closes, he
paints contrasting pictures of the desolations of war
and the blessings of peace, which must have been
most affecting to his hearers, and ends with a solemn reminder of the serious evils existing in the
national character, in part the product of the war

---

* The following letter, now in the possession of Dr. Rodgers' great-
grandson, Mr. Robertson Rodgers, refers to a copy of the printed form of
this sermon:

Philadelpa 5th May 1784

Dear Sir

    The Thanksgiving Sermon which you did me the favor to send
me I read with much pleasure, & pray you to accept my thanks for it, &
the favorable mention you have been pleased to make of me therein.

My compliments await Mrs Rogers—With great esteem and respect

I remain dr Sir—
Yr most obedt & affect Ser
Go Washington

The Rev Docr Rogers

and unhappily surviving it, and reminds the people that of all the good things now restored to them nothing could be compared in importance with the renewed privileges and duties of religion.*

The repairs in the New Church were accomplished at a cost of thirteen hundred pounds sterling,† a large sum, it was thought, but necessitated by the high price of all materials at that time. The first service in the restored church was held on June 27th, 1784, Dr. Rodgers preaching from the text, "I was glad when they said unto me, Let us go into the house of the Lord." It was most encouraging to discover that the demand for pews was at once greater than the supply, showing that the Wall Street Church must also be repaired, and this was done in the course of the next year.

Fortunately, a description of the interior of the church on Beekman Street, as it looked after the restoration, has come down to us. Indeed, with the help of Dr. Manasseh Cutler, whose diary happily includes an account of his visit to New York in 1787, we are enabled to attend both morning and evening service on a certain Sunday in July of that year, which will be much pleasanter than to examine the empty church.

"Attended public worship this morning," says Dr. Cutler, "at the new brick Presbyterian Church. The house is large and elegant. The carvings within

* The original manuscript, from which this abstract is taken, does not correspond, either in form or substance, to the sermon as afterward printed, except in the most general way. The published sermon is in many respects less forcible and less interesting.

† Equivalent to between $3,000 and $4,000. The money was raised by subscription through the energy of Dr. Rodgers.

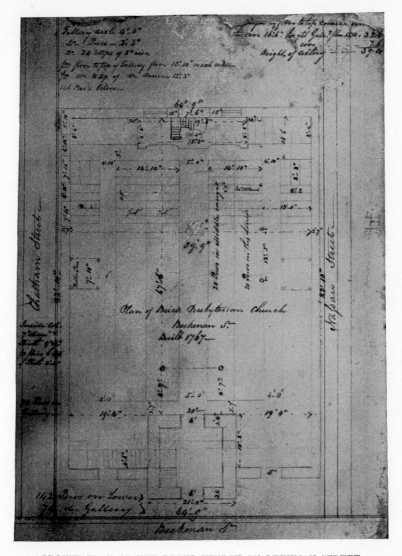

GROUND-PLAN OF THE BRICK CHURCH ON BEEKMAN STREET

are rather plain, but very neat, and produce a fine effect upon the eye. The form of the house is long, and the pulpit near one end, but not adjoining to the wall. It is supported by a single post, which passes up at the back of the pulpit, and is crowned with the sounding-board, not more than two feet above the minister's head. At the end of the house, opposite to the pulpit, are two doors, which open into two long aisles, which extend the whole length of the house. The pews are built on each side of the aisles, one tier of wall pews and two tiers in the centre of the house.* The pews are long and narrow, having only one long seat, except that there are two square wall pews placed opposite to each other near the centre of the side walls, with a handsome canopy over them, supported by pillars. The floors of these pews are considerably elevated above the others, which renders them very pleasant. They are called the Governor's pews, and are occupied by strangers.

"Dr. Ewing, Provost of the College of Philadelphia, preached a very pretty sermon on the advantages and excellency of the Christian religion. The congregation appeared remarkably neat and rich in their dress, but not gay. The house was very full and exceedingly attentive.

"I was particularly pleased with the singing. Around the large pillar which supports the pulpit is a very large circular pew, appropriated to the wardens † of the church and the chorister. In the front of this pew is a little desk considerably elevated.

* In this Dr. Cutler's observation was at fault. There was also a middle aisle, and the number of tiers or ranges of pews, as shown on the still existing plans (see illustration opposite p. 76), were six in number.

† Meaning the elders, and possibly the deacons.

When the psalm is read, the chorister steps up into
this desk and sings the first line. He is then joined
in the second line by the whole congregation—men,
women, and children seemed all to sing, almost without exception. The airs of the tunes were sprightly,
though not very quick; the singing, notwithstanding
it was performed by such a mixed multitude, was
soft, musical, and solemn, and the time well preserved. There is an orchestra, but no organ. The
public service was introduced by a short prayer,
reading the Scriptures, and then singing; but instead
of singing before the sermon, they sing, in the morning as well as afternoon, after the last prayer. As
soon as the last singing is ended, the wardens go out
from the large round pew, with each a large pewter
platter in his hand, each taking a tier of the pews
and walk down the aisles. Every person, great and
small, puts into the platter one copper, and no more.
This contribution is made through the whole congregation in less than three minutes."

Having allowed Dr. Cutler to give us already so
much more than a description of the church itself,
we must go with him a paragraph further in order
to make the picture of this morning service complete, although the bearing of this last item upon the
matter of the church's architecture is, it must be
confessed, rather remote. "I was struck this morning," thus Dr. Cutler continues, "with a custom in
this city which I had never before heard of in any
part of the world. I observed, as I was going to
church, six men, walking two and two toward the
church, with very large white sashes, which appeared
to be made of fine Holland, the whole width and two

or three yards in length. They were placed over their right shoulders, and tied under their left arms in a very large bow, with several yards of white ribbon on the top of their shoulders; a large rose, formed of white ribbon, was placed on the sash. As I came up to the yard of the church, Dr. Rodgers and Dr. Ewing were just before me, going into the church, both in their black gowns, but Dr. Rodgers with a large white sash, like those of the six men, only that the bow and rose of ribbon were black. These sashes, I was informed, were given the last week at a funeral. They are worn by the minister and bearers to the grave, and are always worn by them the next Sunday, and the bearers always walk to and from the church together. To give these sashes is a general custom at the funeral of persons of any note." *

Under so agreeable a guide, the reader, it is hoped, will not object to attending a second service on the same day. For Dr. Cutler, indeed, it was the third, but inasmuch as he went in the afternoon to the service of another denomination, we may reserve our energies to accompany him in the evening. "Attended a lecture," he says, "at Dr. Rodgers' new brick Presbyterian Church. Full congregation. Dr. Witherspoon, President of the New Jersey College, preached. He is an intolerably homely old Scotchman, and speaks the true dialect of his country, except that his brogue borders on the Irish. He is a bad speaker, has no oratory, and had no notes before him. His subject was ' Hypocrisy.' But, notwithstanding the dryness of the subject [and] the bad-

* Cutler's "Life," etc., Vol. I, pp. 231–234.

ness of his delivery, which required the closest attention to understand him, yet the correctness of his
style, the arrangement of his matter, and the many
new ideas that he suggested, rendered his sermon
very entertaining. The attention of the congregation
strongly marked their regard for good sense and clear
reasoning, rather than the mere show of oratory and
declamation. Spent the remainder of the evening
and supped with Mr. Hazard." *

The heavy expense entailed by the restoration of
their buildings was partly offset by the fact that the
Presbyterians, in March, 1784, obtained, by petition
to the Corporation of the city, a reduction of the
annual rental paid for the Beekman Street property,
from £40 to £21 5 s., and, at the same time, the back
rental for the period of the congregation's exile from
the city, amounting to £303, was forgiven. Shortly
after this the treasury received unexpected aid from
another source. In June, 1787, the Corporation of
Trinity Church (which, as is well known, held a large
property from the days before the Revolution) of
its own free will and entirely unsolicited, conveyed to
the First Presbyterian Church of New York a piece
of ground on Robinson Street (now known as Nos.
3 and 5 Park Place), for the purpose of providing a
site for the parsonage of the senior minister.† It

---

* Cutler's "Life," etc., Vol. I, p. 236.

† The following are the extracts from the minutes of the vestry of
Trinity Church, relating to this matter. January 6th, 1786. "The Board
considering that thier fellow citazens of the two Presbytarian Congregations in this City have not convenient lots of ground whereon to build
dwelling houses for their respective senior pastors. RESOLVED that this
Corporation will grant a good lot of ground to each of the Presbytarian
Congregations in this City for the use of thier respective senior pastors for
the time being." Also on April 6th, 1786, it was "RESOLVED that the

was never put to this use, but the income from the property became a part of Dr. Rodgers' salary.*

One other piece of property came into the possession of the church at this time which deserves a passing mention, because, although of no great intrinsic value, it constitutes to-day one of the oldest treasures of the Brick Church. This is a "silver bason," which Colonel Stevens and several other gentlemen presented to the session in March, 1791, "for the use of baptizing children in the New Church." It was in common use for this purpose for over a hundred years.

During the twenty-five years covered by this chapter, that is, the period from the close of the Revolutionary War till the date of the proposal to break up the collegiate arrangement of the Presbyterian Church of New York, there was but one senior pastor, Dr. Rodgers, whose honors increased with his years; but the position of associate pastor was filled in succession by several different men. The Rev. Mr. Treat had not returned to the city at the close of the war, and there were reasons why the session did not desire that he should do so. The somewhat delicate situation was met by a vote of the congregation on July 1st, 1784, that they could

Rector be requested to acquaint the Pastors of the Presbyterian Congregations with the intentions of this Corporation and that they be requested to agree on the lotts thier Corporations respectively [will?] hold that deeds may be prepared accordingly." The two Presbyterian congregations here referred to were the First Presbyterian Church of New York (including the Wall Street and New churches) and the Scotch Presbyterian Church on Cedar Street.

* In 1803 the Presbyterian trustees made a release in fee to William Whyttan in perpetuity, with rent reserved of $250 a year to be paid to the senior Presbyterian pastor. This is still paid. In 1901 this property was assessed at a valuation of $77,000.

at that time support but one minister. Accordingly for the year after the restoration of the New Church, Dr. Rodgers bore the burden alone. In August, 1785, however, Mr. James Wilson, a Scotchman, was ordained as colleague. Two and a half years later, when he was forced to resign and move to the South on account of his health, he had won the "sincere and high esteem" of the church, and was dismissed with regret.

The choice of his successor was complicated by the putting forward of two candidates, with the result that neither obtained a call and nearly two years' time was lost by the controversy. Finally Mr. John McKnight, of Marsh Creek, Penn., was called, and entered upon his duties late in 1789, "to the entire and high satisfaction of all parties."* It soon appeared, however, that the burdens of the position would be too great for his strength, especially the necessity of preaching three times each Sunday, as was then the custom. Rather than lose his valued services or discontinue the Sunday evening meeting,

---

* The following characterization is from a letter by the Rev. George Duffield, D.D., quoted in Sprague's "Annals," Vol. III, p. 374. "Dr. McKnight was a man of slender person, and rather above the medium height. His countenance indicated a considerate turn of mind, and at least a capacity for deep thought. His manners were graceful and dignified, without any attempt at the polish and courtier-like demeanor, sometimes assumed by popular and fashionable clergymen. He was at home in all society, and could adapt himself in his native simplicity of character to every variety of age, temper, and education. . . . As a preacher he was calm and dispassionate. Although there was little variety in either his tones or his gestures, yet his delivery was far from being dull or monotonous: it was well adapted to his matter, which was generally a lucid, logical exhibition of some important scriptural truth. He was a zealous asserter of the Calvinistic faith, which, however, he chose to present in connection with a 'thus saith the Lord,' rather than the subtleties of metaphysics."

as some proposed, it was decided to call a third minister, and on June 5th, 1793, Mr. Samuel Miller became co-pastor with Dr. Rodgers and Dr.* McKnight. He was but twenty-two years of age and is described as having "much more than common advantages in respect to personal appearance. Of about the middle size, he was perfectly well proportioned, with a fine, intelligent and benignant countenance, which would not be likely to pass unnoticed in a crowd. His manners were cultivated and graceful in a high degree, uniting the polish of Chesterfield with the dignity and sincerity of a Christian minister. . . . His work on 'Clerical Manners' could never have been written by one who was less considerate and exact than himself, and indeed, but for his exceeding modesty, one might almost suppose that in writing it he was taking his own portrait."†

In regard to his work as a writer and preacher, we are told that "he had, from the beginning, an uncommonly polished style," and that "there was an air of literary refinement pervading all his performances, that excited general admiration, and wellnigh put criticism at defiance."‡

Dr. Gardiner Spring, writing many years later, selects the word "accomplished" as the one best fitted to characterize his preaching, and tells how, in beginning his sermon, he would remove the Bible from the desk to the cushion behind his back and speak with neither book nor manuscript before him. From other sources we learn that it was his custom

---

* The degree was conferred by Yale College in 1791.
† Sprague's "Annals," Vol. III, pp. 602 f.
‡ Sprague's "Annals," Vol. III, p. 600.

to reduce his material to writing and then memorize it. For "the prejudice against reading was so great, that it was at the peril at least of one's reputation as a preacher that he ventured to lay his manuscript before him. . . . So perfectly distinct was [Mr. Miller's] enunciation that he could be heard, without effort, at the extremity of the largest church. His attitudes in the pulpit were extremely dignified, though perhaps somewhat precise; and his gesture, which was never otherwise than appropriate, was yet not very abundant. . . . He would occasionally deliver a sentence with an air of majesty and a degree of unction that would make it quite irresistible. I remember, for instance," continues Dr. Sprague, to whom we are indebted for this lively description, "to have heard him relate in a New Year's sermon on the text, 'How old art thou?' the well-known anecdote of the Roman Emperor exclaiming at the close of a day which had gone to waste, 'Oh, I have lost a day!' and it seemed scarcely possible that the exclamation should have been uttered in a way to secure to it a higher effect."*

This description conveys to us evidently the impression made by Mr. Miller in his maturity. When he came to New York he was, it will be remembered, at the very beginning of his career, a fact pleasantly suggested in the statement of one of his contemporaries, that in those days, although they were "dressed in full canonicals, not omitting the three-cornered hat," they were commonly called "the boy ministers."

For nearly twenty years these three clergymen, Dr.

* Sprague's "Annals," Vol. III, pp. 603 *f.*

Rodgers, Dr. McKnight and Mr. Miller, labored side by side in the New and Wall Street churches. The addition of the third pastor, in order to lighten the burden, was soon counterbalanced by the opening of a third church on Rutgers Street (in 1798) to supply the growing needs of the northeast portion of the city. In 1805, however, Dr. Philip Milledoler was called to take special charge of this third congregation, with the understanding that his relation there should continue in case of a separation of the churches. Thus the now venerable Dr. Rodgers and his two colleagues were left free once more to devote themselves to the Wall Street and Brick* Church congregations.

A brief review of the work in which they were then engaged will serve to acquaint us with the church life in these years. Besides the six Sunday services, which they shared among them, and the Thursday evening lecture, which Dr. Rodgers himself continued to conduct until 1799, there was now begun, in a very experimental way, a social prayer-meeting. It met at six different churches in rotation on the second Wednesday of each month "at candle lighting," but gradually established itself as a stated feature of the life of each church.

The regular offerings for the poor of the parish, taken on communion Sundays and at the time of the annual Charity Sermon in December, were promptly resumed at the close of the war, and indeed with a generosity that cannot but move us to admiration. Before the New Church had been repaired, in fact but a month after services were resumed, a charity

* For the official adoption of this name at this time see pages 26, 27.

offering of more than £80 was made, and two months later a special offering of £75 for the city poor was added. In December, 1784, the New Church people, now worshipping alone, made a charity offering of £58, an unprecedented sum. It is evident that the exaggerated distress of the time aroused them to extra effort.* Still more remarkable is the fact that, from this time on, their offerings were maintained at a considerably higher figure than formerly. For the first six years after the two congregations were again settled in their respective churches, the charity offering at the New Church was one-third larger than it had been for the same period before the war, and in the next decade (beginning with 1791) the average of the offering was not only increased again, but actually doubled. In some years nearly £100 were given to this cause. In 1801 it is interesting to notice that the sums begin to be given in dollars and cents, the old English system having continued up to that time. The offerings for the first years of the new century ranged from $175 to $225, a still further advance.†

* Dr. Rodgers, in the sermon already described at the beginning of this chapter, had strongly urged the church's responsibility in this direction. After referring to the many "deserving citizens who have lost their *all* in this struggle," and especially to "those who have become widows and fatherless by this great contest," he says: "I most affectionately recommend them to the notice and friendship of their more opulent fellow-citizens, and the attention of the public, not upon the score of charity but of justice. Can no plans be fallen upon for employing such deserving members of the community, which is the best method of providing for them? And can luxury and dissipation, those awkward vices in our present situation (to give them the softest name)—can they spare nothing for the supply of the more indigent among them? The approaching winter enforces the duty before us, with an energy that language fails to express." "Divine Goodness Displayed," etc., p. 36 *f*.

† It is interesting that on at least one occasion (November, 1787), in addition to the usual methods of relieving the needs of the poor, the session

It might be supposed that this increase in the regular benevolence of the church would exhaust the purses of the congregation, but, as so often happens, generosity grew by exercise. Offerings for the sending of missionaries to the frontier were made on more than one occasion; help was given toward the restoration of a church in Savannah, Georgia, destroyed by fire; a collection was taken for the Society for the Relief of Poor Widows with Small Children,* and another for the New York Missionary Society.† The sense of a wider responsibility among the churches was growing, and these occasional extra offerings among the Presbyterians were a happy prophecy of the coming of the new era.

In regard to money required by the church for its own expenses, we have an interesting note recorded in 1795.‡ "The only stated revenue of the church," we are told, "from which they have been enabled to support the gospel from time to time, has arisen from the rents of their pews, in aid to which they have always had and still have a collection at every sermon (a practice in standing use among the churches of every denomination in the city). They have been obliged in four instances, when calling an additional minister, to have recourse to an annual subscription for a few years, but this practice is now laid aside."

voted that wood be bought and stored for the use of the poor through the winter, an early parallel to our modern "coal club."

* The names of three of the other benevolent institutions existing in New York at this time, in which the Presbyterian ministers were actively interested, will help to show the spirit that was now abroad: The Society for the Relief of Distressed Prisoners, The City Dispensary, The Society for Promoting the Manumission of Slaves.

† Founded in 1796. Mr. Miller took a great interest in it.

‡ "Manuscript Hist.," p. 25.

The sum which was thus annually provided was by
no means small. Dr. Rodgers, we are told,* received
a salary of £700. Mr. Miller was called at a salary
of £300; and presumably Dr. McKnight received the
same. Each church had, moreover, its own clerk
or chorister, its sexton, etc., and the annual expense
for repairs and maintenance must have been considerable.

By far the most interesting development of the
church work in this period remains to be described.
On May 1st, 1789, the Presbyterian trustees opened
a charity school for the secular education of the
poor children of the parish. Other churches of the
city had set the example of supplying, in a measure,
the need of a public school free to all,† and whether
we consider their interest in the cause of education
itself or their desire to ensure religious training (in
connection with secular instruction) for the children
of the poor, their endeavor was in every respect an
admirable one.

The foundation for this important Presbyterian
charity had been laid many years before by a legacy
amounting to $750, left by Capt. Jeremiah Owen

---

* By Manasseh Cutler in 1787, who adds that the perquisites amounted
to about £200. Dr. Rodgers was originally called at a salary of £350.

† This important work had not yet been undertaken by the State. In
a sermon by Mr. Miller, delivered in the New Church on July 4th, 1795,
"before the Mechanic, Tammany, and Democratic societies, and the Military Officers," appears the following note (page 29): "The establishment
of public schools, and making their support an object of legislative attention, is so plainly and intimately connected with the welfare of all repub-
lics, that neither proof nor illustration on the subject are necessary. Of
such establishment the Eastern States have set us an honorable and useful
example. The States of New York and Pennsylvania seem to be about
engaging in a similar plan. . . . May we yet see the time when good education shall be extended to every class of citizens."

as a fund whose interest should be applied annually toward the instruction of poor children of the congregation in reading, writing, and the use of figures.*

Unhappily, on the ground that at that time the Presbyterian Church was not, and could not be, incorporated, Mr. Gabriel Ludlow, the administrator, found himself legally unable to pay over the bequest. He was a zealous member of the Church of England, and the vestry of Trinity Church endeavored, we are told, to persuade him that the money might properly be turned over to them, or at least used to maintain, at their school, children of Presbyterian parents. But Mr. Ludlow, who pointedly declared that he was an honest man as well as a churchman, and that he would fulfil the intention of Captain Owen to the best of his knowledge and ability, undertook himself to select needy Presbyterian children and place them under the care of Presbyterian schoolmasters. Thus he expended the income of the legacy for ten years, with singular justness and fidelity.†
The principal of the bequest subsequently came into the church's possession, and after the war, though much diminished by the depreciation of the paper currency, it was still available for its original purpose.

In 1787, with a view to providing more adequately for this work of education, a subscription was opened, and the sum of £500, equal to about $1,250, was realized. In the next year a bequest amounting to $900 was made by Mrs. Elizabeth Thompson, a member of the church, for the same purpose. The

* See "Rodgers Mem.," pp. 167 and 414; also "Manuscript Hist.,"
p. 23.   † "Rodgers Mem.," pp. 168 f.

trustees, acting with a committee of the session, were now able with the funds in hand to hire a master and open a school, which they did in 1789, as has been already stated. This was, however, established in temporary quarters. The next step was to purchase a lot on Nassau Street, between Liberty and Cedar, opposite the Middle Dutch Church, and to erect on it a two-story brick building, measuring twenty-five by forty feet, and containing both an ample school-room and living apartments for the master and his family. Here fifty children were at once gathered, both boys and girls. Their studies consisted not only of the usual rudiments, designated in Captain Owen's plan, but psalmody and the Westminster Shorter Catechism. The minister and a committee of the trustees visited the school once in every quarter and the proficiency of the scholars was carefully noted.

Although the special funds referred to above had made possible the establishment of this institution, they were far from adequate to pay the annual running expenses. Nor did a legacy of £200 in 1792, from Mr. James Leslie, a school-master, supply the deficiency. The trustees were, indeed, forced to depend principally upon an annual collection in each of the two churches. This was very far from being a disadvantage, in that it made the school a genuine and continuing part of the church work. It was thus not merely a monument to the generosity of an older generation, but an appeal to the support and interest of living men and women, and at the same time a striking reminder that the church was called to minister to the general welfare of the people as well

as to their definitely religious needs.   We shall hear
more of this enterprise at a later time.

It has already become evident that, during the
quarter of a century which this chapter covers, the
history of the church was quiet and uneventful.
It was a period suited to normal and gradual growth.
In particular—contrasting decidedly in this with the
period of the war—there were no external events
that seriously affected the church life, either for good
or for evil.   To this, however, one exception must
be made.   The church life must have been affected
not a little by the dreadful epidemics which persistently ravaged the city.   It is hard to realize nowadays
that in the period under discussion New York stood
in constant terror of plague and pestilence, and that
sometimes year after year the scourge returned in
spite of all attempt at prevention.   In 1791, in 1795,
and especially in 1798 yellow fever carried off great
numbers of the inhabitants.   No less than one hundred and eighty-six members of the Presbyterian
Church perished in the last named year.   Again in
1803 and 1804 the prevalence of the plague was great
enough to interrupt seriously the work of the church
and to cause undisguised alarm.

These occurrences must have affected greatly not
only the number of members, but the whole religious
temper of the church.   Considered, as they were, to
be more or less directly an indication of divine dis-
pleasure, these visitations had a very important relation to the religious experience of many people.
Mr. Miller, who, as Dr. Rodgers aged, took the lead
in the church, makes this evident in several sermons
that have come down to us.   He himself, faithful to

his trust, remained in the city throughout the whole of "that melancholy season" in 1798, preaching every Sunday to his trembling fellow-citizens; and his sermon, delivered early in the following year, "On the Removal of a Malignant and Mortal Disease," gives us a vivid impression of the experience and of its appeal to the conscience of religious people.

"There are probably few cases," said Mr. Miller, "in which we feel ourselves more completely helpless, and more entirely in the hands of God, than when he sends forth pestilence, as a messenger of his wrath to chastise a guilty society. . . . Then it is, if ever, that human pride bows its head: then, if ever, that the incorrigible infidel thinks, for a moment, of a God, of Providence, and of prayer. Have you forgotten, my brethren, that such was lately our situation? . . . Have you forgotten those gloomy days, when scarcely any sound was heard but the voice of mourning and death? . . . Have you forgotten the vows which you made, and the resolutions which you formed in those serious and solemn hours? The badges of mourning which I see before me bring to my remembrance a husband or a wife, a parent or a child, a brother or a sister, recently torn from your embraces and consigned to the insatiable tomb." With an exuberant rhetoric, which these brief excerpts but faintly suggest, the hearers were led to acknowledge their unspeakable gratitude to God for his deliverance. "Some he saved by providing a place of refuge, where the salubrious breeze and the hospitable board sustained them till the evil was past; while others were preserved, though walking in the midst of the devouring poison, to discharge the duties of

benevolence and humanity. . . . When the sur-
vivors were helpless, and apprehended a devastation
still more awful, he appeared to stay the plague. . . .
But let all your thanksgivings be mingled with
humility, and all your joy tempered with the recollec-
tion, that sinful beings are continually exposed to
wrath and chastisement. . . . It becomes us to trem-
ble lest we should be again visited by a similar, or a
more dreadful calamity. . . . If I am not deceived,
the spirit of prophecy informs us that the days in
which we live are the 'last days.' . . . Such a general
derangement in the political and moral world has
not, probably, existed since the antediluvian scenes
of depravity. . . . When I look round this populous
city, which was, a few weeks since, clothed in mourning, and contemplate the criminal dissipation and
the various forms of wickedness which have so soon
taken the place of those gloomy scenes, I am constrained, with anxious dread, to ask, 'Shall not God
be avenged on such a people as this?' . . . Do not
hastily imagine, from this strain of address, that . . .
it would be my wish to see every innocent amusement
discarded. . . . But do we see no other than innocent amusements prevailing around us? Are the
lewdness, the blasphemy, the gaming, the unprinci-
pled speculation, the contempt of Christian duties,
and the violation of the Christian Sabbath, so mourn-
fully prevalent in our city and land—are these
innocent? Then were the cities of Sodom and Go-
morrah innocent. Then are the impious orgies of
infernal spirits harmless in the sight of God."

It is perhaps almost unfair thus to subject an
eighteenth-century discourse to the criticism of an

age which in its literary taste and the spirit of its religion is very materially different. But there can be no doubt that Mr. Miller's * sermon was in its day impressive and capable of stirring the most serious emotions in his hearers. The quotation that has been made from it is indeed valuable, not only for the outward picture which it aids us to form of a tragic episode in the city's life, but for the insight which it gives us into the religious condition of the period, and the means which the Christian Church, and in particular the Presbyterian Church in New York, was using at that time for the conversion of sinners and the revival of true religion.

* He received the degree of D.D., in 1804, from the University of Pennsylvania, of which he was a graduate.

CHAPTER VII

THE SENIOR PASTOR

"If solid and respectable talents, if acquirements which enabled him to act his part in various important stations with uniform honor, if patriarchal dignity, if sound practical wisdom, and a long life of eminent usefulness, be worthy of grateful remembrance and of respectful imitation, then the life of Dr. Rodgers is worthy of being written and perused."—SAMUEL MILLER, "Memoirs of John Rodgers," p. 11.

"I will give you pastors according to mine heart, which shall feed you with knowledge and understanding."—*Jeremiah* 3 : 15.

BY the beginning of the new century Dr. Rodgers, as has been already intimated, was beginning to feel his age. He had now served the church for nearly forty years, and in spite of the great growth during that period and the many other able men, both clergy and laymen, who had contributed to the church's welfare and progress, the impress of the personality of Dr. Rodgers upon the whole history was unmistakable. The record of the years to which the last chapter was devoted would be like a watch without the mainspring, unless the senior pastor were given his place in the middle of the scene. The picture presented at the beginning of this history, of the "new minister" just entering upon his city pastorate, must now be completed by a description of the well-known New York divine, whose work is firmly established and whose position as a religious leader is now secure.

And, first, let us take a somewhat casual view of

him as he appeared to the outward eye and upon short acquaintance. Dr. Manasseh Cutler, in whose company we have already attended the church, will now introduce us to the parsonage. The date is July 7th, 1787, a Saturday. "Waited on Dr. Rodgers," says our escort, "and drank tea in company with Dr. Ewing, Dr. Witherspoon, and several other clergymen. The Doctor urged me exceedingly to preach for him, at least a part of the day, on Sunday; but as the two Presidents* were in town, and I had just come off a long journey, prevailed on him to excuse me."†

This cannot be regarded as more than a formal introduction, but on the following Monday we become a little more intimate. "Dined at Dr. Rodgers'," continues the journal at that point, "in company with Dr. Witherspoon, Dr. Ewing, Dr. McCourtland of Newark, Mr. Wilson, colleague with Dr. Rodgers, and two other gentlemen from the Southward, whose names I do not recollect. It seemed like a ministers' meeting. They appeared to be much of gentlemen, and I must do them the justice to say, I was treated with particular marks of attention, notwithstanding my being a New England man. Dr. Rodgers is certainly the most accomplished gentleman, for a clergyman, not to except even Dr. Cooper, that I have ever been acquainted with," ‡ and here we are presented at once to a characteristic that must always have counted much in the first impression of those who came into Dr.

---

* Ewing, of the University of Pennsylvania, and Witherspoon, of the College of New Jersey.

† Cutler's "Life," etc., Vol. I, p. 231.

‡ Cutler's "Life," etc., Vol. I, pp. 236 f.

Rodgers' presence, "the peculiar and uniform dignity of his manners." * He was plainly a clergyman of the old school, conscious of his position, grave in his demeanor, and carefully observant of formalities in his social intercourse. There is a tradition that "the last thing which he and his wife always did before retiring for the night was to salute each other with a bow and a courtesy." † This particular statement is possibly an invention, but of the reserve and dignity of the senior minister of the Presbyterian Church there is abundant testimony, and however much the fashion of such formal manners may now be out of date, they were in his day highly admired, and added, as Dr. Miller says, to his reputation and to his usefulness as a Christian clergyman. The same writer adds, indeed, that Dr. Rodgers was "often facetious and sportive," but these terms must be interpreted in the light of the somewhat serious temperament of the biographer himself. In fact, he adds that the "sportiveness" intended was of a sort that "was always remarkable for its taste and dignity."

It is not difficult, then, to see before us Dr. Rodgers' stoutish figure, of medium height, walking with a majestic step among his neighbors and parishioners, dressed in clothes that were "invariably neat, elegant, and spotless." ‡ To this last matter he always gave

* "Rodgers Mem.," p. 338.

† "N. Y. in 1789," p. 149 ƒ.

‡ "Rodgers Mem.," p. 341. "In this respect he resembled his friend and spiritual father, Mr. Whitefield, whose sayings and example on this subject he not infrequently quoted, and who often remarked that a minister of the gospel, in his dress as well as in everything else, ought to be 'without spot.'" From a letter of Samuel Miller, quoted in Sprague's "Annals," Vol. III, p. 165.

careful attention. Washington Irving, whose family belonged to the Presbyterian Church in New York,* could in his old age still remember his father's pastor, "old Dr. Rodgers with his buzz wig, silver-mounted cane, well-polished shoes, and silver buckles." † If we follow him into his parsonage at No. 7 Nassau Street, we find that "he lives in elegant style and entertains company as genteelly as the first gentlemen of the city." ‡ We find, too, that, as his position deserved, he was on the "dinner and supper list" of Mrs. John Jay.§

These somewhat trivial details and scraps of old gossip will have served a good purpose, if they help us to see the man within the saint. For to Dr. Rodgers the latter title might without reservation be applied, and it would be easy, in reading the long list of his virtues, to feel that he had been reduced to a sort of abstract perfection. But if we have once caught sight of him, as it were, have seen the man himself and felt his human relation to those about him, it will then be a task doubly profitable to set his virtues before us.

Dr. Miller, his colleague and successor, to whom we are indebted for his biography, shall be our guide in summing up this good man's character and work.|| And, first, let it be said that at all the points where he touched the common life of the world, or shared in it, he maintained in himself a notably Christian

---

* One of the burial vaults in front of the Beekman Street Church belonged to his father, William Irving.

† "Life and Times of Washington Irving," (1883), Vol. III, p. 260.

‡ Cutler's "Life," etc., Vol. I, p. 237.

§ "Mem. Hist of N. Y.," Vol. III, p. 99.

|| "Rodgers Mem.," Chapter IX.

JOHN RODGERS
From a painting in the possession of the church

spirit. For instance, in the matter of money, which he did not lack, he was chiefly marked by his generous dispersion of it, and in spite of a prosperous career, not interrupted by any special financial losses, he succeeded in closing his earthly account with a smaller balance than he possessed at the time of his original settlement in New York. In like manner, when he shared, as he did, in the social intercourse of the city, he invariably brought with him such a tone, in conversation and behavior, as was worthy of his calling, and demanded that others should meet him on the same high plane.

In his personal character he may best be described by a few large single words, rather than by much comment. He was *disinterested:* "few men have ever been more free from private and selfish aims than he." He was *upright* in all the dealings of a life of over eighty years: "in no one instance was [his character] ever impeached:" every one who knew him believed in him. And he was *a man of God:* his goodness was the fruit of a deep and utterly sincere religion: "he seemed never, for a moment, to forget that he was a servant of Jesus Christ."

In his work as a minister of the gospel, he was assisted not so much by great genius or extraordinary powers as by a "happy assemblage of practical qualities, both of the head and the heart," and his reward was something better than fame, namely, practical success in the work he had undertaken to do. One or two of his characteristics deserve a special comment in this connection. Together with a determined and not easily daunted spirit, he possessed a certain tactfulness, based on a strong sense of what was both fair and kind, which enabled him to avoid the bitterness of controversy and strife. While most positive in his views, he was ever ready "to take by the hand, as Christian brethren, all who appeared to possess the spirit of Christ," and he was particularly reluctant to take upon himself the task of directly attacking even those with whom he most disagreed. "You must excuse me," he said on one occasion to the officers of his church, when they urged him to take the errors of a certain sect for the subject of his sermon, "I cannot reconcile it with my sense either of policy or duty to oppose these people from the pulpit, otherwise than by preaching the truth plainly and faithfully. I believe them to be in error; but let us out-preach them, out-pray them, and out-live them, and we need not fear." *

One can have but little doubt that the preaching of such a man would speak to the mind and conscience of his time. Its full value, however, would probably not be made evident by giving samples of it to a modern congregation, for times have changed. "Whoever went to hear him at any time," says Dr. Miller with evident approval, "would be sure to find him dwelling on one or another of the following themes," and he proceeds to give a page of titles, such as "Total Depravity," "Sovereign Election," "The Divine Existence in a Trinity of Persons." Even the subjects which admit, and indeed invite, a practical treatment, are stated as propositions in theology. This, however, was exactly the method which the congregations of that day approved and expected, and the question of Dr. Rodgers' power as a preacher

* Rodgers Mem.

of Christianity is not to be determined by an appeal
to modern taste, but by studying the historic church
which by his preaching was built up in the faith.

Of the manner of his preaching and the impression
made by it upon an intelligent stranger we have a
pleasing glimpse in Dr. Manasseh Cutler's journal,
already quoted. The entry is as follows: "Sunday,
July 22d. Attended public worship in the morning at
the old Brick, in Wall Street.* Dr. Rodgers preached.
He made no use of notes, but he arranged his subject
very well; gave us a very pretty sermon on the first
part of our Lord's Prayer. His address is easy, soft,
and engaging—no display of oratory, so called. His
style was pure, sentimental, and nervous, put plain
and familiar. He made me think of Dr. Cooper." †

Yet, after all, it may well be that preaching was
but a small part of this strong man's influence. As
one studies the record of his life, one cannot but be
much impressed by those passages which point out his
patient faithfulness in a multiplicity of occupations.
One of these passages is peculiarly well adapted to
the purpose of the present sketch of Dr. Rodgers'
character and influence; for we are, of course, chiefly
concerned here to learn as far as possible what it was
that the Brick Church owed to the man who brought

* This unexpected designation for the Wall Street Church is probably
due to error, on the part either of Dr. Cutler or his editors.

† Cutler's "Life," etc., Vol. I, p. 296. The journal entry for the evening of this same day is worth quoting for its own sake. "Attended a
lecture at the Old Dutch Church. The sermon was delivered in Dutch
with a great deal of vehemence and pathos, but whether it was good or bad
I know not." Dr. Cutler had in the afternoon heard Mr. Wilson, the
Presbyterian associate, whom he describes as methodical, but not, in his
judgment, a good preacher, adding, however, by way of compensation that
"he was very catholic in his sentiments." (Cutler's "Life," etc., Vol. I,
p. 297.)

it into being and guided it through its first forty years, and this one paragraph, about to be quoted, goes far toward answering that question.

"In preaching, in catechising, in attending on the sick and dying, in all the arduous labor of discipline and government, and in visiting from house to house, he went on with unceasing constancy from year to year, from the beginning to the end of his ministry. He not only abounded in ministerial labors; but he labored systematically, uniformly, and with unwearied patience. Difficulties did not usually appall him. Delays did not discourage him. If he were totally disappointed in the result of his exertions in one case, he did not hastily conclude that all subsequent endeavors in similar cases would be useless. . . . Those who found him busily engaged in pursuing a certain regular and judicious course at one period, would be sure to find him after a series of years, pursuing with steady and undeviating steps the same course."* This is indeed a good description of "a wise master-builder," one who might be trusted to lay firm foundations.

And now when he was nearly eighty years of age, and when it might be supposed that the time for rest had come, we find him still setting an example of energy and faithfulness. In 1805 he writes to a friend, "I am able, through divine goodness, to preach once every Lord's Day, and to do my full share of parochial duty." This was the spirit that controlled him to the end.

* "Rodgers Mem."

New York. Feb'y 26th. 1805.

My dear Sir,

I have but a few moments to thank you for the sermons you sent to me and to extend to you the Beacon — Some time ago I rec'd a letter from Bishop Moore, respecting land, accompanied by a sermon of some Works, respecting some answers which to be employed by our Missionary Some ... which to be employed by our Board of Directors at their last ... these laid before the Board of Directors ... hearing — and they were afraid to accept his offer, till they were better satisfied respecting his Moral Character, which you know had laboured for some time past — Pray what are you and Dr Bishops wished of? the state of that Mission when you & Dr Bishops wished of? what was the result of your Enquiries respecting his Moral Character? Is it likely to be useful among those People? If our Board of Directors could be satisfied on these sub- ject, they would ... be ...

P. S. I wish an answer to this as soon as convenient

CHAPTER VIII

THE SEPARATION: 1809

"And Jonathan said to David, Go in peace, forasmuch as we have sworn both of us in the name of the Lord, saying, The Lord be between me and thee, and between my seed and thy seed for ever. And he arose and departed."—1 *Samuel* 20 : 42.

"No man, unquestionably, who witnessed the scene, would ever again lift his hand in favor of associating several congregations under the same pastors."— SAMUEL MILLER, "Memoirs of John Rodgers," p. 274.

IT will be remembered that in 1784, when the Presbyterian Church in New York was first incorporated, the official title selected was "The Corporation of the First Presbyterian Church in the City of New York." This choice was an indication, we are told,* that a second corporation, "of the New Church," was then thought to be a possibility. The law under which the papers were taken out provided that the estate held by each incorporated religious body must not exceed £1,200 per annum, gross revenue. It was in order to secure the larger liberty which in equity belonged to them as two congregations that the Presbyterians at that time contemplated the future possibility of a separation of the financial affairs of their two churches. It will be remembered that ecclesiastically they were still one body, bound together in a so-called "collegiate arrangement," and so they continued for many a year. But with the practical financial difficulty, which, as just stated,

* "Manuscript Hist.," p. 20.

presented itself in 1784, there appears the first trace
of that tendency toward an entire separation, which
was to bear fruit after a quarter of a century had
passed.

It must not be supposed, however, that at that
early date a complete separation was desired, even by
those who saw the advantages of a two-fold financial
organization.   On the contrary, when, ten years later,
it was definitely proposed to apply for the second
charter, the ministers, elders, deacons, and trustees,
after maturely weighing the subject, voted in the
negative, on the very ground that such an action
would necessarily create a separation of interest,
which might in time result in a dissolution of the
union between the two congregations, an event which
would be deeply deplored by all.*   They chose rather
to apply to the Legislature for special permission to
hold an estate of twice the usual amount, on the
ground that they were in effect two churches, and in
this they were successful.   The act was passed on
March 6th, 1793.†

There were, however, two persons who even at this
time were in favor of a dissolution of the collegiate
arrangement.   These were the two associate pastors,
and, although in so decided a minority, they were outspoken in their opinion and even presented the matter
for formal discussion; but their proposal was at that
time emphatically and almost curtly rejected.   Of the
two, Dr. (then Mr.) Miller ‡ was probably the more
active in this matter.   He had recently arrived and

* "Manuscript Hist.," p. 25.
† See also act of March 27th, 1801.
‡ "Life of Samuel Miller," p. 265.

had been at once impressed, perhaps annoyed, by the difficulties inherent in the situation. He pointed out that every family in both churches expected and claimed visits from each pastor, so that the amount of work which could have been accomplished by a proper division of labor was rendered impossible. Still more unfortunate was the effect of certain partialities for one or another of the pastors, which tended to create unpleasant feeling and to divide the church.

On the other hand, there were recognized advantages. The relation of Dr. Rodgers to both congregations, beloved as he was by every individual in them, made a mighty plea for its own continuance. And the people were content: they did not wish to change. This in itself was enough to determine that at that time no change should be made.

Dr. Miller's opinion, however, did not alter. He still looked forward to the time when "the Siamese twins," as he called them, would be cut apart. With what success his arguments, aided no doubt by the force of circumstances, pleaded the cause of separation during the next decade, is clearly seen in a set of resolutions adopted by the officers of the church in July, 1805. From these we learn that the extension of the collegiate system eight years before, to include a third church,* was by this time felt to be a somewhat doubtful expedient. It is true that the officers voted to continue the union of the three congregations as "beneficial to the interests of the First Presbyterian Church," but only on certain rather radical conditions. The newest church, on Rutgers Street, was

* See above, p. 85.

now to have a separate minister of its own, enjoying his entire and undivided services and paying his salary. It was also to pay henceforth all its own running expenses, instead of drawing on the general treasury, and it was to receive a certain fixed portion of the fees of the burial-ground and of the outstanding debts due to the corporation. It will be evident at once that so far as this third church was concerned the collegiate arrangement had by this new plan been reduced to a minimum. Except that it had no elders or deacons of its own, the Rutgers Street Church was henceforth a practically independent body.

Three years later, in 1808, the tendency of public opinion again plainly declared itself. Still another new place of worship being then demanded by the increasing congregations of the First Presbyterian Church, an entirely separate organization was created. The relation of this new church on Cedar Street to the older collegiate churches * was as hearty as could be desired—Dr. Rodgers laid the corner-stone and preached the opening sermon—but the old

* For the sake of clearness a list of all the Presbyterian churches existing at this time in the city is here given.

(1) The First Presbyterian Church (1706), including:
        (a) The Wall Street Congregation (1719), now the old First Church;
        (b) The Brick Church Congregation (1767), now the Brick Church:
        (c) The Rutgers Street Congregation (1798), now the Rutgers Riverside Church.

(2) The First Associate Reformed Church, originally, and again later, called the Scotch Presbyterian Church (1756), now at Central Park West and Ninety-sixth Street.

(3) The Fourth Presbyterian, known for a time as the First Associate Presbyterian Church (organized, 1787, incorporated, 1803), now at West End Avenue and Ninety-first Street.

idea of an organic union had here been utterly abandoned, and Dr. McKnight, in giving the charge to the new pastor* at his installation, pointedly congratulated him upon his good fortune in being the sole pastor of his church.

The object-lesson, thus provided, of an independent organization "was doubtless," says Dr. Miller, "one of the principal means employed by Providence for breaking up the system of 'collegiate charges.' . . . Though this system, wherever it exists, is injurious to the body of the churches so united, and perplexing and discouraging to the ministers, . . . yet where it has been in operation for forty or fifty years, and where its disruption must invade the feelings and prejudices of many individuals, none can expect to accomplish such a measure without much agitation and trouble. The establishment of the Cedar Street Church, toward the close of 1808, the unusual degree of success which attended the whole undertaking, the numerous advantages which soon began to disclose themselves, as resulting from a separate pastoral charge, and the impression which these advantages made, silently but deeply, on the public mind—all tended at once to hasten and to facilitate the attempt to separate the old collegiate churches." † It should

(4) The second Associate Reformed Church (1797), originally a part of the Scotch Church, and bound to it in "collegiate" organization until 1803. It now forms a part of the Central Church on West Fifty-seventh Street

(5) The Cedar Street Church (1808), referred to in the text, now the Fifth Avenue Presbyterian Church.

(6) The Orange Street Church was founded later in 1808. It is now extinct.

* The Rev. John B. Romeyn, from Albany.

† "Rodgers Mem.," pp. 420 ƒ.

be added, on the other hand, that Dr. Rodgers, not unnaturally, was unable to see the necessity for any change.

As early as December, 1808, the session adopted a resolution * requesting the elders, deacons, and trustees "to meet and confer together respecting the propriety and expediency of attempting a division of the First Presbyterian Church in the City of New York into three separately organized churches." Several such joint meetings were accordingly held, and the main proposition meeting with approval, the following ten articles † were proposed on March 27th, 1809, by way of a definite plan of separation, especially as related to the two older churches. The Rutgers Street Church seems to be concerned in but one of the articles (the fourth.)

1st. The charity school-house and the lot of ground on which it stands shall continue to be held in common, each church, when divided, to bear an equal proportion of the expenses of supporting the school, which shall be under the care of the ministers of the two churches and committees appointed by their boards of trustees.

2d and 3d. The churches on Wall and Beekman streets, with the land on which they stand, shall be the sole property of their respective congregations.

4th. The twenty-four lots purchased from James R. [or K.] Beekman for a burial ground shall be equally divided between the three churches.

5th. The lot on Hester Street and any other real

* From this point the minutes of the trustees and of the session of the Brick Church become our chief sources.

† Given here in condensed form.

estate held or claimed by the corporation of the two churches shall continue to be held in common.

6th. All the personal estate belonging to the two churches shall be equally divided.*

7th. Dr. McKnight shall take the parochial charge of the Brick Church, Dr. Miller of the Wall Street Church, and they are to interchange mutually as heretofore.

8th. The Wall Street Church shall pay to the Brick Church $2,500.

9th. The two churches shall share in paying Dr. Rodgers' salary; Dr. McKnight's salary shall be paid by the Brick Church, and Dr. Miller's by the Wall Street Church.

10th. The annuity of £100 from the lot on Robinson Street shall be enjoyed by the senior pastor of the two churches forever.

These articles were submitted first to the congregations, separately, on Monday, April 3d, and on the following Thursday to a joint meeting held at the Wall Street Church. On this occasion the separation of the Rutgers Street Church from the other two, in regard to which there was general agreement, was determined upon. Besides the property already appropriated to the use of the people worshipping there, they were to receive one equal undivided part of the Beekman lots (see article 4th) and also, what the "articles" did not contemplate, "such part of the personal estate of this corporation as may be justly due." The vote upon this question was unanimous.

* On the basis of this article the people of the Brick Church supposed that they had a claim to half of the silver communion service. When their claim was asserted, however, in 1819, it was challenged, and for the sake of peace they felt constrained to abandon it.

But when the proposal to separate the two older churches was voted upon, it was lost by a vote of forty-seven to forty-six.

The causes for this apparently hopeless disagreement are in part unknown to us. A chief difficulty, however, had certainly arisen in connection with the question of Dr. McKnight's future relation to the churches. Some of the Brick Church people were distinctly dissatisfied that he, rather than Dr. Miller, should now become their sole pastor. Dr. McKnight, on his side, was even more emphatic in expressing dissatisfaction with his assignment to the Brick Church. It is evident that a letter from him, proposing to resign altogether, was an important cause of the adverse vote of April 6th.

All that could be done was to appoint a committee to "consult on the present unhappy state of affairs in the two churches, and make report to the two congregations." This committee, after considering all means of "restoring harmony," recommended the adoption of the original plan of March 27th, and at the same time provided that an endeavor be made to convince Dr. McKnight "of the sincere love and esteem of the congregations for him" and to gain his acquiescence and, if possible, his support.

In one respect this committee failed in its purpose. It could not persuade Dr. McKnight to alter his decision: he persisted in resigning. But the continued canvassing of the matter among the congregation, by changing the views of some and arousing many to action who had not been heard from at all in the first instance, opened the way to a practical solution of the main problem. At a second meeting of the congregation, held on April 12th, the general subject of separation being put to vote without debate, it was found that ninety-two were in favor as against seventy-six opposed. The original plan, with such modifications, of course, as were necessitated by the previous separation of the Rutgers Street Church and by Dr. McKnight's complete withdrawal, was then adopted; and at last this "perplexed and embarrassing situation" was brought to an end.

The Presbytery of New York, meeting two weeks later, approved in two separate articles the formation of the Rutgers Street congregation into a distinct and independent church, and the separation of the Wall Street and Brick churches one from the other.* At the same time they granted the request of Dr. McKnight, that the pastoral relation between him and the united Presbyterian congregations of New York be dissolved. It is noted that in this the congregations concurred "with great reluctance." †

In conformity with these proceedings Dr. Rodgers and seven of the Presbyterian elders,‡ namely, Abraham Van Gelder, John Thompson, Thomas Ogilvie, Benjamin Egbert, William Frazer, John Bingham,

---

* The separation had already been authorized by an act of Legislature, February 17th, 1809.

† The excellent effects of the separation were in a short time very apparent. Dr. Miller, who afterward was inclined to believe that his own part in this matter was his greatest service to the Presbyterian Church in New York, wrote in 1813: "The writer is persuaded that he is chargeable with no exaggeration, when he asserts that all the churches which were once united have become more flourishing since they were separated, and that in the period of four years since that event occurred nearly double the number of members has been added to the aggregate Presbyterian body in New York than was ever added to it in a similar period before." ("Rodgers Mem.," p. 422. Cf. also "Life of Samuel Miller.")

‡ See Appendices C and D, pp. 517, 519.

and John Mills were constituted a new session for the Brick Church, and that body held its first meeting on Monday evening, May 1st, 1809. Besides arranging to pay $15 * a Sunday for the supply of their now vacant pulpit (Dr. Rodgers was too old to preach), they on that occasion nominated Samuel Osgood and William Whitlock for the office of elder. These two gentlemen, who were shortly afterward ordained, thus belonged practically to the first session of the independent church.

Of the five Presbyterian deacons † at the time of the separation three, namely, Mr. Richard Cunningham, Mr. Hutchins and Mr. Miller, became deacons of the Brick Church, and began their work there with the sum of $75.87, brought over from the old treasury.

The trustees ‡ who composed the original board must also be given by name. They were Samuel Osgood, John R. Murray, John Mills, Benjamin Egbert, John Bingham, Grove Wright, Richard Cunningham, John Adams and Peter Bonnett. Their first act was to adopt as the official title "The Corporation of the Brick Presbyterian Church in the City of New York." Immediately their minutes indicate activity in many directions. They divide themselves up into committees on finance, on repairs, and on the charity school. They appoint a collector of pew-rents. They provide for the erection of a fence about the church, consisting of a stone basement twelve inches high, surmounted with wooden pales. They secure the right to build burial vaults in the church-

* This was later increased $5 by the trustees for supplies from New Jersey or Long Island.

† See Appendix E, p. 520.

‡ See Appendices F, G, H, and I, pp. 522, 524, 525, 526.

yard and proceed to build and to sell them. They
provide for a division of the burying-ground together
with its appurtenances, such as the hearse-house, the
hearse, and the silk and the cotton palls. They
appoint James Forrester as teacher of the charity
school at a salary of $250. Several of these items
refer to subjects which will demand fuller attention
in later chapters, but at present it is necessary to turn
to the one great task which now confronted the whole
church, the calling of a pastor.

PART TWO

THE LONG PASTORATE

CHAPTER IX

THE CALL OF GARDINER SPRING: 1809-1810

"And Micah said unto him, Whence comest thou? And he said unto him, I am a Levite of Bethlehem-Judah, and I go to sojourn where I may find a place. And Micah said unto him, Dwell with me, and be unto me a father and a priest."—*Judges* 17 : 9 *f*.

"It appeared to my own mind the call of the great Head of the Church to a field of labor too important to be compared with others."—GARDINER SPRING. "The Brick Church Memorial," p. 14.

IT must be confessed that the independent life of the Brick Church did not begin under very favorable auspices. The separation which created it had been opposed by a considerable minority. As a result the church was to some extent divided. Except the decay of faith and morals, nothing is more destructive of a church's welfare than division of this sort. By it every action of the church is hindered, and especially the work of choosing a pastor becomes, under such circumstances, a very difficult matter.

This proved abundantly true in the case of the Brick Church. Moreover, it was soon discovered that, not unnaturally, the conditions then existing did not prove attractive to such men as were invited to consider the pastorate. The Rev. John Brown, of North Carolina, being earnestly requested by the session to make the church a visit "with a view to further measures," sent word through Dr. Miller

117

"that his engagements were such that he could not make a visit to the city of New York." In September a congregational meeting issued a unanimous call to the Rev. John McDowell, of Elizabethtown, N. J., at a salary of $2,000, but this promising step led to nothing. The elders who had been appointed to prosecute the call before Presbytery reported that they were unsuccessful and that the call had been returned. But the persistency of the session and their promptness in bringing forward a new candidate were certainly admirable. In November they had secured the Rev. Andrew Yates, of East Hartford, Conn., as supply for the Brick Church pulpit, and in the same month he also was unanimously called. Not until January, 1810, was it learned that disappointment must again be borne. The Council of Congregational Churches called to consider Mr. Yates's removal to New York were of the opinion that his present pastoral relation should not be dissolved, and in their decision he acquiesced.

The next name that came before the session was that of the Rev. Lyman Beecher, then of East Hampton, Long Island. It is interesting to think that the father of Henry Ward Beecher and Harriet Beecher Stowe, might have been chosen at this time to guide the fortunes of the Brick Church. He had supplied the pulpit twice in December, and at that time had written to his wife, "if the city clergymen alone were concerned [I] should, I was given to understand, be gladly stationed among them." * Two months later, on February 10th, he tells the result of a later visit. He says, "I preached three Sabbaths in New York

* "Autobiography of Lyman Beecher," Vol. I, p. 179.

for the Brick Church, and came as near having a call as the fellow did being killed who came to the field the day after the battle." * This statement was perhaps not quite just to himself, for after his visit the proposal to call him was by no means summarily dismissed. At four separate meetings of the session or of all the officers of the church together the question of calling Mr. Beecher was under discussion, but such a decided and persistent difference of opinion was discovered that the matter was never brought before the congregation. A friend, writing to Mr. Beecher from New York, says that the opposition came chiefly from two of the trustees, others voting with them in the negative chiefly for the sake of preserving harmony, and that in his judgment three-quarters of the congregation were disappointed in the outcome.† At any rate no pastor had yet been secured.

It is certainly no wonder that after such prolonged discouragement the difficulty of uniting upon a pastor had increased. In May the session passed a resolution which reveals the truly pathetic state of this pastorless church. A committee of two was "authorized to proceed to Philadelphia so as to be there before, or as soon as, the General Assembly meets, and make application to any of the Presbyterian ministers that may be convened there, whose piety and talents would in their judgment render him acceptable to the congregation of the Brick Church, and earnestly solicit such minister to make said church a visit for two or three Sabbaths with a view to a perma-

---

* "Autobiography of Lyman Beecher," Vol. I, p. 183.
† *Ibid.*, Vol. I, p. 188.

nent settlement as pastor of said congregation; and in case they should not find any minister there, suitably qualified, that would be willing to come, that they make inquiry of the ministers present, and if they received well-grounded information respecting any minister whose piety and talents would probably make him acceptable to the congregation of the Brick Church, that they take such measures for procuring a visit from such minister as they may think proper either by writing or by personal application."*

Before this humble quest, in search of some one to take pity on their need, could be carried out, a young man, who was passing through the city on his way to the meeting of the Assembly, and who preached at an evening lecture in the Cedar Street Church in the absence of Dr. Romeyn, was heard by a number of Brick Church people, and made upon them a favorable impression. This was Mr. Gardiner Spring, a candidate for the ministry, who had just completed his theological studies at Andover.† A few days later, after he had returned from Philadelphia, he was invited to preach for three Sabbaths in the Brick Church. The instructions to the committee appointed to invite him seem to suggest the same chastened spirit and sensitiveness in regard to a possible rebuff which have already been observed. The committee is "to call on Mr. Spring and to request him to inform them whether it will be convenient for him to accept the invitation for that

---

* At the meeting when this resolution was passed it was also voted to invite the Rev. Mr. Speece, of Virginia, to visit the church, but of this nothing came.

† "The Life and Times of Gardiner Spring," by himself, now becomes an important source.

number of Sabbaths, and if not, how many Sabbaths he can supply their pulpit."

He made his first appearance in the Brick Church at the Sunday morning service on June 3d, 1810, when he preached from the text, "Wherefore come ye out from among them, and be ye separate, and touch not the unclean thing, and I will be a Father unto you, and ye shall be my sons and daughters, saith the Lord of Hosts." Immediately after this service the session met in the church and voted that at the close of the services that very afternoon and evening a notice be read, calling a meeting of the pew-holders and stated hearers on the next day at noon, to consider the propriety of making out a call for Mr. Gardiner Spring to be the stated pastor of the church. The meeting was held at the time appointed, the call was unanimously voted at a salary of $2,500,* a year, and almost immediately came through Mr. John Mills, the senior elder, the good tidings that Mr. Spring intended to accept. If in the relation between church and minister there is ever such a thing as love at first sight, this was certainly an instance of it.

It must have been gratifying to the somewhat discouraged and humiliated church to know that the delay of a month in Mr. Spring's more formal acceptance † was due to the fact that in courtesy he

* In the signed copy sent to the pastor-elect and now in the possession of the church, the figure was originally $2,000, the extra $500 being added by an interlineation.

† The text of the acceptance was as follows:

"ANDOVER, *July* 6th, 1810.

"To the Congregation of the Brick Presbyterian Church in the City of New York.

"DEAR BRETHREN:

"Your communication containing a call to me to settle among you as a gospel minister has been the subject of advice, prayer,

must first dispose of two other calls, from Andover and the Park Street Church, Boston, and also a request to entertain a call from New Haven. But, no doubt, their own personal assurance that they had found the right man was enough to satisfy them. He himself, it is true, speaking in later years of the sermons preached by him in the Brick Church on that momentous third of June, said that he had "often been filled with wonder that these two jejune and puerile discourses should have decided the question on which so many interests depended." * The fact was, probably, that the young preacher was chosen for himself rather than for his sermons, and, moreover, back of all such explanations, as he himself said, "the hand of God was in the whole proceeding."

Like the proverbial "course of true love" the necessary preliminaries to the formal settlement of the new pastor did not "run smooth." For a time it seemed as though the banns might yet be forbidden. When Mr. Spring was examined before the Presbytery, many heads were doubtfully shaken over the question of his orthodoxy. "My trial sermon," he says, "was a frank avowal of my sentiments, and a

---

and serious deliberation. I hereby accept it. Believe me, dear brethren, that I feel thankful for the unmerited attention and respect which a call from so respectable a congregation has manifested. By the blessing of God I hope to be with you in the course of a few weeks. I have given myself up to God. Without recalling that act, I now give myself to you. Pray for me, fathers and brethren, that I may be sent in the fulness of the blessings of the gospel of peace.

"Wishing you grace, mercy, and peace from God our Father and the Lord Jesus Christ,

"I am, dear brethren,
"Your servant in the Lord,
"GARDINER SPRING."

* "Br. Ch. Mem.," p. 13.

The Congregation of the brick presbyterian church in the City of
New York, being on good grounds, well satisfied of the ministerial
qualifications of you, Mr Gardiner Spring, and having well
founded hopes, so far as they have had experience of your ministerial
labors, that your ministrations in the Gospel will be profitable to our
spiritual Interests, do earnestly call, and desire you to undertake
the pastoral Office in said Congregation: promising you, in the
discharge of your duty, all proper support, encouragement & obedience
in the Lord.— And that you may be free from worldly cares & Avocations,
we hereby promise, and oblige ourselves to pay to you the Sum of
two thousand five hundred dollars annually in regular quarterly payments during
the time of your being and continuing the regular pastor of the
aforesaid Congregation

New York June 4th 1810. Signed by order & in behalf of said Congregation

N.B. the words "five hundred" interlined before signing

Ab. Van Gelder   John Bingham   Elders
Thos. Ogilvie   Wm. Richd. Cunningham
John Thompson   William Miller   Deacons
William Fraser   John Adams
Benj. Egbert   Geor Wright
S. Osgood   John Murray   Trustees
John Mills

FAC-SIMILE OF THE CALL OF GARDINER SPRING

bold and unequivocal statement of the views I *then* entertained upon the subject of human ability," a burning question in that day. Had not Dr. Miller declared that he himself must be included in any condemnation of Mr. Spring's views on this matter, it is likely that an adverse vote would have resulted. As it was, the ultra-orthodox comforted themselves by the reflection that the gentleman was young and that a better acquaintance with Presbyterianism would soon modify his views. Dr. Milledoler, who was one of the first to attempt to acquaint him more fully with the Presbyterian system, and to produce the expected modification, is said to have exclaimed, at the close of a prolonged discussion, that in his judgment the best way of curing a man of such views as those which Mr. Spring obstinately professed was to dip his head in cold water. This incident, however, occurred at a slightly later date, and meantime on Wednesday, August 8th, 1810, Mr. Spring was ordained and installed in the Brick Church. On that occasion Dr. Milledoler preached the sermon, and Dr. Miller and Dr. Romeyn delivered the charges to the pastor and to the congregation respectively. Dr. Rodgers was present and united with the others in "the laying on of the hands of the Presbytery." The pastorate thus begun was destined to last for more than sixty years.

Mr. Spring was of New England ancestry. His father, the Rev. Samuel Spring, of Newburyport, Mass., was a man of ability and influence. He had served with credit as Chaplain in the Revolutionary War, accompanying Arnold's army on the arduous expedition to Quebec, and his subsequent call to the

Congregational Church in Newburyport, on the strength of the single sermon preached by him to the colonial soldiers on the eve of the expedition's departure, was not unlike his son's call to the Brick Church. His entire life was given to the ministry in Newburyport and to the duties which grew out of his position there. Perhaps his greatest public service was rendered in connection with the founding of Andover Seminary and of the American Board of Commissioners of Foreign Missions. Of the spirit which, in addition to his undoubted talents, made him a successful minister of the gospel, enough perhaps is said in quoting the remark of one of his hearers: "I love to hear Mr. Spring pray, because he prays as though he loved God." *

For his mother Gardiner Spring always cherished a very tender affection. "She was a sweet mother," he says of her. "She was our earthly refuge. The church loved her as much as they did their pastor. The whole town, with all their denominational differences, loved and respected Mrs. Dr. Spring. She was at the head of their charitable institutions, alike honored by the rich and sought after by the poor." †

From both his parents Mr. Spring had received the most thorough Christian training, and their influence upon his later religious life can hardly be overstated. It is reassuring, however, to learn that he was a real

* His epitaph is suggestive. It reads in part: "A man of an original and vigorous mind, distinguished for a deep sense of human depravity, and especially of his own unworthiness, and for his exalted views of the character and perfections of God the Redeemer; of great integrity, firmness, benevolence and urbanity; an able, faithful and assiduous pastor, an example to the flock over which he was placed; a kind husband, a tender father, and a sincere friend."

† "Life and Times," Vol. I, p. 51.

boy before he was a good one. Our evidence comes from his own pen when he was over eighty years of age, and it is in a tone of self-accusation that he writes; but, reading between the lines, it is possible for us to take a somewhat more genial view of the youthful perversity which he confesses. "I was born," he says, "in the town of Newburyport on the 24th of February, 1785. I recollect nothing of my infancy, very little of my childhood, and nothing so early as my proneness to evil. As far back as I can remember anything, I can remember that I was a selfish, wilful boy, and very impatient of restraint. As I grew to riper years, my sinful tendencies were expressed, sometimes in bold and sometimes in deceitful forms. . . . I was by nature a child of wrath. . . . I had no outwardly vicious habits, but was impatient of control, and thought it a hard and severe discipline that I was not allowed to enjoy the ordinary amusements of boys of my age, and only wished that I was old enough and strong enough to flee out of my father's hands."* And yet, when at the "ripe" age of twelve, he was sent away to school, he soon showed, according to his own confession, a quite different character. "I had no heart for study," he says, "I had no heart for anything but *home*."† We may say, then, that at the outset he had the good fortune to be very much like other boys of his age.

He was not so fortunate in the fact that his studies were unduly pushed, so that he entered Yale College ‡ when he was but fifteen years old, the youngest of

---

* "Life and Times," Vol. I, pp. 74–76.

† *Ibid.*, Vol. I, p. 76.

‡ He tells us that in the college "at that time there were but three professors." *Ibid.*, Vol. II, p. 285.

his class. He was, he tells us, "a severe student and as ambitious as Cæsar," * and the result was that his eyesight was injured and his health impaired, so that he was forced to drop out of college for a year, and finally graduated in 1805. He was the valedictorian of his class, and in his address, he says, was "foolish and wicked enough to adopt the vainglorious maxim *Aut Cæsar, aut nullus.*"†

The boy of twenty who thus once more assures us that he was entirely human, had, during his college course, passed through a very decided religious experience. During a revival in the college he had been led to give to the subject of religion a measure of that awful consideration which was then regarded as indispensable. He speaks particularly of one Saturday afternoon which he devoted entirely to prayer, endeavoring to reach the assurance that he had secured the divine mercy. "There," he says, "in the south entry of the old college, back side, middle room, third story, I wrestled with God as I had never wrestled before." ‡ For a month he thought he had succeeded in his purpose, and then on the Fourth of July "marvellous to be told, amid the arrangements and speeches, the songs and glee of that memorable day, my religious hopes and impressions *all vanished,* as 'a morning cloud, and as the early dew.'"§ It is noteworthy that although he did not "abandon [his] closet nor forsake the society of [his] religious classmates," ‖ he now considered that he was leading a distinctly irreligious life. This belief was strength-

* "Life and Times," Vol. I, p. 78.   † *Ibid.*, Vol. I, p. 82.
‡ *Ibid.*, Vol. I, p. 80.   § *Ibid.*, Vol. I, p. 81.
‖ *Ibid.*, Vol. I, p. 81.

ened by the fact that at the time of another revival in the college during the next summer, though he "rejoiced to see so many students pressing into the kingdom of God," he himself felt that he had "no lot nor part in this matter." *

It will probably seem to readers of the present day that a less wooden conception of the process of conversion than was then current would at once have assured this young man of the essential Christianity of his thoughts and purposes; but the extreme conscientiousness, which the old view inculcated, certainly played a most important part in the building up of that stalwart Christianity by which our grandparents were distinguished, and unless we have some knowledge of these passages in the early experience of Mr. Spring we shall not be prepared to understand some of the strongest and most characteristic elements of his later life and work.

On leaving college he began to prepare himself for the profession of the law, but this was shortly after interrupted by an opportunity to go as school-teacher to the island of Bermuda. One of his letters, written while in that position, displays in the most singular manner the religious perplexities in which he was then involved. At one and the same time he first expresses in the most feeling terms his inclination to turn to the ministry as his life-work, and then with equal force declares his haunting fear that he is not even a Christian. He tells frankly the best and the worst about himself, as far as he is able to see them. The best could hardly be better, and the worst was not so bad after all. "I am attached to the world,"

* "Life and Times," Vol. I, p. 82.

he confesses, "I am avaricious; and in the present
state of my family, make money my god. I strain
honesty as far as I can to gain a little. . . . I serve
God and Mammon."*

One clause in these damaging accusations informs
us of an important element of the story. The
"family," to which he refers, consisted of his young
wife and their son, three months old. For Mr.
Spring, while still in New Haven, had fallen in love.
Miss Susan Barney was a pupil at the weekly singing
school; Gardiner Spring was the teacher; and
"before I was aware of the attachment," he says, "my
heart was led captive by one who had captivated more
hearts than mine."†

When he first went to Bermuda, however, he was
so ill provided in a financial way, that marriage was
as yet out of the question: indeed, it is evident that his
acceptance of a position so far away, and out of the
line of his intended profession, was influenced by his
desire to provide as soon as possible the necessary
income. Even when, in the spring of 1806, he claimed
his bride, making a hasty journey to Connecticut
for that purpose, and taking her back with him immediately to Bermuda, his circumstances could not
be called affluent. He was still teaching and saving
money, at a little place called the Salt Kettle, when he
wrote the letter to his father already quoted, and one
may conclude therefore that the conditions and
problems of his life, quite as much as original sin,
accounted for that attachment to the world and alarming avarice which he there confesses. But at last

* "Life and Times," Vol. I, pp. 87 f.
† Ibid., Vol. I, p. 88.

enough money was saved to enable them to return to America. In New Haven, Mr. Spring resumed the study of the law, and in December, 1808, he was admitted to the bar.

It was not until now that this essentially good man, who, both in his outward observance and in his inward purposes, had been living a life of which many Christians might be envious, thought himself fitted to unite with the church. The truth was that he was at the same time prepared for a still further step, though he did not at once realize it. The state of his own mind was revealed to him by the sermon preached at the college commencement in 1809, at which he was present to take his degree of A.M. and to deliver an oration. The sermon, preached by the Rev. Dr. John M. Mason, started from the text, "To the poor the gospel is preached," and to tell in a sentence its overpowering effect upon Mr. Spring, he left the church possessed by the one thought that he must devote his life to the preaching of the gospel of Jesus Christ.

It was, as may be imagined, no easy task for a husband and a father to make so radical a change, to abandon the law for which he had now prepared himself and enter upon a preparation for the totally different profession of the ministry. His wife, however, when after some delay he told her of his purpose, rose to the occasion in a brave spirit of loyalty which must have greatly cheered him, and which was all the more creditable to her in that she did not at that time entirely share his convictions.

The new seminary at Andover was the place chosen by Mr. Spring for his theological studies, and there, in the extraordinarily short period of eight months, he completed his preparation.   During that time he had for a number of weeks supplied the pulpit at Marblehead, and for this purpose he had written eight sermons.   With these as his visible equipment, and with such preparation of head and heart as he had received from his home-life, from his own reflection and experience, and from his brief period of study at Andover, he set out, being now twenty-five years of age, on the journey to Philadelphia which led him, by God's providence, to the pulpit of the Brick Church.

CHAPTER X

THE TEMPORALITIES: 1810–1850

"I will make them keepers of the charge of the house, for all the service thereof, and for all that shall be done therein."—*Ezekiel* 44 : 14.

"The house does not belong to us, but to him; and therefore we are bound to husband the property entrusted to us, for the best interests of his kingdom."— GARDINER SPRING, "The Brick Church Memorial," p. 39.

THE period of forty years upon which we now enter is crowded with events, and we are fortunately provided with full information in regard to it, so that we shall be able to follow the history in all necessary detail. It would not, however, be desirable to proceed by a strictly chronological method. Various interests of the church developed side by side, and it would be only confusing to attempt to deal with them all together in one interwoven narrative. It will be best, therefore, to treat each main group of subjects in a separate chapter, with the understanding that each of these chapters covers the same period, and that the events and developments described in any one of them were contemporary with those described in the others. This arrangement is the more feasible because the whole period may be regarded as a unit: it was not divided into parts by any events of critical importance, but consisted of one continuous development.

The material may be conveniently divided into five parts; first, the temporalities of the church, its lands, buildings, and general finances; second, the work of the minister as pastor and theologian; third, the church's religious and moral progress; fourth, the history of the church's schools for secular and religious instruction; and fifth, the growth in the church of missionary and philanthropic enterprise. The present chapter, then, will be devoted to the first of these five divisions, and will give an account of the changes which took place, during the first forty years of Gardiner Spring's pastorate, in the lands and buildings upon and within which the history of the Brick Church was enacted, and of its financial problems and achievements during that period.

The interior of the church itself first demands our attention. Whether in 1810 the old pulpit, lifted high on its supporting post, still existed, is not certain. Mention of the fact that in 1813 certain ladies had presented "the curtains for the pulpit," combined with our knowledge that after the pulpit had been changed to a platform against the rear wall, with the usual desk, curtains were then hung across the window behind it, leads us to suspect that the change may have been made at that date. On the other hand, in 1822 extensive repairs were undertaken with the express purpose of rendering the church more easy to speak in, and we learn, incidentally, that these repairs involved the removal of certain pews, all of which might readily suggest some change in the pulpit. In any case, the change was made at some time during this period.

One other relic of antiquity was early removed. The two "Governor's pews" for the use of strangers, had in 1811 been exchanged for six of the ordinary

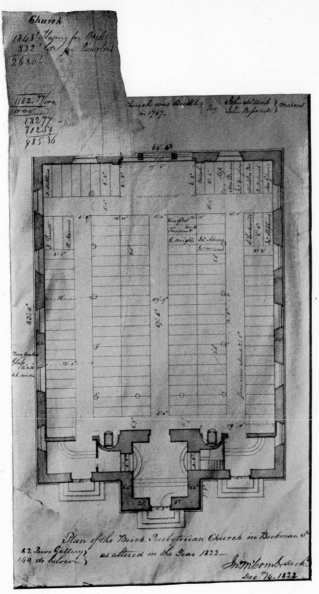

GROUND-PLAN OF THE BRICK CHURCH ON BEEKMAN
STREET AS ALTERED IN 1822

size. A few years later the addition of some form
of mahogany trimming for the pews throughout the
church was authorized, and no doubt added a good
deal to the general appearance. Indeed, any modest
adornment must have been welcome, one would think,
in that severely plain apartment, whose main features,
the whitewashed walls and the plain glass windows
with interior shutters, made a somewhat cheerless
effect. Even the mahogany trimmings did not satisfy
some of the worshippers, who accordingly introduced,
of their own accord, certain decorative changes in
the pews which they had rented. This led to a
curious declaration of the trustees in 1824, in which
they "discountenanced, not to say prohibited, the
lining of pews with green cloth or painting them
the same color." In 1840 the trustees themselves
caused the pews to be lined, but the color is not
mentioned.

There was in the church one decorative feature
which must not be overlooked. This was a shield
surrounded by conventional foliage, carved in wood
and painted in white and gold. Upon it was inscribed in gold letters the words HOLINESS TO THE
LORD. It was placed over the high window behind
the pulpit, and no doubt in those days, as in later
times when it was removed to a corresponding position in the church on Thirty-seventh Street,* it
offered a grateful object of study to the wandering
eyes of the children of the congregation.

How was the church lighted in the early days of
the nineteenth century? A bill of over £30 for

* Though no longer a part of the church's decorations, it is still preserved, together with the large clock from the downtown church.

candles paid in 1813 gives us our answer.* Five
years later brass lamps were proposed, and after a
year of consideration they were installed, a row with
reflectors ranged along the wall in the galleries, and
others, for lighting the main floor, suspended from
the gallery fronts. In 1830 the lamps were in their
turn disposed of, and gas was introduced.

During the first part of this period the heating of
the church was by stoves. Some £23 were paid for
their erection in 1810, and it may be that until that
time the worshippers had had no other source of heat
during the long services than the old-fashioned foot-
warmers. In 1813 two "Russian" stoves were provided, but four months later, whether because of objection to stoves in general or dislike of the particular
design chosen, it was ordered that "the committee
who were appointed to have stoves erected in the
church be directed to have them removed." With
the coming spring the matter was then dropped for
the time, but the frosts of the next December produced
the following resolution: "Whereas it is represented
that a number of persons who worship in the Brick
Church are desirous that stoves should be erected
in said church, . . . Resolved that stoves be erected."
This time they remained, and at about the period
when gas was introduced we hear also of furnaces.†
By that time the idea that worship was best carried on
under a certain degree of bodily discomfort had given
way to the more luxurious modern view.

We now pass to the outside of the building and

---

* The candles were supported in brass "chandeliers," this word then
having its true etymological significance.

† Croton water was introduced ten years later.

SHIELD FROM THE BRICK CHURCH ON
BEEKMAN STREET

INTERIOR OF THE BRICK CHURCH ON BEEKMAN STREET IN ITS
FINAL STATE

consider first its surroundings. Its situation was certainly attractive, for the City Hall Park, which formed its western boundary, was probably, in the early years of Dr. Spring's pastorate, the most attractive part of the entire city. The City Hall, which still ranks among the most admirable of New York's buildings, was completed in 1812, while the Park itself during this period "is described as having been a beautiful place, the walks and grass-plots being trimly kept, and shaded by groves of elm, poplar, willow and eucalyptus."* Fronting upon it were some of the most important buildings of the city in that day, such as the New York Gardens, Mechanics' Hall, the London Hotel, the Park Theatre, then the city's most fashionable place of amusement, and Tammany Hall, besides the Brick Church; while St. Paul's Chapel stood opposite the Park's southern point, for in those fortunate days the open space included the site of the present post-office.

But what was the external appearance of the Brick Church itself? The wooden pale fence, erected, as we have seen, in 1809, continued till 1840, when an iron railing succeeded it.† The earlier structure, besides its natural use in protecting the property, served several picturesque purposes. To it were fastened the chains which, from 1810, were on Sundays extended across Nassau and Beekman streets in order to prevent any noise of traffic from disturbing the services. Against it, moreover, were placed the stands and booths of fruit- and oyster-

---

* "Mem. Hist., of N. Y.," Vol. III, p. 202.

† When the church was finally torn down, this fence was removed to the place of Mr. J. T. Stranahan, in South Brooklyn, where it is still standing.

sellers, and especially of the petty dealers whose rich harvest-time was the third and fourth of July. From 1828 there are frequent indications that these encroachments upon the church's property were making the life of the sexton * miserable. What is of more importance, the same facts suggest that by that time the Brick Church was beginning to be "downtown." On the other hand, the mention in 1815 (not many years before) of a willow tree on the church grounds, whose limbs overhung the street and occasionally needed trimming, reminds us that the scene would nevertheless have looked rural enough to modern New Yorkers.

Standing on Beekman Street, we look up at the front of the church and are at once reminded that its well-proportioned steeple was nearly destroyed soon after the coming of Mr. Gardiner Spring. On Sunday morning, May 19th, 1811, a destructive fire broke out in the region northeast of the Green, and, before it could be extinguished, burned nearly a hundred buildings. In the midst of the conflagration flying embers set fire to the wooden steeple of the Brick Church, and it seemed to the onlookers that at least a portion of the building, perhaps the whole of it,

* A few facts regarding the sexton's office may be of interest. By a minute of the trustees in 1814, it was declared to be the duty of the sexton "to attend to ringing of the bell, opening, sweeping, dusting, and lighting the church; and sweeping and cleaning the streets adjacent, as required by law; opening, sweeping, and lighting the session room, at all such times as are now usual in the day or evening, for the accommodation of the session, trustees, lectures, and prayer-meetings of the church." At the same time his salary was fixed at $125 per annum, while "other emoluments arising from the church," such as burial fees, for instance, were guaranteed to amount to $225 more. During a large part of this period the sexton was also collector of pew-rents, for which service he received five per cent. on collections. See Appendix K, p. 528.

was doomed. How the blaze was extinguished is made plain by the following notice which was ordered to be inserted next day in the daily papers: "The board of trustees of the Brick Presbyterian Church, deeply impressed with a grateful sense for the timely and constant aid offered for the preservation of the said church from the calamitous and destructive fire of the 19th instant, make in behalf of the congregation their most sincere acknowledgments to their fellow-citizens in general, and more especially to the un-daunted mariner and several others who by the [lightning] conductor ascended the steeple and checked the fire that had then broke out, until more effectual means arrived, and were instruments in the hands of God of saving the church." At the same time one hundred dollars was voted to Stephen McCormick (evidently the "undaunted mariner"), and half that amount to four other rescuers, as rewards for the signal service thus rendered, and as the addresses of the persons in question were unknown and several days' inquiry failed to discover them, a further news-paper notice invited them to call and receive the money. It is a curious fact, commonly reported in histories of this period, though it does not appear on what authority, that the hero of the incident never claimed his reward.

If in our examination of the building we now pass around it toward the rear, and if we imagine that it is the week of Mr. Spring's installation, we observe that, adjoining the north end of the church, is a smaller wooden structure just completed. This is the "session and prayer room," which had been projected in the preceding May and was finished just in time for the use of the new pastor. It measured about thirty by fifty feet and contained an assembly room, fitted with a pulpit, and having its walls, like those of the church, whitewashed—"The Old White Lecture Room," as it was affectionately called by those who in later years remembered it. Here the weekly evening lecture and other meetings were now held, and to this room the session, who heretofore had met in the charity school-house, transferred their head-quarters.

By 1829 the needs of the church had outgrown this building, and it was then proposed to tear down the old addition and erect in its place a "large and commodious two-story brick session house." According to the plan then suggested the new building was to contain large rooms suitable for church meetings and for the Sunday-schools which had now been established,* smaller rooms "for the pastor, session, trustees and for school and church libraries, etc." (probably one room was intended to serve more than one of these uses), "and in addition two or more valuable and pleasant rooms to rent." †

There were two difficulties in the way of this proposal. In the first place, the trustees did not feel able to undertake the expense. This was overcome by the guarantee of certain members of the congregation that the money should be provided from other sources. But it was also necessary, if the plan to rent certain of the rooms was to be carried out, to secure the removal of the restriction in the original lease of the Beekman Street lot by which the church

* As will be described in Chapter XIII.
† For secular purposes.

was forbidden to convert the land "to private, secular uses." A petition was accordingly made to the
Common Council, praying for such a modification of
the original grant as would permit the carrying out
of the new plan, and this petition was granted.
This event was important, not only in its relation to
the matter then in hand, but because of the precedent
thus established of removing certain restrictions upon
the use of the church property.

It was now possible to proceed to the erection of the
new building, called at first the session house, but
finally named the chapel, and by December, 1832, it
had been completed at a cost of about $12,000. It
was a handsome structure. Its windows were separated by pilasters which rose to the eaves. The roof
was considerably lower than that of the main church,
and the two buildings together made a harmonious
design. The arrangement of the interior, according
to the best information obtainable, was as follows:
on the first floor directly adjoining the church (but
not communicating with it) were two Sunday-school
rooms, opening into each other, one looking out on
Nassau Street and one on the Green. Over these
rooms was the large lecture room. Still further in
the rear on each floor there were four rooms, two on
each side, and between them, with the entrance at
the north end, a hallway containing the stairs.
Doubtless it was in one of the smaller rooms on the
second story that the pastor kept his books and
prepared his sermons, "that memorable study,"
he calls it, "so enbowered, so retired and tranquil
amid noise and uproar." The two small, rear rooms
on the first story facing Chatham Street (now Park

Row) were the ones originally designed for renting. The trustees in the end determined that they would themselves provide the money expended in the building, which they were enabled to do by mortgaging the property. The interest on this mortgage was provided by renting not only the two rooms just mentioned, but also, afterward, with the permission of the city,* other rooms not required for religious purposes. In about 1840 the chapel was extended fourteen feet to the north so as to provide more space that might be "let for offices."

The tenants to whom the records refer were a physician, an agent for the Foreign Mission Board, and a publisher and book-seller. The last mentioned, Mr. John S. Taylor, opened his store here soon after the chapel was built and continued it through almost the whole of this period. His advertisement, inserted in a publication of 1838, shows that his was a business not inappropriately housed beneath the eaves of a church. It calls the attention of the public to the "Popular Religious Books, published by John S. Taylor, Theological and Sunday-school Bookseller, Brick Church Chapel, New York." In 1846 another publishing house became the church's tenant, that of Baker and Scribner, whose successors, Charles Scribner and Co., and the present Charles Scribner's Sons have continued the firm's long relationship to the Brick Church by becoming the publishers of the principle works of the church's ministers during the last half century.†

* In 1835 permission was given to rent any portion of the chapel.

† According to the terms of the lease of 1846 the trustees rented to Baker and Scribner for five years "the two rooms on the lower floor of the Brick Church chapel, one of which fronts on Nassau Street, the other

THE BRICK CHURCH ON BEEKMAN STREET
Showing Chapel in the rear

It will be remembered that in the original deed of the land on Beekman Street the use to which it was to be put included the burial of the dead. In the days of which we write it was considered a proper and important part of a church's duty to provide a suitable place of burial for the members of its own congregation, and the natural place for this was considered to be the yard about the church itself. Like Trinity and St. Paul's, though in a much more restricted area, the Brick Church had thus surrounded itself with a cemetery. Besides the open. graves there had been constructed early a limited number of vaults which were sold to individuals, and these were increased from time to time until nearly all the available area had been thus utilized, and even some space beneath the sidewalks, by permission of the the city. The flat tops of these vaults, level with the ground and inscribed with the names of the owners, were a familiar sight to all who entered the church or passed along Beekman Street.

In 1823 a city ordinance was passed prohibiting any further burial of the dead south of Grand Street.* The trustees of the Brick Church had barely completed some new vaults at considerable expense and were dismayed at this sudden and unexpected enact-

fronting on Park Row (with the privilege of removing the single partition between the said two rooms for convenience, but at their own expense)." Provision, it is interesting to note, was made for a termination of the lease "in case the said trustees should sell the said premises before the expiration of this lease or in case the Corporation of the city of New York should interfere with the present rights of the said trustees held under certain acts of said Corporation to lease said premises so as to divest said trustees of said rights."

* The plague of yellow fever in 1822 was thought to have started with a burial in Trinity churchyard. See "Westervelt Manuscripts" (Lenox Library), p. 14.

ment, which, they persuaded themselves, was unnecessary or at least premature. One paragraph of
the memorial which they presented to the corporation
of the city, stating their grievance, is sufficiently
interesting to be quoted. "Your petitioners," they
say, "would briefly notice a reason repeatedly urged
against a discrimination in private vaults" (such discrimination was what they had petitioned for) . . .
"namely, that it savored of aristocracy. The suggestion, it is believed, had great weight at the time;
but it is as fallacious as it was popular. Of the whole
number of private vaults in this city, one-half are
supposed to be owned by those who are in moderate
circumstances, and if the remaining half belong to
persons of opulence, who can deny that there are
hundreds, if not thousands, *as well able* to own
them as they." Possibly this argument did not tend
to strengthen their case.

At any rate, the city stood by its ordinance. A
few months later a second memorial was presented
by the trustees, rehearsing the conditions of the
original grant of their land and asserting with some
reasonableness that the city's recent ordinance prevented the church from exercising a right which had,
in return for a certain rent, duly paid, been promised
to them forever "without any let, trouble, hindrance,
molestation, interruption, or denial." At the same
time or shortly afterward an interment was made, in
spite of the ordinance, for the purpose of testing in the
courts the validity of the city's act. In this contest
the church was worsted. But unconvinced, they
again memorialized the city authorities, and followed
this up by instituting suit against the city for $30,000,

damages. The sole issue of this proceeding is told with sufficient clearness by the only subsequent reference to the matter in the trustees' minutes: "Ordered to be paid: H. Holden, Esq., costs of suit for breach of covenant, $123.93."*

The limited area around the church was not, of course, its only burying-ground. The Brick Church had also its one-third part of the Beekman lots on the corner of North (afterward East Houston) and Chrystie streets, where burials were made throughout the whole period now under consideration.†

There still remains to be considered the vital question of the income and financial condition of the church during the forty years covered by this chapter. In the preceding period the revenue had been derived from collections and the renting and sale of pews. It became, however, more and more desirable to devote the collections to benevolent objects, and at length the pews were made to bear the burden alone. To this, after the erection of the chapel, was added the income of such rooms in that building as were rented for secular purposes. In 1835 this amounted to $925.

The buying of a pew meant little more than the renting of it with the right to hold the same year by year thereafter; and on the other hand, there were decided drawbacks to be encountered. Assessments for repairs, or to make up a deficit, or to meet some extraordinary expense, were by no means uncommon.

* The permission of the city, a few years later, to rent certain portions of the chapel (see above, p. 139), was asked and granted as being at least a partial compensation for the loss entailed by the prohibition of burials.

† It may be added that this land was sold in 1866 for $64,200. Ground had been purchased in Evergreen Cemetery in 1856.

And yet from the frequent references in the records, there seem always to have been people who were anxious to buy. It must be added that there seem also to have been people who failed to pay their annual tax or their rent, as the case might be, so that the sale of the pews thus confiscated and of others that were deeded or bequeathed to the church from time to time, provided not infrequent opportunities of purchase.

For the first few years after Mr. Spring's installation the treasurer reported each year a substantial balance. In 1817, however, we learn that an advance in the pew-rents was necessary to keep the church from running behind, and there was a still further increase two years later designed to provide an unsolicited addition of $750 to the pastor's salary. In 1824, the burden upon the pew-holders being evidently a subject of complaint, he offered to relinquish $500 of his salary, if the taxes on the pews should be correspondingly reduced; and the state of the treasury at that time must have been indeed discouraging, for the trustees went so far as to request that he would make the relinguishment unconditional. This he would not do, and they were fain to accept his original proposition. The result was interesting. A meeting of the men of the church was held at once, proposing to restore the pastor's salary without delay to the figure from which it had been reduced, $3,250, by actually advancing the pew-tax. It was thus made evident that, whatever the financial difficulties of the situation might be (and there was no doubt that the church had been forced to borrow money to meet its obligations), the congregation stood behind the pastor and were unwilling that he, rather than they, should be made to suffer.

Whether as a result of this episode, or because of objection to the legal contest, being waged with the city at this time about the burial-rights, at the next election of trustees, in April, 1825, the three whose terms then expired were not reëlected. Immediately the other six handed in their resignations, and although three of these were afterward prevailed upon to remain, the board when it assembled in May was distinctly a new body.

It had to meet, however, the old problems. In the next year with a view to extinguishing the debt and completing certain necessary work on the building, it was again necessary to propose an extra pew-assessment, and to appeal directly to the loyalty of the congregation for support in this unpleasant measure. Yet on the whole the situation as then described by the trustees, though demanding a remedy, was not alarming. "The regular annual revenue," they say, "is barely sufficient to meet the current yearly expenditure," and "the debt, although not now large, will soon become so by the accumulation of interest." Evidently a small increase in revenue would at that time have removed the embarrassment.

From 1832 a new source of revenue was added by the renting of the rooms in the new chapel, as above described, but all of the money so received was required in paying the interest on the debt incurred in the chapel's erection, and in the gradual reduction of the debt itself.

Meantime the difficulty in meeting the ordinary expenses of the church continued. Year after year the treasurer reported a deficit, which even the old expedient of an advance in the pew-tax did not now serve to check.* In 1839 began a series of loans, sometimes for current expenses, sometimes for repairs or alterations. These appear on the records at rather frequent intervals and reveal a condition of affairs which, to say the least, was undesirable.

But now once more the special emergency was the occasion of showing the church's strength. At the request of the trustees in January, 1841, the pastor undertook to raise from the congregation a voluntary subscription for the purpose of obliterating the debt. In less than three weeks' time he was able to put into their hands the sum of $10,077.22. The subscriptions, he says in his accompanying report, ranged from $1 to $370, and came from one hundred and forty different persons. "The claim," he continues, "has received the most prompt and warm response. . . . Six thousand dollars were paid in by the subscribers in a single morning, simply on a public notice from the pulpit." By means of this generous contribution, the entire debt, except the less troublesome mortgage on the chapel was at once paid off, principal and interest, and the congregation set its face to the future with a new spirit of hopefulness.

From this time until 1850 the situation, although not free from anxieties, was more easy. There continued for a time to be a yearly deficit, but a part of this at least could be met from the sinking fund, while by the same means the old debt of $12,000, on the chapel had been finally extinguished. At last, on the very year which closes the period of our

* The financial crisis in 1837 should be remembered in this connection.

present study, the treasurer was able to report that the revenues had exceeded the expenditures.

When it is remembered that the Brick Church had no endowment whatever, that in spite of a narrow income it not only maintained its original building, but twice over made considerable additions to it, that at the same time, as we shall see in later chapters, it was carrying on a missionary and benevolent work of constantly increasing proportions, and that during the very years when it was beginning to lose in numbers through the northward drift of population it nevertheless succeeded in clearing off all indebtedness and putting its work upon a self-supporting basis, we cannot but admire the energy of its officers and the generous loyalty of its people.

CHAPTER XI

PASTOR AND THEOLOGIAN: 1810–1850

"Brethren, my heart's desire and prayer to God for Israel is, that they might be saved."—*Romans* 10 : 1.

"Whatever subordinate ends, therefore, the Christian pulpit may secure in this or the coming world, its legitimate, paramount aim is the glory of God in the salvation of men."—GARDINER SPRING, "The Power of the Pulpit," p. 170.

THE last chapter, although in many of its facts and incidents suggestive of the real life of the church, is for the most part only a description of the outer shell. It presents to us in detail the physical conditions under which the work of the church was carried on. We now turn to study that work itself, and we shall begin by tracing the career of him who was the church's leader throughout this period.

In a sense the whole religious life and activity that then existed in the Brick Church, all those matters, for example, that will be presented in the next three chapters, form a part of his biography. But there are certain more personal facts and events which may well be treated by themselves in a chapter especially devoted to him. And here it will be convenient to deal also with all the church's distinctly theological interests during these years, since in them the church could hardly be said to act at all except in the person of its pastor.

148

GARDINER SPRING IN THE EARLY YEARS OF HIS PASTORATE
From an oil portrait in the possession of his great-grandson, Shepherd Knapp

For the whole period now under observation Gardiner Spring performed alone the duties of minister of the Brick Church. Dr. Rodgers' active work had ended, as we know, before his successor came. Even his service as moderator at the meetings of the Brick Church session in 1809 and 1810 had been performed with great difficulty and frequent interruptions. He was but waiting patiently for the end; and at length the end came when the new pastorate was less than a year old, on May 7th, 1811. It had greatly cheered Dr. Rodgers that, when he was called to go, he had already seen the church moving forward with promise under its new leader. During those last months, his biographer tells us, "he took his young colleague by the hand with paternal solicitude and affection, discovered great anxiety to promote his usefulness, and rejoiced in his talents and success." * Thus the mantle of Elijah fell upon Elisha's shoulders.

The task which Mr. Spring had assumed was arduous, and, except for the force of character, the Christian spirit, and the consecrated purpose which he brought to his work, he was imperfectly prepared. "My theological attainments," he says, "were very limited," † and it was necessary for him to continue as best he could the training and stocking of his mind. He began at once a thorough investigation of Christian doctrine, which he pursued, not only by reading, but also by conference and correspondence with his older contemporaries.

His progress, however, was necessarily slow, for the

* "Rodgers Mem.," p. 277.
† "Life and Times," Vol. I, p. 119.

first demand upon his time was the vigorous performance of his daily ministerial duties, and these were so
engrossing that he seemed to have little leisure for
aught else. "I neglected everything for the work
of the ministry," he says, "I had a strong desire to
visit the courts, and listen to the arguments of the
eminent jurists of the city; but I had no time for this
indulgence. I had none for light reading, none for
evening parties, and very little for social visiting, or
even extensive reading. Everything was abandoned
for my pulpit ministrations. . . . Under God it was
this laborious and unintermittent effort that saved
me from shipwreck." * He was abundantly justified
in asserting, as he did, that a faithful minister is in
the most thorough sense "a working man."

Let him in his own words give us some idea of his
method and habits of work. "There is nothing,"
he affirms, "of which I have been constrained to be
more economical, and even covetous, than time. I
have ever been an early riser, and even in mid-win-
ter used to walk from Beekman Street † round the
'Forks of the Bowery,' now Union Square, before I
broke my fast. I usually went into my study at nine
o'clock, and after my removal to Bond Street, more
generally at eight, though my study was opposite the
City Hall, and more than a mile from my residence." ‡
This description of the prompt beginning of the day
prepares us for his account of the system and regu-

---

* "Life and Times," Vol. I, pp. 104 *f.*

† Dr. Murray in his "Memorial Discourse" (p. 20), says: "He once
told me that his first residence in the city being on Broadway, near Canal
Street, he was obliged to walk across a number of open lots to get to his
Thursday lectures, and on dark nights stood sometimes in dread of assault."

‡ "Life and Times," Vol. I, p. 105.

larity with which he produced his sermons. "For a series of years," he says, "I rarely retired to my pillow of a Lord's Day evening without having selected my subject for the following Lord's Day." *
On Tuesday almost without exception he would begin actual work upon his sermon,† and with the same regularity he brought his writing to an end at Friday noon. Never except in two instances, he declares, had Saturday been devoted to the preparation of the sermon for the next day. It should be added, however, that when the importance of the subject demanded it, and when the assistance of other clergymen made it possible, he would spend two, three, or even more, weeks in the preparation of one sermon.

He preached commonly from a manuscript, but when, as he occasionally did, he employed the extemporaneous method, he went to the other extreme, using no notes whatever, preferring to be absolutely untrammelled; and he records his opinion that some of his best and most profitable sermons were delivered in this way, by a method "so literally extemporaneous that from beginning to end I did not know beforehand what would be my next sentence." ‡ This success, however, he points out, was the result of previous mental discipline, in which the regular use of the pen had played a considerable part.

In regard to his written sermons it is significant in

* "Life and Times," Vol. I, p. 110.

† In his "Letter to a Young Clergyman" ("Fragments from the Study of a Pastor," 1838, p. 117), Dr. Spring says: "One sermon a week, well planned, well digested, carefully written, and faithfully applied, is labor enough for any man who allows himself any time for intellectual improvement." He adds that, in that case, "you may draw upon your Text Book for two or three others without much preparation."

‡ "Life and Times," Vol. I, p. 111.

this connection to hear him say that when sometimes he had begun a sermon without any fixed method in his mind, he had almost always found it lost labor. "For the most part," he says, "my divisions and arrangements have been thoroughly premeditated; and so thoroughly that . . . I have in many instances written the application first, and the body of my discourse last." *

These facts in regard to his persevering and methodical industry go far toward explaining the success of Gardiner Spring as a preacher. But, of course, method could have produced but a mediocre result, had it not been inspired by something more spontaneous and personal in the man himself, and been provided with good material on which to work. For the first of these necessities we have his declaration, uttered with enthusiasm, that he "loved the work of writing sermons and preaching the gospel." † To him the routine and the system of it all were no drudgery, for his whole heart was in it. There was no other occupation in which he took so much delight. And as for the second necessity, material to work on, his strongly acquisitive and fertile brain kept him well supplied. His own reference to this subject is interesting, and especially because it incidentally dispels any notion that he was merely a student of books, as we may have hastily assumed. He was also, as he here shows us, a student of life. "I have rarely been embarrassed for want of subjects," he said in his later years. "The wonderful facility with which one subject leads to another, the state of the congregation, an interview with some individual or

* "Life and Times," Vol. I, p. 112.   † *Ibid.*, Vol. I, p. 106.

family, a watchful observance of the leadings of Divine Providence, intercourse with ministerial brethren, some unexpected suggestion during the night-watches, a solitary ride on the saddle,* my *index rerum* and the inexhaustible treasures of the Bible, furnished me with subjects which I have not yet overtaken." †

But we have yet to observe the most important characteristic of Mr. Spring's plan of work. Of greater significance than his natural talents, his strong personality, his enthusiasm, or his faithfulness, was the high aim which he held constantly before him. He was literally possessed by a great determination to use all his power and opportunity in the reclaiming of sinful men and the establishing of them in the kingdom of God. Not to write learned or elegant or striking sermons was the purpose he had set before himself, but "by the foolishness of preaching" to save men from sin. He was not even content to address himself to the less urgent needs of those who were already Christians, but from the beginning labored "rather with the view of being instrumental in the conversion of sinners, than of comforting the people of God." ‡

How serious and deep-seated this purpose in him was, is shown by the fact that he maintained it in face of the greatest obstacle of all, namely the surprise and

---

* Dr. Murray says, "He loved to recall the incidents of the earlier period of his ministry; and on several occasions, while riding with him to funerals, it seemed to me like the telling of some curious dream to hear him say in the midst of some busy street, shadowed by massive buildings; 'There ran a stream, and there is the spot over which I used to jump my horse in my afternoon rides years ago, during which I composed my lecture for the evening.'" ("Memorial Discourse," p. 20.)

† "Life and Times," Vol. I, p. 112.

‡ *Ibid.*, Vol. I, p. 109.

criticism of some of those who were his best friends. Both the congregation and the officers of the church, he tells us, were eager, when he first began his work among them, that their minister should win the popular ear. Not that this was their chief desire, but they not unnaturally wished to see him cultivate such qualities in his sermons as would draw large numbers to the church and keep them there. And perhaps he would not have been greatly blameworthy had he adopted their point of view. On the contrary, he showed the depth of his conviction by refusing to forfeit anything whatsoever to the lower motive. He boldly preached a sermon to his own people from the ironical text, "Speak unto us smooth things," and by it succeeded in establishing once for all, as the rule of his preaching in the Brick Church and as the test for judging it, that a sermon should aim to please God, whether it pleased men or not.

Perhaps it is not surprising that a man so strongly moved by conscientious considerations, should have had doubts from time to time about the value of his work. This was, at any rate, the case with Mr. Spring. There were periods during his early ministry when he was utterly discouraged. "Many a time, after preaching," he writes, "did I remain long in the pulpit, that I might not encounter the faces of the people as I left the church, and many a time, when I left it, did I feel that I could never preach another sermon." *

This depression in regard to the real usefulness of his ministry was by no means the only great difficulty by which he was beset in those early days. His health

* "Br. Ch. Mem.," pp. 21 *f.*

threatened to give way and frequently caused him serious anxiety. In 1813 it was twice necessary to employ a ministerial assistant for him on account of his "feeble state," and during the next year he was compelled to leave his work altogether for a couple of months.

A still more serious difficulty in those early years was the doubt entertained by a number of his Presbyterian associates in regard to his orthodoxy. As we have seen already, he had been received under care of Presbytery with a good deal of hesitation on this score. After he began his regular preaching in New York, the feeling of uncertainty in regard to him increased rather than diminished. It was a time when theological questions excited the greatest interest in all the churches, so that any supposed peculiarity of doctrine, even on points of secondary importance, would at once be seized upon with avidity. Congregations enjoyed and expected theological preaching from their pastors, so that almost invariably the sermons preached on Sunday supplied to the critics of orthodoxy abundant material for the coming week.

Mr. Spring, moreover, was thoroughly in sympathy with this theological interest and his sermons were distinctly of the theological type. This does not imply that he for a moment lost sight of the sermon's practical purpose. On the contrary, that was constantly and prevailingly before him; but he was convinced that that purpose could hardly be achieved except by the theological mode of approach. "Men who complain of doctrinal preaching," said he, "are strangers to the worth and power of practical preaching. . . . I do not see how any man can preach practically who does not preach doctrinally, for the obvious reason that Christian doctrine is truth in theory, and Christian practice is truth in action." *

From what has been said it will readily be seen that any differences between the theological views of Mr. Spring and those of other Presbyterian clergymen of the city would soon be thoroughly known and become the subject of anxious consideration.

Now Mr. Spring had been somewhat influenced by what was known as the New England Theology, in the midst of which he had grown up; and New England Theology, though Calvinistic in its basic principles, was regarded with grave suspicion by the New York Calvinists. Mr. Spring's father was a follower of Dr. Hopkins of Newport, one of the New England leaders; and the son in his sermons in the Brick Church gave some reason for fearing that he also might be a Hopkinsian. When it was said that Dr. Mason, preaching in the church on Murray Street, in his denunciations of New England divinity made "unmistakable allusions to a rising young preacher, who was suspected of favoring some peculiar views of the New England School," the reference was to the pastor of the Brick Church.† The Rev. Ezra Stiles Ely published a book entitled "The Contrast," which, in its discussion of the difference between Hopkinsian and Calvinistic theology, was plainly aimed at the same person. Such attacks as these he could well afford to ignore except so far as preaching the truth "more plainly and pungently"‡ was an answer. On the other hand, he felt bound to

* "Br. Ch. Mem.," p. 116.   † "Br. Ch. Mem.," p. 136.
‡ "Life and Times," Vol. I, p. 129.

give full and frank replies to a series of questions propounded to him in writing by certain members of the Presbytery, who had been disturbed by his supposed errors, and who in a courteous and straightforward manner sought to learn just how far their fears were well grounded.

Some ground there was. Mr. Spring had, in truth, adopted certain Hopkinsian views and was by no means slow to express them. Especially he made much of a distinction between "natural" and "moral" inability to become holy, the former of which he denied, against the old Calvinists, while the latter he accepted, with them. It would be difficult perhaps to awaken any enthusiasm on the subject nowadays, or to explain the ardor and enthusiasm with which Mr. Spring contended that men have in themselves "all the natural faculties that are necessary to holiness," and, if disposed to use them aright, would be holy, since he at the same time admitted, nay, urgently asserted, that the total depravity of human nature creates "an invincible aversion to holiness," and that the "moral inability" thus produced is actually innate in the human heart.* But at the time of which we write, this subject aroused the keenest interest, and Mr. Spring's position was regarded as more than questionable. There were, besides, other New England views of smaller importance, which, with more or less certainty, he was prepared to urge as a modification of the older Calvinism.

All this, however, was far from amounting to an acceptance of Hopkinsianism as a whole. The most characteristic doctrines in that system, as he took

* Spring's "Essays" (1813), p. 35, note.

pains to assert, he had always emphatically rejected. He did not believe, for instance, that God's absolute sovereignty in all things should be so construed as to make him the direct cause of sinful as well as of holy actions.   Nor did he believe in "unconditional submission," the doctrine that a man ought so wholly to resign himself to the divine will as to be ready to be damned for the glory of God.   The truth was that he remained, after all, a Calvinist of the stricter sort, yet one who had come near enough to the New Englanders to share some of their good points, while maintaining his own freedom and avoiding their extreme positions By degrees this became plain to all, and in the end, instead of being regarded as suspicious in his theology, he was accepted as a champion of orthodoxy.

It should be added at this point that his relation to the Hopkinsians had given him something far better than the few minor doctrines he had adopted from them.   It had early given him the power to appreciate men from whom he continued to differ on many important points.   It was no small thing, at a time of theological controversy and in a man whose own views were always clear-cut and positive, that he could in so large a measure keep his Christian sympathies free from the influence of intellectual prejudice; and the characteristic which we here observe was without doubt one of those that most contributed to the large usefulness of his career.   In this connection it will be interesting to note two passages from his autobiography which exhibit admirably his liberal-mindedness.   In mentioning at some length the published sermons which he had read with most profit, he says, "I do not hesitate to include the name of Emmons" (that name was to strict Presbyterians like a red rag to a bull), "because, while in my judgment he has some errors, he has more truth than any writer whose works have fallen under my notice.   The young minister who refuses to read Emmons because his name has been proscribed by the Princeton reviewers, will remain ignorant of truth which, as a preacher of the gospel, he ought to know." *   The second passage is still more significant.   He has just been speaking at length of certain Hopkinsian doctrines from which he strongly dissented.   Then he continues: "Great and good men have been the zealous advocates of the views here animadverted on, nor are we among those who have called in question the excellence of their Christian character.   As a class I have never known more godly men.   Men of greater humility, greater self-denial, greater devotedness to the interests and enlargement of Christ's kingdom, have never existed in New England than the disciples of Dr. Hopkins.   If their opposers had known them as well as I have known them, I am confident their prejudices would vanish." †

It is certainly pleasant to note these expressions of generous sympathy, and the tolerant spirit which they display.   At the same time, we must not give them an exaggerated meaning.   It must be admitted that outside the pale of Calvinism Mr. Spring's views were not so free from bias.   He had not much patience, for instance, with the so-called New Haven Theology ‡

* "Life and Times," Vol. I, p. 114.

† *Ibid*, Vol. II, pp. 14 *f.*

‡ Yet see below his attitude toward the allied New School Presbyterians.

of Dr. N. W. Taylor, with its complete denial of native depravity; he could countenance the excommunication of a woman from his church for no other reason than that she disbelieved in the eternal punishment of the wicked, the Universalist heresy; he frankly regarded the papacy as antichrist, and affirmed that he actually preferred infidelity to Roman Catholicism. But, as we have seen in the passages quoted above, among the different kinds of Calvinist (and they were many and none too amicable), Mr. Spring set a notable example of liberality. "I do not ask," he said, "that in every particular my brethren should subscribe to my creed. I only ask that they 'sincerely receive and adopt the Confession of Faith of the Presbyterian Church, as containing the system of doctrine contained in the Holy Scriptures.' . . . Few in this age of inquiry, believe every word of it. Nor did our fathers. I myself made two exceptions to it, when I was received into the Presbytery of New York. . . . I could specify more points in which not a few of our ministers and ruling elders do not exactly agree with our standards. Yet they are all *honest Calvinists.* . . . The iron bed of Procrustes is not suited to the spirit of the age."* We shall shortly have occasion to observe how at an important historic crisis he urged in vain that his own liberal attitude be allowed to guide the counsels of the Presbyterian Church.

It must not be supposed that the opinions and characteristics which have been described were, at the beginning of his ministry, as clear-cut and mature as

* "Life and Times," Vol. II, p. 21.

they appear in some of the quotations by which they have been illustrated, and which have been derived in a number of instances from utterances of his later years. Yet in a less complete form they were a true part of his original mental and spiritual equipment. They plainly make their appearance, for instance, in his "Essays on the Distinguishing Traits of Christian Character," published in 1813, to which, as his first printed book, a few paragraphs may properly be devoted.

This small volume, which ran through nine editions, was the outcome of the theological controversy, already described, in regard to the two kinds of "inability," yet I believe a reader of the present day would be surprised at the practical vein in which it is written. It distinctly is not controversial in tone, but makes a direct and continual appeal to the wills of those to whom it is addressed. This was in accord with Mr. Spring's often expressed ideal of what Christian preaching and teaching should be. In the first five chapters he exhibits the several traits of character "that cannot be relied on as conclusive evidence of genuine religion." * These are, a morality which, however excellent, proceeds from selfish motives; observance of the outward forms of religion, however assiduous; a merely intellectual apprehension of religious truth, however orthodox; the conviction of sin without genuine repentance; and a merely inward assurance of conversion and salvation unaccompanied by the evidences of a redeemed character. In the rest of the book he describes, on the other hand, those traits

* "Essays" (1813), p. vi.

which "may be relied upon, without danger of deception." *

It is no small commendation to say that after a hundred years and in spite of all the doctrinal modifications that have taken place in that time, this book still provides profitable reading, is still a practical book. Practical, it should be added, for one sole purpose, the awakening of sinners to the consciousness of their perilous state and of their absolute need of Christian salvation. It does not deal with everyday morals except as they are directly related to that one momentous subject. It does not attempt to apply Christian principles to the details of daily life. It does not even undertake to train the already converted man in higher ways of holiness. Its one aim, pursued with extraordinary force and persistence, is the bringing of the sinner to the feet of Christ.

Occasionally Mr. Spring had some misgivings in regard to a possible one-sidedness in his message. "I early found," he says in a curious passage, "that I could more easily prepare a good sermon from an awakening and alarming subject, than from one that is more comforting. The fact is, I knew more of the terrors of the law than the preciousness of the gospel. . . . The difficulty of preaching well on the more attractive and winning themes, has sometimes alarmed me, and made me fear lest, after having 'preached to others, I myself should be a castaway.'" † In this, it is hardly needful to say, he maligned himself: even

* The titles of the chapters indicate sufficiently what these are: namely, Love to God, Repentance, Faith, Humility, Self-denial, The Spirit of Prayer, Love to the Brethren, Non-conformity to the World, Growth in Grace, and Practical Obedience.

† "Life and Times," Vol. 1, pp. 109 f.

in his early years he was by no means confined to the awful subjects of judgment. But the confession does certainly throw light upon a prevailing tendency of his thought.

Soon after the publication of his Essays he began the custom of preaching sermons in series, sometimes two or three, sometimes as many as twenty or thirty on the same general topic. Indeed, the first series consisted of more than a hundred discourses, and was really nothing more nor less than a whole system of theology. He himself describes it as "the great effort of my life," and says that in the preparation of it he spent "more than three years of laborious and continuous study." * A few sermons from one or another series, written in later years, still exist in the original manuscript, and not only their bulk but the inscriptions on their front pages create a feeling of respect, almost amounting to awe, for both the preacher whose industry and research produced them and the audiences to whom they were delivered. Thus we find that in February of 1826 he was engaged on "System No. VI," on "Divine Revelation," while in November of the same year he had already reached "System No. XVIII," on "The Goodness of God." In 1828 "Series of Discourses No. LII," on "The Method of Salvation" was being delivered. (It is interesting to note that on the cover of the still-existing sermon in this series, its individual theme being "The Nature of the Christian Atonement," is added this instructive legend, "All wrong. G. Spring, February, 1841.") In 1829 "Directions for Anxious Sinners" was the subject of "Series of Discourses No. LXV."

* "Br. Ch. Mem.," pp. 17 f.

Much of the material thus laboriously produced was doubtless incorporated in his later books.

In 1822 Dr. Spring, for by this time he had received the degree of D.D., took the occasion of the church's being closed for repairs to go abroad for four or five months. He had been invited to make the voyage as guest of one of the members of his church, and hoped that this might prove an effectual measure for the restoration of his health. In this he was not disappointed, but the sights of Europe, its "scenes of splendor, and of folly, and of sin," and especially the evidences of superstition which he observed there, seem to have disgusted and depressed him. His chief pleasure had been found in the ocean voyages and the friends whose companionship he had enjoyed.

Thirteen years later he crossed the Atlantic again on a more important and more interesting journey, but before speaking of that, a brief reference must be made to an incident occurring in the interval. In the summer of 1832 there was a dreadful outbreak of Asiatic cholera in New York. More than a hundred persons perished every day, nearly a thousand in one week. The ministers of the Presbyterian churches in earlier days had already set a high standard of conduct in such emergencies, and Dr. Spring was not the one to lower it. He might possibly have withdrawn from the city without special blame, as it was time for his annual vacation, but, instead, he made announcement that as long as the danger lasted he would remain in the city with his people. Through the summer he ministered to the sick and dying by personal visitation, while to those who had as yet escaped he brought cheer and strength, both by the regular services of the church, and still more by a prayer-meeting held daily at six o'clock in the afternoon for many weeks, to which people of all denominations came in large numbers.   This incident is not mentioned here because it was the greatest proof of his faithfulness—there were a thousand days of inconspicuous, and for the most part unrecorded, service which really counted for more in his ministry— but this is at least an incident easily grasped, and it will perhaps serve as well as any to prepare us for the strong bond of reverent affection which had been growing up between the people and their pastor, and which in 1835, when he started on his second journey to Europe, already alluded to, found opportunity to express itself in an appropriate and emphatic way.

He had been appointed by the General Assembly as its delegate to the Congregational Union of England and Wales.   He was also delegate to the meetings of the British and Foreign Bible Society in London and the French and Foreign Bible Society in Paris, and he was to attend besides several other important meetings.   It was almost a diplomatic mission, its purpose being to draw together Christians living on the two sides of the Atlantic, and both the Brick Church and its pastor made extraordinary preparations.   The people collected a purse of $2,500 to pay the expenses of the journey, while he, until then utterly ignorant of the French tongue, mastered it in three months under two teachers, with such success that he was not only able to write in French his address for the French Society, but to pronounce it (as he says with pardonable pride) "almost without

any foreign accent."* Then came the time for his
departure, and on that occasion his people, through a
committee, presented to him a letter which tells more
of the relations that existed between them than could
a whole chapter of explanations. It is possible to
quote but a part of it:

"It is no light matter for any Christian church to
be deprived, even for a few weeks, of the stated ministrations of a beloved pastor; but in a case like the
present, where the church is large, and its members
[are] scattered over the whole extent of a great commercial city, the population of which is ever changing,
and where the separation is not for a few weeks only,
but for months, the trial is vastly greater. . . . But
the objects of the mission were understood to be of
such an interesting nature that the church has not
felt itself at liberty to interpose an objection, however
great the sacrifice—more especially as it feels that the
confidence in their pastor, [expressed] by the General
Assembly, has not been misplaced. . . .

"But however much the members of our local communion may feel honored by the selection of yourself, their beloved pastor, for these high and responsible trusts, or however strong may be their confidence
in your ability, under God, to discharge the duties
devolving upon you, with credit to yourself and your
constituents, and far above all with acceptance to
your divine Master, yet the moment of separation will
be painful to a degree which language can but faintly
and inadequately express. The long and intimate,
the profitable and happy relationship which we have
reason to believe has subsisted between yourself and

* "Life and Times," Vol. II, p. 111.

GARDINER SPRING IN THE LATER YEARS OF HIS PASTORATE
From a photograph

us, the thousand endearing and sweet recollections which rush upon our minds, the depth and the strength of the affection which we entertain for you, and which we fondly believe, however little we may deserve it, is also cherished for us by you in return— all make us to feel that the present is no common parting. . . .

"Allow the undersigned, therefore, Reverend and Dear Sir, in behalf of the church in whose name they have been deputed as a committee to act on this occasion, to give you a parting assurance of their high regard for your person in social life, and their most affectionate attachment to you as a faithful minister of the gospel of Jesus Christ, an attachment that has been increasing through a long series of years, during which, at all times, in seasons of plague and pestilence, of personal peril and public danger, they have observed and marked your devotedness to the cause of your Master, and the zeal, perseverance, and activity with which your laborious and often painful duties have been discharged. . . .

"Allow us likewise and in conclusion to request from yourself a continuance of your prayers in our behalf—prayers that have been so long put up for us, and, we have reason to believe, so often blessed—that we may be preserved in unity and concord, and kept steady in the faith once delivered to the saints, and that through God's rich mercy we may each and all of us be spared to witness your return with renovated health, crowned with abundant success in the objects of your mission, and with increased means of private and ministerial usefulness. Farewell."

Only two other items remain to be added to this

already extended chapter. The first concerns the action of the Brick Church and its pastor in the proceedings that led to the unhappy division of the Presbyterians into the Old and the New Schools. While Dr. Spring was absent in Europe a controversy, due to the spread of the New Haven Theology among some of the Presbyterians, came to a climax, and in 1837 the General Assembly, in which the staunch Calvinists had control, cut off certain western synods by what were called the Disowning or Exscinding Acts. Dr. Spring, as we know, rejected entirely the New Haven teaching; he was prepared to oppose it by all proper means; but he did not approve of the Exscinding Acts and he vigorously protested against them. "Error," he said, "has never been eradicated from the church by the severe process of adjudication. Where errors are not essential in their character. . . the most effectual means of opposing their progress is the diffusion of light and the exercise of love. . . . Let the Church go forth unmanacled to the great work of converting the world." * When however, in spite of protest, the division had been accomplished, Dr. Spring and his church, since it was no longer a question how others should be treated, but what they themselves believed, unhesitatingly took their place in the ranks of the Old School. Blame, Dr. Spring tells us, was imputed to them by both parties, for what was deemed their neutrality. He claimed, however, that they had not been neutral. Their action had been, not negative, but positive throughout. It had been controlled throughout by the same clear and consistent principles. The plain fact was that they had

* "Life and Times," Vol. II, p. 55.

allowed neither their strong personal views to make
them unjust toward those who differed from them,
nor their toleration to modify their own conscientious
opinions; and their position is one that their descend-
ants in the Brick Church regard with peculiar pride
and gratitude.

Finally, it must be mentioned that not long after
the event just described, Dr. Spring began to publish
the books which soon became almost as influential in
a larger field as his preaching had been within the
limits of his parish.*

* He had published, in the earlier days of his ministry, a few small
books and many pamphlets. The first of his larger works, referred to in
the text, was "The Obligation of the World to the Bible" (1839). Next
"The Attraction of the Cross," was issued in 1846. These were followed
at short intervals by "The Power of the Pulpit" (1848); "The Mercy
Seat" (1850); "First Things" (1851); "The Glory of Christ" (1852);
and "The Contrast" (1855). Still later appeared "Pulpit Ministrations"
(1864) and the "Autobiography" (1865). His completed works would
fill twenty-two octavo volumes.

CHAPTER XII

RELIGION AND MORALS: 1810–1850

"Lord, who shall abide in thy tabernacle? who shall dwell in thy holy hill? He that walketh uprightly, and worketh righteousness, and speaketh the truth in his heart."—*Psalm* 15 : 1 *f.*

"In what consists [Christianity's] true glory, unless it is in the fact that where it is thus ascendant millions of intelligent and immortal beings, in the solitude of their retirement and in the noise and bustle of the world, in the depression of their grief and in the tranquillity of their joy, in the secrecy and publicity of their devotions, in the rectitude, truthfulness, and benignity of their deportment toward God and their fellow-men, manifest his glory, who is 'the only begotten of the Father, full of grace and truth'?"—GARDINER SPRING, "The Glory of Christ," Vol. II, pp. 39 *ff.*

A S the last chapter was devoted to the pastor, so this one is devoted to the people of the Brick Church during this period of forty years. But the task now set before us is the harder of the two. Nothing, indeed, is more difficult than to ascertain the facts regarding the inner life of the people of former times, and in spite of a careful use of records and biographies and reminiscences, it is to be feared that we shall but attain to a picture of externals after all. It will be possible to state with some fulness what were the means used to bring the duties of religion home to the hearts of individuals and to control or correct their morals; but when we seek further a knowledge of the actual results, an acquaintance with the regenerated men and women themselves and of the thoroughness of their regeneration, we shall be able to do little more than catch a few tantalizing glimpses, and must rely, far more than we should wish, upon a general knowledge of the church's strength, and a study (in the next two chapters) of the active Christian work of the congregation, in order to assure us that the means employed for moral and religious training were successful.

Most obvious among such means were, of course, the public services of the church. These, except for the necessary reduction of the number of Sunday services from three to two, continued as in the time of Dr. Rodgers. that is, morning and afternoon worship on Sunday, a prayer-meeting on Tuesday evening and on Thursday * evening a lecture. "The Old White Lecture Room," in which, until the building of the new chapel in 1832, these week-night meetings were held, was remembered long after with an affection which assures us of the deep religious impression made by these gatherings. "What a fountain of sweet memories does its simple name unseal," exclaimed Mr. Horace Holden a short time before his death in 1862, "What deep and pungent convictions of sin! What tears of contrition! . . . What songs of triumphant rejoicing! It must be reserved for eternity to recount the triumphs of grace witnessed in the Old White Lecture Room." †

The story of how Mr. Holden himself, who afterward became perhaps the leading layman of the church, was first introduced to this room, almost makes us feel as though we, too, had entered it. "In 1814," he says, "Stephen Dodge, a member of this church, . . . met me in the street and invited me to

---

* Changed to Friday for a time, beginning in March, 1825.

† "Br. Ch. Mem.," pp. 145 f.

accompany him to your* Thursday evening lecture.
I had never attended an evening religious lecture.   I
could not resist his polite entreaty.   He called for
me.   He took me to the Old White Lecture Room,
and seated me near the pulpit among the elders.   The
place was full.   It was a new scene to me.   I well
remember the very spot I occupied on that memorable
evening; and well do I remember the text, 'If thou,
Lord, shouldest mark iniquities, O Lord, who shall
stand?' . . . From that night forward I became a
regular attendant upon your ministry.   That lecture
decided my whole future."†

As will be evident from this passage the "lecture"
was practically a sermon, so that this meeting depended wholly upon the pastor.   Not so the weekly
prayer-meeting.   This, at least at certain periods,
was conducted by the elders in rotation, and even if
Dr. Spring was the leader, there were, he tells us, in
those early days, no less than sixty men whom he
could call upon to offer prayer.   The meetings, under
such circumstances, were, as may well be imagined,
full of interest, and it is especially worthy of note that
they were attended, not merely by the members of
the church, but by many who were as yet uncon-
verted.   In 1820 it was even thought necessary to
establish an extra meeting for prayer on the third
Monday evening of each month, in order that the
members of the church, meeting by themselves, might
have the special benefit of more private and intimate
communion.

Even two regular services between Sundays did not

* This is quoted from a speech addressed to Dr. Spring personally.
† "Br. Ch. Mem.," p. 137.

always exhaust the people's zeal. We learn that in addition "there were maintained for a long period twelve neighborhood prayer-meetings at private houses, on every Friday evening, in different parts of the congregation, sustained by committees averaging seven each, which were so distributed as every week to ensure a continual rotation."* It was certainly a strong church that could thus provide nearly a hundred men to carry on such a work. Other meetings held during the week, throughout the whole or a part of this period were the quarterly meeting, a large adult Bible class, the monthly concert of prayer for missions,† a class for instruction in the Shorter Cathechism, the singing-school, and the inquiry meeting.‡

Only two of these demand at this time a fuller comment. The nature of the inquiry meeting may be learned from the following description, in which Dr. Spring was setting forth, under the form of a narrative, his conception of what such a meeting ought to be like. No doubt the methods here described were employed in the Brick Church. "I should judge there were from one hundred and thirty to one hundred and fifty persons present—chiefly of those who were from sixteen to thirty years of age, together with a few of more advanced years, and a few who were children. All were seated. . . . The meeting was opened by singing. . . . When the hymn was closed, the object of the meeting was briefly stated,

---

* "Br. Ch. Mem.," p. 145.

† Toward the end of the period covered by this chapter this meeting was changed from the first Monday to the first Sunday of each month.

‡ This was probably occasional only, and may have been held on Sunday evening.

and all were requested to kneel and unite in a few words of prayer. After prayer the pastor himself, together with three other gentlemen, who as I supposed were officers of the church, dispersed themselves throughout different parts of the room, and entered into conversation with the individuals who were present. Here and there were clusters of persons with whom they conversed collectively. The conversation with individuals was sometimes continued two or three minutes, and sometimes elicited no answer. Sometimes it consisted of a single enquiry and an appended observation or two. And sometimes it continued for eight or ten minutes. So that at the close of the meeting there were none who had not had the opportunity of a personal interview. . . . The conversation was conducted in rather a low tone of voice, and much as it would have been, had the parties been alone in a private parlor."*

The quarterly meeting, included in the list given above, was held during the week preceding each communion service, on Wednesday evening.† It was evidently what is now known as the preparatory service, and is described at one place in the records as "the quarterly meeting of the church with their children." It would appear that until 1816, new members were received into the church at this or some other weekday meeting, but in March of that year it was decided that this ceremony should take place "in the sanctuary and in the presence of the congregation." The "Profession and Covenant" used in the admission of new members is still in

* "Fragments from the Study of a Pastor" (1838), pp. 57–60.
† So in 1838. The day of the week may have varied from time to time.

existence,* a very solemn and searching document. It required a somewhat extended declaration of faith in God, the Father, the Son, and the Holy Ghost, and a confession of sin which included the following items: "the original and total depravity of your nature, the past enmity of your heart against God, the unbelief which has led you to reject a Saviour, and the manifold transgressions of your lives."

For a few months in 1845, "in view of the difficulties experienced in relation to the public profession and covenant," its use was discontinued, and it was ordered that "no other engagements be required of those received into the church save those entered into at the baptism of adults, as required by the Directory for Worship and those implied in actually coming to the Lord's Table." This change was soon reconsidered, however, and the church returned to its earlier practice.

It need hardly be said that candidates for admission to church membership underwent a careful examination. It was necessary for all such persons to appear before the whole session and reply to such questions as were there propounded to them. In 1844, however, an exception was made in the case of those who in the opinion of the pastor might be "deterred by diffidence or natural modesty" from submitting to this formidable examination. In their case, the pastor, alone or with the assistance of one or more elders, was permitted to conduct a more private inquiry into the candidate's "knowledge and faith." †

Turning now to the Sunday services, we must re-

---

* See Appendix T, p. 539.

† In 1859 the examination of all by the session itself was again ordered.

mark first of all that in those days there was, of course, no recognition of any of the festivals of the church year, so that the Sacrament of the Lord's Supper,* observed four times annually† in the simple and reverent manner of the non-liturgical churches,‡ was the only service that had a peculiar character of its own. To this one service, however, which he regarded as the culmination of Christian worship, Dr. Spring gave a very marked emphasis. It was observable, we are told, that "he brought to it always, so far as he could, the most careful preparation on his own part and that of his people. . . . He gave it the highest prominence in his ministry, as the comfort of disciples, and the preacher of Christ to the world. At the communion table some of his most moving spiritual addresses were made." §

The character of a service upon an ordinary Sunday may readily be conceived by recollecting what has already been told regarding Dr. Spring's preaching, and from the following suggestive account of his

* In regard to the administration at this time of the other sacrament, that of Baptism, we know only that a silver bowl was provided for that purpose (see above, p. 81), and that the service was almost invariably held in the church. Only for very strong reason, such as sickness, was it allowable to hold it elsewhere, and then at least one of the elders was present with the pastor.

† Both the month and the Sunday in the month assigned for this service were changed from time to time. As an illustration may be given the dates assigned in 1827, viz.: the second Sundays of January, April, July and October.

‡ In regard to the silver communion service we have this note under the date, January 5th, 1819. "The committee (of the trustees) also reported that they had procured two pitchers, six flagons, two dishes, and one plate, making with the pieces previously belonging to the church a complete service." Four silver plates had been presented by a member of the congregation in 1813.

§ "Memorial Discourse," p. 25.

manner of conducting public worship. "His prayers were wonderful," we are told by his successor, "rich in the letter and in the spirit of Holy Scripture, varied, most felicitous in all personal allusions, deep in the devotion of a Christian heart, comprehensive in their range, . . . even more remarkable than his sermons for marked impressiveness. . . . His reading of the Scriptures, his reading of hymns, were always according to the maxim so often used by Dr. John Mason, that 'correct emphasis is sound exposition.' One of the leading merchants of the city, whose name is the synonym for Christian benevolence, has told me that he never was able to shake off the religious impression made on him by Dr. Spring's manner of reading the hymn of Doddridge, 'Ye hearts with youthful vigor warm.'"*

Not upon the minister alone, however, did the character of the service depend.† The music during this period attained a considerable importance, and claimed a greater degree of attention than we should probably have supposed. When Mr. Spring came

---

* "Memorial Discourse," pp. 24 ƒ.

† As to the customary or prescribed action of the congregation at the public services we know little. The following minute by the General Assembly of 1849 in regard to "Posture in Prayer" will, perhaps, be surprising to some readers: "While the posture of standing in public prayer, and that of kneeling in private prayer, are indicated by examples in Scripture and in the general practice of the ancient Christian Church, the posture of sitting in public prayer is nowhere mentioned, and by no usage allowed; but, on the contrary, was universally regarded by the early Church as heathenish or irreverent; and is still, even in the customs of modern and Western nations, an attitude obviously wanting in the due expression of reverence. Therefore the General Assembly resolve, that the practice in question be considered grievously improper, whenever the infirmities of the worshipper do not render it necessary; and that ministers be required to reprove it with earnest and persevering admonition." "Assembly Digest," p. 205.

to the church the musical equipment consisted chiefly of the clerk, or chorister, as he was then beginning to be more frequently called. At first this official conducted the church's music by simply beating time and leading in the singing; but gradually his duties were, as we shall see, changed and enlarged. The gradual advance in his salary is an indication of this. The $100 paid in 1811 was soon increased to $150 or $200, with occasional relapses to the original figure. One especially valuable man, Marcus Alden, was allowed to augment his salary by a collection in the church. Later, in the thirties, the figure rose to $500, which was the highest reached up to 1850.

Seventeen different names appear on the list of choristers in the forty years, many of them for very short terms. Evidently it was a difficult position to fill. In 1813, for instance, Mr. Roberts, "a teacher of psalmody from Connecticut," is ushered in with a decided flourish, but even before the year is out Mr. William R. Thompson has succeeded him. Sometimes the difficulty was increased by the fact that a man who could not properly lead the singing was, nevertheless, a faithful worker and an excellent Christian. There was one instance of this sort so striking that it deserves to be recorded for its illustration of victory in defeat. Mr. S. P. Pond, who had served for several years, was told with regret, in 1841, that his work was not giving satisfaction. The committee of the session, who presented the matter to him, reported, "that Mr. Pond treated the whole subject in a kind and Christian spirit, himself cheerfully resigned his place, and suggested Mr. Comes as his successor." Also "that Mr. Pond is willing to continue his services in assisting Mr. Comes until the first day of February next." We are glad to hear that a hearty and appreciative resolution was passed and sent to this excellent man, and also that it was accompanied by a still more substantial recognition of his services.

Mr. Spring had barely been installed when Mr. Holbrook, the chorister of that day, obtained permission to teach sacred music in the session room on two nights in the week. Remembering what an important part the singing-school in New Haven had played in the life of Mr. Spring himself, one fancies that his favorable opinion in regard to such institutions was not difficult to obtain. This new step— new, that is, for the Brick Church—is the first indication of any decided movement toward the encouragement of the congregational singing in the church services. In 1815 Wednesday and Friday evenings were devoted to this enterprise. At first there was apparently no attempt to train any special group of people, general improvement in singing appearing to be the object in view; but in December, 1819, the session records the receipt of a communication from "the singers of the congregation" in regard to their instruction in vocal music. From this we may conclude that the process of specialization had begun. Three years later they had advanced so far as to form a society which went under the formidable title of "The Association for the Promotion of Sacred Music in the Brick Church." What constituted this "sacred music" we do not know. At the church services most probably nothing but psalms in the metrical version and a certain number of hymns were permitted. Possibly a little more freedom was permitted at the "concerts," which from 1819 were given in the church about once a year, partly as a benefit for the chorister and partly for some benevolent purpose or the church funds.

Some idea of the hymns admired and sanctioned in the church at this time may be gained from a little volume published in 1823 "by request of the members" and entitled "The Brick Church Hymns, Designed for the Use of Social Prayer Meetings and Families, Selected from the Most Approved Authors, and Recommended by Gardiner Spring, D.D., Pastor of Said Church." Of the two hundred and fifty-odd hymns in this volume only about one-fifth continue in use, and only one or two of these are among the really good hymns in our modern books; while some of the sentiments which were in 1823 commended to the use of Brick Church people will somewhat astonish modern readers. For instance,

> "Alas! this adamantine heart,
>   This icy rock within!
> Alas! these active powers congealed
>   By the deceits of sin."

It is no wonder that another hymn exclaims:

> 'My heart, how dreadful hard it is!"

Many of the selections dwell with painful persistence upon the lessons of mortality, such as that which begins,

> "Death! 'Tis a melancholy day,"

or that more famous one,

> "Hark! from the tombs a doleful sound!
>   Mine ears, attend the cry—
> 'Ye living men, come view the ground,
>   Where you must shortly lie.' "

Even in singing the glad tidings, the joy was not permitted to be unmixed; witness the uncompromising terms of the following:

> "Go preach my gospel, saith the Lord,
>   Bid the whole earth my grace receive.
> He shall be saved that trusts my word;
>   He shall be damned that won't believe." *

It should be understood that the hymn books of those days contained the words only. The music was in a separate volume, and the bills for "music books" became, as time went on, a considerable item in the accounts of the treasurer. The fitting of tune to psalm (or hymn) was at first the work of a committee of the session, consisting of the pastor and two elders, but afterward was evidently left to the discretion of the chorister.

* Watts's Hymns, with additions by Dr. Timothy Dwight, had been "cheerfully allowed" by the General Assembly in 1802. Four years later they declared that other psalms and hymns than those expressly allowed might be used, but that sessions and presbyteries must keep strict watch to exclude "hymns containing erroneous doctrine or trivial matter." Down to 1820 the following books had been authorized: "Rouse's Psalms," "Watts's Psalms" and his three volumes of hymns, and Barlow's and Dwight's revisions of Watts. In that year the Assembly decided to have a book of its own prepared, which should include "a compilation of the metrical versions of the Psalms" and "a copious collection of hymns and spiritual songs from various authors, giving the preference to those now authorized, so far as good taste, sound sense, and enlightened piety admit." This book was issued in 1830. A revised edition appeared in 1843. At the very end of the period under discussion, namely in 1848, the Assembly appointed a committee on church music with special reference to the preparation of a book of tunes. One paragraph in the Assembly minutes is especially interesting: "It is proposed to add an appropriate selection of set pieces for special occasions, such as anthems and chants, both metrical and prose, adapted to our psalmody, and also to portions of the common prose version of the Book of Psalms and other inspired lyrics from the Old and New Testaments." This tune book, or "psalmodist" was completed in 1850. See "Assembly Digest," pp. 195 f.

The musical society above referred to did not last long, unhappily. Ten months after its first mention in the records it is referred to as "the late association." But meantime it had made one hopeful suggestion. It had proposed that the singers in the congregation have assigned to them certain special pews in the gallery of the church. The trustees gave their approval and bought certain pews for this purpose, making them free of rent for the singers' use. Then for the first time a choir might be said to have been assembled. This was in 1822. Shortly after this either the funds were low or applications for places in the choir became suspiciously numerous, for we learn that the singers, though continuing to occupy their special seats, were required to pay a pew-tax; but finally the more generous policy was resumed. Pews No. 86, 85 and 38 "in the front gallery" facing the pulpit, were set aside for the choir, and permission was even given to make such changes in them as would adapt them more perfectly to their purpose.

In 1825 musical matters were not considered to be in a satisfactory state. The trustees took measures "to make, if possible, some improvement in the singing department of this congregation." Possibly as a result of their activity, a second musical society was formed in the next year, called the "Asaph Association," and a couple of years later we become aware of another innovation. The board of trustees at that time resolves "that Mr. Rolla and his daughters be engaged *to fill the choir* for one year." Besides the somewhat amusing form of this statement, the fact stated is worth noting, for it indicates that in 1828, other paid singers besides the chorister began to be employed.   Mr. Cole, who succeeded Mr. Rolla, was assisted in like manner by a Miss Gould, and the considerable sums of money which soon after this were voted from time to time for "improvement of the choir" suggest that other singers not mentioned by name may have been employed.

In regard to the question of instrumental music our information is meagre.   No mention of any such accompaniment to the singing appears in the records of this period until 1844, when we learn that Mr. Samuel Johnson was paid $25 a quarter to play the violoncello; and from that time on this appropriation continued to be made at regular intervals.   But how are we to interpret the entire silence of the records in regard to instrumental music during the first thirty-four years of Dr. Spring's pastorate?*   Possibly the "orchestra" of which we heard in the days following the Revolution, had been discontinued, a stricter standard having been introduced, forgetful of the biblical warrant for the use in worship of trumpets, psalteries, and harps, stringed instruments, organs, and high-sounding cymbals.   Or it may be that during the earlier part of the nineteenth century the players upon instruments had rendered their service without remuneration, so that the records of the trustees had no need to refer to them.   The most that can be said with certainty is that the violoncello was a regular feature of the Brick Church music, from 1844 and until its place was taken by a more modern instrument.†

* Except that a small organ, evidently for use in rehearsals, was admitted to the lecture room at the desire of the "Asaph Association."

† The General Assembly in 1845, in reply to an overture from the Synod of Cincinnati on the subject of instrumental music, adopted the fol-

Without underestimating in the slightest degree the power of Dr. Spring's impressive eloquence to build up and maintain a faithful congregation, we need not doubt that the improved music and especially the opportunity to have a hand (or even a voice) in that improvement was a decided help. There were, however, times when, it is plain, any such aid was absolutely unnecessary, times when services grew and multiplied as though of their own accord, and when the distinctly religious interest was so great that the problem was to control and apply rather than to create it.

From the year 1792, and still more strikingly after 1800, the American churches had experienced a remarkable series of religious awakenings. Hardly a month passed but some village, some city, or some college reported a "revival." Mr. Spring himself, as we have seen, had been greatly influenced by sharing in such an experience at Yale, and it was manifestly his great desire, as soon as he was settled in New York, that his own church should be visited by the revival spirit. His preaching, as we have seen, was carefully calculated to promote this end, and indeed during his first three or four years there were several "seasons of deep reflection and fervent prayer," which, though of short duration, had made a deep impression upon many individuals.

lowing minute; "Whereas, By our constitution the whole internal arrangement of a church, as to worship and order, is committed to the minister and session; therefore, Resolved, That this Assembly do not feel themselves called and obliged to take any further order on this subject, but leave to each session the delicate and important matter of arranging and conducting the music as to them shall seem most for edification, recommending great caution, prudence and forbearance in regard to it." "Assembly Digest," p. 197.

During the summer of 1815,* there began a much more important and enduring movement. Pastor and people were moved alike by what seemed to be a new earnestness. Days of fasting and prayer were occasionally observed, and what was still more noteworthy, the younger men of the church organized a special weekly meeting for prayer which met at private houses on Saturday evenings. "Our Sabbaths," says Dr. Spring, "became deeply solemn and affecting. We watched for them like those who watch for the morning." † "What days of heaven upon earth!" exclaimed old Mr. Horace Holden, recalling the services of this same period. "No tongue can describe them. . . . Every pew filled, the galleries crowded in every part with anxious and devout worshippers. . . . What a beautiful and sublime spectacle to behold the vast assembly retiring after each service in profound silence, to meditate and pray. Amid these scenes of mercy it is delightful to

* Dr. Spring in his autobiography says "the summer of 1814," and states that the New Year's sermon (to be described presently) was preached on the last day of the same year. But December 31st, 1814, was a Saturday, so that the next day was both Sunday and New Year and the New Year's sermon would certainly have been preached on that day. Moreover, the sermon refers in the following terms to the peace which closed the War of 1812: "In the recent desolations of our land, we were not exempt from our portion of calamity. But the silver clarion of peace has again vibrated on our ears, and the rich blessings of peace have been again restored in unexampled profusion. Worldly prosperity has been flowing in upon us in deep, wide channels, and all classes of men have been growing rich." Now the peace of Ghent was signed on December 24th, 1814, and the news of it did not reach New York till February, 1815. Moreover, it is evident from the above quotation itself that months rather than days had already passed since the peace was declared. Dr. Spring, we must therefore conclude, had made a mistake of a year. The sermon was preached on Sunday, December 31st, 1815, and the summer of revival referred to was the summer of that year, instead of the year previous.

† "Br. Ch. Mem.," p. 22.

know that almost every member of the church was actively employed."*

On the last day of 1815, Mr. Spring put his whole soul into a New Year's sermon, to which later was given the appropriate title "Something Must Be Done."† The pastor, as we learn from this important discourse, was by no means content with the evidences of revival already existing among his people. He felt that as yet there had been no "general out-pouring of the Holy Spirit," and his aim was to secure for them, if possible, this supreme blessing. In spite of the interest already manifested, he felt that the love of riches and the comforts of a time of prosperity and peace,‡ were blinding the eyes of many, even of many Christians, to the higher interests of religion. In view of all this, he declares that "something must be done." He calls upon his people to repent as a church, sincerely to desire a revival, to pray for it, to work for it, and not least, to expect it. If they so act, they will not, in his judgment, be disappointed. But if they neglect their duty in this matter, he cannot but warn them of their responsibility for those who, for the want of this revival, will be overtaken in their sins. This most solemn and fervent address seems to have been, under God, the means of achieving the end to which it so ardently looked. The effect, indeed, was almost instantaneous. The next Sunday, the first of the New Year, was marked by services especially solemn, and from that time, continuing through the winter and even longer, men

* "Br. Ch. Mem.," p. 145.

† It was published and ran through four editions.

‡ The War of 1812 had recently been concluded. See note on preceding page.

and women were continually seeking admission to
the discipleship of Christ in a spirit which had not
been known before.

It must not be supposed that the cruder methods of
evangelistic appeal, which were perhaps more prevalent at that time than at the present day, were ever
adopted in the Brick Church.   Dr. Spring had a very
positive repugnance for "getting up"* a revival.   He
says expressly of the revivals in his church, that in
them "there were no 'new measures,' no 'anxious
seats,' and no public announcement of the names or
the number of those who were striving to enter into
the strait gate."   The means used were simple.
First "there was prayer," and upon this he lays chief
emphasis.   Then "there was solemn and earnest
preaching," and "there were private circles for religious conversation, and prayer, and praise, and these
scarcely known beyond the individuals who composed
them."   He mentions particularly a day of fasting,
humiliation, and prayer, which he shared with some
thirty others of the church one Thursday of January,
1816.   They met at a private house in Church Street,
just in the rear of St. Paul's, "and such a day," he says,
"I never saw before, and have never seen since."†

It is not possible to follow further the details of this
memorable epoch in the church's life, or to describe
other similar experiences in the course of the next
twenty years;‡ nor would it be accordant with the

---

* "Life and Times," Vol. I, p. 219.

† *Ibid*, Vol. I, p. 166.

‡ Dr. Murray says: "That remarkable series of revivals seems to have
ended in 1834. Then came the work of training in Christian knowledge
those who had been converted to Christ by this ministry." "Memorial
Discourse," p. 18,

spirit by which the church was then controlled to
record even now the number of converts or to give
the names of those, afterward pillars of the church,
who were thus claimed for the Master's service; but
there is hardly need of further statement to prove that
the Brick Church in the years which we are here
studying, was a place where deep and genuine religion
was effectively urged and earnestly accepted.

Besides its services and meetings the church employed two other means of caring for the religious
and moral needs of the people, namely, visitation and
discipline. To the work of the pastor in carrying his
message and influence into the homes of the people
emphatic witness is given by one of his parishioners.
He speaks, it will be noticed, with discrimination.
Dr. Spring, he tells us, did not make frequent calls
upon his people as a matter of routine, and it was
well understood that he regarded his preaching, together with the necessary preparation for it, as the
most important part of his ministry. All the more
impressive, therefore, is this testimony of the parish-
ioner to the faithful pastor. The people of the Brick
Church, he says, had been taught by their experience
under Dr. Spring to esteem pastoral visitation a
valuable means of grace. Especially in the memorable seasons of unusual interest had their pastor made
use of this method "going from family to family to
guide enquiring souls, cheer the faint, comfort the
feeble-minded. . . . Not one weary heavy-laden sinner was overlooked. . . . I do not recollect," con-
cludes this witness, who knew the church as few did,
"I do not recollect to have heard of an instance in
which a pastoral visit was neglected, if there was any

real call for it, or the least prospect of doing any good." *

The sharing of this work of visitation in those days by the members of the session is a matter that needs to be brought to the attention of modern Presbyterians, who would probably be astonished to receive from the elders of their church such calls as were customary in the early nineteenth century. Dr. Samuel Miller, in a sermon on Ruling Elders, delivered in 1809, thus describes this particular function of the elders' office. "It is their duty to converse with and admonish in private those who appear to be growing careless, or falling into habits in any respect criminal, suspicious, or unpromising. It is their duty to visit and pray with the sick, as far as their circumstances admit, and to request the attendance of the pastor on the sick and dying, as may be judged desirable. It is their duty to visit the members of the church and their families; to converse with them; to instruct the ignorant; to confirm the wavering; to caution the unwary; to encourage the timid; and to excite and animate all classes to a faithful and exemplary discharge of duty." †

That the elders of the Brick Church did not always live up to the height of this ideal, we may believe without seriously accusing them of lukewarmness in their service, but that they themselves held the ideal before their eyes is made evident on more than one page of their records. Mention may be made of one instance where they undertook "to digest a system of measures with the view to extending their official visita-

---

* Horace Holden in "Br. Ch. Mem.," p. 141.
† "The Divine Appointment," etc., pp. 31 f.

tions to the members of this congregation." And there is another minute which still more clearly indicates the seriousness with which they regarded their own participation in this ministry. In October, 1820, after a meeting "devoted to prayer and friendly conversation on the present languishing state of this church," they appoint a committee to suggest, not merely what may be done in general, but what they themselves can personally do, to better the situation, and, of the four measures afterward adopted, one proposed to consider it "the duty of each individual of the session to converse with a given number of the congregation at least once a week, on the importance of personal piety, and that reports of such interviews be made to the session at each monthly meeting," while another provided "that in his pastoral visits the minister be associated with one of the elders, and that each elder perform this service in rotation."

In the administration of discipline for errors and offences, the final means of supervising and controlling the private life of the members, the elders played a still more prominent part, for this work was always carried on by the session as a whole, in which the pastor had only such superior authority as belonged to his position as moderator. The amount of time devoted to this work, the patience and system with which it was executed, and the conscientious administration of justice which it exhibits make this element of the church life an impressive one. That the record of it is not pleasant, need not be said. It is not agreeable to read here the record of old sins and follies and insincerities, to learn that in those days there were some black sheep in the fold. But, after all, we know well enough that the mere profession of Christianity does not at any time ensure a pure heart and an honest life, so that this record of discipline in the Brick Church of the early nineteenth century merely illustrates by concrete instances a well-known fact; and on the other hand, the courageous facing of the practical problem thus made manifest, the reclaiming of some, and the protection of the church from the accusation of indifference to the sins of its own members—all this serves to give the subject an honorable place in the church's history.

It will be instructive to present an abstract of the procedure in one specific case, as an illustration of the general method. Information having been received that Mr. C., a member of the church, is addicted to the habit of intemperance, a committee is appointed to expostulate with him. He acknowledges his offence, gives "some evidence of penitence" and promises to reform. The session then "consider it their duty to forbear with Mr. C. for a short period, . . . while at the same time they view themselves under obligation to watch over their offending brother with redoubled diligence." Four months later they perceive that he has not mended his ways and that a trial cannot be avoided. A committee is accordingly appointed to obtain the necessary evidence. This, unhappily, is an easy matter, and furthermore there now appears to be ground for adding profanity to the original accusation. Finally, the day of trial is set, and Mr. C. is cited to appear. The trial is duly held * and the examination, in which he is forced to acknowl-

---

* Had he failed to respond after three citations they would have proceeded in his absence.

edge the justice of the charge, is carefully recorded, with questions and answers given in full. As a result he is "suspended from sealing ordinances." A committee informs him of this sentence and urges upon him repentance and reformation. Two years now pass, and it becomes necessary to inquire whether still more severe measures should not be adopted. Evidence is obtained that Mr. C. is now guilty of bigamy in addition to the original offences. The Presbytery is consulted. A second trial is held in which the accused makes a full confession, but without due evidence of sorrow. The Presbytery, again appealed to, counsels the imposition of the full penalty, and Mr. C. is accordingly "excommunicated." The sentence is publicly announced, and is recorded in the minutes of the session in the following terms: "Whereas Mr. C. hath been, by sufficient proof, convicted of the sin of habitual intemperance, and also of the crime of bigamy, and after much admonition and prayer obstinately refuseth to hear the church, and hath manifested no evidence of repentance; therefore in the name, and by the authority, of the Lord Jesus Christ we pronounce him to be excluded from the communion of the church."

The penalties imposed upon the unrepentant were, as we have just seen, either excommunication or suspension, which involved especially exclusion from the Lord's Supper, and which might be publicly announced or not, according to the circumstances. Those who declared themselves to be repentant were required to make reparation in case of injuries done to other persons, and commonly to make a public confession of their sin and of their sorrow for it. No clearer conception of the effect of this last expedient could be given than in the record of one pathetic instance which I shall venture to quote. It may seem, at first sight, to set forth the session of the church as a stern and awful court of judgment, but even in the formal record we can surely hear a deep note of pity and tenderness, by which the judges were really controlled, and which made even so hard a punishment as is here described not altogether unbearable. "The moderator stated," say the minutes, "that information had been communicated, stating the very reproachful conduct of ——, widow of ——, one of the members of this church. . . . The moderator also stated that he had called on Mrs. —— in company with one of the session; that Mrs. —— did not deny the fact; that she appeared penitent for her crime. . . . Mrs. —— herself, being present [at the session meeting], begged the privilege of confessing her folly, and desired the forgiveness of God and the church. She stated . . . that she felt she had sinned greatly against God; that she felt . . . heartily sorry that she had brought reproach on the name of Christ, and that she was willing to humble herself in any shape and seek forgiveness. Whereupon, Resolved, after much deliberation and anxiety, that Mrs. —— be required to make a public confession before the whole [church] this evening, at their quarterly prayer-meeting, and be restored to Christian privileges. Resolved that the moderator publicly address Mrs. ——, and read, and unite in singing the 51st Psalm at the close of the exercise, and finally close the whole with prayer." The purpose of mercy which prompted this judgment is evident, as has been already said, but certainly much love and tenderness in session and congregation were necessary in order to make the bearing of such public shame a true means of grace.

The transgressions that were dealt with by these faithful guardians of the flock were numerous. We may divide them into two separate classes: First, those which were distinctly offences against religion. These were violation of the Sabbath, neglect of prayer, neglect of public worship, neglect of the Lord's Supper, heresy (for example, "the crime of disbelieving in the inspiration of the Holy Scriptures") and infidelity or atheism. The second class consisted of offences against morals. Here intemperance was the most common charge, and there were, besides, keeping bad company, profanity, unchastity, dishonesty in various forms, card-playing and theatre-going. There were between thirty and forty cases of discipline in the forty years we are now studying.

It is a fact not unworthy of notice that discipline for what was regarded as worldly and un-Christian amusement was inconspicuous, showing that the session used its powers in no bitterly inquisitorial spirit. The charges of card-playing and theatre-going above referred to appear but three times in the records, and even then were merely additional to others of a more serious nature. Dr. Spring, it should be noted, held strict views in regard to the grave dangers inherent in "gay amusements and the various pursuits of the present scene." * He was "thor-

* Spring's "Essays," p. 191. See also for quotations which follow, "Hints to Parents," p. 24, and "Life and Times," Vol. I, p. 128.

oughly, and more and more, persuaded that the
great mass of novels and plays exert a pernicious influence, both on the intellectual and moral character."
To dancing he was emphatically opposed. It distressed him greatly that Christian parents would
countenance it for their children, and was led by it
to exclaim that "our mercurial youth live for folly
and fun." "Balls and assemblies," to his mind, were
the natural enemies of the Spirit of God. At the
same time he perceived that "youth" (or as he preferred to call it, "old Adam"), was a very real force
in the world. "It is a foregone conclusion that our
young people will dance," he said with a naïve sort
of sadness; and he had to confess that in these matters he had not been able effectually to stem the tide.
Positive as he was in his own opinion, it was certainly
a sign of moderation that he practically did not use
at all the power of church discipline to enforce his
view.

The control of the morals of Christians by the
session acting in its judiciary capacity is now seldom
attempted. In the more complex life of our great
modern cities it would be almost impracticable in the
absence of any legal power to summon witnesses.
We have not the ready means of knowing the facts
of the inner life of our neighbors as men did seventy-
five or a hundred years ago. Perhaps, moreover, our
repugnance for undertaking this painful work has
something to do with our neglect of the old method.
In this latter reason Dr. Spring would have had no
sympathy with us. "Church discipline," he said,
looking back upon the practice of the Brick Church
in this matter, "is not less truly an ordinance of

God than church Communion. No church can prosper that connives at heresy or immorality among its communicants. . . . It has often been at great sacrifice of feeling, and some of interest and influence, that these acts of discipline have been performed; but, however reluctantly and cautiously, it is a work that has to be done."

It is unfortunate that there was no occasion for the session to inquire formally into the lives of its good and faithful members, whose record would remind us that the offenders, who were dealt with in the way described above, constituted a very small minority. No such authoritative records exist. But we will not admit that Antony in the play was right, and that only "the evil that men do lives after them." On the contrary, the good lived on, in other and better ways than on the pages of minute books; and even in books, though of the less formal sort, some happy memories of the individual members of the Brick Church between 1810 and 1850 have been preserved for us.

Two or three such passages may be quoted, in the hope that, at least, they will help the reader to see with his mind's eye the forms and faces of some of those whose memories are cherished by the church, and to feel that he has gained some personal acquaintance with these good people. The first passage is from an address by Horace Holden, already several times quoted* He is looking back, in memory, to the most faithful and beloved of those officers of the church who had died before the time at which he spoke. They had, all of them, served in the early years of Dr. Spring's

* "Br. Ch. Mem.," pp. 146 f.

ministry. He says, "I may not omit to mention the
sedate and venerable John * Bingham; the warm-
hearted and heavenly-minded William Whitlock; the
meek and childlike Richard Cunningham; the intelligent and upright Peter Hawes; the wise and useful Stephen Lockwood;† the respected and pious Rensselaer
Havens; the courteous Horace W. Bulkley; the conservative and gentlemanly Alfred de Forest; the sober-
minded John Stephens; the urbane and gentle John
C. Halsey; the amiable and exemplary Daniel Oakley; the earnest and devout Abraham Bokee; the
humble, lowly and refined John McComb; the guile-
less and unassuming Samuel Brown; the modest
and diffident William Luyster; the sincere and un-
pretending Elijah Mead; the consistent and devoted Richard Harding; and John Adams the in-
flexible and just." To this list must be added one
other name, in words recorded by the pastor of the
church. Among the members of the original session,
all of them men of worth and influence, "the ruling
spirit," says Dr. Spring, "and the man eminent for
discernment, practical wisdom, ardent piety, and
vigorous action, was John Mills." Thus much for
the elders and deacons of those early days. In regard
to the congregation as a whole we fortunately possess, in an address by one of the later officers, a brief
characterization of the people among whom Gardiner
Spring began his ministry. "As I remember this
community in early life," says Mr. Daniel Lord, "the

* The Christian names, not in the original, are here inserted.

† One of the most competent, most esteemed, and beloved members of
the session. He was killed, almost in the sight of Dr. Spring, by a boiler
explosion on the steamer *Oliver Ellsworth*, in 1827. He and his pastor were
returning together from an ecclesiastical council in Connecticut. ·

Brick Church congregation was composed of men in the middle ranks of life—thinking, working, independent men; men whom you could not drive by fear, nor coax by favor, and with whom you could not deal without intellectual conviction.   Convince them and they were yours; fail to convince them, and they were the most independent body of men that could be seen." *

The other roll of names, which shall form the conclusion of this chapter, is of a different character from that of Mr. Holden, given above. It is only an extract from a reminiscent sketch † in a newspaper, and did we not supplement it from other sources would give us little more than a glimpse of the outer appearance of some of the people who attended the Brick Church in the twenties, thirties, and forties of the nineteenth century, yet even from such a source as this we may be able to gain some impression of the wholesome Christian graces of Dr. Spring's parishioners.

"Let us walk into the church a fine Sunday morning in spring, and see whom we shall find there—you and I, reader—and I will answer all your questions. There is Moses Allen, with his bright, cheery face, [a man generous, active in Christian work, and prominent in all benevolent enterprises,‡ and there

* "Br. Ch. Mem.," p. 154.

† By R. W. Newman, published in the "Evening Mail" in 1873. The text has been slightly rearranged and abridged. Additions are indicated by brackets.

‡ This insertion is from the session records, which add also: "We shall miss his beaming face. We shall miss the affectionate interest with which he regarded his associates. We shall miss his cheering words." Dr. Beven, the pastor at the time of Mr. Allen's death, described him in these terms: "Busy, familiar with earthly pursuits, wise with the wisdom that

are] his pretty daughters, Miss Priscilla * and Miss Charlotte. They live in St. John's Square, and are among the admired belles of their locale. There is Eli Goodwin, of the firm of Goodwin, Fisher and Spencer, with his two interesting daughters, and a little one, Caroline, one of our first young ladies to make the tour of Europe in the old packet-ship days. She and Susan Spring,† daughter of the pastor, were in Paris together, and they were there called the 'beautiful Americans.' That is Jonathan Thompson with his wife; he is Collector of our Custom House. That is Daniel Parish [one of the trustees, a man of energetic temperament, reticent in speech, a strong adherent of Dr. Spring and the Brick Church],‡ and that Drake Mills [a trustee also, and described by his colleagues as uniformly attentive and courteous, one who fully commanded both confidence and esteem].

"In the next pew is Anthony Dey and his handsome family. That is Miss Catherine Patton, an heiress, step-sister of Rev. Dr. Patton. She has since died, leaving handsome bequests to many charitable societies. There is Abijah Fisher, a man of talent and poverty, who rose to great distinction by his merits. That is Joseph Sampson, a large merchant, who lives at 116 Chambers Street. He recently lived

gives a man influence and force among his fellow-men, he still lived as ever in his Master's presence. There was a peculiar sweetness and gentleness, a simplicity of demeanor, a directness of character in him, which belonged rather to the higher than the lower life." He was a prominent and prosperous banker.

* Afterward Mrs. Thomas P. Lathrop.

† Afterward Mrs. Paul Spofford.

‡ The following note in regard to him has an interest beyond its reference to himself: "He was very matter-of-fact and indisposed to argue a point when he knew he was right, so that he kept from discussing doctrinal points which made so large a portion of the church life of that period."

in the elegant house at the corner of Broad Street and Broadway, now [1873] in process of demolition. There are Abner L. Ely [sagacious in counsel, firm in his convictions, scrupulously honest, generous, conscientious, systematic in his benevolence,* and Jasper Corning, whose family has long been connected with the church], and Thomas Egleston [that humble-minded and consistent Christian, 'ever esteeming others better than himself,' much beloved for his uniform courtesy and fidelity].† That tall, straight man is George Douglass, a merchant of good standing and a man of great and good mind.

"That is Horace Holden of No. 34 Beekman Street. He was a great man in the church [the right hand of his pastor and deeply beloved by him—beloved, in fact, by every one, an invaluable friend, 'a Christian lawyer,' prompt and diligent in office, cheerful, useful, and wise].‡ There is Miss Maria Laight, afterward Madame de Gourley; and there are Anson G. Phelps [unostentatious though pros-

* See "A Memorial of Abner L. Ely" (1873). He was a prominent real-estate broker. He failed in the panic of '37. Thirty years later he had the satisfaction of paying off the whole of the old indebtedness. The following is a portion of a letter sent by one of the creditors at that time. "Yours of yesterday, inclosing cheque for ——, principal and interest on an indebtedness to the old firm of ——, is at hand. I hardly know how to express my surprise and pleasure in the receipt of this money; not so much, I trust, in its money value as from its moral worth. Your own experience in mercantile life must bear witness to the rarity of such returns, after having been outlawed and forgotten. So far as regards yourself, it is only the natural outgrowth of those religious principles which you have illustrated by an active Christian life; and I sincerely thank you, and thank God, for such an example by his followers." Mr. Ely's affection for the Brick Church was deep and constant. "That beloved church," he called it in a letter to his pastor, dictated from his dying bed.

† From the session records.

‡ From the trustees' records and Disosway's "Earliest Churches of N. Y.," p. 154.

perous, benevolent, given to hospitality, especially if the guest was a clergyman,]* and Daniel Lord, a great lawyer, a man of uncommon industry, and of the highest Christian character. He united with the church in 1833, at which time he was marked as a rising man. His fame has since increased, and he has been engaged in every prominent case in our courts for many years.†

"There are James McCall, a merchant of high standing, Samuel B. Schiefflin, the druggist in William Street, and Samuel Marsh,‡ of Erie Railroad fame, an old bachelor who lived at the Astor House as soon as it was built, and continued to do so till he died. William Black, of Ball, Black & Co., is yonder, and Isaac Kip, father of Bishop Kip of California. [Mr. Kip was one of those who had been in the church almost from the beginning of Dr. Spring's pastorate; and with him must be mentioned another of the older generation, William Couch, who, in the course of his long connection with the church, served as deacon, elder and trustee].§ Shepherd Knapp, [a leather merchant in the 'Swamp,' and afterward for almost forty years President of the Mechanics' National Bank, a close friend also of

* "Disosway," p. 151.

† His colleagues in the session record their appreciation of his "judgment, charity, cheerful service and consistent example," which "have tended to secure [the church's] harmony and prosperity." Daniel Webster was his intimate friend and often sat in his pew when in New York.

‡ He was a pew-holder, but does not appear to have been a member.

§ As deacon (from 1823) "he cared for the poor with great assiduity and wisdom and in the tender spirit of his Master." To his duties as elder (from 1834), he brought "a firm independent judgment exercised always in Christian modesty." In the board of trustees he served as clerk, then as treasurer, and finally for many years as president. From the session records.

the pastor, and like Mr. Couch, a holder of the three church offices], was, with his family, an attendant at this church; and Guy Richards [admired and loved for his honor, his generosity, his frankness, and his genial courtesy],* was a conspicuous member."

* Thus characterized by one who well remembers him, and who supplies also the following facts: Mr. Richards' New England home training made him ever a sincere and childlike believer in the truths of Christianity, and for more than forty years he was a regular worshipper in the Brick Church. Not until late in life, however, did he make an open confession of his faith, being deterred by conscientious motives. The persuasion of his pastors, who had no doubt about his fitness, were for a long time ineffectual. One evening, in 1867, Dr. Newman Hall preached in the Brick Church to a crowded audience, from the text Gen. 24 : 31, "Come in, thou blessed of the Lord; wherefore standest thou without?" Mr. Richards, being hard of hearing, was provided with an arm-chair and sat directly beneath the pulpit. That sermon brought him into the church, he being then above eighty years of age. He was a graduate of Yale, had studied law, followed the sea for several years, and later was highly successful in commercial life. The present pastor of the Brick Church is his great-nephew.

CHAPTER XIII

THE SCHOOLS: 1810–1850

"What children are to be at a more advanced age depends on the character they form in childhood. . . . Here, then, at this most interesting period of their existence, . . . when the understanding is docile, the memory tenacious, the fancy vivid, the sensibilities tender, and the character accessible by a thousand avenues which will be closed in maturer age—are parents called on to decide the deterioration and degeneracy or the improvement and progression of human society."—GARDINER SPRING, "Hints to Parents," pp. 44 f.

"Your children, which in that day had no knowledge between good and evil, they shall go in thither, and unto them will I give [the land], and they shall possess it."—*Deuteronomy* 1 : 39.

IT will be remembered that, when in 1809, the Brick Church became a separate ecclesiastical body, it retained, according to the terms of the agreement, its one-half interest in the land and building of the Presbyterian charity school on Nassau Street, and a proportionate responsibility for its support and management. Almost immediately, however, there came an opportunity to sell the property at an advantageous price, and thus dispose of the joint control, which, had it long continued, could not but have caused inconvenience. The sale, for $6,500, was effected in the spring of 1810.

The trustees of the Brick Church, although now without any school-building, did not intend that the charity school should cease. They entered at once into an arrangement with one Seabury Ely to take such charity scholars as the Brick Church might send to him, and to instruct them, in quarters provided by himself, under the superintendence of the school committee of the trustees. He was to be paid at the rate of nine dollars a year for each child, books and stationery being furnished by the church. Under this arrangement thirty * children were instructed in "all those branches of literature which it is supposed will be most useful to them," by which, however, it is likely that nothing more "literary" was intended than reading, writing, figuring, and the catechism. The church also provided for the "cloathing" of these scholars. (It is noticeable that in those days spelling was never explicitly mentioned as an essential element of education.)

Our first inquiry concerns the sources of income for the carrying on of the school. In November, 1812, the annual accounts showed that $1,291.22 had been received "by collections and otherwise," and of this $654.60 had been expended. The word "otherwise" here employed refers evidently to certain assistance from the State. For the State had by this time begun tardily to feel its obligation to share the burden of educating the poor. A movement had been started by a group of people in New York City in 1805 to establish free schools for such children as were not provided for by any religious organization. A society then formed to accomplish this end, and known afterward as "The Free School Society of New York," succeeded in opening in 1809, in a building on Chatham Street, the first non-sectarian school in New York City. School No. 2 followed promptly in 1811. These events had had an indirect effect upon public policy, and the State Legislature

* Forty for a limited period, beginning May, 1811.

had, before the time of the separation of the Presbyterian churches, made a grant for schools, of which the Presbyterians had received £626, 6s., 5d., to be held as a fund whose interest should be used for the charity school maintained by them. The Brick Church, after the separation, had its proper share of this annual income.

In 1813, provision was made for still further State aid. The Legislature voted an appropriation and ordered that that part of it received by the City and County of New York should be apportioned among the Free School Society, the Orphan Asylum Society, the Society of the Economical School, the African Free School, and those incorporated religious societies in the city by which charity schools were supported. In return it was necessary to make regular reports to the State Commissioner. The funds thus secured, added to the collections taken in the church, evidently provided ample money for the Brick Church school expenses.

The provision of a permanent school-house, on the other hand, proved to be a difficult undertaking. At first, however, the prospect was hopeful, for soon after the sale of the old school property on Nassau Street, the Brick Church was so fortunate as to obtain from the city the grant of "Lot No. 21 in Augustus Street," agreeing to pay for it a low annual rental. This piece of land was given with the express stipulation that the church should erect a school-house upon it and maintain a charity school therein: otherwise it should revert to the city.

No doubt the expectation had been to build at once, but almost immediately a time of depression in business intervened, caused by the political disturbances which resulted in the War of 1812. The city authorities in May, 1813, deeming that the failure of the church to raise the necessary sum at that unpropitious time was excusable, were pleased to extend the period for erecting the school-house until the end of the war. When, however, peace had been declared and the months still increased to years without the fulfilment of the church's part of the agreement, the patience of the Corporation of the City was exhausted, and at some time prior to November, 1817, the lot on Augustus Street had been declared forfeited. The trustees of the Brick Church, when they applied for another similar grant, were refused, and were fain to be content with receiving back from the city some $671, which they had already paid on the first lot. Thus ended the last attempt to provide a permanent school-house; for by the time that returning prosperity made the church able to carry out its plan, the necessity no longer existed.

Meantime, during all the years covered by these futile negotiations the Brick Church scholars had continued to be taught in the manner already described, and for five years of that time Seabury Ely continued to be the teacher.

We learn from a report to the State, made in 1814, that the school was held throughout the entire year, and that the largest number of scholars (31) attended during the quarter extending from the middle of May to the middle of August. The ages of the children ranged from four to fifteen years. As to the supervision of the trustees we know that in 1812 they ordered "that the charity scholars be examined in the session room quarterly, the teacher being present at the examination." To the first of these awful encounters the children were summoned on Saturday, June 6th, at three o'clock in the afternoon.

But our fullest information in regard to the management of the school, and indeed, concerning its whole character, is provided by "The Rules of Government of the Charity School," which were presented by the school committee of the trustees and adopted by the board in November, 1814. They are comprehensive, and tell us in considerable detail the things we most desire to know. We learn from them, for instance, that there were at this time about thirty children, boys and girls, and that they were not now received at such an early age as formerly, the girls not till they were six, and the boys, evidently a duller species, not until they were seven. Many of these little people were orphans, for to such children preference was given, but in any case they were children of Presbyterian parents who were, or during their life-time had been, in full communion with the church.

All applications for admission were entered in a certain book which the teacher kept, and were submitted in due time to the school committee of the trustees, who made selection of the fortunate names. No doubt the children themselves might have questioned this assertion of their good fortune in being selected, for the school was by no means intended to be a place of recreation. At nine o'clock each morning and again at two each afternoon the scholars must be at the school door, and punctuality was greatly emphasized. Still more trying was the regulation that scholars must "appear in school with their clothes clean and whole." The teacher was strongly admonished to see to this important matter.

The first study that is mentioned in the rules— and it has a whole rule to itself—is the Shorter Catechism. All the scholars were "obliged" to commit to memory the whole or (merciful provision!) "such parts of it, as they may be found competent to"; and on Wednesday afternoon of each week, or at such other times as might be appointed, they must be at the church to recite what they had learned. This important study having been arranged for, another single rule of much less length was enough to cover all the remaining subjects in the curriculum— reading, writing, arithmetic, "and, if circumstances permit, the principles of English Grammar."

What penalties and punishments the teacher may have been allowed to inflict upon disobedient or negligent scholars we are not told. The rules discreetly refrain from inquiring too curiously into that subject. But under certain extreme conditions the trustees themselves, we learn, would step in and cause a scholar to be expelled. If a child was absent without adequate excuse for six days in succession or for more than eighteen days in one quarter "———— or ————" (these long dashes, suggestive of a very ominous pause, are copied accurately from the official text of the rules), "if any scholar shall be guilty of misbehavior, and, being admonished by the committee, shall continue such misconduct," the sentence of expulsion must be imposed.

If a scholar did indeed thus misbehave, the record of his conduct was set down in that same book of the teacher's, already mentioned, and there it was carefully preserved for the eyes of the trustees. It was not necessary to send the record to them, for every week the school was visited by at least one of the board's school committee, and once a month the committee appeared in its entirety to "inspect" and "receive returns," especially as to the matter of conduct. Once in each quarter occurred the chief visitation, when the entire board of trustees of the Brick Presbyterian Church "in a formal manner" made their appearance to "inquire into the proficiency of the scholars and the attention of their teacher."

If Saturday was a holiday, no mention is made of that fact. At least Sunday was not, for here is the description of it. All the children of the school must attend divine service, morning and afternoon, and they must occupy the seats provided for them. Moreover, "during the whole of the service, and in coming into and departing from the church" they must "demean themselves peaceably and quietly" and must "return from church direct to their places of residence." Finally, they must "remain at home during the day and evening" and remember that the Lord's Day is to be kept holy.

Poor little charity scholars; their life, as outlined in the "rules," does not sound very cheerful; but after all, if Mr. Seabury Ely had any true love for children in his heart, perhaps their school-days were happy in spite of the committee; and in any case there was open the usual expedient of children, who turn even a stiff rule to some cheerful human use by regarding it as something to be broken.

In 1816 took place another change even greater than the abandonment of the school-building, and still further indicative of the fact that the denominational schools were on the wane. The Presbyterians in that year ceased to hire their own teacher and sent their charity scholars to Free School No. 1, paying over to the commissioners of that school the portion of State funds received by the Brick Church, only stipulating that the Bible should be read in the school daily. The sole direct responsibility, therefore, which continued to devolve upon the trustees was the clothing of their scholars, and for this purpose they still caused a collection to be taken annually, in November or December, until the year 1829. Then a legacy from Mrs. Catherine Ryan, expressly for the use of the charity scholars, provided the trustees with all the money needed, and accordingly the collections ceased. At last in May, 1834, we find recorded a vote that any balance at that time remaining in the Ryan legacy should be turned over to the Sunday-schools of the church, from which it is evident that the whole charity school system had come to an end.

For the full explanation of this we must refer to a few facts outside of the history of the church. Ten years before this time there had begun a decided movement to remove the schools from religious influence. The churches themselves had largely contributed to this result by their denominational rivalries, as we perceive in an incident of the year 1824, when the suspicion that a certain church was trying to claim as scholars children belonging more naturally to other congregations, led the Free School Society and certain churches, including the Brick

Church, to protest vigorously and demand a firm restriction of the offending church to the limits of its own parish.

It was significant, too, that at this time, New York State, and a year later New York City, excluded the clergy and the churches from administering the school fund. The gradual relinquishment by the Brick Church of its charity school was, therefore, not peculiar to that church, but a result of the general situation. As reported by Dr. Spring in a speech some years later, the Brick Church was solicited to surrender its individual rights and denominational feelings for the sake of the general good, and promises, he said, were made, not in writing, but "as a solemn matter of compromise and contract," that if the Brick Church withdrew from the field, the Public School Society should hold itself free from any other religious control or influence. From this time the Brick Church took no further part in the work of secular education.

It will have been noticed above that when the Ryan Fund seemed about to lie idle through the discontinuance of the charity school, the trustees were able to transfer it to a kindred institution. The fact was, that as the church's secular school waned to its extinction, two Sunday-schools, which the Brick Church people had founded, were flourishing more and more, and had gradually become a chief interest of the church. We must now turn to study their origin and growth.

In New York at the beginning of the nineteenth century Sunday-schools were a decided novelty.

Even in England the idea was but twenty years old, having been originated by Robert Raikes in 1781 to meet the needs of the poor children of Gloucester. In Great Britain the movement spread with astonishing rapidity, and more slowly it made its way to America. In New York it is said that the first school was opened by a poor negro woman in 1793, but with more certainty the beginning there may be dated from the school of a Mrs. Graham and her daughter, Mrs. Bethune, who had seen the English schools in operation, and now started one in New York in a private house in 1801. By this time the teachers, who in the earlier schools elsewhere had been paid at the rate of a shilling a Sunday, were volunteers. It is noticeable, also, that from the beginning they had been women.

Two more schools were started in the city by 1804, and these also were the work of private individuals. It was not until nine years later that a Sunday-school was started by one of the churches, the old Dutch Church on Garden Street. But the advantages of this plan were at once apparent, especially in giving more permanence than private management could secure; and when in February, 1816, the "New York Sunday-school Union" * was organized, for the purpose of encouraging the establishment of schools throughout the city, the church-school had practically won the field.

Dr. Spring was among those who joined in the formation of this Union, and one of its early meetings was held in the Brick Church; but the best evi-

* See "Semi-Centennial Memorial Discourse of the Sunday-school Union," by Isaac F. Ferris, D.D., 1866.

dence of the church's hearty interest in the movement was its establishment of two Sunday-schools of
its own in the very first year of the Union's existence.
These were "No. 3," * on Fair (now Fulton) Street,
and "No. 23" on Henry Street.

Why, it may be asked, was no school started in
immediate connection with the church itself? The
"Old White Lecture Room" would have been available for the purpose, and very convenient for a majority of the children of the church. But it must be
understood that these early Sunday-schools were not
intended for the children of the church at all. These
were trained by their own parents at home, the
church undertaking merely to assure itself of the
thoroughness of their home instruction, by bringing
the children together for the recitation of the catechism on a week-day afternoon. The Sunday-schools,
on the other hand, were distinctly missionary institutions. They were intended for children belonging
to the poor and ignorant classes, and were regarded
merely as a substitute for the home teaching which
was lacking in their case.

Of the history of the first sixteen years of the
Brick Church Sunday-schools we unfortunately know
but little. The records prior to 1832 have been
lost,† and the references in the session and trustees'
minutes are few and fragmentary. We do not even
know the number of schools maintained throughout this period—whether, for example, there were

---

* No. 1 was the school of the Garden Street Dutch Church referred to
above. No. 2 was started by the Wall Street Presbyterian Church.

† A note written in 1837, states that these earlier records were then "in
the possession of Miss Delia Stevens." She moved from New York about
May, 1838.

ever more than two, or how long precisely the second
of the original schools, "No. 23," was continued.*
We know nothing of the manner in which the schools
were governed, except that they had superintend-
ents,† as at the present time, elected, apparently,
by the teachers, and that the general rules of the
Union provided for a board of management, and
systematic visitation by a committee. Apparently
the instruction was biblical, for there is reference to
the committing of passages of Scripture to memory
(reward tickets were given for proficiency in this,
as well as for attendance and good behavior), and
one at least of the Brick Church schools seems
early to have tried with success a plan of "selected
and limited lessons," first put forth in New York in
1824. All the further details that we possess on this
period are given in a report to the Union for 1827,‡
from which we learn that at that time School No. 3

* The facts known to us are very perplexing. In 1817 and 1818 there
are references in the trustees' minutes to "The Sabbath school [singular]
connected with this church," yet, apparently, schools No. 3 and No. 23
were both in existence long after that. From 1819 to 1825 "schools" are
consistently referred to in the records. Then again in 1826 the singular
number is used, and this falls in with the fact that the report of the Sunday-
school Union for the next year (which happens to be in existence) includes
no mention of School No. 23. We should, therefore, be certain that this
second Brick Church school had been discontinued by this time, were there
not references in 1828, 1831 and May, 1832, to "schools" once more.
Before October, 1832, some sort of a "union" had taken place in connection with the schools of the Brick Church, and after December, 1833, there
was certainly but one school for several years. In 1839 the girls' department of the school is referred to as "The Female Sabbath-school attached
to the Brick Presbyterian Church." Possibly this suggests the explanation
of the plural used between 1828 and 1832, and also of the "union," in the
latter year.

† See Appendix J, p. 527.

‡ See "Semi-Centennial Memorial Discourse of the N. Y. Sunday-school
Union," 1866, by Rev. Isaac F. Ferris, D.D., p. 14.

was for boys only, sixty-seven being enrolled; that there were twenty-one teachers, all men; that there was a library connected with the school including nearly four hundred volumes; and that the school was then situated at 208 William Street.*

When, beginning with 1832, our information becomes more detailed we find that a number of important changes have taken place. For one thing, as soon as the new chapel was completed, in December of that year, the Sunday-school took possession of the rooms in that building which had been especially designed for its use, and this change of location, as might be supposed, was indicative of another change still more radical. The scholars were no longer drawn exclusively from the poor and unchurched families, but included the children of Presbyterian parents. We do not know when or how this change had taken place, but at the time now referred to it was an accomplished fact, as is evidenced by an appeal issued to the church-members in January, 1834, in the hope that they would interest themselves either "to obtain new members or bring in such of their own children as they may have previously withheld." Another important change that had taken place was the admission of girls, and the introduction of women teachers, although "the male department" continued to be the larger portion of the school.†

* From 1819 till 1826, it was the custom in appointing the annual offering for clothing the charity scholars, to direct that the surplus, if there were any, should be used to defray the expense of a room or rooms for Sunday-school uses.

† In December, 1833, there were seventeen men and fourteen women enrolled as teachers.

In 1833 and 1834, it is evident from the records, the school was undergoing a thorough reorganization, and when this had been accomplished a good deal of satisfaction was felt in the result. The secretary, having been requested to "furnish some brief statement of the present situation of the school to such of the church and congregation as would probably feel willing to exert their influence in the cause," wrote "that the school is in a flourishing condition under the immediate supervision of Mr. Seward,* and is well supplied with faithful, devoted and efficient teachers," and "that there has been ample provision made for an additional number of scholars." The organization of the school effected at this time remained practically unchanged until 1840, and the description about to be given may therefore be taken to apply to the whole period ending in that year.

There were five officers elected annually by the teachers, namely, a superintendent, an assistant superintendent, a female superintendent, a librarian, and a secretary. The treasurer, on the other hand, was appointed by the session of the church. The teachers were apparently chosen with great care and entered upon their duties in a spirit of serious consecration. Before being appointed they were required to answer the following questions: "Are you so situated in the providence of God that you can probably hereafter attend to the duties of a teacher with vigor and punctuality? Can you attend ordinarily to a faithful examination and study of the weekly lesson? When your scholars are absent, can you promptly visit them?"

* Mr. B. J. Seward was agent of the Sunday-school Union.

A fuller description of the teachers' duties is contained in an appendix to the constitution * wherein is stated what the superintendent expects the teachers to do. They are to be in their seats at least five minutes before the hour of opening and "ready to greet their scholars as they appear," thus "approbating punctuality and reproving delinquency." At the ringing of the bell and throughout the devotional exercises they are to maintain in their classes "perfect silence." They are to allow "no idleness in any class for a moment." At the close of the session they are always to "accompany their classes to the door of the church, maintaining order among the scholars." And finally, teachers who are necessarily absent are expected to provide substitutes.

Perhaps more important than rules and statements of duties was the spirit in which the work was undertaken, as expressed in the preamble of the constitution just referred to. There "the teachers and conductors of Sunday-school No. 3" make it evident that in their opinion the work of teaching in the Sunday-school was to be regarded as no merely routine exercise, no mere providing of a safe and suitable occupation for children on the Lord's Day, but as a genuine preparation of boys and girls for Christian life and especially for Christian service. It is very noteworthy that they mention with most emphasis the need of missionaries to heathen lands and of ministers at home, as their incentive to "unremitting labor." Their object, as they finally state it, is "to win souls to Jesus Christ, and to prepare them for usefulness in his kingdom."

* Adopted on December 21st, 1833. See Appendix W, p. 545.

Until 1839 two sessions of the Sunday-school were held each Sunday, the first beginning at nine o'clock in the morning throughout the year, while the second began at half-past one in the afternoon from the first of October to the first of May, and at two o'clock from May to October. In June, 1839, it was decided to omit the afternoon session for three months, and later in the year it was voted to make this change permanent.

The sessions began and closed with devotional exercises, the interval being filled by the teaching of the lesson. For the most part the subject of study was a passage from the Scriptures aided apparently by some sort of "Question Book," but the fourth Sunday of each month was devoted to the teaching of the shorter catechism. At the close of the afternoon session it was customary for the superintendent to examine the scholars on the lesson for the day. Teachers' meetings for the preparation of the lesson were a regular institution. They were held on Saturday evenings "in the committee room of the chapel," * and were conducted by Dr. Spring.

The library was evidently regarded as an important department of the work of the school, though it may be feared that the "select books" which were purchased from time to time were of the sort that has caused the name "Sunday-school book" to be regarded as a title of opprobrium. Select though the books were, the children were not allowed to choose among them for themselves, but it was the duty of the teachers to "choose such books from the library as they may judge most proper for their scholars."

* Referred to sometimes as "the missionary room."

Once a year, on a Sunday morning in April, the school celebrated its anniversary by exercises held in the church. We do not know the nature of the service except that the secretary read a report which, sometimes at least, included a sort of history of the school, that Dr. Spring preached a sermon appropriate to the day, and that on that occasion it was customary "to have the female scholars and their teachers sit in the front seats of the gallery next the Park, and the male scholars and teachers opposite."

In the summer of 1837 a new light broke upon the Brick Church Sunday-school. Then for the first time it was suggested that a small amount of play be mingled with the school's discipline and study. One cannot but be impressed, in reading the accounts of the treatment of children in the time of our great-grandparents, with the almost utter ignorance of the men of that time in regard to the child-nature. Children were then commonly dealt with much as though they were merely old men and women dressed in bibs and pinafores. There was barely any attempt to appeal to distinctly childish tastes. There was very little consideration for the inevitable immaturities of childhood. Especially there was almost no appreciation of the fact that all teaching, and religious teaching quite as much as any, should be adjusted accurately to the children's intelligence and experience.

An illustration of this is provided by the use made in the Brick Church Sunday-school one Sunday in 1850, of the tragic death of a scholar resulting from injuries received in an accident on Hague Street.

Dr. Spring, with reference to the melancholy event, "addressed the children," we are told, "on the necessity of being prepared for [Christ's] coming, and the danger of provoking God's wrath and curse in this life and that which is to come." Another incident, which occurred a few months earlier, and which is curious enough to be quoted for its own sake, was no doubt made the text for a terrifying address upon the crime of theft. It seems that in May, 1849, the superintendent received from some unknown person a Bible in which, written in pencil on a slip of paper, was found the following pathetic message: "To the Superintendent of this School. Dear Sir, about three years ago, when the School was downstairs, this Bible was stolen with some others from the bookcase. Will you inquire for the owner in the school and ask him to forgive and pray for the thief."

But to return to the proposal which in 1837, marked the beginning of a fuller appreciation of the needs of childhood. As it happened the plan then proposed could not be carried out at once, but it afterward bore fruit, and even the proposal of it must have made the life of the little scholars distinctly more worth living. The full record of the incident may be quoted: "June 27th, 1837. By agreement the teachers met this evening to take into consideration the utility of celebrating the coming 4th [of] July with the scholars. The committee reported verbally as follows: They have taken in consideration all the places in the neighborhood suitable to visit, and found that they would probably be filled by many visitors and thus defeat the object in view; and also the lateness of notice prevents suitable arrangements for the occasion. It was therefore concluded to postpone until another year."

In 1840 a radical change in the whole management of the Sunday-school was made by the session of the church, who were dissatisfied with the conditions which then existed. Up to this time the school, though closely identified with the church life, had been in a large degree independent. It had appointed its own officers,* made its own rules, determined its own policy, without any reference to the session whatsoever. The only superior authority to which it looked was the New York Sunday-school Union, an outside and undenominational society.

As early as 1836 the session had expressed some uneasiness in regard to the situation, and had appointed a committee to consider "the measures to be pursued for the religious education of the children," and especially to provide for some direct intercourse between the children and the officers of the church. At that time, however, they did not undertake to interfere with the Sunday-school, but merely adopted additional means of ensuring the children's proper instruction. They were content to appoint "an afternoon service in the session room once a month,† in which the children and youth of all the church and congregation may meet for instruction in the catechism." ‡ The older members of the congregation

---

* Except the treasurer. See above.

† On the fourth Sunday.

‡ At an earlier time, before the day of Sunday-schools, such a service had been held weekly. In 1835, the General Assembly had expressed deep regret that the Sunday-schools seemed to have superseded very largely the catechetical instructions of the pastor.

were invited to participate, and the pastor and elders were to superintend the course of instruction.

This expedient, however, after about three years' trial, proved to be inadequate, and on January 9th, 1840, the session, "having taken into consideration the existing state of the Sabbath-schools * and the present plan of instruction," referred the whole subject to a committee. The report which this committee presented two weeks later is of such interest from several points of view that it must be quoted in its entirety.

"The committee appointed to take into consideration the present system of instruction in the Sabbath-schools connected with this congregation, beg leave to submit the following suggestions and plan as their report:

"It appears to your committee that the original design of these schools has been to a great extent lost sight of, in the almost exclusive instruction of the children of families belonging to our own congregation and the gradual withdrawing from them of the poorer and more ignorant population around us.

"It may be assumed as a fact which will not be questioned that those who receive instruction in these schools are almost exclusively made up of our own congregation.† This circumstance throws no small weight of responsibility on this session to inquire into the condition of the schools, both as it regards the system of instruction, the qualification of

* The plural is frequently used at this period, though it is evident that but one school existed, including a boys' and a girls' department.

† Three years later when 114 scholars were enrolled, all but fourteen were from Brick Church families.

the teachers, and the number and progress of those who are taught.

"In the prosecution of these inquiries your committee have been persuaded that there is a diminution in the number * of young persons who receive religious instruction among this people which must awaken solicitude in the minds of all who feel the importance of bringing up the youth in the nurture and admonition of the Lord.

"Your committee have no doubt that this is to be attributed in part to the widely scattered condition of the congregation and the great distance of many families from the place of instruction. But they are convinced that this is not the only evil. From a variety of circumstances neither necessary nor proper to be mentioned in this report, there has been unhappily so great a change of teachers in the school and, with few exceptions,† such instability in their attachment to this particular field of labor that more than once the whole system has been not a little embarrassed by this single circumstance.

"It will at once be seen that these frequent changes must originate incompetency in the teachers themselves as well as a want of confidence in parents in the whole system of Sabbath-school instruction, and both these things are lamentably true. Nor is this the whole evil. While parents have relinquished the instruction of their children to the Sabbath-school, and while the Sabbath-school has in too great a de-

* Whereas there were thirty-one classes in 1833, there were but twenty-two at the end of 1839.

† Among the notable exceptions were Abner L. Ely, Henry K. Bull, Albert Woodruff, Charles J. Steadman, John K. Starin, Henry Brewster, J. F. Donnell, and Miss Delia Stevens.

gree failed to supply the place of parents, it is to be feared that parents have not themselves resumed their former wonted care of the religious instruction of their offspring; so that while the Sabbath-school has taken this great work out of the hands of parents and out of the hands of the pastor and elders, the work itself remains to a great extent unfulfilled.

"There are other evils also in the very constitution of the Sabbath-schools which in the judgment of your committee call for the kind but decisive inter-position of the session.

"The system of instruction in the Sabbath-school, designed to meet the views of various denominations of Christians, necessarily omits very important truths, and truths with which the youthful mind ought to be familiar. It is feared that teachers from among us, with some honorable exceptions, have lost their interest in the established institutions of the Church, so that there are few 'to guide her among all the sons she hath brought up'; and there is that in the system which, while it is independent of the Church of God, is insensibly weakening her influence and govern-ment and relaxing those bonds by which the mem-bers of a church as individuals are bound and obliged to walk together in truth and love.

"In view of these things your committee recom-mend the following plan and resolutions:

"1. Resolved that the Sabbath-school connected with this congregation be placed under the immediate superintendence of the pastor and an assistant elder by whom all its teachers are to be appointed and all its lessons assigned.

"2. Resolved that, with the exception of those

whose age, infirmities or distance may excuse them, all the elders of this church attend upon this service, each one having the superintendence of assigned portions of the school, for the special purpose of securing the attendance of its classes and, in connection with their teachers, visiting the families of which they are composed.

"3. Resolved that it be the duty of all the members of the church—and their Christian fidelity is confidently relied on for this purpose—to take such parts in the instruction of the school as shall, upon a full view of their relations and condition, be assigned them by the session.

"4. Resolved that the session look with confidence to parents and guardians connected with this congregation to send their children to the school attached to their own church, to teach them carefully the lessons at home, and to make it a business of more serious importance to furnish their minds with instruction in the doctrines and duties of religion.

"5. Resolved that the pastor of this congregation attend a weekly meeting on every Saturday evening with all the teachers, for the purpose of examining the lesson for the ensuing Lord's Day and that all the Sabbath-school teachers belonging to this congregation, in whatever schools they may teach, be invited to be present at this weekly exercise.

"6. Resolved that the monthly prayer-meeting established for Sabbath-schools be discontinued and henceforth united with the monthly prayer-meeting of this church, at which it shall be considered a leading object to implore the divine blessing upon the instructions of the Sabbath-school and the youth and children of this people."

Unfortunately the school records close abruptly after announcing the succession of the pastor to the superintendency. Perhaps it was thought that since the session was in complete control, no separate records were longer necessary. At any rate, for the conditions that existed during the next six years we must seek elsewhere for our information. Enough, however, is known to assure us at least that the change of policy was beneficial. One evidence of this is the fact that at some time prior to 1844 a branch or "mission" school* was started, an attempt to reach once more the poorer children for whom the schools were originally intended. We know also that the original Brick Church school (No. 3) was slowly increasing in numbers under the session management. In three years it achieved a gain of over twenty per cent. Further, the afternoon session was probably resumed at this time, for a little later we find it a regular feature of the school.

Exactly how long the session of the church retained control we do not know, but probably it was until about 1846, for when the school records are resumed at that time the superintendent is found to be a layman once more, and the minutes give the impression that some important readjustment has just taken place. A new constitution, for example, is prepared and adopted, which resembles in substance (though not in form) the old constitution of 1833. Probably the session felt that its object had now been ac-

* Mr. Woods was superintendent. This school is probably the No. 12 referred to later in the records.

complished, and at this time gladly surrendered the burden of direct management which it had temporarily assumed.

In any case the school continued to prosper. In 1847 it maintained thirty-five classes, including an infant class and Bible classes, and had on its roll one hundred and seventy-five scholars, much the largest number recorded up to that time. The standard of its scholarship, also, seems to have been high, for when the children who had memorized the whole of the Shorter Catechism were from time to time rewarded (according to a custom introduced in this period) the lists were surprisingly long, while a still larger number of boys and girls received Bibles, Bible dictionaries, Bible geographies, "Illustrated Skethes," or "small books" as rewards for punctual attendance and good behavior. On one occasion a scholar named Miss Catherine Halsey received a "gilt Bible," which must have betokened a most extraordinary degree of goodness and punctuality.

But perhaps the two most interesting developments were those which still remain to be described. One was the system of visitation, which was at this time devised and put into practice. Here once more we see the reawakening of the old sense of responsibility for the children of the ignorant poor, the children of the slums as we should say to-day; and this awakening was due, no doubt, to certain important changes in outward conditions. For the neighborhood of the Brick Church on Beekman Street was now becoming more and more a downtown region, full of the bustle of business, and used for residence by the poorer classes only. How to reach the many neglected children who lived within hearing distance of the Brick Church bell became, therefore, a more and more urgent problem. The officers and teachers of the school gave themselves earnestly to the solving of it. The section of the city in the vicinity of the Brick Church * was by them subdivided into convenient districts which were assigned to individual teachers for "thorough" visitation. Full reports were then presented at the teachers' meetings, of the whole number of children in the district, of those attending the Brick Church school or other schools, and of those who attended none. Special pains were taken "to ascertain the wants and supply the necessities of those applying for aid," and especially to provide proper clothing for poor children, whose parents desired them to attend the school.† A "charities committee" was at the same time appointed to solicit funds from the congregation and to relieve the cases of need reported by the visitors.

Finally, and this will complete the subject of this chapter, we must notice that the Sunday-school, toward the close of the period we are studying, began to take a direct and practical interest in missions. We have seen already that the moving purpose of the workers had long been, in no small part, the provision of such religious training as might in the future prepare their scholars for the work of the

* The Sunday-school Union at that time apportioned a certain district to each church, much as the Federation of Churches proposes to do at the present day.

† One entry states that arrangements are to be made for visiting "malignant children," but probably the secretary did not intend to refer to the young reprobates of the community. "Indigent," the word used in several similar passages, was no doubt the adjective he meant to use here.

gospel at home and abroad. But now, in addition
to this, the school began to make direct contributions
to the work of missionaries already in the field. The
initiative in this movement came originally from one
of the school's own teachers, Miss Cowdrey, who
when on a visit to Cincinnati, in 1836, was moved by
the sight of "the destitute of the West," and wrote to
her fellow-workers in the Brick Church Sunday-
school, begging a donation of old question books,
hymn books, etc. A prompt response was made,*
and a precedent was set which had important consequences. Not until the late forties, however, was
anything like a habit of missionary giving established. After that we read of comparatively frequent
appeals for aid from Sunday-school missionaries
in the West, asking still for books, but new books
now, not old ones. "Raising a library" became
accordingly a familiar undertaking among the Brick
Church teachers. At last in 1850, at the very close
of the period to which this chapter is devoted,
occurred an incident which was dramatic in its effect
and launched the school suddenly upon the high
seas of benevolence.

At the teachers' meeting on Sunday, February
17th, a Mr. Chidlar made an address on "The
Needs of the West." What anecdotes he may have
told or what arguments he used we do not know, but
at length, pausing in his appeal, he unfurled a worn
and faded banner which had evidently seen long
service in some Sunday-school. While his hearers

* The secretary with singular accuracy records that 247 question books,
35 new hymn books, bound in leather, and 31 of the same bound in paper,
were sent by dray No. 1304 to Mrs. Cowdrey, in Albion Place, to be for-
warded to her daughter,

were wondering what this meant, he told them that this banner was one that the Brick Church Sunday-school had itself sent out to Illinois eighteen years before. It had now come back from the faithful workers on the frontier, with the message that they had done with it all that they, unaided, could possibly do, and that to send it westward again, unaccompanied by the means for carrying out its glorious object, would be a kind of cruelty to those brave but exhausted workers in the West. It is needless to say that in a school which was, as we have seen, not unfamiliar with the cause of missions, such a direct appeal as this could not be disregarded. At once, there was proposed and adopted a resolution, which, brief as it is, still communicates to us something of the noble emotion which prompted it: "Resolved, that we will support a missionary to be our standard-bearer for the West, and will supply him with ten libraries to aid him in his labors."

But this growth of practical benevolence in the Sunday-school * was, in reality, part of a much larger movement of the same kind in the church itself, and this is the subject of the next chapter, to which we must now turn.

* It should be remarked that up to this time no attempt seems to have been made to interest the *scholars* in these practical enterprises. When money was needed it was raised by the teachers from other members of the congregation. The Sunday-school was apparently supposed to consist of two parts, opposite in character—the scholars, who were expected to be for the most part entirely passive, and the teachers and officers, by whom the whole active work was to be done.

CHAPTER XIV

MISSIONS AND BENEVOLENCE: 1810–1850

"In those great and benevolent enterprises, for which the age in which we live has been distinguished, it has been the privilege of the Brick Church to bear her part. Taking the forty-six years of my ministry together, no church in the land has given more bountifully to the cause of domestic and foreign missions."—GARDINER SPRING, 1856, "The Brick Church Memorial," p. 29.

"As ye go, preach, saying, The kingdom of heaven is at hand. Heal the sick, cleanse the lepers, raise the dead, cast out devils: freely ye have received, freely give."
—*Matthew* 10 : 7 f.

WHEN Gardiner Spring came to the Brick Church, almost all the money received in the collections was used for the church expenses. The two established exceptions, it will be recalled, were the annual collection for the support of the charity school * and the provision that on communion Sundays and at the time of the annual charity sermon the collections should be devoted to the needs of the poor of the church.† We have also seen that occasional exceptions had begun to be made from time to time in response to special appeals, but as yet the instances of these were so few and scattered, that they must be regarded only as a prophecy of greater things to come.‡

Under Dr. Spring the collections for the poor § and, as long as was necessary, for the charity school

---

* See page 90.   † See page 85.   ‡ See page 87.

§ This money was administered as formerly by the deacons, except that a small sum was put into the hands of the pastor for special cases. The funds appear to have been ample till about 1842, from which date there was frequently a small deficit, easily made up.

231

continued as before; but the growth of occasional benevolences was for a time checked, apparently by a combination of two causes. First, the period of business depression before and during the War of 1812 made it necessary to observe great economy in the management of the church's finances. And, second, a custom had by this time been adopted of taking up a special annual collection which should be in part devoted to missions.* This was usually set for a Sunday in April, and at first (in 1810), the sum received was divided into three equal parts, one-third being "for the use of the Presbytery," one-third "for missionaries," and the rest "for the use of the Commissioners of the General Assembly." Five years later a different apportionment was made. Two-thirds were now to be given to "The Education Fund," and the remaining third to be "divided between the Commissioners and Missionary Funds." This regularizing of the church's benevolence, though it was but a small beginning, was a distinct advance upon the irregular and indiscriminate offerings of the earlier period. Moreover, the change in the apportionment which has just been mentioned, omitting altogether, as it does, the contribution to the purely ecclesiastical expenses of Presbytery,† and empha-

* The General Assembly as early as 1791, had resolved "that the Presbyteries composing the Synod of New York and New Jersey and that of Philadelphia, use their best endeavors to forward yearly to the General Treasurer a collection [for missions] from each of their churches." The only evidence that this was carried out in the Presbyterian Church of New York City is the record of three offerings, in whole or part for the purpose of sending missionaries to the frontier, in 1791, 1792, and 1796. (See above, p. 87.) The next allusion to a stated yearly collection is the one referred to in the text (1810).

† Of course the church by some other means than a collection must have continued to bear its share in these expenses.

sizing missionary and benevolent objects, indicates a most wholesome tendency.

This one stated annual collection seems to have provided a sufficient outlet for the church's missionary benevolence for about eight years, but in October, 1818, the trustees passed a resolution which, simple as it appears to be, marks the beginning of a new advance. It was the granting, to the directors of the African School, of the use of the Brick Church for their anniversary sermon, and of permission to take up a collection at that time for the institution which they represented. It is plain from this action and from other instances of the same sort which followed in the succeeding years that the church's sense of missionary responsibility had again begun to outgrow the means provided for its exercise.

Moreover, from without the pressure at this time had greatly increased. To this the General Assembly had called attention in a notable communication in the year 1817. It had then declared: "The gradual increase of gospel light; the extension of the blessings of education to all classes and ages; the growing diffusion of missionary zeal and exertions; the rapid multiplication of Bible societies, and through their instrumentality, the wonderful spread of the knowledge of the word of life in languages and countries hitherto strangers to the sacred volume; the numerous associations for evangelical, benevolent, and humane purposes, which have arisen, and are daily arising, in every part of our bounds; and, above all, the converting and sanctifying influences of the Holy Spirit, which have been poured out for some time past, and especially during the last year, in many of the congregations belonging to our communion—form an assemblage which cannot fail to be in a high degree interesting and animating to the friends of pure and undefiled religion; an assemblage which, while it gratifies for the present the pious and benevolent heart, must excite the most precious hopes for the future. Such mighty plans of benevolence, such wonderful combinations, such a general movement to mankind, in promoting the great cause of human happiness, were surely never before witnessed.

"At such a period, dear brethren," this utterance of the Assembly continues, "let it be impressed upon the mind of every member of our church, that we are called to humble, diligent, persevering exertion. Much has been done, but much more remains to be done; and much, we hope, will be done by us. Every day makes a demand upon the time, the affections, the prayers, the property, the influence of the people of God, which it would be ingratitude, cruelty, nay, treachery, to repel." * To the great appeal which the times were thus making the Brick Church responded, slowly for a while, but more and more as the years passed. From 1821, there is in the church records constant allusion to the granting of the use of the church,† and of collections, sometimes at special services on week-days, but more commonly at one of the regular Sunday services. The number and variety of the causes to which the Brick Church thus rendered material aid is really astonishing. Widows, orphans, and other poor persons, both young and old,

---

* "Assembly Digest," p. 313.

† A nominal charge of two dollars was charged in most cases as a fee for the sexton.

students, sailors, negroes, churches in America, in Europe and in Asia, Sunday-schools, hospitals, and more kinds of missionary enterprise than one would suppose possible, were among the debtors to the hospitality and liberality of the Brick Church.* The collections given to these causes (thus diverting money, be it remembered, that would otherwise have gone into the church's own treasury), amounted frequently to more than $100 each, and the sum total must have attained to a very generous figure.

It will readily be imagined that as appeals for these special collections increased in frequency, the officers

---

* The following is a list of societies, etc., aided from 1818 to 1838, in the ways described in the text: The African School; Society for the Relief of Poor Widows with Small Children; Institution in Amherst for the Classical Education of Poor and Pious Youths; N. Y. Evangelical Missionary Society; * N. Y. Sunday-school Union Society; * N. Y. Religious Tract Society; Auburn Theological Institution; United Foreign Missionary Society; * Church in West Farms; * United Domestic Missionary Society; * Society for Promoting the Gospel among Seamen; Church in Scipio; Orphan Asylum Institution; Presbyterian Education Society; Female Sunday-school Union Society; Church in St. Augustine; * Mariners' Church; * Marine Bible Society; Young Men's Auxiliary Education Society; Palestine Mission Association; widow and children of late James C. Crane, the Missionary; *American Colonization Society; * Bethel Union (for Seamen); Greek Committee; Colored Church lately under pastoral charge of Mr. Cornish; * Port Society of New York; *African Presbyterian Church of N. Y.; N. Y. City Bible Society; Infant Schools Nos. 1 and 3; Female Lying-in Asylum; Sunday-school No. 42 on Orange Street; Society for Relief of Respectable, Aged, Indigent Females; * Board of Education; * General Assembly's Board of Missions; Commissioners' Fund; Five Points Sunday-schools; Matron Association; * Young Men's Missionary Society; Seaman's Friend Society; American Board of Commissioners of Foreign Missions; *N. Y. Young Men's Bible Society; American Sunday-school Union; *N. Y. Colonization Society; Church in St. Petersburg, Russia; Church in Brussels, Belgium; N. Y. Academy of Sacred Music; *Poor of the City. The names are given in the form in which they appear in the church records. Those marked with asterisks received aid from the church two or more times. The N. Y. Sunday-school Union, for instance, was granted five collections in the twenty years.

of the church would again grow dissatisfied with such a haphazard and unorganized method of distributing the benevolences. In giving full opportunity to the growing spirit of liberality, the absence of a hard and fast scheme had, for a while, been advantageous, but the time was bound to come when it would be desirable to control, in a more systematic way, the habit of generous giving which had now been well established. There was, moreover, another objection which made a change expedient. The admission to the Brick Church pulpit of the agents, who came to plead the cause of the various institutions, interfered seriously with the regular ministrations of the pastor, without supplying an altogether satisfactory equivalent.

Accordingly, early in 1838, when the subject of organizing the church's benevolences was seriously brought forward in the session, the first step taken was to exclude agents altogether, and to provide that "hereafter all appeals on behalf of the religious charities be made by the pastor and, whenever necessary, be followed up by the session and members of the church."* This, however, was but a preliminary step. A month later a plan was presented and adopted by which, it was hoped, the current evils would be

---

* In this matter the Brick Church was evidently helping to form the opinion of the Church at large. In the next year the General Assembly passed the following resolution: "That while the necessity for agents is at present felt and recognized by the Assembly, in order ultimately to remove this necessity, and thus to reduce the expenditures of the Board, the individual agency and coöperation of every minister and church session, in forwarding the interests of this Board, would, in the opinion of the Assembly, if faithfully employed, with least expense and the greatest certainty advance the cause and multiply the resources of the Board." "Assembly Digest," p. 315.

remedied, and a more adequate use made of the church's present opportunity. What they really proposed to do was to expand the old idea of the three-cause offering taken in April, into a much broader and more inclusive scheme adapted to the later conditions. To this end it was resolved that, with the concurrence of the trustees, five specified causes should "receive the stated and annual patronage of the congregation." In January of each year the Presbyterian Board of Education was to receive its collection, in April the American Board of Commissioners for Foreign Missions, in June the American Tract Society, in October the Sunday-school Union, and in November the Presbyterian Board of Domestic Missions. Nor was this all. Almost equally significant was the appointment of five special committees, of two elders each, to watch over the interests of these five causes.

Thus two important results were sought to be accomplished; first, it was insured that henceforth the chief appeal to the church's liberality should be made by causes of paramount importance, and second, the people were to be trained by pastor and elders to feel that these causes were worthy of their regular and generous support. There was, it is true, a special provision that collections should from time to time be taken for "such other occasional charities as the urgency of the case may require," but at the same time, there was an evident intention that these occasional appeals should become much less frequent than heretofore. The money formerly available for them was now to be appropriated by those five objects selected by the session as the ones which the Brick Church ought most strongly and constantly to aid. As a matter of fact, the special offerings became, after this, noticeably rare, and two years later a regulation that outside organizations should usually be charged $25 for the use of the church, tended still further to diminish their number.

Reviewing briefly the thirty years of development which reached a culmination at this time, we observe that the advance had been by a sort of pendulum movement. In 1810 an enlarged capacity to give to missions, etc., evidenced by a growing readiness to respond to occasional appeals, was met by the establishment of a regular annual offering mostly devoted to benevolent objects. At once the irregular benevolences ceased. Eight years later, although the annual collection still continued, the occasional offerings once more made their appearance and rapidly multiplied, showing again that there was a surplus for benevolence, over and above the sum which the existing scheme demanded. Whereupon steps were again taken to adapt the scheme to the advance. The one annual offering, mostly devoted to benevolent objects, was replaced by five annual offerings, entirely devoted to benevolent objects. Once more the custom of occasional collections ceased at once, from which it might be inferred that the change had accomplished its purpose.

The chief test of success, however, must, of course, be sought not merely in the orderly working of the scheme, but chiefly in the amount of money produced by it for benevolent purposes. From this point of view, also, the result was eminently satisfactory. In 1838, although the month for the offering for the Board of Education had already passed before the plan was adopted, no less than $3,516.96 was received in the four remaining collections. Indeed, in this the congregation had apparently outrun its real ability. It was a case of the new broom performing a service which, as it grew old, it could not maintain. The next year all five offerings amounted to but little more than $2,700. Even this, however, was not unsatisfactory, and the average annual total for the years from 1838 to 1850 was certainly excellent, namely, $3,330. Each year in this period, except the last, the cause of foreign missions took the lead, receiving always more than $1,000. Domestic missions came next; and the other three were about equal claimants for third place. Miscellaneous offerings were exceedingly variable; sometimes there were none reported, and sometimes they amounted to several hundred dollars.

This chapter would be incomplete without some account of the part played, directly and indirectly, by the Brick Church in some of the important religious organizations through which its benevolences were distributed. It will have been evident already that the forty years which we have been studying were marked by an extraordinary development of such organizations. When Gardiner Spring was installed one could almost have counted upon the fingers of one's hands the important societies then carrying on benevolent work, and as for societies whose work was distinctly Christian, Christian in definite purpose as well as in general spirit, there were almost none. But in 1850, as we have seen, the question for the Brick Church was not so much, How shall we put our money at work? but, How shall we prevent it from being dissipated among a hundred different channels of Christian usefulness? In the marked change of condition which had thus taken place, the Brick Church and its pastor had played an active part.

The American Bible Society, for example, had Dr. Spring for one of its founders. It was, he tells us, his privilege, as delegate from the New York Bible Society, to sit in the convention in New York in 1816, when the national society was organized. He was afterward one of its directors, served on one of its standing committees, and contributed not a little to its progress and efficiency.

In a still more interesting manner was the Brick Church connected with the origin of work for seamen in America. In the summer of 1816—and, by the way, it will have been noticed that this was a very eventful year in the history of the Christian activities of New York—some of the members of the Brick Church held meetings in the lower part of the city with the general purpose of reaching, if possible, the neglected and churchless people of that section. It was noticed that certain of these meetings, held in Water Street, were attended by numbers of seamen, which suggested the holding of meetings for sailors only, an entirely new idea in America at that time. The first meeting of this sort was held in a house at the corner of Front Street and Old Slip, and out of it grew, in time, the Mariner's Church in New York, similar organizations in many other Atlantic ports, and finally the American Seaman's Friend Society.

On one occasion an unsuccessful attempt on the part of Dr. Spring to organize a movement was, nevertheless, so excellent an illustration of his relation to the larger interests of practical Christianity, that a description of it may be here included, especially as he himself speaks of it at some length in his own autobiography. The object which he had in view was Sabbath reform. In 1827, the year in which he made his attempt, conditions in respect to Sunday observance had materially changed from those which had formerly existed. "When I first came to New York," wrote Dr. Spring, "Sabbath desecration was by no means so flagrant as it became at a later period. Carriages and carts were not allowed to run wild by our churches; an iron chain was stretched across Nassau and Beekman streets in order to protect the church, at whose altars I served, in the quiet enjoyment of its religious services. . . . The leading minds of our fellow-citizens strongly favored a decent observance, of the Lord's Day." *

But as the years passed "the men and the times changed." In 1827, Dr. Spring preached a series of five sermons on "The Obligations of the Sabbath," the last of which, on "The Sabbath, a Blessing to Mankind," † made so decided an impression upon Mr. Stephen Allen, then mayor of the city, that he wrote to Dr. Spring, asking him to publish it, and afterward consented to give his hearty coöperation in some general effort for Sabbath reform. He "engaged to preside at a public meeting of the citizens in the City Hall, summoned through the public press, for the consideration of this important subject."

* "Life and Times," Vol. II, pp. 141 *f.*

† This was printed, not only in English, but in Italian and Modern Greek.

"I was warmly zealous in the cause," says Dr. Spring. "The meeting was called. Able speakers, both clergymen and laymen, saw the importance of the discussion, and the city was in a glow of excitement. But long before the appointed time the place of meeting was *preoccupied* by those who had taken the alarm at this supposed, and clerical, invasion of their civil rights. . . . It was not without difficulty that we got into the Hall; our friends earnestly entreated me not to attempt it. Those on whom we relied to advocate our cause, one after another, deserted us, and the Rev. Alexander McLeland and myself were left alone, of the ministers of the gospel, to face the storm. We forced our way through the crowd, and found ourselves in the midst of an indignant assemblage, passing resolutions *requesting the ministers to mind their own business.* We were marked men. The excited multitude looked daggers at us. They would not listen to us. Our persons were in danger, and we left the Hall without the opportunity even of bearing our testimony for God and the Sabbath. There was more zeal than wisdom in that movement. It was a failure." *

But to return to the successes. The relations of Dr. Spring and the church to the creation and development of the New York Sunday-school Union has already been alluded to. A still closer connection existed between them and certain societies which represented the cause of home missions. The New York Missionary Society, a very old organization,† whose work was done in "the Indian territory in the remote

* "Life and Times," Vol. II, pp. 142 *f.*
† See above, page 232.

West," was aided after 1809, by an auxiliary, known as The Young Men's Missionary Society of New York. This society was composed of young men from all the evangelical churches in the city and, "by the enthusiastic spirit which animated it, gave a powerful impulse to the good cause, and promised to be one of the important agencies in the missionary work." Most unfortunately, however, the society after a few years, was greatly hindered by internal differences and jealousies. This state of things reached a climax in 1817, at which time Dr. Spring was a member of the board of directors. In November of that year a Mr. Cox was nominated as a suitable missionary to be sent by the society, but after a prolonged series of meetings, held, as it happened, in the session room of the Brick Church, he was rejected by a majority of the members, for the reason that he represented a somewhat less extreme form of Calvinism than did these opposers themselves. The minority, which included Dr. Spring, held that the objections were conceived in a spirit of bigotry and represented an attempt to achieve by main force such a theological narrowing of a supposedly undenominational society as would virtually exclude many of the members themselves. The result was that the minority withdrew and formed a new organization, known as the New York Evangelical Missionary Society of Young Men, declaring it their belief that the great needs of the time called upon true Christians, even if differing "in important articles of faith," to unite as laborers for the harvest, This new society at once achieved a striking success, enrolling more than four hundred members in a few weeks. In its beginning Dr.

Spring was a moving spirit, and his connection with it was afterward still closer. "It was my privilege as the secretary," he says, "to correspond with the missionaries, and to address the communities to which they were sent; and much as it added to my labors, it is with thankfulness that I look back to the part I was called to perform in originating and sustaining this society. It was an honor to be a fellow-worker with them. . . . They gathered around me, encouraged, and strengthened me, and gave a hallowed influence to the church of which I was pastor and so many of them were members."

The second home missionary organization in which Dr. Spring and his church were directly interested was one of larger scope. Up to 1826, the missionary work in the United States had been carried on by a number of State or city societies, but the need of a national institution had for some time been felt, and at length, in the year mentioned, a committee of the home missionary workers in New York City "addressed a circular to a large number of churches, inviting them to convene at the session room of the Brick Presbyterian Church in the city of New York, for the purpose of forming an American Home Missionary Society. . . . The response to this invitation was a large assemblage in convention, of one hundred and twenty-six ministers and laymen from thirteen States and Territories of the Union, men of high character in Church and State and from four different Christian denominations," * the Dutch, Scotch, Congregational and Presbyterian Churches. The plan was successfully carried out, and three Brick Church rep-

* "Life and Times," Vol. I, p. 265.

resentatives were among the first officers of the new society, Dr. Spring as one of the directors, Peter Hawes as treasurer, and Stephen Lockwood as recording secretary.

If, in the founding of the first great American foreign missionary society, the Brick Church did not play an equally prominent part, this was because the American Board of Commissioners for Foreign Missions had already been organized while Gardiner Spring was studying theology at Andover. He was present, however, as a spectator, at the meeting in Bradford, Mass., in 1810, where that famous Board was first projected, and heard his fellow-students from the seminary, Mott, Mills, Newall, and Judson, present that "respectful and earnest memorial" which led directly to this result. Associated as he was with these men, he could hardly fail to feel a deep interest in the subject of foreign missions. Moreover, his own father, Dr. Samuel Spring was, as has been already stated in an earlier chapter, one of those who joined in the creation of the American Board. Dr. Gardiner Spring narrates one interesting incident which occurred in his father's church, on the Sunday immediately following the Bradford meeting. "On his return to Newburyport," he says, "my father, on the Sabbath morning, gave a brief narrative of the devotement of the young men, . . . and also gave notice that he would preach on the subject in the afternoon, and that after the sermon a collection would be taken up for missions to the heathen. In the days of my youth," Dr. Spring continues, "the town of Newburyport was an active, commercial village of great enterprise and wealth. My father's congregation had a large share of the wealth of the place, and a large share of its mercantile marine, composed of sea-captains and native mariners. At the close of the [afternoon] service, one of the old and rich sea-captains remarked, as he came out from the church, 'the Doctor has given us a grand sermon, and he has preached all the jack-knives out of the sailors' pockets.' On returning to my father's house and laying out the collection on the parlor table, there was gold, silver and copper, and not a few jack-knives. The sailors had little else to give. . . . I know not now the amount of the collection, and only know that such men as William Bartlett, Moses Brown [and others] contributed something besides jack-knives. And this, the first collection in the United States for foreign missions, was taken up in the North Church in Newburyport, where, by my father's hands, I was baptized." *

Interest in the American Board may thus be said to have been a part of Dr. Spring's inheritance, and it continued and increased after he became pastor of the Brick Church. In 1820 he published a life of Samuel J. Mills, one of the participants in the historic "Haystack Prayer Meeting" † in Williamstown, from which the whole foreign missionary movement

---

* "Life and Times," Vol. I, pp. 279 f.

† It is interesting that, according to Dr. Spring's own statement, he was the first to make known the story of this meeting, in the book referred to in the text. For this reason it may be worth while to give his description of it in full. "He [Mills] led them out [two or three of his more intimate fellow-students] into a meadow, at a distance from the college, to a retirement probably familiar to himself, though little exposed to observation or liable to be approached, where, by the side of a large stack of hay, he devoted the day to prayer and fasting, and familiar conversation on this new and interesting theme [of foreign missions]; when, much to his sur-

in America started, and one of those who presented themselves for service at the Bradford meeting. In 1824, Dr. Spring was chosen one of the corporate members of the American Board, and he and his church were its faithful friends and supporters through a long series of years.

It has been already stated that, in accordance with the organized system of benevolences inaugurated in the Brick Church in 1838, the American Board was the organization appointed to receive the church's foreign missionary offering. This is especially interesting because the Presbyterian Church had formed a Board of Foreign Missions of its own in the preceding year, whereas the American Board was at that time interdenominational.

It is natural for us to wish that in both their home and foreign missionary work the Christian churches of America might have continued to work together, instead of starting independent and, in some cases, rival organizations. But apparently the times were not propitious. Men of differing views within the national organizations seemed more and more inclined to come into open conflict, and if this could not be avoided in any other way, it was better, as even those who were themselves most liberal agreed,

---

prise and gratification, he found that the Spirit of God had been enkindling in their bosoms the flame which had been so long burning in his own. The reader will not be surprised to learn that, from this hour, this endeared retreat was often made solemn by the presence, and hallowed by the piety, of these dear young men. . . . The operations and existence of this Society were unknown to the rest of the college, and have remained concealed by a veil which has never been removed till now. Though some of this little company yet remain on earth, I am forbidden by very sacred ties to lisp any other than the name of Samuel J. Mills." "Life of Samuel J. Mills," by Gardiner Spring (N. Y., 1820), pp. 29 f.

to create separate societies, which might provide congenial opportunity for all sorts of Christians without danger of internal contention.* Accordingly the different denominations proceeded to create mission boards of their own.

When a distinctively Presbyterian Board had been thus formed, it was natural, indeed almost inevitable, that Presbyterian churches should sooner or later rally to the support of their own organization. In home missions this had happened comparatively early. In the Brick Church's benevolent system of 1838 the American Home Missionary Society, which the church had itself helped to found ten years before, had no place. Instead, the allegiance of the church was pledged to the Board of Domestic Missions of the Presbyterian General Assembly.

The church and its pastor had been criticised in some quarters for this change of front, especially as they had always been forward to urge a liberal and

* The following extract from an act of the Presbyterian General Assembly in 1840 throws further light upon this subject. "The relation in which we stand to other denominations furnishes another reason why we should consolidate our strength and foster our own institutions. It is obviously for the interest of the evangelical churches in our country that they should preserve a mutually good understanding with each other. Perhaps the best way to secure this is for each to act in its own appropriate sphere, the different denominations uniting together only in those plans and organizations which require no sacrifice of their distinctive principles. Our sister churches are, it is well known, actively engaged in fortifying their respective positions and extending their boundaries. We are so far from complaining of this, that we commend them for their fidelity to their principles; and in so far as they are propagating the truth, we bid them Godspeed. But we urge their activity as a motive why we also should be up and doing. If it becomes them to be active, it becomes us much more. For they are imbued with a denominational feeling of long standing and mighty energy; among us this feeling is in its infancy." "Assembly Digest," p. 313.

comprehensive attitude toward all the large interests of Christianity. There is little doubt, however, that their action was made necessary by the conditions then existing. In 1837, the American Home Missionary Society had come under the control of men who represented that New Haven Theology which influenced the New School Presbyterians, and led, first to the Exscinding Acts, and then to the New School secession. One of the acts of the General Assembly, in the course of this unhappy development, was to declare its belief that the American Home Missionary Society had been conducted by such methods as were "exceedingly injurious to the peace and purity of the Presbyterian Church," and in particular, that some of its managers designed, if possible, to "break down" the Presbyterian Board, and to "introduce and propagate opinions at war with the standards" of Presbyterianism. It was, therefore, recommended that the Society should cease to operate in Presbyterian churches.* We can hardly be surprised that under such circumstances the Brick Church, which, however tolerant toward others, was itself firmly convinced of the truth of the Old School views, should feel compelled to transfer its allegiance to the Presbyterian Board of Domestic Missions.

In relation to foreign missions the change from national to denominational allegiance was deferred for some years longer, and was less abruptly made. From 1839 small sums, from five to fifteen per cent. of the whole foreign missionary offering of the Brick Church, were given to the Presbyterian Board, probably by the expressed desire of the givers. In 1842,

* "Assembly Digest," pp. 754, 757.

the Presbytery having urged the churches to do as much as they felt they could to strengthen their own organization, the Brick Church session declined to do more than regularize the special designation of offerings for that purpose. Undesignated offerings were still to go to the American Board. But in the next year, pressure no doubt continuing, it was ordered that the undesignated money for foreign missions be equally divided between the two societies. Not until several years later did the American Board cease altogether to be one of the stated beneficiaries of the Brick Church.

As we look back over the forty years whose history has now been completed, it is hardly necessary to call attention to the great changes in benevolence, and, indeed, in every department of the church life, that these years had witnessed. At the beginning the church was comparatively weak, unformed in method, confined to a rather narrow programme of Christian work. From this it had grown to be a strong, efficient, and highly influential organization, active in every important movement, sharing liberally in the growing work of the Church at large, and itself notable for the type of Christian character and conduct which it had succeeded in creating in its members.

Perhaps it was well that such a church was not permitted to rest on its laurels. At about the time which we have now reached it was called upon to face a new and serious difficulty, which threatened almost to cause its overthrow. What this was, and how it was met and conquered, the next chapter will show.

CHAPTER XV

THE LAST YEARS ON BEEKMAN STREET:
1850–1856

"Had any one told me twenty years ago that I should live to see [this church] abandoned as a place of religious worship, I should have thought him a romancer, if not a madman; yet the hour of abandonment has come."—GARDINER SPRING, 1856, "The Brick Church Memorial," p. 35.

"Lord, I have loved the habitation of thy house, and the place where thine honor dwelleth."—*Psalm* 26 : 8.

SEVERAL allusions have already been made to the great changes that had taken place in the neighborhood of the Brick Church. The truth was that during the eighty-odd years from the building of the church to the middle of the nineteenth century, the relation of the site on Beekman Street to the rest of New York had been completely reversed. In 1768 the church was at the extreme north end of the city; almost all the residence quarter lay southward toward the Battery. In 1850, on the other hand, so greatly had New York grown, that the church found itself practically at the extreme south end of the city; the homes of the people lay almost all to the north of it. The change from residence to business was not yet complete, for hotels and boarding-houses were still to be found in that vicinity in considerable numbers, but the private houses had moved away northward and they had taken the congregation of the Brick Church with them.

251

The difficulties produced by this state of things will readily be perceived. In order to carry on the work and worship of a church, it is necessary that the members should come together at frequent intervals in the church building, and it is desirable that they should be known to one another, so that they may work together in a friendly and cordial spirit; but when they have moved to a distance from the church, and, not improbably, at the same time have moved in different directions, these desired conditions are very difficult of attainment.

It will surprise most people to learn that the Brick Church had at least begun to experience this supposedly modern difficulty more than twenty years before 1850, long before one would suppose the city large enough to make even the greatest distances in it a very serious obstacle to social intercourse or church attendance. It will be necessary for us to turn back thus far in the narrative and to trace through the interval the development of these conditions and their effect upon the church's life and the church's policy. We will begin for this purpose with the year 1828. None of the Brick Church people were then living above Fourth Street,* and yet the preface of the little church catalogue, issued in that year, remarks that

---

* It will, perhaps, be interesting to note the addresses of the officers of the church at this time (as given in the catalogue of 1833):

ELDERS.—Rensselaer Havens, Lafayette Place; William Whitlock, 80 Franklin Street; John Adams, 144 Thompson Street; Alfred de Forest, 26 Bond Street; Horace Holden, 34 Beekman Street; Moses Allen, 113 Hudson Street; Silas Holmes, 8 College Place; Jasper Corning, 60 Walker Street; Abner L. Ely, 394 Pearl Street.

DEACONS.—William Couch, 50 Bleecker Street; John McComb, 193 Fourth Street; John C. Halsey, 189 Water Street; Daniel Oakley, Jamaica, L. I.; Shepherd Knapp, 76 Beekman Street; Elijah Mead, 48 Cliff Street; Nichol H. Deering, 110 Grand Street.

"the great obstacles to a personal acquaintance and familiar intercourse among Christians, in a city like this, are their wide dispersion, the continual change in their places of residence, and the consequent difficulty of ascertaining where they reside from year to year." Indeed the catalogue itself, which contained chiefly a list of the names and addresses of the congregation, was issued with the express hope that it might in a measure counteract these tendencies of the time, and lead to the cultivation once more of "that spirit of mutual intercourse which has in former years been so productive of good to this people."

Apparently, in 1828, the members still managed to attend the church services with regularity, but a little more than ten years later the session felt called upon to prepare a special circular, of which 250 copies were printed, expressing to delinquent members the concern with which the session had observed their "habitual absence from the public worship of God" in the church of which they were members. The cause of this, the circular says, has no doubt been in large measure "the distance of [their] residence from the House of God," although the session is constrained to attribute it in part to a blameworthy neglect of duty also. "Exemplary churches," the elders pointedly add, "are composed not of members whose *names* simply are upon their records." If this was the state of things among the grown-up people, it was no wonder that at this same time, as was related in a former chapter, the children were similarly affected, and that the Sunday-school had diminished in numbers as a result of "the widely scattered condition of the congregation and the great distance of many families from the place of instruction."

In view of such real difficulties as these, the question began to be asked whether the Brick Church would not be forced to move, and already various rumors were current concerning its probable new quarters and its successor on the site at Beekman Street. A New York writer in 1839, informs us, for instance, that "for a year or two past there has been some talk of removing the Brick Meeting House to make room for a post-office building. But I believe," says he, "that the danger is now past, and the venerable edifice will still continue to grace our city, and serve for many years to come as a temple for the worship of the Most High." *

The rumors here referred to were not altogether without foundation. At least, it was certain that the removal of the church had been seriously considered, and indeed, all but accomplished. The initiative in the matter had come from the city. In February, 1836, the chairman of "the Committee on Lands and Places, of the Board of Assistant Aldermen" had written officially to ascertain whether the trustees of the Brick Church would be willing to surrender to the Corporation of the city "the triangular piece of ground now in their possession on Nassau, Beekman, and Chatham Streets leased from the Corporation," and, if so, what sum of money they would be willing to accept by way of compensation.

The trustees, even at that early date, regarded the matter with sufficient favor to name a figure,

* "Familiar Conversations on the History of the Evangelical Churches of N. Y.," by R. Carter, 1839, pp. 176 f.

$150,000, and even when the Corporation replied to this, offering $20,000 less, the trustees determined to bring the matter before the pew-holders, in order to gain their necessary consent. The pew-holders, however, by the smallest possible majority rejected the proposition. The vote stood fifty-one to fifty. It was thought that they might view the matter differently if the compensation were held at the trustees' original figure, but when, four days later this also was put to the vote, it met with a still more decisive defeat, sixty-one noes against forty-nine ayes.

It would appear as though the incident had now been closed, but evidently a good deal of private argument had been indulged in, and in this manner a large number of converts made, for another meeting of the pew-holders was held after a month's time, and at it the former action was reversed. In the preamble to the resolutions then adopted the objections to the Beekman Street site were again succinctly stated. "From the residence of a large portion of the families of the congregation at a distance from their present place of worship," this preamble said, "and the increasing changes of residence into the upper parts of the city, the present site of the church is deemed less promotive of the interest of religion than one which may be selected." Moreover, "the contemplated improvement of streets * in the vicinity will render the place less quiet than it is, and will be accompanied with heavy expenses." On these grounds the pew-

* The property had already suffered from the improvement of streets, the widening of Beekman Street in 1831, and of Spruce Street (affecting the north end of the lot) in 1834. The assessment in the one case was $750, in the other $2,000.

holders voted to relinquish the property for $150,000. But now, when, apparently, this difficult step, from which many shrank, no doubt even some of those who voted for it, had been irrevocably taken, one word reduced the whole scheme to ruin. The Chancellor of the city, whose order was necessary to the completing of the transaction, refused to give it, "on the grounds both of law and expediency." As a consequence the Board of Aldermen withdrew from the negotiations, and the trustees necessarily allowed the matter to drop.

All this occurred, it will be remembered, before 1838. Ten years now passed, during which the difficulties perceptibly increased. The officers of the church realized more and more that the removal from Beekman Street was becoming a matter of the utmost importance. Something must be done before the whole organization should be imperilled. It was true that, as yet, though the conditions were highly inconvenient and calculated to create alarm for the future, the church was in a prosperous condition, as the preceding chapters have abundantly shown. If only the Beekman Street site could by some means be exchanged for another before the tide turned, the church might yet be carried through the crisis without any real loss.

Toward the close of 1847, the trustees themselves reopened negotiations. They sent a formal address to the Common Council requesting that body either to buy the church's interest in the property in question, or for a consideration to remove all restrictions from it, and transfer to the church "all the right, title, and interest of the Corporation of the City of New

York therein." This communication, however, produced no effect.*

In May, 1850, the trustees, who must by this time have been a good deal troubled by the situation, again endeavored, without success, to bring the Common Council to some agreement. But even had they succeeded, they would now have been too late to bring the church through unscathed, for in this year of 1850, which we have already marked in preceding chapters as a turning-point in the church's history, the difficulties under which the church was laboring had become acute. The church had visibly begun to lose ground, and when this process had once set in there was no telling how rapidly it would advance.

Of course the strongest and most valued friends of the church stood by her. She had no lack of wise and faithful men to fill her offices. Her treasury was well sustained by a generous constituency, which more than made up for any falling off in the pew-rents. Indeed, it will be remembered that in this very year of 1850, the treasurer had the pleasure, for the first time in a long period, of announcing a balance, and

* It is a rather amusing circumstance that at the same time when these deeply important matters were the subject of correspondence between the church and the city government, the following somewhat insignificant matter was also thought worthy of being carried direct to the attention of the city's Executive: "Repeated complaints having been made to the board of trustees that the noise by collections of boys in the neighborhood of the chapel is a very serious annoyance and frequently an interruption to the religious meetings held therein; therefore, Resolved, That a communication be addressed to his Honor the Mayor, desiring his interference in the premises and the urgent request that he may adopt suitable measures effectually to remedy the evils complained of." Had the city fathers permitted themselves to be guided by their sense of humor, they might have sent word to the Brick Church trustees, "We regret our inability to buy your church site or remove the restriction in your title, but, on the other hand, we will see that the 'collections of boys' are 'effectually' dealt with."

this comfortable state of things, so far as finances were concerned, continued even for two years longer. The first danger, then, did not lie in this direction. Rather it was the spiritual life of the church that was primarily imperilled. Its practical work was being curtailed, its habits of religious observance were being weakened, its accustomed meetings and services, upon which its influence was so much dependent, were being neglected more and more.

The first direct effect was felt in the week-day services. For some time it had been difficult to maintain them, but now they were apparently about to die out altogether. Judging by the ominous silence in regard to it for the next six or eight years, the prayer-meeting did actually expire at this time; but an attempt was made to save the Thursday evening lecture by holding it in quarters uptown, secured for this purpose. "Hope Chapel," a building erected not long before, on Broadway nearly opposite Waverly Place,* was accordingly hired.†

Three years later, in 1853, the session proposed that the second Sunday service also should be held uptown, a still more radical suggestion. We do not know that it was ever carried out, but if not, it is probable that the service was at once abandoned altogether, for we know that a little later this had occurred. Indeed, there were periods, possibly of

---

* It was built by certain members of the Stanton Street Church who took their letters and organized a church of their own in 1846. Mr. Bellamy became their pastor. It became later the Broadway Baptist Church. "A History of the Churches of All Denominations in N. Y.," by J. Greenleaf (N. Y.,1850), p. 412.

† The precise date on which this was determined was October 17th, 1849, but for the convenience of the round number, 1850 has been used in the text to date the "turning-point."

a year at a time, when even the Thursday evening lecture was not held, in Hope Chapel or elsewhere; and finally in May, 1856, Dr. Spring, in showing how utterly impossible the condition of things had become, tells us that the weekly lecture, the prayer-meeting, and the Sunday-school had all perforce been discontinued, while it was with no small difficulty that a single service was maintained on the Lord's Day. That the Brick Church, which a few years before had been one of the most prosperous and influential churches in the city, should be reduced to this state, was an unhappy, and, to those who loved it, a heart-breaking fact.

But meantime the officers had not been idle. On the contrary, as conditions grew worse and worse, in the years between 1850 and 1856, they redoubled their efforts to liberate the church from the position in which it was manifestly starving to death. Baffled as they had been in every attempt to dispose of their rights in the Beekman Street lot, they proposed in 1852, to abandon that endeavor, but at the same time held to their purpose "to procure or build another church edifice in the upper part of the city, to be occupied as an associated or colleague church, with their present establishment." Where the money was to come from for this costly enterprise is nowhere explained, and it was probably this financial difficulty that caused the matter to be tabled from meeting to meeting without any progress toward a definite result. At any rate, the scheme was at length abandoned, and the trustees once more, with what discouragement we can well imagine, were forced back upon the attempt to effect a sale.

It may be well at this point to refresh the reader's memory in regard to the conditions which complicated this endeavor, and had thus far thwarted it. To state the matter in a sentence, the church did not own its property. It merely held it on a perpetual lease, and, moreover, with the restriction that it must never be converted to "private, secular uses." It is true that, carefully interpreted, these words did not imply the prohibition of every use that was *either* private *or* secular, but only such use as was *both* private *and* secular; that is, it was no doubt allowable to put the property to a use which was secular but not private, such as a custom-house or an armory, or to a use which was private but not secular, such as a church or a cemetery. It was only forbidden to put it to a use which was both private and secular, such as a dwelling-house or a dry-goods store. From this interpretation there was some gain, and yet not very much, when it came to making a sale; for though some other church or the federal or State Government, if one of them acquired the Brick Church's rights in the property, could use it for some of the purposes mentioned above, they would not be very much inclined to acquire land which was so strictly conditioned, and which would, therefore, be transferred again with great difficulty, if that should ever become desirable. Furthermore, it was questionable whether the church, acting by itself, had the power to transfer its rights at all.

At one time, as has been described in an earlier chapter,* the Corporation of the city had shown a certain disposition to modify the restrictive terms of

* See pp. 138–140.

the original grant. In 1831, when the new chapel was being built, permission had been given to rent for ordinary business purposes "two smaller rooms fronting toward Chatham Street," "without affecting the validity of the grant or lease." In 1835 the Corporation granted still greater liberty, for they then so modified the terms of the grant "as to authorize and permit the said church, from time to time and at all times during the continuance of the said lease, to rent so much and such parts of the new edifice erected on the rear of said church as may not be required for religious purposes." From this the church derived decided benefit, in that the rental of its rooms added materially to its income; but it is evident that nothing in these modifications of the grant concerning the use of the chapel made a sale of the entire property any more easy.

To sum the whole matter up, it appeared that in the ordinary course of affairs there were but two ways open by which the church could proceed. Either it must obtain from the city, for an equitable consideration, a complete removal of all restrictions, so that the property could be sold to any one for any purpose whatsoever, or else the city itself must be induced to take the property and pay the church the value of the church's rights. In 1847, as we have seen, an attempt had been made to accomplish either one of these two things, but without success. This was still the situation of affairs in 1853.

But we have as yet spoken of only one set of difficulties by which a sale was prevented. There were also other difficulties of a different sort. The church had been in the habit of selling its pews from time to time to individuals. It had also sold in like manner certain burial vaults in the churchyard. The purchasers in each of these cases had thus acquired certain rights in the property and must be reckoned with if the property should be alienated. In regard to the vault-owners, it was at first proposed to satisfy them by the promise of a reasonable indemnity, but finally, before the end of the negotiation which we are about to study, it was deemed wise for the church to buy back the vaults and so remove this complication altogether. It so happened that a second widening of Beekman Street just at this time, which forced the removal of a number of vaults in any case, aided the church materially in this undertaking.*

The rights of the pew-owners could not be dealt with in this way. The sum required would have been very considerable and, moreover, they themselves did not wish to sell. They preferred, if the church moved, to have their rights transferred to pews in the new building. Meantime, as we have seen, it was considered necessary to gain their consent before any sale of the property could be consummated; and they had a will of their own, which they occasionally asserted in opposition to the measures proposed by the trustees. Happily, however, as time went on, practically all of them were convinced that the change of location was necessary. In February, 1853, it was found, after a careful inquiry, that there was only

---

* The city officials in 1853 claimed that the opposition of the vault-owners to a sale of the property had up to that time been not only one, but the chief obstacle to an agreement. This, however, is extremely unlikely.

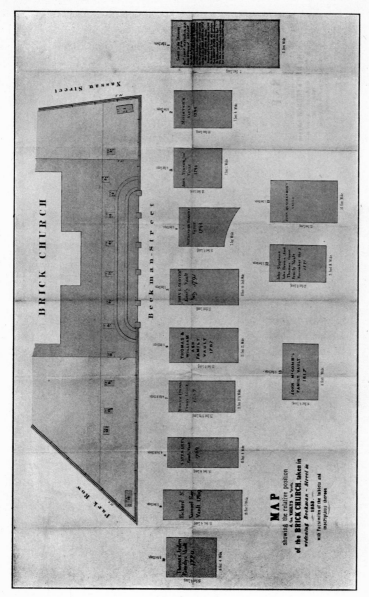

PLAN OF BURIAL VAULTS ON BEEKMAN STREET

one pew-owner who expressed decided opposition to the measure.*

At the same date all nine trustees and nine members of the session, including the pastor, put themselves on record as being of the opinion that the change must be made, and the remaining two elders declared that they would at least offer no opposition. Backed by this almost unanimous approval, the board of trustees took an entirely new step; they made application to the Supreme Court for an order authorizing the Brick Church to dispose of its property "and to execute to the purchaser or purchasers good and sufficient conveyances therefor."

In this the trustees scored their first real success. The order was issued on February 15th, 1853.† Exactly what power it gave must be thoroughly understood. It did not alter in any way the original restriction upon the property, that it should not be converted to private, secular uses, but it authorized the Corporation of the Brick Church "to sell and convey all their church property, lands, and tenements, situate in the Second Ward of the City of New York . . . either at public or private sale, subject to the conditions and restrictions contained in the grant." That is, it was now declared that, if the church could find a purchaser, able and willing to use the property for other than private, secular uses, a legal sale could be made without any permission or coöperation of the city. On the other hand, a new restriction was added. The proceeds of the sale must be applied "to the

* Twenty-one others did not favor it, but agreed not to oppose, and of five the opinion was not known, they being absent from the city. See Appendix S, p. 537.

† See Appendix X, p. 547.

purchase of other lands in said city and to the erection of a new church edifice thereon." This, of course, was an entirely just provision.*

Greatly encouraged by this evidence that the tide had at length turned, and assured of their position in a degree that had not before been possible, the trustees approached once more the authorities of the city. They had several interviews with the Commissioners of the Sinking Fund, and made the offer to give $15,000 to the city for a removal of all restrictions. This, however, "was considered a sum too trifling." The Commissioners called attention to the facts, that for eighty years the church had been exempt from taxation and had enjoyed freely the city's protection. Moreover, the value of its property had been greatly increased by many improvements which had involved the city in a heavy debt and burdensome taxation. It was urged that the trustees should, in view of these facts, concede something to the public benefit, "and it is believed," say the Commissioners in their report to the Common Council, "that these considerations have had their influence in bringing the trustees up from their proposition of $15,000," to the acceptance of the plan which was finally agreed upon.

By this it was proposed that the property be put up at auction, the minimum price being fixed at $225,000, and that of the proceeds, twenty-five per cent. should go to the city, the rest to the church. By this arrangement the city would receive at least $56,250, and the church at least $168,750. It was thought, however, by the representatives both of the

* For this and other details to follow see "Board of Aldermen, Document No. 37" (1854).

city and of the church, that the property would bring at least $250,000, and probably much more.

This plan in its entirety was accepted by the trustees on April 6th, 1853,* who even appointed a committee to confer regarding the "time, the terms, and conditions of site," but although the Commissioners of the Sinking Fund and afterward the Committee on Finance of the Board of Aldermen reported favorably, no final action was taken by the city at this time. The trustees, disgusted by the delay, employed legal counsel to aid them, and even secured opinions on the subject from Judge Bronson and Charles O'Connor. They attacked the city authorities through the Comptroller † and through the Mayor.‡ They even considered § "the expediency of instituting legal proceedings against the city Corporation, with a view to ascertain what the rights of this church are under its grant." But, although they were apparently led to believe that the city would at some time act favorably upon the matter, no action could be secured until 1856.

This tedious interval, however, had not all been spent by the trustees in a state of discouragement. At one point in it they had strong reason to believe that they had the whole matter in their own hands, that, armed with the Supreme Court's order, they might accomplish a sale without any coöperation of the city authorities at all. The circumstances were

---

* Their committee, in recommending this, gave as one reason "the present peculiar condition of the city government." Politics in New York at this time were in a somewhat confused state. Corruption had already infected many lower officials. Two years later the notorious Fernando Wood was elected Mayor.

† In February, 1854. ‡ In January, 1855. § In August, 1855.

these. In September, 1854, the agents of the United States "advertised for proposals for the purchase of a site for a post-office and for courts, etc.," in the city of New York. Here was the very chance that the church needed,* and for which it had not even dared to hope. For the purposes here expressed the church had full legal right to sell, and the United States Government to buy and use, the property on Beekman Street, without the aid or consent of any other party whatsoever.

The trustees very quietly went to work, considering the matter from every point of view, and finally sending a committee twice to Washington to confer with the proper officials there. From the second of these two visits the committee returned, feeling that the prospect of a sale was favorable. There was, indeed, a difficulty (was there not always a difficulty in this struggle to dispose of the church's "angular lot"?). Congress had so left the matter, that it was a question whether the President could act without further sanction. Still Mr. Pierce, who was at that time the nation's Chief Executive, and with whom the church's committee had conferred, gave them the impression that he considered himself to have the necessary authority. The Secretary of the Interior, the Hon. Robert McClelland, had also received the church's proposition in a friendly way; and indeed the offer was, in the trustees' opinion, so highly advantageous to the Government, that they expected every effort would be made to accept it.

They had offered the property at $300,000, which

* For a curious prophecy of this proposal fifteen years before, see above p. 254.

was one-fourth less than what would be the value, it was said, were there no restrictions, the reduction being made because of the government's being ready to use the land for purposes not prohibited by the original grant, so that the city need not be consulted and the whole sum would go to the church. If, moreover, the valuation was thought to be too high they would willingly submit that matter to any competent judges for revision. They asked for a reply within twenty days and also "that unless accepted and the contract signed, the proposal shall not be made known to any but the gentlemen connected with the service of the United States, whose interference may be deemed useful to the government."

But the reader knows, of course, that the New York Post-Office was never built on the church's land. Within the twenty days, on May 22d, 1855, word was received "that the President, after mature reflection, had concluded that it would be of doubtful propriety to take any action in the matter of the purchase of the Brick Church property without further sanction of Congress."

This, it is a pleasure to state, was the last of the many disappointments which these patient church officers were called upon to endure. At the very meeting when the declination was received from Washington, two applications for the purchase of the property were received from other quarters. These were conditioned, no doubt, upon that coöperation of the city which had been so long delayed; but still there was distinct encouragement in the knowledge that the property was in active demand, and that pressure would now be exerted, not only by the sellers, but by prospective buyers, to have the matter speedily settled. The trustees had, it is true, felt all along that their property possessed an assured value, which was bound to be realized in time—they had even trusted so far in this assurance as to open negotiations already for new land uptown, as we shall see in the next chapter—but the result would be doubly and trebly welcome if it could come at once.

In January, 1856, they received a definite offer of $175,000, for their rights in the property, but they stood out for $200,000. And three months later, this course was justified, when their figure was definitely accepted by Frederick P. James, Edward B. Wesley, and Henry Keep, who became the purchasers, for the sum named above, of all the rights of the Brick Church in the property which it had occupied for nearly ninety years.*

* The contract was signed on April 11th, and the deed delivered a month later. The church was given "the right to remove from the church edifice the bell and furniture and fixtures in the church" and also "the right to remove at their own cost the remains of the dead contained in the vaults and in said ground." The church was to receive the award for damages for the widening of Beekman Street; but agreed to pay the assessment for the same, and also to settle the claims of all vault-owners who should not have been previously bought out. In the process of removing the dead, as here provided for, there arose the "novel and interesting question, Who is legally entitled to the custody of the dead?" In order to settle this point a friendly suit was instituted. The remains of one Moses Sherwood (identified "by the ribbon, by which his hair was tied in a queue, found lying with his skull and bones") were claimed by his daughter, although the grave in which he had been buried was now the property of the church. The trustees raised no objection, but desired that the rights in the matter should be legally determined. They received with pleasure the decision of Judge Davies, in committing the dead exclusively to the next of kin, and thanked both the Judge and Samuel B. Ruggles, Esq., who had "vindicated the rights of the dead," for the achievement of a result so distinctly in accord with "Christian sentiment, taste and feeling." See "An Examination of the Law of Burial," by S. B. Ruggles.

This sale was consummated, "subject to the proposal made by the church to the Corporation to sell said property at auction," for this proposal had finally been accepted by the city, and the auction did actually take place on Wednesday, May 14th, at twelve o'clock noon, at the Merchants' Exchange. In this the church, of course, was not directly interested. It had already sold its rights and received the payment therefor in full. Yet the trustees could not but regard with interest the event which, in accordance with the city's agreement, would once and forever wipe out those words "private, secular uses," which had so long chained the Brick Church, against its judgment, to its downtown site.

When the auction took place, and the property was sold for $270,000, it was found that Messrs. James, Wesley, and Keep had bought it in.* It was reported that the only bidder against them was Mr. A. T. Stewart. As is well known, upon the ground in question were afterward erected the Potter and Times office buildings.

After following the history of the church through these trying years, the reader will certainly agree that only a very strong organization, sustained by devoted members, could have withstood the effects of such a prolonged period of discouragement and increasingly adverse conditions. How much reserve strength the church possessed, and how soon that strength manifested itself in the reëstablishment of the old work in a new field, as soon as that was possible, and also in the establishment of new work, even before the move uptown had

---

* The property therefore cost them $267,500.

been fully accomplished, will be told in the next chapter.

It is but fair to say that a large element in this ability of the church to outlive such a long wandering in the wilderness was the devotion of all the people to their now venerable pastor. A very convincing evidence of this, and at the same time, a notable proof of the fact that the adverse conditions of the years between 1850 and 1856 had not exhausted the financial resources of the congregation, are supplied by the fact that in June, 1854, in the very midst of the period of discouragement, Dr. Spring's salary was increased to $5,000.* In voting this, the trustees expressed some contrition that for a series of years their pastor had been receiving a salary "below the average amount paid to many of the clergymen of this city." But that this delay had been due to no lack of appreciation, their act at this difficult juncture, and perhaps still more the words of unbounded confidence and love by which it was accompanied,† proved beyond any doubt.

* From $3,250. *Cf.* p. 144.

† The letter which conveyed the notice of the increase of salary was as follows:

NEW YORK, *June* 13th, 1854.

REV. DR. SPRING:—

DEAR SIR: The undersigned have been appointed a committee to communicate to you the accompanying resolutions, passed unanimously at a meeting of the congregation, and subsequently in like manner ratified and confirmed by the board of trustees.

It affords us great pleasure to discharge this duty, and it is only embittered with the regret that this act of justice has been so long delayed, much of which delay may be chargeable to our own negligence or forgetfulness, not to use a harsher name.

It is gratifying to be able to state that on this occasion but one sentiment pervaded the entire meeting; not the slightest dissent was manifested in thought, word, or deed. It was the spontaneous expression of grateful feelings from full and thankful hearts.

On Sunday May 25th, 1856, the Brick Church congregation met for the last time in their old downtown church. We need not be told that, in however remote a part of the city they might then be living, they found the distance no bar to their attending on that memorable and affecting occasion. We are even sure that many who had transferred their membership to other churches, or had even moved

For almost half a century you have occupied the same post and the same sphere of labor and of duty. Some of us have sat under your ministry for more than forty years, and during that long period can bear testimony to your untiring industry, your unbending integrity in the exhibition of gospel truth amid conflicts and parties, and your entire devotion to the appropriate duties of the ministry.

We feel, too, that it is neither flattery to you, nor vain boasting in us, but a thankful expression of gratitude to God, to say that yours has not been an unprofitable ministry, nor [has] your influence been confined to this church. We can see traces of your faithful preaching, marked by the divine Spirit, not only in our city and vicinity, but in almost every State of this vast republic; and we expect, if we are ever so happy as to arrive at our Father's house on high, to meet multitudes there, of those whom neither we nor you have known in the flesh, brought home to glory through your instrumentality.

It is a source of delightful reflection to us that in the early evening of your days, after so long a ministry among us, you retain the undiminished confidence and affection of your whole people, an affection as warm and fresh as crowned the day when first you devoted your youthful prime in this church to Christ and his cause.

Our beloved Pastor, these expressions but feebly represent our own sincere emotions. We would humbly commend you to the Great Head of the Church, and earnestly pray that he may preserve you yet for many years to come, to preach the everlasting gospel to this people; that he may make you perfect, stablish, strengthen, settle you; and finally, when our warfare is accomplished, that he may receive you and us to that blessed communion where our love shall be forever perfect, and our joy forever full.

Respectfully and affectionately,

HORACE HOLDEN,
SAMUEL MARSH,
MOSES ALLEN,   } *Committee.*
IRA BLISS,
GUY RICHARDS.

Quoted from "Br. Ch. Mem.," p. 32, note.

out of New York, were found in the pews that day, their hearts full of old memories which made it good to be there.*

We may leave it to Dr. Spring himself to express the emotions which characterized that last meeting in the familiar place, and to interpret its significance. The following extracts from the farewell sermon which he that day delivered † will fitly bring this chapter to its conclusion.

"The present service," he began, "closes the public worship of God in an edifice where it has been enjoyed for eighty-eight years. For whatever purposes this hallowed ground may be hereafter employed, experience has convinced us that it is no longer a fit place for religious worship. We have admitted this conviction reluctantly; we have resisted it too long. It is now forced upon us by considerations which we have no doubt God approves, and the best interests of his kingdom demand.

"With the future," he continues, "we have less to do on the present occasion, than the past"; and with this introduction he proceeds to tell briefly that history which has already been told with greater fulness in the preceding pages of the present volume, including an account of the discouragements and losses of the last six years. One detail only needs to be added at this point. "The question has been asked," says Dr. Spring, "Why not leave this church as a church for strangers, and for the hotels and boarding-houses in this part of the city? To this we have this conclu-

* When the building was torn down many were seen rescuing "bricks" from the ruin, and one of these, preserved by Miss Sarah Casper, now of Fort Lee, N. J., is to-day among the church's relics.

† The text was Psalm 48 : 9–14.

sive answer, We ourselves have proposed to do so. At a meeting of the Presbytery of New York I myself made the proposition to the churches, that this congregation would subscribe $50,000, for that purpose, on condition that the other congregations would unite in raising the balance of $150,000. The Presbytery received the proposal with favor, and appointed a committee to take it into consideration. That committee reported against the proposed arrangement, and the Presbytery and the congregations dropped the subject.

"And now," says Dr. Spring, after he has completed his historical survey, "in this brief review, what shall we say? One thought forces itself upon your minds and my own. It relates to a theme on which I have so often dwelt in this sacred desk: *The goodness of God*, how wonderful it is! The rising and setting sun proclaim it, and every star of the dark night. . . . Every sea, every lake and fountain, every river and stream and sparkling dew-drop, receive alike their riches and their beauty from this uncreated source. How much more richly and purely, then, does it flow here in the sanctuary, where all its streams are confluent, and from the mountain tops of Zion send gladness through the city of our God. . . .

"On an occasion like the present something is due to this ancient sanctuary. The speaker stands here for the last time; and you, beloved friends, meet for the last time in the consecrated place, where we have so often assembled for the worship of God. . . . We call upon you to witness, we call upon the sacred spirits of the departed to witness, we make our appeal to the walls of this hallowed edifice, if the truth of

God . . . has not been proclaimed from this pulpit.
This house has also been greatly endeared to us as
'the house of prayer,' as 'the house of prayer for all
people.' . . . This house has been our thankful resort in prosperity; in adversity it has been our refuge.
Here the aged and the young have come for the first
and the last time to commemorate the love of Christ
at his table. Here our children have been baptized,
and their children after them, and here we have wept
and prayed together as God has called them from
these earthly scenes. . . . I seem to stand to-day
amid generations that are past, so vividly does my
imagination people these seats with faces and forms
whose place now knows them no more.

"This house has also been the stranger's home. Of
this and of that man it shall one day be said, that 'he
was born here.' Many a wanderer from other lands,
and more from distant regions of our own broad territory, have here sought and made their peace with
God. 'We have thought of thy loving-kindness, O
God, in the midst of thy temple,' that 'we may tell it
to the generations following.' . . .

"But our work and our privileges in this house of
God here have an end. It is his voice which to-day
says to us, 'Arise ye, and depart hence, for this is not
your rest.' We have occupied it too long; and, although it has been for the benefit and enlargement of
other congregations, it has been not only to the diminution of our strength, but to the injury of our habits
as a people. . . .

"We have been a harmonious people for six and
forty years; and we are now harmonious in this great
and agitating question. . . . We bid [this house]

adieu, to follow the guidance of [God's] providence, and pitch our tabernacle under the pillar and the cloud. . . . Farewell, then, thou endeared house of God! Thou companion and friend of my youth, thou comforter of my later years, thou scene of toil and of repose, of apprehension and of hope, of sorrow and of joy, of man's infirmity and of God's omnipotent grace, farewell! *

"But not to thee, O thou that hearest prayer . . . do we say farewell. . . Even now, at this late, this last hour, from the bottom of our hearts do we say, 'If thy presence go not with us, carry us not up hence.' . . . Nor, my beloved people, is it to you that your pastor says farewell. These brick walls and this plastered ceiling, and these pillars and seats, do not constitute the Brick Presbyterian Church. Ye are these constituents, and 'ye are our glory and joy.' . . .

"These days of solicitude and agitation will soon be over. 'The root of Jesse' yet stands as an 'ensign to the people, and his rest shall be glorious.'

---

* In "Frank Leslie's Illustrated Newspaper," for May 10th, 1856, appeared pictures of both the exterior and interior of the church. The following is a part of the accompanying text: "It is probable that in the course of a few weeks the Old Brick Church in Beekman Street, known for so many years as 'Dr. Spring's' will be torn down to make way for 'modern improvements.' It is thus that one old landmark after another disappears, and the time is not far distant when 'old fogies' will not find a familiar wrinkle upon the entire face of New York. . . . Our engravings make any allusion to the architecture of the building and its interior unnecessary. Suffice it to say that, with all our wealth and extravagance, but little advance has been made upon the real beauty and picturesque effect of the old churches, built when New York had but little wealth, and was really but a country village. Embalmed in our columns, the antiquarian will, in future times, turn to them with pleasure, and learn what was the appearance of the Old Brick Church before it gave way to the wants of our ever-increasing population."

Only take diligent heed and *be very courageous* to do his will, to love the Lord your God, and to walk in his ways, and to keep his commandments, and to cleave unto him, and to serve him with all your heart and all your soul, and his presence and blessing shall be with you and yours for a great while to come. The Lord bless you and keep you; the Lord cause his face to shine upon you, and be gracious unto you; the Lord lift up his countenance upon you, and give you peace. His name be upon you and your children. Amen and Amen. And let all the people say, Amen." *

* "Br. Ch. Mem.," pp. 7–42.

CHAPTER XVI

THE MOVE TO MURRAY HILL: 1855–1858

"So David and all the house of Israel brought up the ark of the Lord with shouting, and with the sound of the trumpet. . . . And they brought in the ark of the Lord, and set it in his place, in the midst of the tabernacle that David had pitched for it."—2 *Samuel* 6 : 15, 17.

"We have lived to see the top stone of this edifice laid, and its doors open to us. We have nothing to ask in the external and material arrangements of this house. It is not a gorgeous edifice; it has no decorated walls and arches, and no splendid magnificence. Yet there are stability and comfort and tasteful architecture, which do honor to the genius and fidelity of those employed in projecting, erecting, and embellishing it. '*Strength* and *beauty* are in his sanctuary.'"—GARDINER SPRING, 1858, "The Brick Church Memorial," p. 71.

A PERIOD of fifty years in the life of a city does not seem very long, but when we realize the changes that have taken place in New York in the last half century, we cannot but realize that, counted by results, it may be a very long time indeed. It is, in truth, hard to picture to ourselves the city that existed on Manhattan Island in 1855, when the Brick Church first definitely began to look at new sites. One is almost inclined to doubt that Thirty-fourth Street, which to-day is fast becoming the centre of the retail shopping district, was then almost at the northern limit of the built-up part of the city, with open fields beyond, and indeed many unoccupied spaces below it; but such was, indeed, the fact.

An extract from some unpublished reminiscences of New York in the forties and fifties * will serve to

* By the author's mother.

277

introduce us to the conditions then existing in the neighborhood of the present Brick Church. In 1848, we are told, the last houses on Madison Avenue were just above Twenty-seventh Street. "A grove of trees was where the next block now is, and nothing obstructed the view from our windows, so that we could see as far as Hoboken. . . . I could roll my hoople before breakfast to the end of Madison Avenue, which stopped at Forty-second Street." One detail of the life of the city at that time I venture to add from the same source. It goes far toward showing how different conditions then were from those with which we are now familiar. "I walked generally to school and back. If I rode, it was by stage. They were white stages, filled with straw for your feet, and with cornucopias containing flowers painted on the sides. After a heavy fall of snow there would be stage-sleighs, and there was enough snow then to give us fine sleigh-rides. The traffic was nothing, compared to to-day. I remember that we knew generally to whom the private carriages belonged, usually from the coachman, who stopped long enough on the box in those days to impress his features on the rising generation." Street railways were, in certain parts of the city, beginning to make their appearance, but they were as yet very far from being the typical mode of conveyance. In 1856, as another writer tells us, "the slow stage still travelled its weary way along Wall Street and Broadway." *

The fashionable quarters of the city were then Broad Street, Washington Square, East Broadway, St. John's Park and Second Avenue, while Chelsea

* "Memorial Hist. of N. Y.," Vol. III, p. 447.

THE BRICK CHURCH ON MURRAY HILL

Taken in March, 1908

was regarded as a very select neighborhood.* Some "splendid ranges of private residences" † had been built on lower Fifth Avenue, and a very few, like outposts of the advancing city, had even reached as far north as Murray Hill. "The wealthy Dr. Townsend," for instance, had erected at the corner of Fifth Avenue and Thirty-fifth Street a mansion of "almost royal splendor," as contemporary observers described it. The curious public were admitted by ticket, we are told, the proceeds being devoted to the Five Points Mission.‡ A new fashion in domestic architecture, by the way, had just invaded New York at this time. Houses of red brick and built in the London style, such as were then to be seen on Broadway and may still be seen on the north side of Washington Square, were being replaced by the brownstone, high-stoop structures,§ which for many years became almost universal throughout the city, and which went far toward making New York, in the day of their ascendancy, one of the homeliest cities on the face of the globe.

This sketch of the conditions which existed, when the trustees of the Brick Church began to look for their new site, will help us to appreciate what it really meant for the church to "move uptown." We soon discover that in order to build for the future rather than for the fleeting present, the church proposed to move practically out into the country. This was certainly a bold plan, but no less certainly it was a profoundly wise one.

* The region about Ninth Avenue and Twentieth Street.
† "Putnam's Magazine," March, 1854.
‡ "Leslie's Hist. of Greater N. Y.," by Daniel Van Pelt, Vol. I, p. 344.
§ "Memorial Hist. of N. Y.," Vol. III, p. 447.

The trustees took their first definite step toward securing new land at the time when the sale of the old site to the United States Government still seemed a possibility. And, indeed, they almost bought, in April, 1855, a plot of ground on the south-east corner of Fifth Avenue and Thirtieth Street.* It was only the discovery of a possible defect in the title that prevented the purchase from being made.

No further steps were taken in this matter until April, 1856, when the old property had finally been sold. Then preparations were made to proceed at once. To a committee of two, consisting of Paul Spofford and Shepherd Knapp, the task was entrusted, and for their guidance it was formally voted that the site selected should be somewhere between Twenty-third and Forty-second streets, and between Sixth and Madison avenues. A week later the committee made its first recommendation. Of all the sites examined by them within the prescribed area they favored one on the north-east corner of Fifth Avenue and Thirty-sixth Street.† They also mentioned verbally that a piece of land on Twenty-third Street, belonging to Mr. Am s R. Eno, and held at $72,000, was available, but they did not recommend it.

The trustees, however, "after mature deliberation and discussion," decided upon Mr. Eno's land,‡ and the committee, although they were unconvinced, and although Mr. Knapp requested that "his decided

---

* It measured 96 feet on the avenue, by 175 on the side street. The price was $58,000.

† It contained eight city lots and was held at $60,000.

‡ It consisted of 100 feet "east of Mr. Arnold's house" on Twenty-third Street, and extending through to Twenty-fourth.

choice" of the Thirty-sixth Street site be noted in the minutes, consented to make the vote unanimous. A month later an irreconcilable difference as to certain conditions of the sale arose between Mr. Eno and the trustees, with the result that they ceased to negotiate. The majority of the board, however, still favored Twenty-third Street as the most suitable location for the church.

It is interesting that in spite of this expressed preference of the board, the committee on the new site, had so far the courage of their convictions as to report at the next meeting Murray Hill sites only; and what was more, they succeeded in bringing the majority to their views. Before they rose from this meeting the trustees had voted unanimously that the committee "be directed to purchase one of three plots of ground reported by the committee, and that the north-west corner of Thirty-seventh Street and Fifth Avenue have the preference, and the corner of Thirty-sixth Street and Fifth Avenue have the second preference, and the corner of Thirty-eighth Street and Fifth Avenue, west side, have the third preference." Six days later, on September 15th, 1856, the committee reported that the first choice had been actually bought * for $58,000. This, it will be observed, was $14,000, less than had been asked for the Twenty-third Street property.

The newly acquired land, upon which the present Brick Church was to be erected, measures ninety-eight feet, nine inches on Fifth Avenue and one hundred and forty-five feet on Thirty-seventh Street, and the purchase included "all the stone, brick, lime,

* From Mr. U. Hendricks.

and cement that are now on and in front of said lots."

The property, as this added clause suggests, had been previously occupied. In about 1845, Mr. Coventry Waddell, who, we are told, had held for a long time a confidential position in the State Department at Washington, had here built himself a residence of "yellowish gray" stucco with brownstone trimmings. It was in the Gothic style and was regarded as a handsome specimen of domestic architecture. The following account of it is taken from Lamb's "History of the City of New York." * Mr. Waddell's mansion "was a famous social centre, although at the period of its erection Fifth Avenue above Madison Square was little more than a common road, and the old farm fences were visible on all sides. . . . The place, when improved, was called a suburban villa; its grounds, beautified with taste, covered the whole square between Thirty-seventh and Thirty-eighth streets. . . . When Fifth Avenue was graded, the edifice was rendered still more imposing and picturesque by its elevated position." A writer in "Putnam's Monthly," March, 1854, gives a contemporary description: "It is remarkable for being enclosed in its own garden ground, as high as the original level of the island, and descends by sloping grass banks to the street. There is also a Gothic cottage-lodge on the north side of the garden, of which and of the whole ground, a fine view is obtained from the terrace of the Croton Reservoir." The house, we are also told, "was finished in a style of costly elegance, and a large conservatory and picture-gallery were among its

* Vol. II, pp. 756*f*.

attractions. From its broad marble hall a winding
staircase led to the tower, from which a charming
view was obtained of both the East and Hudson
rivers, the intervening semi-rural landscape, and the
approaching city. It was the scene of many notable
entertainments, Mrs. Waddell being a leader of
society." *

There is probably no district in New York to-day
whose character exactly corresponds with that of
Murray Hill in the years while the Brick Church was
building, 1856 to 1858. To-day one must travel out
into the more distant suburban towns in order to see
an entire community of the better sort coming into
existence all at one time, the homes and churches of
the well-to-do, with schools for their children, all going up together. Where, on the "frontier" of the
city itself, new regions are now suddenly developing
amid open fields, the buildings are usually of an inferior sort. The wealthy residents of New York in
our day have ceased to be pioneers. But in the
middle of the nineteenth century Murray Hill was
suddenly seized upon and developed by people of position and means, who there set about the transformation of a region of almost open country with scattered
suburban residences, into a district of city streets,
with costly houses built in solid blocks. Dr. Townsend's somewhat pretentious house, which had been
erected in 1855, and which stood two blocks below the
site of the church, has already been mentioned. In
1857 and 1858 houses were going up to the west of
the church site on Thirty-seventh Street and immediately north of it on the avenue. The building of

*Lamb's "History." See above.

the church itself was, of course, a most important factor in these operations, for it helped greatly to fix the character of the neighborhood and to attract as residents the most desirable class of people.

Even before the site for the church had been secured, the trustees had begun to consider in a general way, the plans for their new building, but when Thirty-seventh Street was finally determined upon, they began in earnest. A committee consisting of Messrs. Spofford, Knapp, and Holden of the trustees, and Mr. John M. Nixon, representing the congregation, presented tentative plans for the new church and lecture room in November, 1856. It seems to have been agreed by all, from the beginning, that in its shape and in the general arrangement of its pews the new building should resemble the old one, and especially that, while each pew might well be made more commodious and the aisles increased in width, the seating capacity should not be enlarged. "No church [to be under the charge of one pastor]," it was said, "should contain a greater number of pews" than did the old place of worship on Beekman Street.

In regard, however, to several other important matters, there was some uncertainty. It was first proposed, for instance, that the lecture room should be under the church, but fortunately it was at length decided that a chapel should be erected in the rear of the main building, although it was feared that this would add $10,000 to the cost. Another important question related to the placing of the pipe organ; for it had been determined that the violoncello should no longer supply the church's music. This innovation, which the trustees had early made a part of their plans, was, it is interesting to know, heartily desired by the congregation and by the session, "in the hope," as they said, "of adding interest to the public worship of the sanctuary." * The debated question in regard to the organ, therefore, was not whether there should be one, but where it should be placed, some favoring the front of the church above the entrance, and others the west end behind the pulpit.

The architect employed for the preliminary work was Mr. Leopold Eidlitz, but after February, 1857, the work was in the hands of the firm of T. Thomas and Son,† to whom doubtless the final plans, from which the church was built, should be altogether attributed. Several months were spent in this all-important work of preparation, and then, in the summer of 1857, the walls began to rise.

They were built of two materials. The first was, of course, that which tradition and the church's name prescribed: it was still to be the "Brick" Church. But in deference to the accepted fashion of that particular time, referred to a few pages back, the base, the trimmings, and the greater part of the steeple, whose strong and graceful lines have made it ever

* The session at this time were aroused to an increased interest in the music of the church. Possibly they felt that the trustees had too entire control of it. At any rate, mindful of "the sacred privilege and the appropriate duty of the session to conduct that part of public worship which consists in praise to Almighty God," they now appointed a special committee for this purpose. The committee's first task was to secure an organist, who was to receive a salary of $500 a year.

† On May 18th, 1858, and from that time on, the architect's fees were paid to Mr. Griffith Thomas, who is subsequently referred to as "the architect of the church."

since one of New York's noblest architectural monuments, were of brownstone. * The tower, from which the steeple rose, contained the old Beekman Street bell and a clock, † whose four faces told the time to the whole neighborhood. There were three main entrances to the building from Fifth Avenue, and high windows lighted the church, the vestibule, and the chapel, on either side. The style chosen for the architectural details was the somewhat late classic, and the design as a whole was simple and dignified. On both street and avenue the church was surrounded by a high iron fence with lamp-posts at the entrance gates. In short, without continuing further this description, it is enough to say that except for the stained glass in the windows and the vine which now covers the entire south wall and is making its way across the front, the exterior at the present day tells us precisely how it looked at the time of its erection.‡

The same thing cannot be said of the inside of the building. The plaster walls were then almost white in color, and divided into rectangles to give the effect of courses of stone. The windows, filled with plain glass, were fitted with great folding shutters,§

* The tendency to scale off which this stone developed in the moist climate of New York, has caused the repair of the steeple from time to time to be a very troublesome and costly operation.

† The clock was ordered while the church was building, but it did not arrive until after the dedication. The gossip of the time gave out that, when installed, it would have "illuminated dials." See "The Presbyterian," November 6th, 1858.

‡ In March, 1908, new clock faces of glass replaced the original wooden ones, of which one was blown down in a strong wind in the preceding fall.

§ The writer well remembers with what interest, as a boy, he would watch the sexton manipulate them, if by some good fortune they needed readjustment during service.

INTERIOR OF THE PRESENT BRICK CHURCH AS IT APPEARED IN 1858

while the ceiling, now so richly adorned, was then a
perfectly plain white surface. Yet it is interesting to
observe that those features of the newly completed
interior which were selected for special mention by
a contemporary journal * a week after the building
was first opened to the public, are, with one exception,
to be seen in the church to-day. The "Scagliola columns" still support the half dome of the apse behind
the pulpit.† The floors of the vestibule, "laid
with marble," have withstood admirably the tread
of almost two generations (though at the present day of costly buildings their material would
hardly be deemed worthy of any special admiration). The stairways to the galleries are still of
the same "solid oak," of which they were constructed in the beginning, and we hope that those
who climb them still find that they "are of easy
ascent."

The one exception referred to a moment ago was
perhaps the most magnificent object of which the new
church could boast, the sole extravagance, one might
say, in which the trustees had indulged. It was a
huge brass chandelier of a hundred lights, which hung
from the centre of the ceiling, and, except for a few
single brackets under the gallery and two lamp-
stands in the pulpit, lighted the entire church. It
cost no less than $1,300. Its place now knows it no
more. Long ago, no doubt, it was broken up and sold
for old metal, but it was greatly admired when the

---

* "The Presbyterian," November 6th, 1858.

† Their position, however, was slightly changed a few years after the
church was built. Originally the six columns were all at equal distances
from one another. The reason for the change will be explained at the
proper place.

new church was first opened and for many a year after.

Three other features of the church need to be mentioned before the reader will be able adequately to picture to himself the original interior. First, the pews were painted white or cream-color and had the same mahogany trimmings that exist to-day, though now almost overlooked amid the generally dark tones that prevail. Secondly, the organ-loft had been placed at the west end, above and behind the pulpit. The marble columns in those days stood free, and through the openings between them one could look into the gallery, where the organ * had been erected, and from which the chorister led the congregation in the singing. Finally, as many people of the present day will remember, there were, in the east wall of the interior, over the central door, three niches. It was originally intended that all of these should be used, as the following action of the trustees informs us. At a meeting held the day before the church was dedicated, they resolved "that whenever the lady friends of the Rev. Dr. Spring shall procure a bust of his person, in bronze or marble, semi-colossal in size, and executed with artistic skill, the central niche in the inner front wall of the new Brick Church be, and is hereby appointed, to its reception, and the side niches to urns or vases as shall most appropriately embellish the same." The embellishing urns or vases were never introduced, and the bust of Dr. Spring did not take its place in the centre until after his death.

If the interior of 1858, with its light color and

---

* The organ was built by Mr. Richard Montgomery Ferris, for $2,300.

severe simplicity, would seem strange to persons familiar with its present appearance, it seemed no less strange to the members of the old Brick Church, when they first entered it, for, aside from the most general resemblances to the older building in shape and arrangement, there were but two familiar objects in the whole church. As they came in at the central door they could see, on the left-hand wall of the vestibule, the old dedicatory tablet of black stone which had been removed to this place from the front of the downtown building, a visible memorial of the "Presbyterian Church erected in the year of our Lord 1767," * and when after entering the church itself, they had taken their seats and begun to look about them, there, in its familiar place, high on the wall above the pulpit, was the old white shield with its gilt letters, beloved by all the Brick Church people, still proclaiming that this house was "Holiness to the Lord." †

---

* Opposite, on the right-hand wall was (and is) another tablet of the same style and material, bearing the inscription:

THIS EDIFICE
ERECTED
In the Year of Our Lord
1858.

† See p. 133. Some other facts, which should not be altogether omitted may here be set down indiscriminately. At the west end of the church there were, on each side, above the entrances to the side galleries and just below the cornice, two smaller galleries which have been described as "the slave galleries," but they could hardly have been put to such a use in New York in 1858. They are now bricked up, so that they are no longer visible from the church, but the spaces still exist, and in one of them the old seats remained until a few years ago, when the room was fitted up as a robing-room for the choir. The pulpit of the church in 1858

When the church was complete, and ready for occupancy, one delicate problem still remained to be solved. Those who had owned pews in the old building must in some just manner have their rights transferred to the new. At first it was hoped that in planning the uptown church the plan of pews might be made identical with that on Beekman Street, and the rights of the pew-owners simply transferred to new pews, exactly corresponding with the old ones. This, however, proved to be impracticable, and a more complicated method was adopted. First, $140,000, a figure somewhat arbitrarily fixed upon as the value of the pews in the old church, was apportioned among the said pews according to their size and location, and scrip for the proper amounts was issued to the owners. Second, minimum prices were assigned to the pews on Murray Hill.* And, third, the pews were put up at auction "in order," as the trustees somewhat naïvely remarked, "to give

was furnished with an enormous sofa and two equally enormous armchairs. The coverings of these, and of the cushion on which the Bible rested, together with the valance which surrounded the marble-topped communion table, were of brilliant red damask. The carpet also, I believe was red. The chapel (and this name, by the way, was applied to the entire building in the rear of the church) contained on the first floor the lecture room, fitted up with pews like a little church. The square entrance hall was then open all the way up to the roof. On the second story were the pastor's study or "library," and the Sunday-school room. It had been proposed to place the Sunday-school in the basement, and possibly this was done for a time. The entire building, church and chapel together, cost about $150,000. (This was $25,000, more than had been expected at the outset.) The furniture and carpets had cost nearly $5,000. Including the land, therefore, the trustees had paid out about $213,000. The proceeds from the sale of the old site, with interest, provided 203,000, so that $10,000, had to be borrowed. Other needs increased this loan to $15,000.

* The prices ranged from $150 to $1,500.

every person an opportunity to locate according to his wishes." Before this plan had been entirely carried out, however, the church had been opened for public worship.

And happy must the people have been as the time approached when they would once more have a church of their own. For more than two years they had been using Hope Chapel, maintaining there, as well as they could, their church life. * And, indeed they had succeeded nobly. This is sufficiently indicated by the mention of a single fact, namely, that it was at this very juncture, while they were struggling to reëstablish their own organization on a new basis, that they found time and energy to go outside of their own immediate interests, in order to inaugurate another work of the utmost importance. This refers to the opening of that Sunday-school on the west side of the city which has since developed into Christ Church; but the complete story of that unselfish and most successful enterprise must be reserved for a future chapter.

And now, at length, the time had come to take possession. The period of exile was over, or, since these pilgrims were not minded to return to the land from whence they had come out, we may rather say that their ship, which had left the old harbor and put to sea two years before, had at last been brought

---

* Dr. Adams had "very kindly and cordially" offered the use of the Madison Square Presbyterian Church for the holding of the Communion Service on at least one occasion, and this was gratefully accepted. The trustees' meetings during the two years had been held in the directors' room of the Mechanics' Bank, the session meetings in the pastor's temporary study.

in safety to her desired haven. On October 31st, 1858, the church on Murray Hill was dedicated to the worship of Almighty God. *

* From contemporary newspapers and other periodicals, the following account of this event has been compiled. The people, assembled by the same bell that had "sounded the call to worship for so many years in the old church," came together in great numbers. When the service began "an immense crowd filled the spacious edifice, even to the aisles and portals." Ex-President Fillmore and his wife were observed to be among the congregation. The service was, of course, conducted by Dr. Spring, "the venerable pastor, who seems yet to retain a large portion of the vigor of his younger days." The order of service was as follows:

1. Opening Prayer.
2. Psalm (sung by the congregation),
   "Where shall we go to see and find
   A habitation for our God."
3. Prayer.
4. Psalm 132.
5. Collection, "A Thank Offering, for the benefit of the Princeton Students."
6. Sermon, on "The Sanctuary," from the text Leviticus 19 : 30. (It "held the unwearied attention of the audience for an hour and a half.")
7. The Dedication (the people standing).
8. Hymn.
9. Benediction.

"Fifth Avenue was completely blocked with carriages for a long time after the close of the services." Afternoon and evening services were also held, Dr. Samuel Spring of East Hartford officiating at the one, and Dr. Phillips of New York at the other. See "N. Y. Tribune," "N. Y. Evening Post," and "N. Y. Times" for November 1st, 1858, and "The Presbyterian" for November 6th.

CHAPTER XVII

WORK RESUMED: THE CIVIL WAR:
1858–1863

"We enter upon our new career under few circumstances of discouragement and many of bright anticipation. . . . In the name of the Lord, therefore, we set up our banners. It is an eventful age of the world in which our enterprise receives this new impulse."—GARDINER SPRING, 1858, "The Brick Church Memorial," pp. 74 f.

"Ye shall hear of wars and rumors of wars: see that ye be not troubled: for all these things must come to pass, but the end is not yet."—*Matthew* 24 : 6.

THE members of the Brick Church had not waited for the new building to be ready before they began to revive the work which was to occupy it. At least one discontinued enterprise had been zealously taken up again as soon as the new site had been purchased, and even before the plans for the new church had been fairly begun. This was the Sunday-school. At the call of Dr. Spring, eighteen persons came together in Hope Chapel on a Sunday afternoon in November, 1856, "to organize a Sabbath-school which should be connected with the Brick Church and located for the present at the Hope Chapel." One of the first acts of the teachers, after the school had been started, was to inquire whether during the interval the old title, "School No. 3," had been assigned to any other institution. If not, they voted to reassume it. We do not know whether they were successful, for this is the last time that the old name appears in the records.

293

But the school itself, at any rate, was reëstablished, ready for the new opportunity that was about to open, and on the day of the new church's dedication, the first service was that of the Sunday-school, which, at quarter after nine assembled in its own room in the chapel in the rear of the church. The immediate renewal of this important department of church work was certainly an auspicious opening, and indicated that the people were eager to regain as soon as possible whatever ground had been lost.

As soon as the church was established on Murray Hill, preparations were made to take stock, as it were, of the congregation, and to exploit the neighborhood. Districts were laid out for visitation by the pastor and elders, and we still possess a copy of a printed street-plan which was used to facilitate this work. It represents the section between Thirty-sixth and Fortieth streets and between Sixth and Lexington avenues, divided up into sixty visitation districts. Dr. Spring, in his dedication sermon, had called attention to the fact that no other churches had located in the immediate neighborhood, * so that there was a free field for the Brick Church to work in, and he declared also that the surrounding population had already shown a disposition to receive the church in a most friendly spirit. Many, indeed, of those who were now neighbors, had in former days attended the old Brick Church, and these welcomed the opportunity of restoring the old relationship.

* The Madison Square Church had been built on Twenty-fourth Street in 1854 and the "Marble" Dutch Church at Fifth Avenue and Twenty-ninth Street in the same year. There were less important churches at Eighth Avenue and Thirty-fourth Street, Broadway and Thirty-ninth Street, and Lexington Avenue and Thirtieth Street.

For all reasons, therefore, it was desirable that a very patient and thorough visitation of the whole region should be made, and this the session now undertook.

But this very undertaking must have brought forcibly home to them a truth long evident to all, that their pastor, now over seventy years of age, was ill able to do the full work of a city pastorate, and least of all, to break ground in a new field. Indeed, there was already an understanding between them that as soon as the new church was complete, steps should be taken to lift a part of the burden from his shoulders.

As early as 1848, it had been necessary to provide a considerable amount of pulpit assistance. The sum of $1,000, was then put at the disposal of the session for this purpose, and this act was repeated three years later. But some months before the departure from Beekman Street it became evident that a more radical change was necessary. The situation was one that the officers desired to treat with the greatest delicacy, not wishing to seem in any way impatient of the growing infirmities of their beloved pastor; and we may well believe that he, for his part, lover of the church as he was, and of his work in it, was reluctant to begin the laying aside of the powers and responsibilities he had borne so long.

The letter which he wrote to his elders in October, 1855, is, therefore, touched with that inevitable pathos of the old workman who is conscious of the coming night. "It must be quite as obvious to you as to myself," he said, "that I am not able to discharge the duties of my office to any such extent as satisfies my own mind. Though my health is vigorous and my courage for labor undiminished, the calamity * with which it has pleased a wise and righteous Providence to visit me, unfits me for the toil in which it has been my privilege to be so long employed." But aside from this special affliction, his age itself, as he said later in this same letter, made some decided assistance an immediate necessity. He made several suggestions as to the means of providing this, evidently thinking himself that the best plan of all would be to call a colleague; and in this the session concurred, but upon full consideration of pastor and session together, it seemed so difficult to secure a proper person for this office while the church was still struggling for the sale of one property and the purchase of another, that delay was decided upon, until the new land should be secured.

As a matter of fact, the church, as we have seen, was already at work on Murray Hill, before any active measures were taken for calling a colleague. For the first few months in the new church the Sunday afternoon service was supplied by students from Princeton Seminary. But finally in March, 1859, a call was issued to the Rev. William James Hoge, D.D., Professor of Biblical Literature in Union Theological Seminary in Virginia. Dr. Spring and two of the elders had gone to Virginia expressly to see him, and had returned with the report that, in their opinion, "the intellectual, religious, and social qualifications of this gentleman, as well as his public performances in the pulpit, are such as in no ordinary degree qualify him to become the associate

* His failing eyesight.

WILLIAM J. HOGE

pastor of the Brick Church." He had been licensed
to preach in 1850, and, previous to entering his professorship, had been for four years pastor of the Westminster Church in Baltimore, where his former parishioners regarded him with high esteem. The call
now issued to him by the Brick Church was unanimous.*

It must be confessed that in accepting, as he did,
Dr. Hoge was undertaking a difficult work, which
would require not only high talents and great industry, but an unusual degree of tact and Christian
grace. Dr. Spring and his people had worked together, without any other person between them, for
almost half a century, and it was only with the utmost reluctance on both sides, and in answer to an
imperative necessity, that the expedient of a colleague had been adopted. At the congregational
meeting which called Dr. Hoge, a set of resolutions,
offered by Mr. Holden, was adopted, in which were
feelingly expressed the love of the Brick Church
people for Dr. Spring, their sense of obligation to
him for past service, their ever-increasing appreciation of "his richly matured and invaluable instructions," their joy that, though "his eye is dimmed by
excessive devotion to his chosen work," yet "his
natural force and mental vigor are not abated,"
and their assurance that "it will always be our
pleasure and anxious desire to hear him preach once
every Sabbath and to render such other assistance at
our weekly evening services as may be agreeable to
his own feelings and wishes." It would almost have
seemed to an onlooker at the meeting that it had

---

* His salary was $5,000, the same as that received by Dr. Spring.

been assembled with special reference to the old rather than to the new pastor.

But both pastor and people had determined that the newcomer should be given all the help that could be conveyed by a hearty and affectionate welcome, and Dr. Spring, especially, had determined that his young colleague should be as free as was possible from the difficulties inherent in the situation. Those who were present on the evening when Dr. Hoge was installed in the Brick Church * were much impressed by the generous spirit in which the venerable Dr. Spring said of his youthful associate, "He must increase, but I must decrease. My sun is setting; his has not yet reached its zenith." "And when," says one of the eye-witnesses, "the senior pastor stopped in his discourse, and took his associate by the hand, assuring him of the cordiality of his welcome to take part in the work, there were few dry eyes in the house. Such scenes are rare," this writer continues, and points out that all the circumstances of the occasion were such as could only be produced by great personal qualities in the chief participants.†

The Brick Church had not been mistaken in regard to the man they had chosen. His "lovely Christian character and thrilling pulpit eloquence," to quote the words in which one of his successors in the Brick Church has referred to him,‡ soon won

* May 22d, 1859. The Rev. F. G. Clarke presided as moderator of the Presbytery. The Rev. S. D. Alexander offered prayer. Dr. Spring preached the sermon. The charges to pastor and people were given by the Rev. Dr. Krebs and the Rev. Dr. Potts, respectively. The Rev. Dr. Phillips offered the concluding prayer.

† "The Presbyterian," May 28th, 1859.

‡ Dr. Henry van Dyke "An Historic Church," p. 23.

him a place in the people's affection and drew great numbers to hear him preach. He delivered the gospel message with all the fire and passion of the Southland, from which he came, and soon the younger generation, who naturally did not share all the enthusiasm of their parents and grandparents regarding Dr. Spring, were again thronging the Brick Church.

Certainly a church that could thus appeal to all ages and varying tastes was well calculated to do a great work. Dr. Spring in 1860, at the time of his fiftieth anniversary, which was celebrated with great enthusiasm,* declared that the church's change of locality had resulted in great gain; and spoke with gratitude and joy of the fact that the services in the new edifice were "filled to overflowing." A study of the benevolences of the church at this time tells the same story and with a most decided emphasis. It will be remembered that for a number of years before 1850 the average annual benevolences had amounted to a little over $3,000. The highest figure for any single year up to that time had been about $5,800. Until 1860, this figure had not been exceeded. But in that year, it suddenly rose to $8,500, and from this time continued to rise by leaps and bounds, year after year.†

* The anniversary sermon was preached by Dr. Spring on August 5th. Owing to the illness of Mrs. Spring at that time and her death soon after, the rest of the celebration was deferred till October 15th. On that occasion a magnificent silver service was presented to Dr. Spring, while the words spoken by his oldest and dearest friends in the Brick Church were a still richer expression of esteem and love.

† 1861, $9,300; 1862, $9,600; 1863, $14,600; 1864, $14,700; 1865, $19,200. This increase was partly due to growing interest in the mission Sunday-school to be described in the next chapter.

One evidence of the church's increased activity is directly traceable to the influence of Dr. Hoge. It has already been pointed out that his great opportunity was with the younger people. It was surely by no accident, therefore, that "The Young Men's Association of the Brick Church" was organized during the first year of his pastorate.* It is easy to believe that the following words from the preamble of the society's constitution were suggested by Dr. Hoge himself, and that they represented with some exactness a chief purpose of his own New York ministry. "The disciple who leaned on Jesus' bosom once said, 'I write unto you, young men, because ye are strong.' It is to the young men . . . that [our churches] must look as the future depositories of that Christian and moral influence which is to protect and advance the highest interests of the church and the world."

It was, accordingly, the purpose of this organization to draw together as many as possible of the young men of the Brick Church, from fifteen years old and upward, into a comradeship whose objects were "to promote Christian friendship and social intercourse among its members, to improve their spiritual and mental conditions, and to take such measures for benevolent action as may be deemed proper, especially such as will tend to exert a salutary influence in the neighborhood of the church." The regular meetings were held on the second Monday of each month (except July and August), and no

---

* The constitution was adopted on February 27th, 1860. The officers for 1860–1861 were: Pres., George de Forest Lord; Vice-Pres., Robert Stewart, M.D.; Sec., Arthur Gilman; Treas., William D. Black; Managers, George A. Bennett, Charles T. White, Thomas C. M. Paton.

special regulations were made as to their nature, except for the provision that "all remarks or discussions of a political or controversial character shall be excluded."

When we remember in what year of our American history this society was formed, the year namely, in which Abraham Lincoln was first elected to the Presidency, we perceive a very special appropriateness in that one restriction just quoted, and when we realize further that Dr. Hoge was a Southerner, we can see that "political and controversial" subjects were especially dangerous to the peace of the Young Men's Association. But more than that, they were a danger, we may readily believe, to the peace of the whole church. How had it happened that on the very eve of the war a Virginian had deliberately been installed over the Brick Church in the city of New York?

We cannot but regard this occurrence as the result of a serious error in judgment on the part of the church and its officers, and of a singular lack of foresight. Dr. Hoge, on the other hand, urged to come to a great church in America's greatest city, was more pardonable. And yet upon him, of course, the chief punishment for the mistake fell. Some of the very qualities that made him eloquent, the qualities of a sensitive and high-strung nature, made him also the more quick to suffer from any of the thousand bitter words that filled the air in those days of controversy; while to avoid giving offence, on his side, required perhaps more tact than any ordinary man was likely to possess, and it must be confessed that tact was not his strong point.

In 1861, when war had actually broken out, the situation soon became acute. Dr. Hoge had many warm friends in the church, men who, although, as he himself declared, they totally differed from him in everything relating to the national crisis, believed that he was following a wise and blameless course,* and were "unwilling to allow a dissolution of the pastoral relation on grounds of political opinions." Such prominent officers in the church as Daniel Lord, Abner L. Ely, Moses Allen, James Darrach, and Thomas Egleston, held this view of the matter. On the other hand, the preponderant element in the church felt that the situation was intolerable, and that the presence of an avowed Southerner in the Brick Church pulpit could not but cause continual and increasing friction, however careful he might be to avoid in his public utterances all controverted subjects.

The ideal of conduct which Dr. Hoge had set before himself was in theory admirable.† On the one hand, he assumed that as a free citizen of the Republic he had an unquestionable right "firmly to hold and calmly to express," in private, his opinions. His position, to be sure, required him to declare them "unobtrusively," and sometimes to waive conversation on such topics, but "when fairly approached by any responsible person" in private conversation, he claimed his right to make known "frankly and courteously" his political faith.

On the other hand, he purposed to exclude absolutely from the pulpit the questions that divided

* "Farewell Discourse of Dr. Hoge," p. 8.
† The following outline is taken from his "Farewell Discourse," pp. 9*ff*.

men's minds. His prayers he designed to make of
such a character as would express the proper petitions of men in South or North, and his sermons he
undertook to keep entirely out of the realm of politics. Indeed, he held, and had held even before the
war, that the rigid exclusion of politics from Christian preaching was the duty of every minister of the
gospel, even if he and his congregation were in agreement on every point.

In much of this, without doubt, Dr. Hoge was in
the abstract quite right. But whether his plan fitted
exactly the existing situation, or would work among
ordinary human beings at a time of heated excitement, was another matter. The practical question
was whether a man whose approval of secession was
well known, could be listened to with composure by
a Northern congregation week after week; whether
he could go in and out as pastor among a people to
whom he was a "rebel"; whether the studied avoid-
ance of direct allusions to the war in prayer and discourse would really keep the services free from all
political significance, so long as the minister stood
there as a personal representative of the enemy.

One concrete instance may be given by way of
illustration. In the petitions for those in places of
authority, Dr. Hoge had used such expressions as
would include (of course without mentioning them)
the rulers of the Confederate States. Now without
doubt, such obedience to the apostolic exhortation
that "supplications, prayers, intercessions, and giving of thanks, be made for *all* men," is, as Dr. Hoge
declared, in full accord with the truest Christian spirit.
In every Christian Church in time of war the enemy

ought certainly to be prayed for. But for a Southerner, who frankly hoped that the North would be annihilated, to lead a Northern congregation in asking, however vaguely, for a blessing upon the rulers and fighters of the South, was, not unnaturally, a little more than average Northerners could stand.

At length in July, 1861, a meeting of the session was called for the declared purpose of discussing "the relations of the church and its pastors to the present state of the country." But Dr. Hoge felt that the time for discussion was over, and as soon as the meeting opened, he offered his resignation. It was accepted by a bare majority.

Dr. Hoge, as was very natural, felt some bitterness toward those who had plainly desired him to leave. The unfortunate tone of sarcasm and accusation in which he allowed himself, in public utterance and in print, to speak of them * makes this evident. And not a few of the congregation were inclined to feel that his personal qualities and his work in New York had not been fully recognized. On the day after that on which his resignation had been accepted by the session, a number of them expressed in writing to Dr. Hoge their sorrow at his parting from them, and their veneration for his consistent preaching of the gospel, and for the Christian moderation and gentleness of his bearing "in the midst of angry, political excitements." Yet it must in time have become evident to his most warm admirers, and indeed to Dr. Hoge himself, that his position in the church at such a juncture was unnatural, and could not possibly have long continued.

* "Farewell Discourse," pp. 7 f., 24.

At the time when the resignation was accepted, the session voted to submit their action to a congregational meeting one week from that day. But for this Dr. Hoge refused to wait. On the intervening Sunday he preached a farewell sermon to a congregation in which the tension was extreme. One incident of the occasion was especially significant of the irreconcilable differences which no attempt at fairness of statement could overcome. While the sermon was being delivered Dr. Spring sat in the pulpit. Dr. Hoge, at the close of a passage in which he had spoken of recent events in the country and the church, turned to Dr. Spring and said: "I appeal to my venerable colleague whether this is not in substance correct." Dr. Spring shook his head in the negative, and in a decisive tone, loud enough to be heard by many in the church, declared, "It is *not*, Sir."* The truth was, no doubt, that a Southerner and a Northerner at that time inevitably saw the same events with different eyes.

Early in the following week, and before the arrival of the day set for the congregational meeting, Dr. Hoge took his departure, and thus passed out of the history of the Brick Church. He was soon at work again in a Virginian parish, and now threw himself, untrammelled, into the work that opened for him there on every side, exhibiting that Christian zeal and devotion which had always characterized him. The truth was, that when he went back to the South, he went to lay down his life for that Southern cause in which he conscientiously believed. Almost a year

* This scene has been described to the writer by an eye-witness. See also "N. Y. Tribune," July 23d, 1861.

before the war was over his labors in the army hospitals, added to his work among the people of his parish, had worn out even so robust a frame as his, and made him an easy prey to the typhoid fever which then attacked him. He died on July 5th, 1864.

From the time of Dr. Hoge's departure, the Brick Church stood, without reservation, for loyalty to the Union, and that in no uncertain manner. Dr. Spring did not at all agree with the view that at that time the pulpit should hold aloof from the discussion of current politics. Rather he held that the national situation was such as to demand from the Christian Church a strong and unmistakable declaration of its attitude.

He was not, it should be said, one of those who, from the beginning, had bitterly opposed the policy of the South. He said himself: "When the first indications of this conflict made their appearance, all my prepossessions, as is well known, were with the Southern States."* As early as 1839, and again in 1851, he had delivered and published lectures designed to rebuke the extreme abolition spirit of the North, and even a short time before the war, he was strongly drawn to espouse the Southern cause, through his horror of a dismemberment of the Union. Slavery, he felt, was recognized by the Constitution of the United States, and the rights of the South in this matter could not be ignored, however much slavery itself might deserve extinction. It was only when he became convinced of what he regarded as a wicked and determined disloyalty in the South, and

* "State Thanksgiving during the Rebellion; A Sermon." N. Y., 1862, p. 32.

especially when the seceding States had actually broken the Union, that his sympathy for the Southern position came to an end.

It was not, therefore, because he was carried away by excess of passion that, after the war's beginning, he gave himself, in private and in public, in the pulpit and out of it, to the support of the government, but because he felt that loyalty had been made the issue, and that the church ought openly and officially, to withstand the destroyers of the nation, as they would withstand any other enemies of public morals. "Strong as have been my predilections for the South," he said, " . . . I have not been able to see, nor do I now see, the justice, the equity of her demands. We regard the act of secession, so causeless, so rash, so fratricidal, so ruthless—as unequalled in wickedness. I do not know that the history of the world records a more criminal procedure." *

In May, 1861, at the General Assembly, then convened in Philadelphia, Dr. Spring introduced and urged certain resolutions, declaring the loyalty of the Presbyterian Church, which were, with slight modifications, passed by a large majority. The part of these "Spring Resolutions," as they were called, which now especially concerns us was as follows: "Resolved, that the General Assembly, in the spirit of that Christian patriotism which the Scriptures enjoin, and which has always characterized this Church, do humbly acknowledge and declare our obligations to promote and perpetuate, so far as in us lies, the integrity of these United States, and to strengthen, uphold, and encourage the Federal Government in the

* "State Thanksgiving," etc., pp. 34 f.

exercise of all its functions under our Constitution; and to this Constitution, in all its provisions, requirements, and principles, we profess our unabated loyalty." *

By this declaration, which Dr. Spring had led the Church at large to make, the Brick Church was guided throughout the war. The stars and stripes flew from her steeple. The sermons to which her congregations reverently listened were filled with the love of country as with the love of God. The prayers in which the people were led, from Sunday to Sunday, asked in all plainness that the endeavors of the national enemy might be brought to nought.

We who live so long after that tragic conflict, and who, with the disappearance of old prejudices, know now that honor and truth and love of country were by no means the exclusive possession of one side, do not care to dwell more than is necessary upon that period of division and bitter strife; and it is more congenial to us to note, as we may, in concluding the account of the attitude of the Brick Church through the war, that even in the heat of those passions which war inevitably arouses, the Brick Church people were not permitted to forget the bond of Christian brotherhood which bound them to the people of the Southern States. "We reluctantly take up the sword in defence of the rich heritage God has given us," said Dr. Spring in the Brick Church pulpit in November, 1861, "and most cheerfully will we return it to its scabbard when this heritage is secure. . . . It will be

---

* Dr. Hoge did not resign till two months after these resolutions were passed. Their effect upon his continuance in the Brick Church pastorate will be evident.

the joy of our hearts and the thank-offering of our
lips to sound the retreat the moment the voice of rebellion is silent. We have no bitterness against the
South. We do not wish to reign over them, but to
reign with them, and wish them to reign with us, as
they have ever done, in all the rights and immunities
of the Federal Government." *

While the war was in progress the church had
once more called and, to the great regret of all, lost
again, an associate pastor. On February 6th, 1862,
the Rev. William G. T. Shedd, Professor of Ecclesiastical History and Pastoral Theology in Andover
Seminary, was unanimously called to be the colleague of Dr. Spring. Dr. Shedd hesitated not a
little to change his field of labor from that of teaching, in which he had been engaged for seventeen
years, to that of the active pastorate; and probably,
had it not been that the call also offered him an opportunity to enter the Presbyterian Church, whose
doctrine and polity were peculiarly congenial to him,
he might not have accepted. At length, however, his
duty in the matter seemed to him clear, and he entered with gladness into the service of the people of
the Brick Church, and into the close fellowship which
it offered with "their revered pastor, whose praise
and influence," as Dr. Shedd said, "are in all the
churches." †

It was a remarkable fact that Dr. Spring, though
so far advanced in years, was still able to carry a very
large part of the burden of the church's work. But
Dr. Shedd had not long been settled in New York

---

* "State Thanksgiving," etc., p. 42.
† The installation took place on April 13th, 1862.

when it appeared that the senior pastor must withdraw largely from active service. Upon the associate,
therefore, the responsibility fell more and more
heavily, and toward the close of 1863 it became evident that soon he must bear the whole burden alone.
This sudden increase of demand upon his strength
Dr. Shedd had not anticipated, and his health began
to break down under it, so that when in September,
1863, he received a call to the chair of Biblical Literature in Union Theological Seminary in New York,
he felt constrained to accept it.

The church allowed him to go with the greatest
reluctance. He was most affectionately regarded by
the people and by his senior colleague. His brief
work in the church was felt to be "eminently useful
and acceptable," and had given to all "encouragement
and hope for the future." If at the last moment he
had been willing to remain, his decision would have
been hailed with joy, and such assistance would have
been given him in his work as would have freed him
from all anxieties on the score of overtaxing his
strength. But Dr. Shedd persisted in his decision,
and his subsequent life abundantly proved that in
returning to the work of a teacher and a writer, he
was following the natural bent of his genius. It was
a happy circumstance that, after leaving the pastorate of the Brick Church, he continued his allegiance
to her as an attendant upon her services until the
time of his death.*

The choice of a successor to Dr. Shedd was de-

* In November, 1894. He had continued as Professor in Union Seminary until 1891, but had been transferred to the chair of Systematic Theology in 1874.

WILLIAM G. T. SHEDD

layed for some time through the failure of the church, on two occasions, to secure the persons whom they desired to call, and the year 1864 had almost come to a close before this important undertaking was accomplished.

PART THREE

THE MODERN PERIOD

CHAPTER XVIII

"THE OLD ORDER CHANGETH": 1864–1875

"Behold, the former things are come to pass, and new things do I declare; before they spring forth I tell you of them."—*Isaiah* 42 : 9 *f.*

"It is the duty of those who have anything to do with sacred song, to educate the Christian popular heart in the very best and highest forms of devotional experience."—JAMES O. MURRAY, "Christian Hymnology," p. 37.

ON December 12th, 1864, the church called to be its associate pastor the Rev. James Ormsbee Murray, who, ten years before had been one of Dr. Shedd's pupils at Andover, and was now recommended to the church by him. Although ostensibly his position was the same as that held by Dr. Hoge and Dr. Shedd before him, the conditions under which he entered upon his pastorate were in one respect essentially different. Dr. Spring had now so far withdrawn from active work that his associate became in everything but name the sole pastor of the church.

Six months before Dr. Murray was called, Dr. Spring had communicated to his people the fact that "by reason of his age and increased infirmities" he felt unable to continue even so great a measure of service as he was then rendering. The name "pastor emeritus" was not used, but the understanding was that he should now be retired on a reduced salary of

315

$3,000, and that the associate, about to be called, should assume practically the whole burden of labor and responsibility.

During the eight remaining years of Dr. Spring's life it was his joy to take such part in the services of the church as his strength permitted, and to his old parishioners the sight of his venerable head and the sound of his voice seemed like a benediction upon the church's work. By the thoughtfulness of the trustees a railing was erected beside the steps at the right-hand side of the pulpit in order that he might ascend and descend in safety. He was now almost totally blind, yet so richly was his memory stored, that he could, if there were need, conduct an entire service, repeating the Scripture lesson and the words of the hymns with as much accuracy as though he were reading them from the book. Not only by his own congregation—the grandchildren and great grandchildren of the generation among whom he had begun his work—but also by the whole city, the presence of this aged saint was counted a blessing: "the patriarch of our metropolitan pulpit," Dr. Adams called him.

It was regarded by every one as a peculiarly happy thing that Dr. Spring lived long enough, not only to see, but to take some part in, that reunion of the Old and New Schools for which he had long been hoping and praying. It will be remembered that in 1837 he had been one of those who deeply deplored the division, and that he had done his best to prevent it. Thirty-two years later, in 1869, he rejoiced in the coming together again of the two schools in a reunited Church. The Assemblies that year, with a special

MEMBERS OF THE LAST NEW SCHOOL ASSEMBLY

Taken outside of the Church of the Covenant

view to facilitating this happy consummation, were both held in New York and within four blocks of one another, that of the New School at the Church of the Covenant at Park Avenue and Thirty-fifth Street, since incorporated into the Brick Church, and that of the Old School at the Brick Church itself.

In spite of the strong movement toward reunion, which had been gathering strength for several years, there was at the last moment a feeling on the part of many that the attempt was, after all, premature. Dr. Spring, eighty-four years of age, and knowing that his time on earth could not be greatly prolonged, was one of those who would not listen to the word delay. At the opening of the Old School Assembly, sitting in the pulpit beside the presiding officer, he suggested to him the propriety, as the first business, "of notifying the other branch of our readiness to consummate the reunion immediately." This did not at the moment appear to be practicable, and Dr. Spring, called upon to make the opening prayer, felt that there was still work to be done by him in his Master's vineyard. "When this majestic and veteran pastor . . . rose in prayer," says Dr. Jacobus in the official history of the reunion, "he uttered such exalted petitions, in such glowing and godly words, as even he, perhaps, had never excelled." *

In the course of the succeeding debates and conferences, Dr. Spring's voice was still heard. He urged that any delay in the consummation would be "flying in the face of the prayers of God's people." "If you postpone this union another year," said he,

* "The Presbyterian Reunion." N. Y., 1870., p. 334.

"I shall probably not see it, but shall die a member of a divided Church." * As is well known, his fears, so feelingly expressed, were not to be realized, and meantime, on Friday, May 28th, at the joint Communion Service in which the members of the two Assemblies shared, he, with the two moderators, officiated at the table. "It was," says the historian, "as if Moses or Elias had come down to talk on that Transfiguration Mount, of the decease accomplished at Jerusalem." †

After sharing in this historic event Dr. Spring might well feel that his work was accomplished. "The closing years of his life," wrote Dr. Murray, "were marked by what he himself used to call 'a gentle decay.' It was, indeed, very gentle. His faculties were clear, his interest in things about him keen, his enjoyment of life healthy and true, almost to the very close."

Of the days just before the end there is but a single incident that need be here repeated. We are told that during those last days he was never tired of hearing what he called the bairns' hymns, and it was a striking illustration, says Dr. Murray, of how the mightiest disciple must enter the kingdom of God only as a little child, to hear the old man, lying like an aged patriarch in the midst of his household, repeat in broken accents the children's prayer, "Now I lay me down to sleep," adding at the end, as though the words had carried him back to his childhood days, "and make me a good boy, for Christ's sake. Amen." On the 18th of August, 1873, he died. He

* "The Presbyterian Reunion," p. 349.
† *Ibid.*, p. 360.

had been the pastor of the Brick Church for sixty-three years.*

Mr. Murray, who came to take up the work of the church as Dr. Spring was laying it down, was in the prime of life, and was fitted in an exceptional degree for the office upon which he now entered.† He had graduated with honors from Brown University in 1850, and had at that time already become known for his Christian character and his scholarly taste and attainments. He had especially devoted himself to the study of English literature and throughout his whole later life he was distinguished for "the true literary spirit" with which he was imbued.

The next period of his life, spent at Andover in his theological preparation, is admirably described by one of his classmates, Charles Tiffany, afterward Archdeacon of the Episcopal Diocese of New York. "Mr. Murray at Andover," wrote Dr. Tiffany, "showed as a student just the same qualities which made him efficient and beloved in his later career. He was faithful in his work and commanded respect

---

* Although he received several calls to other spheres of work, he never seriously contemplated any change. During his early ministry he was offered the presidency of both Dartmouth and Hamilton colleges, and later he was sought as teacher of Sacred Rhetoric in Princeton Theological Seminary. Even in 1865, eight years before his death, there remained alive but four persons who had been members of the church at the time of his call. He had, in one instance, baptized the great-great-grandchild of one of those early parishioners. New York's population during his pastorate had increased from something under a hundred thousand to more than a million. So far back in our national history did his memory reach that he could say, "I well remember the day when Washington died." "Life and Times," Vol. II, pp. 212, 282 ƒ.

† He was born November 27th, 1827. On his father's side his ancestors were Presbyterians and Episcopalians, and partly of Scotch stock (the Murrays), partly of English, settled in Ireland, (the Syngs). On his mother's side his blood was wholly English and Puritan.

as a scholar; and his literary felicity, even at that early period of his life, made a marked impression on all who heard him in his addresses in the chapel and on other semi-public occasions. Every one prophesied for him a future of eminence and distinguished usefulness. Those who were privileged, as I was, to be of the number of his intimate friends felt the spell of his charming and genial personality, and loved him as much as they respected and admired him. His religious character was too deep to be ostentatious, but it was manifest in his profound earnestness and in a high tone of thought and simplicity of expression which marked his intercourse with others. He was so genuinely human and so unconsciously true and spiritual that one knew he would reach men and elevate them by merely being what he was. . . . His humor added a glow to his more solid qualities, and his refinement of nature gave him the distinction and influence so commanding in a genuine gentleman. He belonged to the very elect both by nature and by grace." * Such, even in his seminary days, was he who, after two Massachusetts pastorates,† was called to the Brick Church in 1864. His ten-year pastorate in New York will be described in this chapter and the next.

It was characteristic of the man and a sign of the beginning of what may be called the modern period of the history of the Brick Church, that Mr. Murray early gave his attention to the improvement of the

* From a letter quoted in "James O. Murray: a Memorial Sermon." By John DeWitt, Princeton, 1899, pp. 23 f.

† In South Danvers, near Salem (1854–1861), and in Cambridgeport (1861–1864), where many students of the University were drawn to his services.

JAMES O. MURRAY

music of the church services. Already, as we have seen, the changed spirit of the times had caused the introduction of the pipe organ, but the singing was still led by the chorister, and, with the removal from the old site, even the volunteer choir had evidently been discontinued. No doubt the congregation were ready to welcome a change in these conditions, but there had been lacking some one in authority who was in sympathy with the more modern taste, and willing to exert himself in an endeavor to satisfy it. Mr. Murray was both able and ready to undertake this work.

He had not long been in the church when he was asked to become chairman of the session's music committee, and the attempt to improve the quality of the music, evidenced by a decided increase in the chorister's salary at this time, was no doubt the immediate result of his influence.*

These changes, however, were merely preliminary to another of much more importance. In April, 1866, the committee on music reported to the session that upon inquiry a very general desire had been found among the congregation for "a change in the present method of conducting the singing," by substituting for the precentor or chorister "a choir of at least four voices." It was not intended, they said, that "congregational singing should be superseded by the performances of a quartette, but only that the choir should lead the congregation in the service of song in the house of the Lord."

---

* It now became a part of the chorister's duty to sing at the meeting on Tuesday evenings. In 1872 a small pipe organ was erected in the lecture room.

"In the judgment of some of our best professional musicians," the report continues, "the only method of maintaining congregational singing successfully is by putting it under the guidance and assistance of a choir of voices, where all the parts are represented; and the musical education of many among us, especially the young, as also the musical tastes of the community, are such that the change suggested is thought to be needful in order to make them interested worshippers in this most delightful part of our worship of God. In the case of persons seeking a new place of worship, an attractive form of church music is often a controlling element in their choice." The committee were of the opinion that any additional expense, entailed by the proposed change, would without difficulty be met by means of private subscription.

The proposal involved, as it happened, something more than the hiring of a quartette. No proper place had been provided in the new church for a choir, even of four voices, and it was at first thought that the best way of dealing with this difficulty would be to open an entirely new gallery under the tower at the east end of the church. But Mr. Thomas, the architect, recommended a less costly change, by which the gallery behind the pulpit might still be utilized. Under his supervision the columns, whose arrangement had interfered with that gallery's use, were now moved to their present positions, providing a clear space of ten feet in the centre.* Here it was designed that the quartette should stand, while the organ, considerably enlarged,† was moved back as

* See p. 287, note.   † It was reconstructed by Mr. William J. Stewart.

far as was necessary, a certain portion of the room in the rear being appropriated for this purpose.* When these structural changes had been made, a quartette † was engaged and a new era in the history of worship in the Brick Church was begun. The trustees had dealt with the matter in a generous spirit and provided out of the church treasury the additional sum which the change involved. The music, which had been costing $1,400, now called for $2,500.

The next musical problem to which Dr. ‡ Murray gave his attention was the providing of a suitable hymn-book. Already the volume entitled "Songs for the Sanctuary" had been purchased, in 1866, for use at the weekly meetings, but to find a satisfactory book for the use of the Sunday services was a matter much more difficult, and in November, 1867, the session decided to undertake the preparation of a hymn-book of their own, which should include a selection "as well from the psalms and hymns of Watts as from all other published hymns." This task was entrusted to Mr. William S. Gilman, Mr. Daniel Lord, and Dr. Murray.§

The report of this committee, at the time when the

---

* A wall was built running west from the north end of the organ loft and cutting off entirely the whole southern end of the room in the rear, then used for the Sunday-school. It was necessary, in consequence, that the Sunday-school be moved to the third story, where it was held for a number of years.

† This first quartette was composed as follows: Miss Kellogg, soprano; Miss Gordon, alto; Mr. Emerson, bass; Mr. Millard, tenor.

‡ He received his Doctor's degree in 1867.

§ Mr. Lord, whose "discriminating taste and excellent judgment" were highly prized, died before the book was complete. Dr. Spring made the selection of metrical versions of the Psalms.

completed manuscript was submitted to the session, may be regarded as a part, not only of the history of the Brick Church, but of the history of hymnology in the Church at large. For two years, the report tells us, the committee had devoted itself to the work of making a select list of hymns from American and English publications, with a view to securing "the best hymns upon the various topics." During this time weekly meetings had been held, at which the hymns were discussed one by one, while the considerable literature on the subject, "on which," they say, "more has probably been printed during the past ten years than for a generation preceding," was thoroughly canvassed.

The aim pursued had been to select hymns "which show forth the praises of God and the glories of his attributes in the glowing language of the emotions," such hymns as "appeared best to express Scripture truths regarding man's lost estate and the means of his recovery through Christ," and to be most "expressive of the warmest love and nearness to God. . . the most fervent zeal, and the most touching and comforting religious experience."

In pursuing this purpose the committee had "cast aside a large mass of mediocre hymns," * and had chosen in their place "those which in Watts, Steele, Wesley, Doddridge, Toplady and some more modern writers prove themselves the offspring of deep religious convictions based upon a sound and true

---

* They add, however: "Your committee has not hesitated to retain some hymns apparently subject to criticism by a cultivated taste, but which, by general consent of Christians, appear to be of such merit as to defy ordinary rules of criticism. Among such we regard Newton's ''Tis a point I long to know,' and 'I asked the Lord that I might grow in grace.'"

theology." On the other hand, they had added a large number of valuable hymns which were not to be found in the General Assembly's book * nor in "Watts and Select," † the book which the church was at that time using. The result was a collection of six hundred and sixteen psalms and hymns, of such a character that the committee believed no other recent compilation for congregational use was "more rigidly confined to the productions of the great hymn writers," or more free from the second-rate material by which in recent years the hymnology of the church had been debased.

The book was rendered still more valuable by the inclusion in it of certain of the ancient hymns of the Church, such as the "Gloria in Excelsis" and the "Te Deum," ‡ also a selection of other chants, especially from the Psalms, and a collection of sacred

* "As a sample we name the following, namely: by Toplady, 'When languor and disease invade'; by Charles Wesley, 'Soldiers of Christ, arise'; by Needham, 'Rise, O my soul, pursue the path'; by Cowper, 'The billows swell, the winds are high'; by Montgomery, 'Prayer is the soul's sincere desire.'" Committee's report.

† "As a sample we name the following, namely: by Doddridge, 'How gentle God's commands'; by the same, 'My gracious Lord, I own thy right'; by Tate and Brady, 'As pants the hart for cooling streams'; by Doddridge, 'Awake, my soul, stretch every nerve'; by Cowper, 'Jesus, where'er thy people meet'; by Wesley, 'Come, O thou Traveller unknown'; by Gerhardt, 'O Sacred Head, now wounded'; by Charlotte Elliot, 'Just as I am, without one plea'; by Mrs. Adams, 'Nearer, my God, to thee'; by Henry Francis Lyte, 'Abide with me, fast falls the eventide'; by an unknown author, 'Ye Christian heralds, go proclaim.'" Committee's report.

‡ The committee quote with approval the opinion of Dr. Hamilton "that in churches where the Apostles' or Nicene Creed is not audibly repeated by the congregation, great advantage is derived from confessing with the mouth the doctrine of our holy faith in song, especially in this chant [the Te Deum] which was praised by Luther as a good symbol not less than a perfect hymn."

lyrics,* which, although from their nature unfitted for congregational singing, "are exceedingly profitable in private devotions and are calculated greatly to benefit young persons in the family, cultivating in them a taste for the very best order of religious verse."

In November, 1869, the book was published under the title, "The Sacrifice of Praise." It was at once introduced into the church, and with its aid the regular committee on music, with Dr. Murray still at the head, took up their work again with renewed interest, and especially directed their attention to the development of the congregational singing to the fullest possible extent. †

In raising additional subscriptions for the music, the committee proved themselves equally zealous, and for several years, they thus provided about $1,400, for by this time the annual cost of the music had come to be nearly $4,000.

The singing was by no means the only element of public worship that engaged the attention of the session at this time. Indeed, in 1870, a committee was appointed to consider whether in general there were any changes that ought to be introduced into the manner of conducting the services in the Brick Church. We do not know what proposals they may have made, except that at the suggestion of their chairman the gown, which had been worn

* "Exquisite gems such as Wesley's 'Wrestling Jacob,' and Montgomery's 'Poor wayfaring man of grief,' and Keble's celebrated hymn on complete resignation to God." Committee's report.

† We learn that besides the congregational singing of psalms and hymns there was now an "opening piece," sung presumably by the choir alone.

by the minister in Dr. Rodgers' day, but had been disused during Dr. Spring's pastorate, was now resumed. We may, perhaps, infer from this that their recommendations were in the direction of an increased orderliness and dignity in the worship of the church. It should be added that the manner of celebrating the Lord's Supper * was, during Dr. Murray's pastorate, given careful consideration.†

It was during this period, moreover, that certain changes were made in the number of the services and meetings and in the time at which they were held, by which some of the customs, still prevailing at the present day, were originated. Thus the change of the hour of Sunday morning service to eleven o'clock was first broached in 1873, "for the accommodation of families with children, Sunday-school teachers and scholars, persons living at a distance from the church, and the many others whose convenience would be promoted by the change." Earlier than this a more radical departure from established custom had been introduced: in 1866, the weekly lecture, which was at that time held on Tuesday evening, was temporarily discontinued, "with a view to increasing the interest and attendance at the weekly prayer and conference meeting on Friday evening." ‡ A year later the holding of but a single meeting between Sundays was still further established as the accepted custom—it consisted of "a brief lecture connected

* After 1865, this Sacrament was administered five instead of four times yearly.

† See Appendix V, p. 543. For order of Baptismal service at this time see Appendix U, p. 542.

‡ Although the nights had been changed, these were, it will be observed, the same two week-day services as were held in Dr. Rodgers' time.

with a prayer-meeting, to continue for one hour and a quarter," * —and by 1869, when the meeting was held, as at present, on Wednesday evening, it was referred to as "the weekly church meeting," as though a second week-day service were not so much as thought of.

Among the changes which during Dr. Murray's pastorate marked the beginning of the present era, one of the most important concerned the activities then commenced among the women of the congregation. In Christian work of every sort the part played to-day by the women of our churches is so important that we find it difficult to conceive what the conditions would be, were they to become inactive. Yet it must be remembered that this great importance of women's work is a very modern development. When Dr. Murray came to the Brick Church the women had only begun to discover their powers, but before his departure their work had assumed definite shape and had already acquired a place of unquestionable prominence and practical value in the church's programme.

Long before this time women had, of course, been active in Sunday-school work and their benevolent impulses had no doubt found abundant expression in personal charities, and to some extent in money-raising auxiliaries of the prominent missionary and benevolent organizations of the church at large,†

---

* It was held on Tuesdays that year.

† A "Female Auxiliary Tract Association of the Brick Church," for example, had been in existence before the middle of the century. The account book of the treasurer of this organization for the years 1837 to 1861, is preserved in the church archives. Its subscription lists constitute an interesting roll of the givers and workers among the Brick Church women for that period.

but for women alone the only distinctive organized work in the Brick Church had been a struggling little "Dorcas Society," concerning which but few facts have come down to us. We do not even know when it was founded. Its chief purpose, as its name implies, was to provide garments for the poor; but occasionally, we are told, it also superintended the sending of a home missionary box. Aside from these scanty facts, the only thing we know about the Dorcas Society is connected with the burning of Dr. Hoge's house one night in February, 1860.

It seems that on that occasion the entire clothing of Dr. Hoge's family was either burnt, or spoiled by the water used in extinguishing the fire, so that the children were forced to stay in bed till clothes could be borrowed for them from the neighbors. But the Dorcas Society came to the rescue. The members were promptly called together and worked to such good purpose that by Sunday the minister's family had all been refitted and could appear in church with new clothes of their own. *

In January, 1869, some of those who had been active in this society decided that, by adopting a somewhat different plan of work, they could accomplish a great deal more good. If, instead of making with their own hands the garments to be given away in charity, they employed for that purpose poor women who needed work and especially work that could be done at home, it was evident that the value of the benevolence would be doubled. This plan was already in use in a society in the Marble Collegiate

* These facts are taken from a letter written by Miss Sophia Ely in 1902.

Church on Twenty-ninth Street, and the women of the Brick Church now adopted it, forming for that purpose what has ever since been known as the Employment Society.* For some time the old Dorcas Society continued its work in coöperation with the newer organization. The latest mention of it was in April, 1871.

The work of the Employment Society, which was carefully systematized, is worthy of being described in some detail. The first necessity was to secure capital for running the business—for "business" is the proper word to use: the society was really engaged in a small way in the manufacture and sale of clothing. The needed capital was provided by annual subscriptions from the members, by donations, and, after the work had been started, by the proceeds of the sales.

A certain portion of the money was then expended for materials, and the records show that the buying committee were constantly on the alert to lay in their supply when prices were most favorable. The rest of the money was set aside for the payment of the women employed to do the sewing.

Meantime the garments must be cut out, and for this purpose the cutting committee met in the

---

* The following were the members whose names appear in the records of the first year: Mrs. Barbour, Beebe, Blakeman, Bonnett, Brown, Buchan, Buchanan, Burr, Church, Clark, Comstock, Corning, Downer, Dunning, Gilman, Holbrook, Holden, Lathrop, Morgan, Murray, Odell, Paton, Shedd, Stafford, Talmage, Tucker, Watson, White; Misses Bonnett, Donaldson, Houghton, Lord, Parish, Phelps, Smith, Vernon, Vose. To Mrs. W. G. T. Shedd, who was first directress for several years from the time of the society's organization, much of the success of the society was due. The minutes of the board of managers from the beginning till the present time have been carefully preserved.

church rooms on Friday mornings, while many of the
members continued this work at home between the
meetings. Frequently from three to four hundred
garments would be cut in a single month.

The employment of women to do the sewing was
managed by a system of "permits." Each annual
subscriber had the privilege of sending, in the course
of a season, a certain number of applicants. If the
subscriber's recommendation and her guarantee of
the return of the materials were satisfactory, a permit
was issued which entitled the applicant to receive
work from the distributing committee. When finished, the work was brought back and submitted for
inspection. Here was encountered one of the chief
difficulties: the women were often found to be far
from skilful with their needles. Various expedi-
ents for solving the problem thus created were proposed from time to time, such as, the absolute
refusal of work to persons not competent; the re-
quirement that work be done over when not satisfactory; the imposing of some sort of penalty upon
the sewer or upon the subscriber who had recommended her; or the offering of some sort of reward,
especially the promise of double the amount of work,
to those whose work was well done. But the happiest
expedient attempted was one which responded to the
need by introducing, in addition to the society's designated work of "employment," some features properly belonging to a sewing-school.

A concrete instance may be given. At a meeting
in January, 1871, the subject of poor sewing "was
enlarged upon," the minutes tell us, and in the course
of the discussion "one girl was alluded to as a great

object of charity, but a very poor sewer." There-
upon, the record continues, "Mrs. Odell cut the discussion short by kindly offering to give her instruction in her own house, to see if she showed any
disposition to improve under proper teaching." It is
pleasant to read in the minutes of the next meeting
that Mrs. Odell's pupil already showed "decided
improvement."

When the garments had been completed and the
women paid for their work, the next problem was to
dispose of the finished product. Occasionally, when
a large stock had accumulated, donations were made
to the Dorcas Society or other similar organizations,
but for the most part the goods were sold. The prices
were adjusted in accordance with a double standard:
members of the society and their friends paid the
full, or nearly the full, cost of materials and making;
while to the poor and to charitable societies garments
were sold at a small percentage of the cost-price.

In order to give some conception of the amount of
work accomplished by this useful organization, the
results of a single season chosen at random, that of
1871-1872, may be noted. Including the work done
by the members during the summer months two
thousand and ninety garments were cut out, and by
the end of the season all but one hundred and eight
of these had been finished. The sewers, who ranged
from forty to seventy in number, had been paid
$911.25. Garments sold had brought in nearly $900,
and over $400 had been received in subscriptions
and donations. As the years passed all these figures
were materially increased.

Out of the Employment Society there grew another

organization. In order to follow up, in a more distinctly personal and religious way, the work which the society was doing, a Bible reader, or visitor, had been employed, Miss Margaret Griffiths, whose duty it was to visit among the poor women of the mission. In the course of her visitations Miss Griffiths found a great many sick children whose need appealed to her most strongly, and to the women of the Brick Church, also, when she brought her report to them.

The proposition was made that the Brick Church children be organized to meet this emergency, under the direction, of course, of their elders. The result was the Children's Society, which flourished for many years, and did an excellent work, not only for the sick children on the west side, but also for the boys and girls of the Brick Church, whom it trained in Christian service.*

At the meetings of the society the girls were set to work at making simple children's garments, and the boys, who are, it must be confessed, somewhat hard to make useful under such circumstances, were fain to be content with making scrap-books. Besides this, a good deal of money was raised, and with it a work begun which was destined to extend far beyond the sphere to which it was originally limited. We shall in a subsequent chapter have a glimpse of the Children's Society during the next pastorate, and at a still later time shall learn how, in dying, it gave birth to another organization which remains and works to the present day.

* The originators of this plan were Mrs. Norman White and Mrs. James O. Murray. Others who aided them were Mrs. Alexander McLean, Miss Mary M. Roberts, Mrs. John E. Parsons, Mrs. W. G. T. Shedd and Miss Houghton.

In this account of the activities of Dr. Murray's pastorate, which mark the beginning of the present era, we come finally to the benevolences, which, with the growing wealth of the time had so increased in amount as to render the old schedules quite inadequate, and which were now reorganized on a modern basis. The five annual offerings arranged in 1838 had, with some changes in the objects, continued until 1864, when a sixth offering was added; but two years later the number was increased to nine, and in 1870 there were ten stated objects of Brick Church benevolence.* Except for the division of some of these into two or more, and the addition of two others,† the present schedule is practically the same.

In 1871, in response to a recommendation of the Presbytery, an entirely different system was temporarily adopted, the so-called "plan of weekly giving," by which the members were invited to pledge a stated sum for each Sunday throughout the year, the entire amount so received being then apportioned by the session among the various causes. For a time the results of this change were highly satisfactory. In October, 1872, for example, it was reported that "the aggregate contributions for the past year have considerably exceeded those of the preceding one, although the new system was not inaugurated until the middle of December." But at the end of four years' time, when the excellence of novelty had worn off, it

---

* These were, Church Erection, N. Y. Bible Society, Brick Church Mission, Board of Freedmen, Domestic Missions, Board of Education, Foreign Missions, Aged and Infirm Clergy Fund, City Missions, Board of Publication. These offerings were taken on the third Sunday of each month except July and August.

† For Hospitals and Church Federation.

was felt that for the Brick Church the old arrangement was, on the whole, more successful, and the
schedule of ten specific annual collections was resumed.

The spirit in which the church at this time approached this whole subject of giving is well illustrated by the brief address on the subject of "Christian Beneficence" which the session prepared in 1865
and published in the "catalogues" of the congregation for 1866 and subsequent years.   In this little
publication, it may be added, no other department of
the church's life, except the duty of Christian discipleship as a whole, was given so much space.

"That our prosperity as a church," the session
declare, "is closely connected with the use of property for religious objects, is apparent from the Word
of God.   As an explanation of our frequent public
contributions in the church, members are here reminded of first principles made known in the Scriptures."

They then proceed to show that the religion of
the Old Testament was inseparably connected with
"statedly recurring tithes and offerings, so that no
conscientious Hebrew could fulfil the duties of the
sanctuary without necessarily becoming a systematic
giver"; that the prophetic teaching of later Israel
was no less emphatic on this subject; that "the pre-
cepts and example of the Saviour confirmed all previous teaching as to the importance of alms-giving,
and gave assurance of great spiritual benefit resulting therefrom," and finally that "apostolic authority
enjoins Christian liberality as a *grace* in which
Christians were to abound."

Therefore, they conclude, "regarding alms-giving as an imperative Christian duty, an exalted Christian privilege, a means of grace, and an act of worship, the session of the Brick Church recommend all its members to accord to Christian beneficence a high place in their Christian life, and to see that it be unostentatious, cheerful, systematic and prayerful."

That this appeal of the session to the spirit of generous giving in the people met with a large response, the statistics of the offerings for these years plainly testify. Though not so eloquent, in the form of expression, as the words of the church officers just quoted, the figures reported by the treasurer from year to year did certainly possess a certain eloquence of their own. In 1865, the people had given about $19,000, a very large figure, it was thought at the time, and more than twice as much as had ever been given in any one year up to three years previous. But in 1866, the next year, the people of the Brick Church gave $61,550. The special work * which caused such an amazing increase at this time will form the subject of the next chapter, and for the present it is necessary only to notice the amount contributed. The next year, when the same special demand continued, the contributions reached almost the same figure, amounting to over $59,000. This was remarkable enough, but when, after the special need of those two years has been met and left behind, the offerings continue, in 1868 and 1869, to aggregate as much or more, we become aware of a new standard of giving adopted by the people of the Brick Church.

* The building of the Brick Church Mission on West Thirty-fifth Street.

After that there was, indeed, some falling off, but even so, there was no return to the old low figure of 1865. The congregation had learned how much they could give, if they chose, and were plainly disposed to take a large part in the religious and philanthropic work of their day.

CHAPTER XIX

A WIDER HORIZON: 1857–1875

"When I ceased my active connection with the mission, I felt, and I had occasion frequently to say, that I looked upon the twenty years of my service there as the most profitable of any work in which I had been engaged. I doubt if there is any work in this city which bears larger or more satisfactory fruit than this."— JOHN E. PARSONS, from an address in "The Story of the Christ Church Work," pp. 43 f.

"Behold, I have set before thee an open door."—*Revelation* 3 : 8.

O F all that was accomplished during Dr. Murray's pastorate nothing can be compared in importance with the opening in 1867, of the Brick Church Mission Chapel. The work for which this building was provided has already been several times alluded to in this history, for it had been started ten years before the date just mentioned. We must now turn back to trace its progress through those earlier years. It is fortunately possible to tell the story almost entirely in the words of those who were themselves the foremost workers in the enterprise.*

* An address of Mr. John E. Parsons, first superintendent of the Brick Church Branch Sunday-school, delivered November 27th, 1905, and published in "The Story of the Christ Church Work," N. Y., 1906. Also a minute of the Brick Church session in 1866, on the origin of the mission, printed in the same pamphlet. It was signed by Dr. Murray as pastor, Mr. John E. Parsons, whose controlling influence in the work will be made abundantly evident in the succeeding narrative, and Mr. George de Forest Lord, another devoted laborer in the school "who taught the boy's Bible class," says Mr. Parsons, "I think down to the time of his death, certainly down to the time when I ceased to be superintendent [1877], and toward whom, during all his life, I entertained feelings of the warmest and most affectionate regard."

"In the winter of 1857–1858," we are told—and we should remember that the present Brick Church was not then completed, "by a simultaneous impulse, two enterprises, one at No. 654 Sixth Avenue and the other at No. 1272 Broadway, were started for the purpose of furnishing religious instruction on the Sabbath to the children and young persons of the destitute section of the city lying to the westward of the Sixth Avenue. The former was principally sustained by members of [the] Brick Church and of the church at the corner of Fifth Avenue and Nineteenth Street, * while the latter owed its origin mainly to persons connected with the Scotch Presbyterian Church, † though each extended an earnest invitation for aid to all those connected with the churches in the upper part of the city who felt a desire to assist in the Master's work. A description of the origin of one will explain the origin of both. It was in literal obedience to the injunction, 'Go out into the highways and hedges and compel them to come in, that my house may be filled.'" ‡

"In October, 1857, six or eight young men, with more faith and fervor than financial strength, were impelled to start in this part of the city a mission school. . . . On a bright Sunday afternoon one of the number took his place at the head of the stairs, while the others went out to bring in boys from the street. First came one, then a second, then two or three more. Then there was a rush, and the room was taken possession of by a considerable number of

* The present Fifth Avenue Presbyterian Church.
† Then in Fourteenth Street between Fifth and Sixth avenues.
‡ "Session Minutes."

the young roughs of the neighborhood. They had been found playing ball,* had accepted an invitation, with the idea that more amusement might be afforded in the school than in the street, and they, with the others who had preceded them, formed the nucleus of what later on was to become the Brick Church Mission.

"They very quickly discovered that an essential feature of the fun was to obey orders. The first lesson on that line was taught that afternoon. It was followed up on succeeding Sundays, until there was established as a characteristic of the school . . . absolute good order." †

"The twin movements continued separate until the spring of 1859, [when] it was deemed by those having them in charge (they happening to be on terms of personal friendship) desirable to coalesce. The large hall ‡ at the north-east corner of Broadway and Thirty-second Street was accordingly engaged, and there, on a pleasant Sunday morning in the month of March, 1859, teachers and scholars met." §
From the time of this union two sessions of the school were held each Sunday, one in the morning, the other in the afternoon. Thus the children were fully provided for.

But it was soon found that another class of people had been drawn within reach of the influence of the work, for which the school did not provide at all.

---

* "And finally a company of boys found playing at ball, who at once contributed some fifteen or twenty hardened little Sabbath-breakers." "Session Minutes."

† Narrative of Mr. Parsons.

‡ On the third story.

§ "Session Minutes."

These were "the parents and adult friends of the children." So good an opportunity as this, for enlarging the scope of the enterprise, was not to be lost, and accordingly "the services of a faithful missionary," the Rev. John Kimball,* "were secured, and in the succeeding winter [1859–1860], a church service on Sunday afternoons † was started." ‡

It will be observed that during all this time the work was entirely independent, connected neither with the Brick Church nor with any other, except through the individual church members who carried it on and contributed to its support. The Brick Church provided such devoted workers as Mr. Thomas C. M. Paton and Mr. A. Gifford Agnew, but the superintendent, Mr. John E. Parsons, though in later years so closely identified with the Brick Church, was then a member of the Scotch Church, and it was from two of his fellow-members there that a considerable part of the money for the school's support during its early years was derived. Mr. Parsons himself tells us in a peculiarly interesting manner how this came about.

"I received one day," he says, "a note from a member [of the Scotch Church] asking me to call. I did so. He began to speak about the school, and asked how we proposed to meet its expenses. In the

---

* See Appendix Q, p. 535.

† "As the child is father to the man, so the school was parent to the church. The need of a congregation for adult worshippers became apparent as soon as the school was fairly started. Some assembly for worship must be available for parents interested in the work through their children, some household of faith into which scholars could be received when they were ready to make their personal profession of the religion of Jesus." The Rev. James M. Farr in "The Story of the Christ Church Work." p. 16.

‡ "Session Minutes."

enthusiasm of youth I expressed strong confidence that what we could not do ourselves would in some way be provided, we did not know exactly how or from what source. He asked what our rent then was. I told him $600 a year. He said he thought that would be about his share. And he went on to say that (although he would make no promise for the future), until I received notice to the contrary, I would, on the first of every month, receive his check for $50.

"Within a year or two he died. Not long subsequently I received a line from his brother asking me to call. I called. He told me that in looking over his brother's accounts and papers, he found that once a month I was receiving this payment of $50. He asked me to explain what it was for. I did so. In almost the same words which had been used by his brother, he said that (although he would make no promise for the future), until I learned to the contrary I would receive on the first of every month, toward the expenses of the school, his check for $50, and for a year or more it was sent. I refer to this, not only because it shows how was justified the trust in Providence upon which we had relied, but particularly because Mr. Samuel Cochran and Mr. Thomas Cochran, the two brothers, were the great uncles of Mr. William D. Barbour, and it was not long after this that there began Mr. Barbour's connection with the school which, to its very great benefit, has lasted down to the present time."

And here it is pleasant to record that three others among the present workers in this school, the Misses Hatfield and their sister, Mrs. Alexander McLean, have served for a term of years only slightly shorter than that of Mr. Barbour. They entered the work in 1864 and 1865, and it would be hard to estimate the value of their devoted service in the more than forty years that have since passed.

But to return to the progress of the work: at the same time that the school was showing a tendency, as has been related, to grow beyond itself into a church, its own members were rapidly increasing, so that larger quarters, especially for the accommodation of "a numerously attended infant class," * were found to be necessary. In response to this demand "the three upper stories of the building No. 1285 Broadway" were obtained, and thither the mission moved in the month of April, 1860.†

"The standing of the school was by this time assured. There had gathered together a large corps of teachers, all young, all personal friends, and all devoted to their work. There had become established the morning Sunday-school service, preceded by a short prayer-meeting, the afternoon Sunday-school service, succeeded by periodical teachers' meetings, a Wednesday-evening service, and, with the assistance of students from Union Seminary, a preaching service," ‡ on Sunday evenings. "The enterprise as thus constituted continued until November, 1862, without special church connection, and sustained by the voluntary efforts of those engaged in it." §

* "Session Minutes."

† Between Thirty-fourth and Thirty-fifth streets, where the store of R. H. Macy and Co. now stands.

‡ Narrative of Mr. Parsons.

§ "Session Minutes."

"At this time there was being agitated in the Brick Church the question of establishing a mission school of its own. It meant," says Mr. Parsons, "that there would be withdrawn from our school a considerable number of valuable teachers, male and female. It meant that there might be two weak missions in near competition, instead of one strong mission." The result was an invitation to Mr. Parsons' school to become the mission of the Brick Church.

This plan had, indeed, been under consideration for some time, and the church had more than once extended this invitation in an informal way; but in 1862, the matter was taken up with a more definite purpose, and in November of that year the Brick Church officially assumed charge of the enterprise. The relation thus established was well defined in the following minute prepared by Mr. Daniel Lord and adopted by the session in April, 1863: "The session, having had in consideration the relation of the mission school lately patronized by the congregation, express their view of that relation as follows: That by their pastors, elders, and other officers of this church they will foster and favor it in every way, and will favor its aid and support by the contributions of the people. They will visit it, or see to its visitation by proper officers and delegates, and will generally supervise and promote its welfare. That the session, on the other hand, expect that their counsels and advice will be deferred to, and that between the school and those engaged in its management and government, and the pastors, elders, deacons, and members of the church, a cordial, active, and hearty coöperation will be kept up."

During the first half year of this most profitable and providential union the Brick Church people gave to the work of the mission $1,195,* a true prophecy of the constant and generous support of later years. Immediately the second story of the building which adjoined the one already occupied was secured, and "the division wall sufficiently removed to make one larger room." Had it not been that the Civil War, which was at this time raging, checked the advance of every sort of aggressive enterprise, the mission would no doubt have been provided almost at once with a building of its own. That it was worthy of such accommodation had soon become evident to all.

The work was, in truth, growing in all directions. The Saturday morning sewing-school, which was to become an important institution, was started at this time. A children's prayer-meeting, and, a little later, a reading-room and library for adults were other new features. But especially the development toward a church, to be the centre and focus of the whole work, had become very marked. Mr. Kimball, the first missionary, had been succeeded, in 1862, by the Rev. A. E. Rulifson, and he, two years later,† by the Rev. Govello B. Bell. By this time Sunday services were held in the morning as well as in the evening, and in 1865 it was proposed that the Sacrament of the Lord's Supper should be celebrated at the mission on the evening of the same day on which it was celebrated in the Brick Church, one of

* The average annual contribution for the first seven years was $4,194.00.

† In the interval between these two, the Rev. Mr. Tait preached for a few months.

the pastors of the Brick Church and the missionary officiating.

Of course, under the conditions then existing, all who, through the work done at the mission, were led to a personal acceptance of Christianity, became members of the Brick Church, and made their public profession there; and until this time it had been necessary for all such persons to go to the Brick Church in order to receive the Communion. But the session, when the matter was brought to their attention by Mr. Bell, now decided * that there were convincing reasons for making a change. It was thought that the people of the mission, coming to the Brick Church for Communion only, felt themselves in some degree to be outsiders and strangers at a service where such a feeling was peculiarly unfortunate, that possibly some were actually deterred from becoming professed Christians because of these conditions, and that the effect upon the regular worshippers at the mission, of having the ordinance administered there, could not but be good. This important step toward the transformation of the mission into a church was accordingly taken.

In the winter of 1865–1866, the most pressing problem connected with the work advanced toward its solution. At that time "the great and general prosperity which followed the close of the war, afforded the hope that success might attend an effort on the part of the Brick Church to erect a building for its mission, and for the accommodation of the various services which had grown about it." † A

* In June, 1865.
† "Session Minutes."

committee was accordingly appointed by the mission workers themselves, and so energetically did they take up the task, that when they laid their plans before the trustees of the church in May of 1866, they had secured pledges amounting to $40,000,* and had actually bought "three lots on the south side of Thirty-fifth Street, west of Seventh Avenue," † where they proposed to begin building at once. ‡

A year and a half later, on October 20th, 1867, the Brick Church Mission Chapel, at No. 228 West Thirty-fifth Street, was dedicated. § The building (known in more recent years as Christ Church) will be well remembered by many readers of this volume. It was built of brick, with light stone trimmings, and presented its gable end to the street. Below, on the

---

* The pledges for definite sums amounted to $38,200 and four gentlemen had promised to bring it up to the figure named in the text. The sum subscribed had increased to $41,370 by April, 1867, while over $26,000 was added the next year.

† In turning over the undertaking at this point to the trustees, the committee said: "It is thought proper that the title shall be taken in your name, that the fund raised shall be paid into and drawn from your treasury, and that [it] be under your control, with no legal restraint upon you, and only on the honorary obligation (to be evidenced by suitable entries in your minutes) that the contribution shall never, unless in view of circumstances which cannot now be foreseen, be diverted from the purpose for which it has been subscribed. The Brick Church has received a mission at the hands of the donors represented by us. Time, which has worked such wonderful changes in the past of our city, may again compel a removal of the Brick Church. By this gift it is desired that the trustees shall feel committed to the application of these funds for the maintenance *somewhere* of a Brick Church Mission so long as there shall be a Brick Church."

‡ Before the building began, it was proposed that the site be exchanged for one on Thirty-seventh Street, and the trustees were asked to supply $7,500, the difference in price, but they refused, deeming the site first chosen to be preferable.

§ A portion of the building had, however, been in use for several months before this. The opening of the Sunday-school had taken place on May 27th.

street level, and reached through three entrances, was the church, adjoined by smaller rooms for church meetings and the pastor's study. Four staircases, one at each corner of the building, ascended to the Sunday-school room, which covered the entire upper story. Its lofty roof, large windows, and especially the commodious gallery at the south end, filled with the boys and girls of Mr. Barbour's intermediate department, made it a place that one remembers with peculiar pleasure.

Not long after the new building was occupied "the numbers in attendance had increased from the three hundred and twenty-five who were present at the opening service . . . to seven and eight hundred, the full capacity of the hall. The very first Christmas festival had an attendance of some fifteen hundred— nine hundred children and six hundred adults."* And, by the way, this was probably the very first time that the word "Christmas" was used officially in connection with the Brick Church. The year before, 1866, special exercises were, it is true, held in the mission school on Sunday, December 23d, but in the printed programme it was carefully described as "The Anniversary of the Brick Church Mission School," and not a word in the order of service, which appeared below, suggested in the slightest degree the beautiful story of Bethlehem.† Apparently, however, the sight of those eager children's faces, and the experience of their childish needs, had at last broken down the old objection to an observance which had

* "The Story of the Christ Church Work," p. 10.

† The hymns were "Saviour, like a Shepherd lead us," "Jesus loves me," "Am I a soldier of the Cross," "Jesus paid it all," and "Nearer, my God, to thee."

THE BRICK CHURCH MISSION CHAPEL

been supposed in earlier years to be unevangelical;
for in December, 1867, the children were invited,
not to a mere "Anniversary," but to a "Christmas
Festival," and joined their voices in singing "This is
Christmas Day" and "While Shepherds watched
their flocks by night."

Coincident with the opening of the new chapel was
the coming to the mission of the Rev. Joseph J.
Lampe, whose pastorate there was to continue for
nearly thirty years; and at the same time, another
prerogative of an independent church was given to
his congregation. It was then decided that those at
the mission who desired to make a profession of their
faith need no longer go to the Brick Church for this
purpose, but might be received into membership of
the Brick Church *at the mission chapel;* thus in everything except its government the mission became practically an independent organization.

From this time the growth of the congregation
there, both in strength and in members, was phenomenal. Not long after Mr. Lampe had taken up
the work, so many names of applicants for church
membership were presented by him to the session of
the Brick Church, that at the close of the session
meeting the ministers and elders were constrained to
unite "in a season of special thanksgiving to God for
his blessing on the mission."

One special feature of the work at this time calls
for particular mention, a dispensary started in 1872.
Like the sewing-school and the reading-room, already
referred to, this was an early indication of the need
of various forms of activity supplementary to the
purely spiritual. This dispensary, for the assistance

and relief of the sick poor of the church was, the session records tell us, "in charge of Dr. E. D. Morgan, Jr., who had generously tendered his services in connection therewith." * This work was continued at the mission for two years.

Meanwhile, the Sunday-school which had been from the beginning, and continued to be, the foundation of the work, was enjoying great prosperity. For this it was indebted, under God, to the unselfish devotion of the workers and especially to Mr. John E. Parsons, who, during all these years and until 1877, was at its head. "For twenty years he has occupied that post," said the session, in reluctantly accepting his resignation, "He has been enabled by the good providence of the Head of the Church to gather around him a devoted band of Christian workers. By the inspiration derived from his own energetic leadership these teachers formed and maintained one of the most extensive and flourishing missions in the city. The regularity, devotion, and wise management of the superintendent were exemplary to all associated with him, and the estimate which the friends of the mission have formed, during a long continuance of years, of Mr. Parsons' work, has been

* In a memorial address on the life of Dr. Morgan, delivered by Dr. C. R. Agnew before the Medical Society of the County of New York, the following reference is made to this enterprise: Dr. Morgan "graduated from Bellevue Hospital Medical College in 1871. He soon opened an office on the west side of the city, near the quarters of the poor, and from that moment until broken down in health, in the spring of 1879, devoted himself, as the writer of this very well knows, to the unpaid care of the sick poor. I take back that word 'unpaid.' He got his reward; for although he, with exemplary reticence and meekness, tried to hide his beneficence from the gaze and applause of his fellow-men, it was seen, we must believe, by One who never allows a cup of cold water even to be given, in true charity, to a sufferer without a note in his book of remembrance."

heightened by the consideration that it was sustained throughout the severe and growing pressure of professional duties." During this whole period, we are reminded by the present pastor of Christ Church, "the school met in both morning and afternoon sessions. These long years of exacting service, the many hours of the Sabbaths which he used, not for rest, but for the Master's service, the energy and intelligence with which he directed the work of the school, should insure to Mr. Parsons a grateful memory among the people of Christ Church, while his example of consecrated service should be an inspiration to us all."* For the subsequent development of this whole enterprise, we must wait until we reach a later chapter of the history.

In January, 1875, Dr. Murray expressed his desire to resign from the Brick Church pastorate that he might accept a call to the Chair of Rhetoric and English Literature in Princeton College. The affection with which the congregation regarded him was very deep, and they had learned to prize very highly the intellectual and spiritual quality of his ministrations. One or two concrete facts will serve to suggest the esteem with which he was regarded. In 1868, when he had been pastor but three years, his salary was raised to $8,000,† a very emphatic indication of the

* "The Story of the Christ Church Work," p. 11.

† It will be interesting to note, as an indication of the make-up of the church at this time, the names of those present at the meeting of men of the congregation at which this increase was voted. They were: Hon. E. D. Morgan, Messrs. White, Ely, Gilman, Dunning, Nixon, Bennet, Joscelyn, Black, Griswold, Parsons, Comstock, West, Knapp, Paton, Spofford, Downer, Sperry, Faxon, Parish, Hull and Lord.

value that was placed upon his services. In the next year another act of the congregation showed with equal clearness their personal attachment to him. They gave him, on their own initiation, a leave of absence for five months that he might cross the ocean "for purposes of culture and relaxation"; and as in the case of Dr. Spring, many years before, his departure was made the occasion of expressing in words the affection of the congregation.* It was impossible they said, to express fully "the feeling of attachment, respect, and confidence with which our people are most closely bound to you. We truly compose but one Christian family, guided, as we believe, by God through means of your ministry, on which a great blessing has been bestowed."

As the years passed, these sentiments were still further strengthened, and it is evident from the records, that his friends of the Brick Church learned with sincere sorrow of his proposed resignation and departure to Princeton. He, on his part, was for many reasons most loath to go. He said with feeling that his ten years in the Brick Church had been the happiest of his life. But the work which had been offered to him at the college had peculiar attractions for him, and there were, moreover, reasons why his departure from New York had come to appear desirable, if not necessary. "The large executive business and the distracting details of his office [in the Brick

---

* The regular summer holiday at the time of Dr. Murray's coming to New York consisted of six weeks. It may be added here that during the pastor's absence it was customary to hold union services with a neighboring church, and we note with special interest that the records at this time speak repeatedly of such an arrangement between the Church of the Covenant and the Brick Church.

Church] and, above all, the glaring publicity in which of necessity he did his work, for a man of his temperament, were hard, and they wore upon him." *

The session acquiesced in his resignation with great reluctance. "Did we yield to our own desires," they said, "or to our views of what the interests of the church dictate, we should without dissent feel it impossible to agree to Dr. Murray's request." But the most emphatic and expressive protest against the acceptance of Dr. Murray's resignation was that which was presented to the session in the name of the children of the church, as soon as the unwelcome news reached the ears of the people. This letter, though it was not the production, we may suppose, of the youthful signers themselves, did express the thoughts of the parents in regard to Dr. Murray's beneficent influence upon their children, and their belief that upon the boys and girls he had made a definite and favorable impression. This in itself was surely no small commendation of his ministry.

"We feel," the letter to the session says, after a brief introduction, "that we, the children of this church, who have been so blessed with his instructions, always so full of affectionate, earnest, and prayerful solicitude for our best good, so tenderly striving to win us to the truth, cannot rest without earnestly begging you to reconsider your action in this matter. We beg you to consider the blessing we have in the prayers and instructions of the pulpit, ever given in language so rarely fitted to guide the young mind to all that is pure and elevated in thought and action, while it is so fully in the spirit of the

* "James O. Murray," by John De Witt, p. 26.

meekness and tenderness of our blessed Saviour. We beg you to compare it with much of the instruction of the present time, so unsuited to the dignity and solemnity of the sacred desk. We also beg you to consider our loss in not only losing these sacred instructions, but also the devoted, affectionate, and earnest efforts that Mrs. Murray and the family have made for our pleasure and improvement in all respects. *

"And, dear Sirs, in view of these considerations, to our minds and hearts more weighty than we have power to express, we pledge ourselves that, if we may be blessed with the continuance of the labors and instructions of our beloved pastor, we will stand by you and him by every effort we can make to sustain you in enlarging the church, by striving by our example and effort to bring others into the Sabbath-school, and in seeking to win them to the enjoyments of the same rich privileges that have been our own, and of which we earnestly hope we may not now be deprived; and beg you to use all your influence and efforts to persuade Dr. Murray to reconsider his resignation, both as a session and as individuals; in proof of which, with great respect, we hereto affix our names."

We may be sure that after such an appeal as this, the like of which it is safe to say, not many pastors have received in relinquishing their charges, Dr. Murray would, if possible, have reversed his action, refused the alluring call to Princeton, and taken up

* Mrs. Murray had been one of the founders of the "Children's Society," as was related in the last chapter. In memory of this service rendered by her, the Murray Kindergarten, when started at the mission in 1891, was named in her honor.

once more the work for the grown people and the children of the Brick Church. But this was clearly an act that he felt to be neither wise nor right. The most that he could do was to continue for a time to occupy his old pulpit, and this he did for nine months until the beginning of October, but then at length the time came for good-bye and Godspeed.*

Such work, however, as he had done, does not perish when the worker is called away to another field. Writing twenty years later, one of his successors in the Brick Church thus paid his tribute to Dr. Murray: "A scholar of fine literary attainments, a Christian gentleman of the most beautiful character, and a preacher of profound spirituality, the influence of his ministry still abides in the church." †

* He spent the rest of his life in the service of Princeton as Professor and Dean, highly influential and greatly beloved. He died in 1899.

† Dr. van Dyke, "An Historic Church," p. 24.

CHAPTER XX

A MINISTER FROM ABROAD : 1876-1882

"What is the result of my ministry amongst you? I am not careful for you to answer in respect to external things. A growing congregation, an extending interest, a public reputation—these are small matters compared with the effect of that ministry in your hearts and lives."—LLEWELYN D. BEVAN, Pastoral Letter, 1878.

"Moreover, concerning a stranger that is not of thy people Israel, but cometh out of a far country, for thy name's sake."—1 *Kings* 8 : 41.

UNTIL 1876, the Brick Church had owned no parsonage, nor had it felt the need of one until the more frequent changes in the pastorate, combined with the increased difficulty of obtaining a residence in the neighborhood of the church, brought the matter into special prominence. At the initiation of Mr. Morgan, at this time president of the board of trustees—"Governor" Morgan, as he was always called*—an opportunity to secure No. 14 East Thirty-seventh Street was improved, and the house, "together with the mirrors, console tables, gas fixtures, and white patent shades," was purchased for $35,100. The furnishings increased this outlay by about $5,000, and the entire sum was borrowed by the trustees, largely by a mortgage on the property. This added nothing, however, to the annual burden of the church, since the pastor's salary would, of course, be proportionately reduced, † while

* He had held that office in New York State for two terms, beginning in 1858.

† From $8,000 to $6,000.

356

to the new pastor himself the provision of a suitable
and commodious house, ready for his use, would be
a great convenience.

The man chosen to be the first occupant of this
parsonage was the Rev. Llewelyn D. Bevan, LL.B.,
of London, England.*

He was pastor of the congregation which worshipped in the church on Tottenham Court Road,
known as Whitefield's Chapel,† having been erected
in 1756 by the same George Whitefield whose preaching exerted a strong influence on the religious development of the first pastor of the Brick Church, as
has been described in an earlier chapter; but except
for this coincidence of association the new pastor
was a complete stranger, and to the country as well
as to the church that had called him.

This going abroad for their minister had no doubt
been suggested to the Brick Church officers by the
example of other churches, for there were at that
time a singularly large number of foreign ministers in
New York pulpits. "It must be somewhat discouraging to our native preachers," said an editorial in one
of the newspapers, "to find so many leading pulpits
taken possession of by ministers brought from
abroad. . . . We have already, in New York, Dr.
John Hall at the great Fifth Avenue Presbyterian
Church, the most popular preacher in the city, and
a north of Ireland Scotchman; Dr. Ormiston,‡ of

---

* He was called on October 4th, 1876, his letter of acceptance was dated
November 16th, and he was installed on January 16th, 1877.

† It was replaced in 1899 by a new building now known as the Whitefield Memorial Church.

‡ In 1864, when he was settled in Hamilton, Canada, he was considered for the associate pastorate of the Brick Church.

the Fifth Avenue Collegiate Dutch Reformed Church, an eloquent sermonizer and a thorough Scotchman; and Dr. Taylor, at the Broadway Tabernacle, also a very gifted preacher and also a Scotchman, and now the old Brick Church on Fifth Avenue follows its neighbors in sending abroad for a pastor. . . . Our theological seminaries," this editorial adds, "must be turning out indifferent preachers, if the instances we have named—and they are only a part of the number—prove that, in order to get ministers whose sermons shall be satisfactory to critical congregations, the wealthiest churches must send across the Atlantic for them."

It was, however, no mere following of a fashion that influenced the people of the Brick Church in calling Mr. Bevan. They had strong grounds for their belief that in him they had found an exceptionally able preacher and pastor. He had for more than seven years worked in London with great success, as his parishioners there testified in commending him to his new charge. "We in sorrow submit [to his decision]" they said, "and transfer him to your love. . . . We pray earnestly that the loss we hereby sustain may prove the gain of the whole Church." Mr. Bevan had also been a prominent supporter of the Working Men's College in Great Ormond Street,* founded by his friend the Rev. Frederick Denison Maurice,† and a letter from the Council of the New College, London, "to the officers and members of the Presbyterian Church usually assembling for

* Moved to Crowndale Road in 1905.

† Especially, the Bible class, which Mr. Maurice had begun, but which had been dropped at his departure, was reëstablished and successfully carried on by Mr. Bevan.

LLEWELYN D. BEVAN

worship in the old Brick Church, New York," expressed in a very emphatic way the regret with which such institutions, quite outside of his own church, viewed Mr. Bevan's departure from London.

He himself could not but feel the greatest sorrow in leaving such an important and prosperous field of work. "The step which I have thus taken," he said in his letter of acceptance, "is fraught with serious issues. I leave here a broken-hearted people whom I have gathered together in the name of the Lord, a large and perfectly united communion. There are many duties within the church, with others belonging to our denomination and our country, which I hereby lay down. I need the grace of the Master, the help of the Holy Spirit, and the sympathetic association of a loving people. That these should be mine is my hourly prayer."

Personally Mr. Bevan had many peculiarly attractive qualities; "gifted, generous, vigorous, warm-hearted,"[*] thus his successor in the Brick Church has described him. He was a Welchman, as his name betokens, and he had, in full measure, the zeal and enthusiasm, the ready utterance, and the impulsive affections of that interesting race. In social intercourse he was genial and human, a man sure to make friends of those with whom he was closely associated.

In spite of all that he was leaving behind and the inevitable hardship involved in taking up his work in a foreign land among a strange people, he came nevertheless with great courage and hope. One large element, probably, in his enthusiasm—it had

* "An Historic Church," p. 24.

also been a large element, no doubt, in his decision to make the change—was the thought that he was coming to a new country, where he could bear a more influential part in laying the foundations of the later life of the people, than was possible in England. That was the kind of work to which he was especially drawn, and, we may add, for which he was fitted in a marked degree, as has been proved by his striking career in Australia in later years, where, it is reported, he has been an important factor not only in the religious, but in the social and political life of the Colony.

But it must be added that Mr. Bevan had apparently overstated to himself the newness of the field to which he was coming. He knew, of course, that the Brick Church represented, not the pioneer life of nineteenth-century America, but an older and more settled portion of its society. Indeed, the letter quoted above, in which the *New* College, London, commends him to "the *old* Brick Church," suggests that he and his English friends had noted—with a genial smile, perhaps—the antiquity, from the American point of view, of the church whose call he had accepted. Nevertheless, as was natural for a citizen of the old world, he evidently had assumed that even the oldest things in America must still be in the formative period.

It is not difficult to see that he was genuinely surprised and disappointed when the real conditions became apparent to him, when he discovered that, far as New York life was from representing a venerable civilization, it was almost equally removed from that youthful state in which any determined and courageous worker can become a founder of social and political institutions, the architect of the future on a large scale.

In an interview published on the eve of his return to England, Mr. Bevan, in a frank and interesting way, described the facts of the case as he had seen them and their effect upon himself. "Your professional men," he said, "especially clergymen, seem to be restricted to purely professional work in a fashion that we do not dream of in London. Here . . . [the clergyman] is outside of politics entirely: he is not expected to lecture much, not expected to concern himself with social questions, and not expected to concern himself much with education, justice, or temperance. To a Londoner this seems all wrong, but it is useless to question it. . . . Clergymen [in America] are well paid and kindly treated, but they are not expected to work for the good of their fellow-men, except in certain defined lines. In England the clergy of the Establishment are frequently justices of the peace. We of the non-Conformist party are members of the School Board, Public Works, and so forth, and take a part in all public movements. . . . You Americans are far more conservative than Englishmen. . . . I was asked to go to a great meeting on a public topic soon after I got here, to find that all I was expected to do was to open the meeting with a prayer and close it with a benediction. I was dumfounded." *

While this statement may seem to an American to be somewhat exaggerated, it must be confessed that

* From the "Evening Post," March 6th, 1880. To some other statements in the interview, not quoted in the text, Mr Bevan took exception in a letter printed in the "Post" on March 8th. He accepted the rest as in substance an accurate report of "a very informal conversation."

it contained a certain amount of truth. In many respects, the field of public life in New York at that time was, as Mr. Bevan says, more difficult of entrance for any but politicians than it was in London. Moreover, the work of the Brick Church was so exacting and its standards of pastoral efficiency, especially in the matter of preaching, were so high, that its pastor would find almost all his time and energy exhausted in the performance of his parish duties. It would be difficult for him to go outside of that more limited sphere and engage effectively in public affairs without some slighting of the work of his own parish. In all this Mr. Bevan not unnaturally found cause for disappointment.

The officers of the church, also, had, on their part, made a miscalculation. They had assured themselves of Mr. Bevan's success in his London pastorate, but they had not sufficiently considered whether he could so far adapt himself to the materially different conditions of the Brick Church as to achieve there a work equally successful. Perhaps they thought that to succeed as a non-Conformist among the middle class people of London, and even among the workingmen of that city, was so much more difficult than the problem presented by a prominent and well-established Presbyterian Church in New York, that no anxiety on that score need be felt. But, after all, the problem of every church is peculiar to itself, and a man, very successful in his own appropriate sphere, may be seriously handicapped when he is moved out of it.

We are thus warned from the outset of the difficulties which Mr. Bevan was called upon to face.

But in spite of them he made a vigorous beginning. The spirit and result of his work during the first two or three years cannot be better described than in his own words, quoted from two pastoral letters which he issued to the congregation in December, 1878, and November, 1879.

"The revolution of another year," he says in the earlier of these epistles, "has brought us to the second anniversary of the day when your pastor first took his place in the pulpit of your church, and it seems fitting that once again I should address you with words of affectionate greeting, grateful retrospect, and joyous forecasting. . . . The increase of familiarity has only added to my respect and affection for those who welcomed me with kindness and have never for an instant ceased to extend that sympathy and evince that hearty regard which, next to the blessing of God, are a minister's chief support.

"Another year of labor amongst you has added also to the strength of the church. We are steadily advancing in consolidation and stability. The flutter of novelty has passed away but only to leave a deeper interest and sense of obligation in the hearts of all associated in our communion. The scattered congregation has been regathered, and a large number of new friends have been added, not only to the attendance upon public worship, but to the regular seat-holders in the congregation, and to the membership of the church.* We had to wait long for the reorganization of our congregation after the summer

* In 1878, fifty-three members were added to the church, thirty-two of these joined at the Brick Church proper, seven by confession and twenty-five by letter. The rest were additions to the congregation at the mission. The figures for 1877 had been slightly larger, similarly distributed.

and autumn vacation; but when it came the increase in numbers was so marked, and the growth was so evidently a solid one, that our hearts have been greatly cheered and encouraged.

"There is one aspect of the growth of the church which I am very anxious to bring before you, and that is, the addition to our numbers of those who make profession of their faith, and are thus not only increments of our community, but gains to the whole Church of Jesus Christ. These, I know, are often the direct effects of a powerful and convincing ministry, and for some that have been thus impressed, I am deeply thankful to him whose grace and power are alone sufficient to affect the changes; but in this work the preaching of the pastor is not alone sufficient; there must be also the prayer of the people. Brethren, I beseech you, pray for me and for my ministry.

"The various spheres of our common activity have been well sustained, and, in some cases greatly enlarged. Our mission work is seriously in need of helpers, and the school only requires teachers, to be filled to its utmost capacity.

"The labors of the ladies of the congregation have been unremitting in behalf of the poor, and the Employment Society, while increasing in the number of those whom it can aid, is able to sustain its efforts only by the continued and increased generosity and activity of the members of the church. . . .

"One of our chief causes of satisfaction has been the interest taken amongst the children, in our Sunday-school and in the Children's Society. There has been a remarkable revival and quickening of atten-

tion. A church in the position of ours must grow
chiefly along the lines of its families, and we have,
therefore, been greatly encouraged by the healthful
energy of the institutions belonging to the children.

"There is one point which I desire to press home
upon your attention, namely, the services of the
church upon the week-days. May I beg of you not to
neglect these opportunities of assembling in the house
of God for instruction and for prayer? To me, these
services are the most refreshing of any that we hold.
To those who wish to hear the preacher when most
living and instructive, I would venture to say, hear
him on Wednesday nights; but especially I beg
for a larger attendance at the prayer-meeting on
Saturday evenings. That is, I believe, a peculiar
source of strength for the entire church. Were it
fully and warmly sustained by a people pressing in
to prayer, the revival which we desire would not be
long delayed.

"One other special point of importance demands
our attention. After several experiments, and after
much deliberation, we have determined that the second Sunday service of our church shall be in the
afternoon, to be held regularly and without break.
May I not beg the fullest attendance of the congregation upon that occasion? The universal dwindling
of the second service of the Lord's Day is not a healthy
sign of modern church life. Let it at least not be
known amongst us. . . . If a congregation be not
in its place, why should the minister be found in his
pulpit? These shall be the only notes not altogether
cheerful in my words to you, and even these I will
close with the expression of the hope of a regular and

large afternoon congregation, in which hope I beseech you not to disappoint me."

The rest of the letter being of a more general and discursive character need not be quoted here, but two or three topics already referred to in the earlier part of it deserve further notice. The attention given to the children of the church was certainly a happy feature of Mr. Bevan's ministry. The present writer well remembers the children's service held from time to time on Sunday afternoons, when all the arrangements were designed to make the boys and girls feel that the service distinctly belonged to them. Particularly important, if depth and permanence of impression are to be regarded as indications, was the fact that even the taking up of the collection was at that service entrusted to the children. It was, it is true, a somewhat awful moment to boys of eight or ten, when they must pass from end to end of that interminable Brick Church aisle, while the possibility of passing by some man or woman, hidden away at the inner end of a pew, added a further cause of dread to the exercise; but the boys liked it, and, what is more important, it gave them a feeling of personal participation in the life of the church which helped to root them there for later life.*

These services were connected with the work of the Children's Society, whose organization in Dr. Murray's time has been already described, and whose quickened interest Mr. Bevan mentioned with gratitude in the letter that has been quoted. The collections at these services, for which the boys "passed the plate," were for the replenishing of the society's

* These children's services had been started in the time of Dr. Murray.

treasury. Another means used for the same purpose was the holding of an occasional fair for the sale of those "fancy and useful articles" which church members are asked to contribute in the morning and buy back in the afternoon.

From these sources considerable sums of money were realized, and used, not only for the regular work which the society had from the beginning undertaken among the poor children connected with the mission, but also for the furthering of special enterprises of a character in harmony with the society's general purpose. Thus in one year the object was stated as "The Children's Convalescent Country Home," in another as "The Sanitary Home for Sick Children." Mr. Bevan was especially anxious that the Brick Church should start a home of its own in the country, to which the sick children in its charge might be sent for rest and refreshment. But although a beginning of the collection of the necessary funds was made, the plan could not then be carried out; and one reason for this was a period of decline into which the Children's Society entered not long after the time at present under consideration. The causes for this decadence and the happy result to which it ultimately led, will be described in the next chapter.

In connection with the Children's Society, it will be appropriate to speak of another organization in which Mr. Bevan took a special interest. When he came, he found no society for the young men of the church, for the "Association," which came into existence in Dr. Hoge's time had meanwhile disappeared. Mr. Bevan had not been in New York three months when he brought about the organization of a

"Young Men's Society," he himself accepting the responsibility of being its first president The session took occasion to express their special satisfaction at the launching of this enterprise and their "hope that it will prove an effective agency in developing Christian fellowship and promoting Christian activity in the church and congregation." And, indeed, the social gayeties which this society introduced into the church life in the year 1877 must have been astonishing to people of the older generation. In April, in May, and again in November engraved invitations from the young men requested the pleasure of the church's company (including the young women) at an evening reception in the church parlors "from 8½ to 10½." How long this society continued we do not know, but the sudden ceasing of all allusion to it makes us fear that it soon perished.

The matter of the second Sunday service, to which reference was made in the pastoral letter already quoted, had evidently been discussed at considerable length, and indeed it was not settled to the satisfaction of every one till a still later date. The officers of the church seem to have been very emphatically in favor of the old afternoon service, but the pastor and perhaps some of the congregation were so anxious to have the hour changed to the evening, that they returned several times to the discussion. They succeeded in obtaining permission to try their plan for brief intervals, but the original hour was always soon restored. A further reference to the same subject will be found in a second letter, issued in the year 1879, which may now be quoted.

"The welcome accorded to my previous communication," Mr. Bevan says in his introduction, "has determined me not to break through the custom so pleasantly begun." Then after referring to the "serious family anxiety" by which the year had been marked (an accident to Mrs. Bevan from whose effects she suffered, with great patience, for many years), he takes up the affairs of the church. "Labor," he says, "has been unbroken. Increase, steady and marked, has attended the church's history, and we are permitted to commence the duties of a new season with promise of still greater achievement and growth. The successful endeavor to deal with the debt which our community had incurred has been a cause of much cheer and congratulation. All have been interested, while to some, whose generous gifts and unceasing energy have combined to render the often ungracious work of debt-raising assured and pleasant, my best felicitations and esteem are due. It is thus that we would blend our thankfulness to God and our recognition of those whom he has inspired with affection and zeal. That kindness which greeted a stranger grows into the confidence and regard which attend the friend and pastor."

We may interrupt the course of the letter at this point to say that the paying off of the church's debt at this time was, indeed, a most happy incident. Partly the purchase of the parsonage and partly still earlier obligations from the days of the double pastorate, had forced the trustees to borrow some $49,000. But now, under the leadership of Governor Morgan, who was always found in the forefront of the church's work, almost the whole of this amount was raised, a tremendous relief to the treasury, which had all it could do to meet current expenses.

But to return to the letter. "I invite the younger members of the congregation," Mr. Bevan continues "to give us all the aid they can in our mission work. This is our practical and aggressive duty. Its social influence will be found pleasant as well as strengthening to all our interests, while nothing but the lack of helpers prevents the limitless increase of the good we can thus accomplish. I shall, therefore, cordially welcome any who may attach themselves to either our Sunday-school or our mission-school work. To the former send your children, to the latter let the young men and women of the church give themselves with complete consecration.

"Amongst the growing interests of our church are the Sunday afternoon service and the service of Wednesday evening. In respect of the former it is well known that your pastor would personally prefer an evening meeting. But many friends are averse to change, and unless it prove necessary, for a while at least, we shall continue with all fidelity the afternoon service. But this fact is a strong argument for a good regular attendance. The second service of the church is that which may generally be expected to prove the chief opportunity for the ingathering of those who are outside her pale. But meagre attendance will render inaffective the most earnest pleas, the most convincing argument. Give your minister the aid of your steady, unbroken, enthusiastic presence at this service. The Sunday afternoon, under any circumstances, is a difficult time for public discourse. The difficulty becomes almost insuperable when the

preacher is greeted by the empty places of those upon
whom he ought to lean for sympathy and support.
Many more, also, ought to be present at the week-
night service. It is hoped that the course of sermons
upon the Book of Revelation, which has been commenced, will sustain and increase the interest which
has already been kindled. An hour snatched from the
home circle or social pleasures, and spent in the
house of God, and in attendance upon his word,
cannot fail to result in confirming life's strength, and
heightening its enjoyments. When the church is open
for service its members ought surely to be present
there. . . .

"The most careless observer of our church cannot
fail to notice not only an increase in the external
signs of church life, but also a stirring of the deeper
elements of faith and character amongst us. The season of prayer lately observed resulted in a deepening
of conviction and a quickening of earnestness. I
have no great faith in sudden, temporary so-called
revivals, but I long for a greater decision of Christian
character. I yearn for the signs of changed hearts,
and kindled spiritual sentiments. I solemnly summon
to profession of faith those who so long have held
back and are disciples only in secret. I pray for the
conversion of sinners and the decisive choice of the
wavering, the careless, the indifferent. . . . Once
again, therefore, I cast myself upon the sympathy
and prayers of the people, thanking all for unremitting personal kindness. Looking forward with
much joyful expectation to the promise of work and
results therefrom which seem to lie in the future,
lifting up to God the voice of praise, and solemnly re-

consecrating myself to your service in the Lord, whilst I claim from you a similar renewal of your vows, I remain, my dear friends,

"Your affectionate pastor."

The two letters that have been quoted carry us but a little more than half-way through Mr. Bevan's pastorate, for he remained in New York over two years more; but no later pastoral letter has come down to us, if, indeed, the custom of issuing one each year was continued. The records of the church, moreover, give us for this period little more than the bare outlines, so that it will not be possible to follow in detail the history of those later years.

Yet to this one exception must be made. The continued prosperity and growth of the mission is fully recorded, and demands our attention. The Sunday-school, of which Mr. Daniel J. Holden was superintendent, he having succeeded Mr. Parsons in 1877, could hardly have been more prosperous. Mr. Holden gave his whole heart to the work and the many who love to remember him know how much that meant. Seldom have there been united in one man so much strength and sweetness. "The soundness of his judgment" on the one hand, and "the peculiarly genial and lovable qualities of his nature," on the other, "visibly irradiated, as it was, by the spirit of a true disciple of Christ," * made him one of those rare personalities under whose influence any good and wise work is bound to prosper. †

---

* From resolutions by the board of trustees at the time of his death.

† In 1880 there was in the school an enrolment of 650 scholars; average attendance, 450; number of officers and teachers, 52.

Mr. Lampe was now on his second decade as pastor at the mission, and in numbers his congregation was fast overtaking that of the Brick Church itself,* while, under the wise leadership of the Brick Church session, it was being prepared as rapidly as possible for an independent existence. Especially a decided advance had been made toward self-support. In January, 1878, the people of the mission requested that they might be allowed to put in an organ at their own expense, and at the same time steps were taken toward placing upon their shoulders some definite share of the responsibility for their church's support. Later in the same year the cost of the music was selected as an appropriate portion of the expenses to be borne by the Thirty-fifth Street congregation, and it was voted by the session that "for the purpose of encouraging the mission to meet the responsibility, the church aid for music at the mission be for the present withdrawn." In 1879, in addition to a general invitation to contribute to the support of the church, the special proposal was made that the people of the mission provide for an increase of $500 in their pastor's salary. Thus, little by little, the spirit of independence and the habit of self-support were being encouraged.

In April, 1882, Dr. † Bevan offered his resignation.‡ He had been called to the new Congregational

---

* In the official reports, the members of the two congregations were, of course, given together in one figure. More than a third of the members received during Dr. Bevan's pastorate worshipped at the mission.

† He received the degree of D.D. in 1880.

‡ His intention to return to London had been made public several weeks earlier, as will be seen from the dates of an interview and a letter quoted in the earlier portion of this chapter, page 361, note.

Church in Highbury Quadrant, London, and, as he said in the meeting of the Brick Church at which his resignation was accepted, he regarded as a compelling summons this invitation to go "back to the field of his former labors." The truth was, no doubt, that his return to England seemed to him like the regaining of his freedom. In some important respects, as has been already said, he had not found in New York the opportunity he had anticipated, the opportunity for whose sake he had abandoned the evident advantages of work among his own countrymen; and the thought of taking up again his life in London could not but be welcome to him.

He left behind him many warm friends. In 1885 and again in 1886, he was invited to revisit America for the special purpose of preaching in the Brick Church during a whole or a part of the summer, but his duties at home prevented his acceptance. In 1891, however, he did visit New York and occupied his old pulpit at that time. He had then moved once more from London, and had found in Melbourne, Australia, a most congenial field of service. Of his great success there his former parishioners heard with joy.

CHAPTER XXI

REJUVENATED: 1882-1893

"Moreover, because the preacher was wise, he still taught the people knowledge; yea, he gave good heed, and sought out, and set in order many proverbs. The preacher sought to find out acceptable words: and that which was written was upright, even words of truth. The words of the wise are as goads, and as nails fastened by the masters of assemblies."—*Ecclesiastes*, 12 : 9-11.

"Our church is not like an ancient sign-post which the weather is wearing to decay; nor like a graven image which can neither hear, nor speak, nor grow, but like a tree planted by the rivers of water. Its roots run down deep into the past. Its trunk rises strong and unbroken in the present. And, please God, it shall still lift its head to greet the future, putting forth new buds and blossoms with every season."—HENRY VAN DYKE, "An Historic Church," 1893. p. 6.

AT the same meeting at which Dr. Bevan's resignation was accepted a committee of twenty-seven * was appointed "to take measures for filling the vacancy." This was in April, 1882. Almost at once the name of Henry J. van Dyke, Jr., minister of the United Congregational Church of Newport, R. I., was mentioned. Governor Morgan, the chairman of the committee, who knew him and his work, and thought him "a very fine young man," believed, nevertheless, that he ought not to be asked to leave the charge which he then held;

* The names of these men, who made up a large part of the strength of the church at this time, are here given: Gov. Edwin D. Morgan, Chairman, George de Forest Lord, Frederick W. Downer, Benjamin F. Dunning, Ezra M. Kingsley, John E. Parsons, Frederick Billings, Isaac N. Phelps, John G. Adams, M.D., Ronald M. Buchanan, Hamilton Odell, Caldwell R. Blakeman, Daniel J. Holden, Daniel Parish, Jr., Robert Watts, M.D., William B. Isham, Shepherd Knapp, Edward W. Davis, John G. Davis, Charles G. Harmer, George W. Comstock, William D. Barbour, Nathan C. Ely, John Campbell, John A. Gilbert (John Q. ?) Clark, Walter Squires.

but happily at about this time there came rumors that Mr. van Dyke was considering a call to London. If Newport was to lose him in any case, Governor Morgan was very clear that the place for him was the Brick Church, and in this the rest of the committee, after the matter had been given the most thorough consideration, heartily agreed. On September 20th, the congregation addressed to Mr. van Dyke a unanimous call.

The pastor elect was not quite thirty years of age, having been born in Germantown, Penn., on November 10th, 1852. Not long after his birth, his father, Dr. Henry J. van Dyke, the eminent Presbyterian clergyman, began his long pastorate in Brooklyn, and there the son grew up and received his elementary education.

Of these early years and of the chief companionship they brought to him, his daughter writes pleasantly in her sketch of his life.* "From the first," she says, "his relationship with his father was a particularly beautiful one, for besides the natural trust and reverence, there grew up the closest kind of a friendship. It was as comrades that they went off for their day's holiday, escaping from the city and its flag pavements and brownstone fronts, and getting out into the fresh country air, to walk through the woods and watch the leaves turn red and gold and brown and drop to the ground, or to skate in winter, or to listen to the song of the first returning bluebird in the spring. It was under the wise and tender guidance of his father that the boy's instinctive love of nature grew and developed."

* "The Van Dyke Book," p. 159.

In 1869 he entered Princeton and four years later graduated, after showing in a conclusive manner his ability as an orator and as a student of literature. His theological training was acquired in Princeton Seminary (1874–1877), and in Germany, at the University of Berlin (1878). Upon his return to America, he was ordained and entered upon his ministerial work as pastor of the church in Newport, where it was soon evident to all, including certain distinguished Americans, who in the summer season became his parishioners, that he was destined to do an important work as a minister of Christ. It was in Newport that Governor Morgan knew him and marked him as a rising man.

On January 16th, 1883, Mr. van Dyke was installed as pastor of the Brick Church.* The task which he had undertaken was difficult but inspiring, for it was his purpose that the Brick Church, finely situated in the best part of a great city, and inheritor of a noble past, should become once more an acknowledged leader in the work of Christ's kingdom, as she had been in the earlier years of the century.

Before any decided advance in this direction could be made, there was needed first of all an honest stock-taking of the materials available for the work. Speaking at a later day to the Brick Church people about the period of his coming to them, he said, "If report speaks truly, you were somewhat discour-

---

* The moderator of Presbytery presided; Rev. W. G. T. Shedd, D.D., conducted the devotional exercises; Rev. Henry J. van Dyke, D.D., preached the sermon from Eph. 3 : 8, "The unsearchable riches of Christ"; Rev. Howard Crosby, D.D., delivered the charge to the pastor; Rev. John Hall, D.D., delivered the charge to the people; Mr. van Dyke pronounced the benediction.

aged. You had a nominal membership of one thousand, and an actual membership of less than three hundred; a congregation which half filled the church in the morning and varied from fifty to a hundred in the afternoon; a floating debt and a sinking revenue. But you had also a company of people who were devoted to the church and willing to work for it in the face of discouragements." *

Almost the first problem attacked was that of the roll. The statements quoted in the last paragraph seem at first thought almost incredible, but they found their explanation in two facts. First, about three hundred and fifty of the members of the Brick Church attended the chapel in West Thirty-fifth Street. This accounted for half of the discrepancy between the "nominal" and the "actual" membership. Second, the other half of the discrepancy was explained by the fact that for a long time the church roll had not been revised, so that it included the names of many who had moved and left no trace behind, or who had otherwise disappeared. In a large city church, especially if it includes the more unstable dwellers in the tenements, as the Brick Church did through its chapel, this sort of loss is always considerable; but three hundred and fifty was

* "An Historic Church," pp. 25 f., cf. footnote above, p. 373. A few of this honorable company, "Gideon's band" as their pastor sometimes called them, are still at their posts. To those who were called away by death during the first decade of his pastorate, Dr. van Dyke, in the sermon already quoted above, made the following reference. "Strong and generous men," he called them, "who seemed indispensable to the maintenance of the church—E. D. Morgan, Frederick Billings, S. H. Witherbee, Charles G. Harmer, John C. Tucker, George de Forest Lord, and many more. How much we mourned the loss of these good soldiers in the cause But their spirits continued with us" (p. 30).

HENRY VAN DYKE, 1892

a tremendous proportion of the entire roll, and the necessary removal of so large a number from the active list made it seem in the records as though the church had suddenly shrunk to an amazing degree. Yet to know the true facts was really a source of strength. The visible three hundred members who emerged from the enumeration were worth far more for the work that lay before them than the vague and largely imaginary thousand who had been supposed to occupy the strategic position on Murray Hill.

A second task immediately undertaken, and one of much greater magnitude, was the introduction of such changes as would make the church more attractive in the best sense. It was the purpose of the new pastor to create in the Brick Church such conditions that the Christian message would there be commended to the hearer by every help that art and learning could properly provide, or, as he himself has characteristically expressed it in a single phrase, "to light the fire on the hearth." In the young preacher who had been chosen to deliver the message, the church was sure that it had found a man capable of speaking God's truth in a manner so full of interest and grace that a congregation could not choose but hear. As events proved, they had succeeded far more fully than they knew: they had chosen as their leader one of those rare men whom God has endowed with double and triple gifts.

But although they had thus secured for their pastor this man who was prophet and poet as well, they were not so foolish as to leave him to work unaided. On the contrary, they responded to his own strongly ex-

pressed desire that all the accompaniments and surroundings of the church service should measure up
to the standard of beauty as well as that of use. At
the very first trustees' meeting after Mr. van Dyke's
installation, the question of an improvement in the
music was the subject of discussion, with the immediate result that the appropriation for that purpose
was increased almost twenty-five per cent.

But the most momentous change proposed was
the complete renovation of the interior of the church.
There had, indeed, been a distinct understanding
before Mr. van Dyke accepted the call, that this
should be undertaken without delay. The old interior, which had stood practically unchanged since
the erection of the church, some twenty-five years before, was dignified, but it could not be called beautiful. According to the standards of taste that had
arisen in the interval, the bare walls, the white plastered ceiling, the plain, unornamented character of
all the fittings and furniture produced an effect of
coldness and severity which to many of the younger
generation was positively repellant. It was intended
that as soon as Mr. van Dyke was settled in his work
all this should be changed.

An unexpected catastrophe threatened to overthrow the entire plan at the very outset, and indeed,
to cripple the church in all its undertakings. On February 14th, 1883, Governor Morgan died. His death
was a national loss, for he had been not only merchant and philanthropist, but statesman and patriot,
and his service to his country during a most critical
period of her history, first as "War Governor of the
Empire State" from 1858 to 1863, and then as

United States Senator from 1863 to 1869, had won for him a place in the admiration and gratitude of his countrymen.* But nowhere was his loss felt more keenly than in the Brick Church, of which, at the time of his death, he was without dispute the leading member.

Governor Morgan, who had been chairman of the committee by whom the new pastor had been chosen, had joined heartily in the promise that the church should be renovated, and when he made such a promise he meant to back up his word by a substantial gift from his generous purse. At his death, it became at least a serious question whether the old bare interior must not be allowed to stand.

But the question was soon answered by an order to go ahead. Possibly the officers of the church were wise enough to see that to abandon the project would almost amount to a vote of lack of confidence in their pastor. On the other hand, he had certainly inspired them with something of his own enthusiasm for the enterprise; and the result was that the laymen of the church undertook to raise the necessary sum, between thirty and forty thousand dollars, and Mr. John La Farge, the distinguished artist, was engaged to direct the work.

* A list of some of the organizations which passed resolutions in regard to his death will give some idea of the varied usefulness of his life: The National Bank of Commerce; the American Tract Society; the Assembly of the State of New York; the Association for the Relief of Respectable, Aged, Indigent Females; the Woman's Hospital in the State of New York; the Chamber of Commerce; the Maritime Association, Port of New York; Union Theological Seminary; the Presbyterian Hospital; the New York, Lake Erie, and Western Railroad Company; the New York City Mission; the Union League Club; the Board of Aldermen of New York City.

"The building or adornment of a church," Mr. van Dyke said, "is not like the building or adornment of a dwelling-house. It is not a work of private ostentation, but a work of public beneficence; not a work of selfishness, but a work of charity, just as truly as the building of a hospital or the endowment of a library. For it stands with open doors, and, if it be a true church of Christ, offers its privileges to all who will receive them." * Such was the generous aim with which the work was begun in June, 1883. On October 28th of the same year, the church was reopened, totally and splendidly transformed.

Instead of the cold grays and whites of a New England meeting-house, which had been familiar to generations of Brick Church worshippers, both on Beekman Street and on Murray Hill, the spacious interior now possessed some of the warmth and richness of color characteristic of the Byzantine churches of the old world. Indeed, so skilfully and with such perfect taste had the artist worked, that one realized with difficulty the newness of the decoration; it seemed already to have acquired the dignity and mellowness which usually age alone is able to produce.

The prevailing tone selected for the broad surfaces of the walls was a soft or broken "Pompeian red," while the color of the woodwork and upholstery of the pews was somewhat similar, a choice which produced the effect of warmth already alluded to; while lightness and variety were secured by the use of

* "The Joy of the Christian when He Is Invited to Enter the Lord's House: a Sermon," p. 10.

REDECORATED INTERIOR OF THE BRICK CHURCH

mosaic of various colors, relief work in majolica,* embroideries, † and colored glass in windows and lanterns. But the most important work was done in the ceiling and the cornice. There the richness of sombre colors on a background of weathered gold, the wealth of varied and intricate design, the significance imparted by a pervading, yet unobtrusive use of Christian symbol and inscription, produce together an effect of great and enduring beauty, and make this work of Mr. La Farge one of the most important examples of church decoration in America.‡ It was felt at once that a spirit of reverence and worship, not unlike that which is characteristic of many Gothic churches, though produced by entirely different means, had been imparted to the very building of the Brick Church, and must be felt by all who entered its doors. §

* This was imported from England, being the product of the "Minton" works. It follows closely the form of decorative work to be found in the Cathedral of Torcello (1008), and in other churches of the same period or earlier, in Ravenna, Venice, and elsewhere in Italy.

† Designed by Mr. La Farge and executed by Miss Tillinghast.

‡ A prominent New York architect, in a letter to the author, after remarking that the original interior of the Brick Church "was even plainer than most New England meeting-houses," adds, "This later proved to be a great advantage, for when John La Farge took hold of it to decorate it, it furnished him a base of operations that was comparatively untrammelled, and the result is probably the most beautifully decorated interior of any public building in the country. I have never seen one that, on the whole, seemed so satisfactory, and it would really be a calamity if anything happened to destroy or deface it. In decorating it, the interior was so devoid of character that Mr. La Farge was at liberty to follow any school that he chose, provided it inclined to the classic. He chose that of the early Italian churches, from the eighth to the tenth centuries."

§ One important change made at this time was the removal of the organ and choir from the gallery above and behind the pulpit (where the spaces between the columns are now filled in with mosaic-covered walls) to a new gallery opened at the east end of the church. This gallery and the organ were greatly enlarged at a later date (1898), as a thank-offering

It will not be necessary to follow in chronological order the remaining events of the first decade of Dr.* van Dyke's ministry. A better conception of the period will be obtained by presenting its salient features without special reference to date. But first of all, the period as a whole must be characterized as one of marked or even of phenomenal progress, from every point of view, material and spiritual alike. The New York "Tribune" was but expressing a matter of common knowledge when it said, in an editorial in 1888, that the Brick Church, which, on Dr. van Dyke's arrival "was very respectable, but very small," had since that time "been growing largely and steadily, and [was] once more full. Christian work," the editorial continued, "is thoroughly organized and actively pushed, and the old Brick Church has completely renewed her youth." † It would be difficult to overstate the esteem and deep personal affection with which Dr. van Dyke was soon universally regarded. His genial and sympathetic nature, added to his great intellectual powers, made an appeal which was wellnigh irresistible.

for the first fifteen years of Dr. van Dyke's ministry. Two of the stained-glass windows on the south, of different design from the others, were given as memorials, one of Governor Morgan, the other of Dr. E. D. Morgan and his wife. The only important changes since that time, in addition to the one already mentioned above, were the placing of a screen of colored glass behind the rear pews, and the introduction of electricity, by which the beauty of the decoration, especially of the ceiling, was revealed as never before. The present communion table, presented in 1890, is a memorial of Mrs. Maria Brower McNeel, while the font was given in 1899 by Dr. van Dyke as a memorial of his little son Bernard.

* He received the degree of Doctor of Divinity from Princeton in 1884 and subsequently from Harvard and Yale. The degree of Doctor of Laws has been conferred upon him by several colleges and universities.

† Quoted in the "University Magazine," for April, 1892, p. 416.

EAST END OF THE CHURCH INTERIOR, 1883
Showing choir gallery

During the whole period there seems to have appeared but one cloud upon the horizon. This was the threatened departure, on two occasions, of the leader to whom, under God, the church's prosperity and enlarged usefulness were plainly due. This recurring danger is worthy of mention, not for its own sake, for it was happily averted in both cases, but because of the expression which it called forth from both pastor and people of the strong bond holding them together.

The first suggestion that Dr. van Dyke might be contemplating a surrender of his office came in December, 1885. He had now been at work three years and he felt constrained to use an opportunity which had presented itself, to submit to the congregation the question whether they approved of what he had done and aimed to do, and desired him to continue his ministry among them. The opportunity consisted in offers, made to him from several quarters, to enter a new field of work in which he would be able, as he said, to gratify "a long-cherished desire to pursue certain theological and literary studies, and to accomplish certain work in that line."

Peculiarly significant and worthy of preservation are the words in which Dr. van Dyke, in his letter to the session on this subject, set forth his own ideal "of the true mission and purpose of the church, his conception of the true history and spirit of Presbyterianism in its relations to the catholic kingdom of Christ, his belief that order and beauty in the worship of God are thoroughly consistent with true piety, his desire to dwell on the great essential points of faith which are common to all Christians, rather than on minor doctrinal differences and traditional questions of conduct, his faith that the mission of the church to minister to the distinctively religious wants of all the people is unchanged and that it must be fulfilled in adaptation to the circumstances of the age, and that its success depends more upon the spirit and effort of the whole church than upon the minister."

Dr. van Dyke's offer to resign took the officers completely by surprise, and indeed, filled them with consternation. It need hardly be said that they "affectionately and unanimously" assured him of their complete unwillingness to join in any course that would tend toward a severance of the relation between them. They stated in the most emphatic terms "their opinion that there had not been within many years past so much reason for both pastor and session to feel encouraged and satisfied with the prospects of the church," and they especially reassured him, by a strong declaration, that any fear of a lack of sympathy with his purposes and aims, on the part of officers or congregation, was "entirely unfounded and imaginary." This answer brought instant conviction to Dr. van Dyke that his work in the Brick Church should be continued. No other consideration could outweigh in his mind her needs, clearly ascertained. "Honestly," he had said, "I love the church better than life," and he took up his ministry again with joy and confidence.

The second appearance of the same danger eight years later, in 1893, was more serious, because the ill health, which Dr. van Dyke had then experienced for some time, made him feel that it was almost imperative for him to embrace the opportunity of less

arduous service, offered in a call to a professorship in
Andover Seminary. That the strain of the constantly enlarging work of the church was seriously
affecting their pastor's health, had been realized
with concern by the session before this time, and
special arrangements had been made to lighten the
burden, including ministerial assistance * and leave
of absence. Still further measures of the same sort
were now proposed. Any possible expedient by
which their beloved pastor could be assisted and
strengthened in his work was welcomed by them, but
of his resignation they would not hear, and their will
once more prevailed.

At this result no surprise will be felt after reading
the session's resolution on this subject, which shall
be given in full:

"Resolved, that Dr. van Dyke be requested to at
once and forever dismiss all thought of a call to
Andover or to any other place. If he desires other
assurance of the affection of the church and of its devotion to him, it will be given at any time, at all times,
and in any way that will best satisfy him of the
depth and sincerity of our feeling.

"We have never doubted that God sent Dr. van
Dyke to us. We believe that it is his divine will that
Dr. van Dyke shall remain with us. We resent all
efforts to detach him from us. We are his people.
Will he leave us without the pastor of our choice?
God forbid.

"To the providence which has smitten his health

---

* For a time Dr. van Dyke had preached on Sunday mornings only,
the afternoon service and the prayer-meeting being conducted with great
acceptance by Dr. Henry M. Booth.

we bow submissively, but we cannot let Dr. van Dyke go. He has endeared himself to all, young and old, high and low. Here his lot has been cast: here is opportunity for a career, for work in and out of the church, work for our own particular church, for the Church at large, and for the cause of Christ and his kingdom, beyond what is possible elsewhere.

"Resolved, therefore, that from sincere conviction of duty we beg Dr. van Dyke immediately to decline any further consideration of the Andover call, and that Messrs. Parsons, Ledoux, and Odell be appointed to present this action to Dr. van Dyke and to press it upon him." *

We must now return to the earlier years of the pastorate and observe in more detail some of the labors whose results have already in a general way been indicated.

Two enterprises, undertaken almost simultaneously in 1885, indicate in a suggestive way the diversity of the labors into which Dr. van Dyke had thrown himself. These were an evangelistic campaign and the task of paying off a debt of some $15,000 which the church was carrying. The former, which took the shape of a special series of Sunday evening services, not only was a valuable stimulus to the Brick Church itself, † but "resulted

---

* Resolutions were passed by the congregation expressing the same confidence and affection, refusing to let him go, and providing for indefinite leave of absence and regular assistance in the pastoral work on his return.

† They were continued throughout the season, the usual afternoon services being discontinued in their favor, and in February and March were varied by a special course of sermons preached by the following well known clergymen: the Rev. Drs. L. T. Chamberlain, R. S. Storrs, James McCosh, J. M. Bulkley, F. L. Patton, James S. McIntosh and Lyman Abbott.

in an evangelistic movement throughout the whole Presbytery in the following year." * The raising of the debt, in which the pastor took vigorous part, not only was achieved in less than a year's time, but ran $1,000 beyond the mark that had been set.

Meanwhile the regular services of the church had, under Dr. van Dyke's guidance, taken on a new character and had acquired a new importance in the religious life of the city. Of the preaching to which the Brick Church listened in those days, something has been already said. Not often have a people been privileged to hear Sunday after Sunday such a series of strong, clear, and compelling sermons, each one rising, as it seemed, to a greater height than the one before, and all aimed, with peculiar singleness of purpose, to express and enforce the greatest Christian truth, and to reach the hearts and wills of the hearers, as well as their minds, in the interests of Christian living.

In the worship of the church the influence of Dr. van Dyke was as clearly felt as in the preaching. Under his direction the order of service was rearranged and enriched. The Psalter was placed in the pews in 1891. A new hymn-book took the place of "The Sacrifice of Praise," now out of print, and much attention was given to the music. † A special endeavor was made to extend a genuine welcome to the strangers who now attended the services in large numbers, and so thoroughly was this matter taken

* "An Historic Church," p. 27.

† It was rendered by a quartette under the direction of Mr. Carl Florio, organist.

to heart that Dr. van Dyke, in 1893, could say, "You have completely lived down an undeserved reputation of coldness, so that now your true hospitality is known unto all men, and there are many strangers within your gates to remember the Sabbath day with you in the joy of a warm and generous Christian fellowship." *

The Wednesday evening service came in for its share in the church's revival. How this was accomplished the following circular, issued in October, 1889, will show better than much explanation.

"You are cordially invited to spend an hour out of your busy week in the study of the Bible with us, and in social worship. The meetings will be held on Wednesday evenings at eight o'clock, and this is what we hope to do:

"First, we shall sing together for a little time, not in a formal way, but as we often sing on Sunday evenings in our homes; and those who wish may suggest beforehand to the leader their favorite hymns.

"Then we shall pray together for a little time, for the things that we really need and want, and for the Church of Christ, and for our fellow-men; but no

* Several significant additions to the regular services of the church were made during this period. In 1885, at the special request of the pastor, it was decided to keep the church open all summer, a custom that, with a few interruptions for special reasons, has been followed ever since. In 1888, a service was held in the church on the morning of Christmas Day. In 1891, a service was announced for the Friday preceding Easter, but it is interesting to observe that the name "Good Friday" was avoided in the notice. A special appeal from the pastor urged all the members of the congregation to make an effort to attend. No allusion whatever to "Easter" was made in the printed announcements for Easter Sunday that year, though the day was doubtless recognized in the sermon and the music. In 1893, an "Easter Service" in the Sunday-school was announced by name.

one will ever be asked to lead in prayer unless the minister knows that he is willing to do so.

"Then we shall study together for a little time; and the subject during this winter will be the life of St. Paul. . . . Every week a paper will be distributed giving an outline of what the minister is to speak about on the following Wednesday. . . . If any suggestions or difficulties occur to you during the week, the minister begs that you will make a note of them and send them to him beforehand. You may feel very sure that they will be welcome; and you may feel equally sure that you will not be called upon to answer any questions in the meeting, if that would embarrass or displease you.

"You can easily understand, then, what it is we want to do with this Wednesday evening hour. It is to make it a little less formal and more really useful and helpful and pleasant. It will not be merely a feeble copy of a Sunday morning service; it will be a common-sense meeting, in which we can come closer together in our study of the religion of the Bible and the Christianity of Christ. . . ." *

One immediate result of the meetings thus announced was a movement to change the character of the room in which they were held—"the lecture-

---

* This programme for the mid-week service was only one of those adopted during this decade, the danger of too long a continuance of "one good custom" being realized. Thus in December, 1892, the following plan was adopted, having been proposed by Dr. van Dyke: "The first Wednesday evening in each month, a meeting in the interest of missions; the second Wednesday evening, a lecture or Bible study; the third Wednesday evening, a conference meeting; the fourth Wednesday evening, a lecture or Bible study; the fifth Wednesday evening, a conference meeting." Two elders and a committee of the men of the congregation were to "aid the pastor in carrying out the details of the plan,"

room" as it was called—and to make it, like the meetings, "a little less formal and more really useful and helpful and pleasant." Without any expense to the trustees a committee of the laymen removed the old set pews and the pipe organ, which had made the room a sort of little church, and provided instead a large open room, whose simple, cheerful decoration, movable chairs, inconspicuous platform, and piano for the singing, made such a meeting as Dr. van Dyke projected much more easy and natural.

What the practical Christian activities of the congregation were during this period is compactly stated in the historical sermon of 1893, already several times quoted. "Ten years ago," said Dr. van Dyke, "your home Sunday-school was dying; there were, perhaps, ten children in it; two faithful teachers and a loyal assistant superintendent watched by its bed. To-day it is a vigorous little school of about a hundred members, well equipped for work, growing, and sending out generous contributions to missions and a steady supply of teachers for your branch Sunday-school of seven hundred members in West Thirty-fifth Street. * Ten years ago your Deacon's Fund for the care of the poor was in debt $500; to-day

---

* This resurrection of the Sunday-school was one item in the long and varied service rendered to the church by Dr. Albert R. Ledoux. Upon his resignation of the office of superintendent of the school in 1892, the session in a resolution declared that they "accept with regret Dr. Ledoux's resignation. . . . and that they place upon record their grateful sense of the large value of the service he has rendered to the church in this office for the last ten years, strengthening its spiritual life, and bringing its young people into close and living connection with the work and worship of the church. For this work so faithfully and so quietly done the session would express the thanks of the church to Dr. Ledoux."

it has an emergency fund of nearly \$1,000. Ten years ago there were two active working societies in connection with the church; to-day there are eight: The Woman's Employment Society,* The Industrial School, † The Woman's Home Missionary Society, ‡ The Woman's Foreign Missionary Society,§ The Sick Children's Aid Society, The Young People's Guild, The Woman's Prayer-Meeting, The Pastor's Aid Society. You have sent out a missionary of your own to China. You have supported a missionary of your own in the City Mission, and two visitors among the poor. You have sent thousands of poor children into the country in the summer time. You have contributed \$10,000 as a memorial offering to the Presbyterian Board of Relief for Disabled Ministers. You have established a flourishing free kindergarten ‖ among the poor of the city. . . . During these ten years your total contributions for the support of the gospel and the work of Christianity in this city and throughout the world amount to about \$390,000. And your gifts for home and foreign missions, as reported in the minutes of the General Assembly, have risen from \$3,000 a year in 1883, to \$6,000 a year in 1892. It is your hope and expectation to do more in the future, but for the past you thank and bless God who has prospered your labors and given to you so liberally that you have been en-

* See above, p. 329.

† That is, the sewing-school in West Thirty-fifth Street. See above, p. 345.

‡ Founded in 1886.

§ Founded in 1884.

‖ The Murray Kindergarten in West Thirty-fifth Street, organized under the direction of the N. Y. Kindergarten Association, by the women of the Sick Children's Aid Society. See above, p. 354 note.

abled to do something for his kingdom and for your fellow-men." *

Of the numerous societies mentioned in Dr. van Dyke's summary two or three deserve a more extended mention.

The Sick Children's Aid Society was the outgrowth of that other organization with a somewhat similar name which, as we have seen, had been founded in Dr. Murray's time, but subsequently had more or less declined, because the boys and girls who originally composed "The Children's Society," grew up in the process of time, and there did not seem to be others in the church to take their place. Their work, however, whose purpose was to minister to the children connected with the mission, especially those who were sick, was not abandoned. The children of the society had always been directed by their mothers and other older women, and by these the work was carried on. There was an intermediate period during which the society hardly knew whether to regard itself as a children's organization or merely as an organization that worked for children—this transition state is indicated in the records by an evident uncertainty in regard to the society's name, which appears now as the Sick Children's Society and again as the Chil-

* "An Historic Church," pp. 27–30. In introducing this summary of the decade's achievements, Dr. van Dyke had said: "It is the custom of ministers, in preaching their anniversary sermons, to give an account of their labors, to tell how many discourses they have delivered, how many visits they have made, how many baptisms, weddings and funerals they have performed. I shall not follow this custom, for I do not feel I have done anything to speak of. I will only confess that I have worked hard, both from necessity and from inclination. But my purpose to-day is to tell what you have done during these ten years, for this is your church and you have made it what it is." p. 25.

THE SEWING-SCHOOL IN THE SUNDAY-SCHOOL HALL ON WEST THIRTY-FIFTH STREET
Taken in 1905

dren's Aid Society—but finally, at the time of Dr. van Dyke's arrival, the transformation had become complete, and at his suggestion the work was entirely reorganized as a work of the women of the church, and called the Sick Children's Aid Society, a combination of the earlier tentative titles, and the name under which this beautiful work has ever since been carried on. *

At about the same time, it may here be parenthetically observed, a new organization was created for the boys and girls, and in order that it might not be avoided by the older ones among them, who might object to being classified as "children," it was diplomatically called the Young People's Guild. Its work resembled that of the earlier children's society, —the dressing of dolls, the making of garments, the pasting of scrap-books, the holding of an annual fair —and it continued to exist until 1895.

But to return to the related organization among the older women. Soon after it had begun work under the new name, the need arose to procure a visitor to take the place of Miss Griffiths, who had died in the service. The Sick Children's Aid Society determined to assume responsibility for her salary, and secured the services of Miss Mary Ziesse. † To this devoted worker, whose ministry has continued to the present time, the success of the work has been in

---

* Among those who joined in the reorganization of the society were Mrs. W. D. Barbour, Mrs. James F. Bills, Mrs. C. R. Blakeman, Mrs. L. D. Bulkley, Mrs. M. P. Corning, the Misses Harmer, Mrs. D. J. Holden, Miss Louise Knox, Mrs. A. R. Ledoux, the Misses Martin, Mrs. Alexander McLean, Miss Anna Olyphant, Mrs. Robert Olyphant, Miss Susan Parish, Miss Porterfield, Miss Roberts, Mrs. W. T. Shedd, Mrs. van Dyke, Mrs. A. A. Wilson.

† She began work on January 1st, 1885.

a large measure due. Her "untiring faithfulness and discriminating good sense" * were early recognized and have constantly called for grateful acknowledgment. †

The special work undertaken by the Sick Children's Aid Society is indicated with sufficient clearness by its name, but the service actually rendered was limited by no set boundary. Beginning with ministry to sick and destitute children connected with the West Side Sunday-school—the provision of food and medicine and medical attendance, and the arrangements for summer outings in the country— the visitor soon discovered all sorts of other needs by the way, and wherever a need was met the effort was made to meet it. If a family was found to be insufficiently clothed, garments were provided. The summer outings were extended to include not only the mothers with their babies, but working girls, who were neither "children" nor "sick" but none the less in need of this service. At Christmas and Thanksgiving the society adopted the custom of providing dinners for worthy poor families. Mothers' meetings were organized; a station of the Penny Provident Fund was opened; a kindergarten, as we have seen, was established. There was no telling to what new enterprise the energies of this vigorous society might not be directed. And all the time its blessed

* "Year Book, 1888–1889," p. 27.

† No one person has known the people connected with the West Side work of the Brick Church—men, women, and children—during the past twenty years, as thoroughly as Miss Ziesse has, nor would it be easy to tell of how many of them she has been the best friend. In addition to her work as visitor she has had charge of several important departments of the work.

work of personal visitation was going on from day to day—hundreds, sometimes literally thousands, of visits in the course of a year.

The Pastor's Aid Society, another of the new agencies in the list given a few pages back, was organized by the men of the church at the very beginning of Dr. van Dyke's pastorate, for the purpose of giving assistance to him by furnishing teachers in both the home and branch Sunday-schools and to aid in any other work that might present itself. It was thus a successor of the similar organizations started in the time of Dr. Hoge and during Dr. Bevan's pastorate, but it was destined to run a much longer course.

As might have been expected, its labor increased as time passed. In 1887, we find it carrying on its work through five committees, including one on "charities," * and one on "strangers." † At this time monthly meetings were held at the parsonage or some other private house, and included an address by one of the members or by a friend from outside. ‡ Subsequently the meetings were held at the church rooms and were "entirely social and informal in their character." In the report for the year 1889–1890, the following matters are mentioned as having been discussed and acted upon: "the transformation of the Wednesday evening prayer-meetings into a most valuable course of Bible instruction; the change

---

* For rendering aid to the sick, persons out of employment, etc.

† This included the ushering at the church services.

‡ The first recorded list of subjects (for the season 1886–1887) is interesting: "The Subway Commission and its Work," by Dr. A. R. Ledoux; "East and West" (historical), by Prof. William M. Sloane; "Bohemia, Its People, and Their Religious Work in this Country," by Rev. Vincent Pisek; "Things in Heaven Above and Below," by Mr. W. S. Gilman.

from pulpit notices to the publication of a weekly bulletin of announcements; * the adoption of better methods of welcoming occasional visitors to the church services; the alteration and improvement of the chapel and the charitable disposition of the replaced furniture; the interchange of information with a view to obtaining positions for unemployed persons; the voluntary and unremunerated assistance rendered by our doctors and lawyers to the suffering and wronged poor"—from which enumeration it will be evident that several of the important enterprises mentioned in an earlier portion of this chapter were either originated or furthered by the Pastor's Aid Society.

The most interesting single event of the decade under discussion remains to be described. It concerned the work which had grown out of the mission Sunday-school on the West Side. This work, which from the beginning had taken a chief place in the hearts of the Brick Church people, and which at some periods of discouragement had been the one really bright and hopeful feature of the church's life, continued to hold its place of importance after Dr. van Dyke's arrival. In 1885, the cost of maintaining the whole group of enterprises on West Thirty-fifth Street was between four and five thousand dollars, from which it will be evident to what large proportions the work had grown.

In 1888 it appeared to many, especially to the pastor of the mission, Mr. Lampe, that the time had come when the chapel, which was gradually being prepared for independence, as has already been re-

---

* A most valuable part of the machinery of the church, edited with great faithfulness and skill for many years by Mr. C. M. Bergstresser.

lated, should now be organized as a church. The Brick Church session were disposed to view this measure with favor and took up with patience the devising of a plan by which the evident difficulties incident to such a step might successfully be met.

The problem was to secure to the new church the advantages of a genuine independence, without endangering through possible mismanagement the large interests of the kingdom which were involved. To effect the merely ecclesiastical part of the separation was easy enough. It was merely necessary to organize a new church according to the prescribed form and dismiss to it the chapel members of the Brick Church, some three hundred and fifty in number. Beyond this point the way was not so clear.

Should the management of the Sunday-school, for instance, be turned over to the new church, or retained by the Brick Church session? In spite of considerable discontent among Mr. Lampe's people, the latter course was firmly insisted upon. A second question concerned the future ownership of the property involved, though this could hardly be called a question, for the Brick Church held that a surrender of its rights and duties in that connection was not to be thought of; and the wisdom of this position was strikingly proved almost at once by the discovery of a strong disposition on the part of Mr. Lampe and his congregation to leave the neighborhood of West Thirty-fifth Street altogether and migrate to some point farther uptown. Had they had a deciding voice in the matter, this undoubtedly would have been attempted.

The third question, and the one that most ad-

mitted of debate, concerned the future relation of the
Brick Church to the support of the independent congregation. A chief object of the whole plan, of
course, was to encourage and hasten complete self-
support. It was felt that, as long as the older and
stronger church held itself responsible for the ongoing of the work, there would be but little incentive to
the daughter organization to shoulder the burden in
earnest. Could not provision be made, in connection
with the granting of ecclesiastical independence, for
the speedy achievement of financial independence also?

With this object in view it was proposed that, beginning with $2,000 for the current year, * the Brick
Church contribution should be $300 less for the year
following, and should be decreased by $400 annu-
ally thereafter until discontinued altogether, as
would occur, according to this plan, in the course of
six years. Not unnaturally Mr. Lampe's congregation took fright at this rapid promotion to complete
responsibility, and expressed themselves as unable
to accept these conditions. A new proposal was
then made by the Brick Church to the effect "that
the amount already raised this year, as suggested in
the former proposition, should be paid, and for the
year 1889 the sum of $1,850; and that on or before the
first day of January, 1890, a new arrangement should
be entered into, based upon the prospects of the new
enterprise, as they should then appear." This proposition was at once unanimously accepted, "the committee of the mission further pledging themselves to

---

* It should be borne in mind that this provided for the expenses of the
new church only; the Sunday-school, sewing-school, etc., were still to be
supported directly by the Brick Church.

make every effort in their power to raise as large a sum as possible." *

On June 6th, 1888, the session accordingly authorized the clerk to issue, to the three hundred and forty-six members worshipping at the chapel, letters of dismission to the new church, when it should be organized. They also nominated six elders and four deacons, and they recommended that the new church adopt the name "Christ Presbyterian Church in the City of New York." On the same evening Christ Church was duly organized by the committee of Presbytery, and Mr. Lampe was chosen as the pastor.

Thus was completed an undertaking in which the Brick Church, disregarding its own feeling in the matter, and seeking with singleness of purpose to act for the best interests of those who had formed its mission and of the Church at large, had set an example of unselfishness and established a precedent in the management of so-called "mission" enterprises, whose influence has been far-reaching. The new and peculiar relationship was not always, it must be acknowledged, free from its perplexities in succeeding years. Misunderstanding and friction occasionally made their appearance; and time and the grace of God were needed to show the full possibilities of fellowship and mutual service, which were presented by this league of two "affiliated" † churches.

---

* In 1890 the sum contributed by the Brick Church was $1,600. In 1891 and again in 1892 it had been reduced to $1,350. After that this item being merged apparently in the expenses of the branch Sunday-school, cannot easily be ascertained.

† This name was not used at the beginning. References to Christ Church in the records commonly employ the term "Auxiliary" until 1894, when the more fraternal word begins to take its place.

In a later chapter we shall arrive at the period when at length patience had her perfect work.

It would carry us too far afield to notice in detail the share which the Brick Church pastor was taking at this time in the larger movements of the Presbyterian Church. It must suffice to say that in this period the question of a revision of the Presbyterian standards was being vigorously discussed, and especially that the Church was called to go through a severe experience in a famous trial for heresy before the New York Presbytery, afterward appealed to the General Assembly. In both these matters, Dr. van Dyke took a prominent and influential part, and, what is here most important to note, his influence, due primarily to his own acknowledged wisdom and personal power, was greatly increased by the fact that he spoke and acted as the minister of a church which had taken its place in the front rank of the churches of the denomination. In short, Dr. van Dyke's ideal, as he set it before himself in the beginning of his pastorate, had been realized in full measure: the Brick Church was now once more an acknowledged leader in the work of the kingdom of Christ.

But no sooner was the fulfilment of this purpose in sight, than another came forward to take its place. It was not enough to make strong the church's position in the present; the future must also be provided for, that future in which the northward movement of population, responsible already for one change in the location of the church, would make it increasingly difficult to maintain a strong church on Murray Hill. "Endowment" was the word that seemed to point out clearly the next problem for the church to face and solve, and this, it is important to notice, constituted the practical application of Dr. van Dyke's tenth anniversary sermon, from which quotations have been freely taken for the material of this chapter. *

"Let us provide for the future," he said, "by taking measures at once to secure the permanence of this historic church where it now stands, in the centre of the city, as a tower of strength, a landmark —nay, better than that, a light-house, a source of saving illumination, through the coming years. . . . There is very little that endures in this city; localities are altered, houses vanish; how beautiful it would be to think that this house, where you and those whom you love have prayed and communed with God, shall not vanish, but that in the distant years others shall come, and kneel here, and say in their hearts, 'Here my father and mother, here my grandparents, here those whose memory I love and cherish, worshipped and served the living God!' How beautiful it would be, to think that the influences of grace

* The church up to this time had practically no invested funds, nor did it own other land than that which it actually used in its work. A few small legacies had, from time to time, been received. Early in the nineteenth century a few hundred dollars had been bequeathed by William Irving, father of Washington Irving, and Ebenezer Turwell (or Turrell). The Catharine Ryan legacy for the use of the charity scholars has already been mentioned (p. 210). In 1847, Mr. Colin Read bequeathed $5,000 to the Brick Church to be used in aid of candidates for the ministry. After 1873, in accordance with the more modern view that theological students should not be taught to regard themselves as objects of charity, the interest from this fund has been paid to divinity students (usually of Union Theological Seminary) in return for services rendered in the Sunday-school on the West Side. In 1876, a bequest of $5,000, whose interest should be used for the mission school, was received from Mr. Peter Naylor. Mr. John C. Tucker, who died in 1892, left $1,000 for a similar purpose.

should flow from this place forever, and the gospel of Christ be preached here to all comers." *

A partial accomplishment of the purpose thus expressed was speedily to be achieved in an unexpected manner, not by the gathering of individual subscriptions for an endowment fund, but by the incorporation into the Brick Church of another distinct church of Christ, whose property would make at least a substantial beginning of the endowment needed. What this event signified, however, and how much greater treasure than that of money the Church of the Covenant brought into the Brick Church in 1894, can be appreciated only after some account has been given of the Covenant people and what they stood for, and the work they had been doing. To give this will be the purpose of the next chapter.

* "An Historic Church," pp. 36–38.

CHAPTER XXII

THE CHURCH OF THE COVENANT:
1862–1894

"I will make an everlasting covenant with you."—*Isaiah*, 55 : 3.

"Come and let us join ourselves to the Lord in a perpetual covenant that shall not be forgotten."—*Jeremiah*, 50 : 5.

"A church, after all, is a sort of religious home; its peculiar offices and attachments are largely domestic in their character; its members are a Christian family, bound together by ties of Christian sympathy, labor, and fellowship."—GEORGE L. PRENTISS, "Eleven Years of the Church of the Covenant," 1873, p. 28.

IN the fall of the year 1860 were taken the first steps which led to the formation of the Church of the Covenant. * Dr. George Lewis Prentiss, formerly pastor of the Mercer Street Presbyterian Church, had just returned from a two years' absence in Europe, made necessary by ill health. † He came back restored in vigor, and a number of his friends and former parishioners immediately began a movement for the establishment of a new church on Murray Hill with Dr. Prentiss at its head. Like the

* The history contained in this chapter will be told, wherever possible, in the words of those who were the leading figures in it.

† Dr. Prentiss was born in Gorham, Maine, May 16th, 1816. He was graduated from Bowdoin College, studied later in New York and in Europe for several years. In 1845 he was ordained and installed as pastor of the South Trinitarian Church of New Bedford, Mass., and shortly after married Miss Elizabeth Payson of Portland. In 1850 he accepted a call to the Second Presbyterian Church of Newark, N. J., as associate pastor, but a few months later resigned to take the pastorate of the Mercer Street Church in New York, which he served until compelled by illness to resign in 1858.

Mercer Street Church, of which it was practically an offshoot, it was to be a Presbyterian Church of the New School, which accounts for the choice of a location so near to that of the Brick Church.

The beginning of the movement is described for us by Dr. Prentiss himself. * "The first religious service," he says, "which issued in the organization of the Church of the Covenant was held in the chapel of the Home of the Friendless, in Twenty-ninth Street near Madison Avenue, on the last Sunday in November, 1860. It had been decided upon, after much thought, and was the result of a strong and general conviction, that a new Presbyterian church was needed uptown in the vicinity of Murray Hill. . . . But although the movement itself was felt to be highly important, the time seemed most unfavorable for entering upon such a work. In my first sermon on the Sunday mentioned (it was, you will remember, November 25th, 1860, only two or three weeks after the election of Mr. Lincoln, and more than four months before the attack on Fort Sumter), I thus referred to this point: 'The state of the times, I confess, does not, at first thought, seem auspicious for the success of our work. Our dear country is in the throes of a great trouble; fear is on every hand; the most hopeful patriotism is smitten with anxious forebodings; we know not, we dread to guess, what awful calamity may be impending over us. . . . But, after all, is such a time as this really unfavorable to the beginning of a new religious work? . . . God can make the hardest times illustrate all the more beautifully at once his own providential hand and the

* "Eleven Years of the Church of the Covenant," (1873), pp. 4 ff.

GEORGE L. PRENTISS

munificent temper of his children. "Troublous times" are the very ones in which the walls of Zion have usually been built; in which the grandest monuments of the faith and patience of the saints have been erected. . . .'

"During the spring and summer of 1861, the long-gathering storm burst upon the country in all its fury. I need only recall the attack on Fort Sumter, the great uprising of the people that instantly followed, and the disastrous defeat at Bull Run. As I look back to those terrible days, my sole wonder is that we did not disband on the spot. We should certainly have done so, had not the movement been sustained from the first, not only by strong and devoted hearts, but by the special favor of God.

"In the autumn of 1861, our place of meeting was changed to Dodworth's new studio building, on the corner of Fifth Avenue and Twenty-sixth Street. Here, on the evening of March 21st, 1862, at a meeting of the congregation, of which Dr. Skinner was the moderator, and B. F. Butler, secretary, the church was organized, and three ruling elders were appointed. * The original members were eighty-three in number." †

The next step was the election of Dr. Prentiss to be the pastor, and on May 11th he was installed. Not until this time was a name for the new church selected. "It was a question of some interest," says Dr. Prentiss, "what the name should be. A strong repugnance was felt to the custom of calling a Christian sanctuary, and the Christian people who occu-

* See Appendix, M, p. 530.
† See Appendix, L, p. 529.

pied it, after a street or a corner of a street and avenue. To say nothing of the question of taste, the historical identity of some of our most important churches had thereby, upon the removal of the congregation to a new locality, been wholly lost to the public mind. After a good deal of conversation on the subject, we unanimously adopted the *Church of the Covenant*. It has become a name exceedingly endeared to us and to many all over the land."

The church was now named and duly organized, but as yet it had no place of worship of its own, and the awful events of the war then raging made difficult the decision to enter upon an enterprise which would have been far from simple even in a time of prosperity. "I shall not easily forget," says Dr. Prentiss, "the hour or the incident which led to this decision. It was on Tuesday evening, January 6th, 1863. Somewhat wearied, not to say disheartened, by our long waiting and inaction, I called upon a friend to talk the matter over with him. To be, or not to be—that was the question. . . . 'Well,' said my friend, 'I believe in work. If you can induce two others of the same mind to join with me, I am ready to put my hand at once to the plough.'"

Mr. Benjamin F. Butler was the speaker, and the two others were soon secured, Mr. Charles H. Leonard and Mr. Enoch Ketcham. As a result of the untiring energies of these three, aided materially by Mr. George B. de Forest and Mr. William E. Dodge, the lot on the north-west corner of Park Avenue and Thirty-fifth Street was secured, and on November 5th following the cornerstone was laid.

THE CHURCH OF THE COVENANT

Of the circumstances of that auspicious service a picture is presented to us by one who was a witness, and upon whom the event made a deep impression. He recalls "the pleasant autumn afternoon, with the heat of summer over, and the city once more made cheery by the presence of dear friends and neighbors; the attractive neighborhood of Thirty-fifth Street and Park Avenue—then far less built up than now; the fine assemblage of interested and interesting people gathered upon the church site; the scaffolding of new lumber rising above the crowd and elevating those taking part in the brief service; the heartfelt prayer; the profoundly touching hymn by the late Mrs. Prentiss, a hymn filled, not only with holy aspirations for the new enterprise, but a fine sentiment of patriotism that in those days of the war for the Union was deeply felt by all present." * The chapel was the first part of the building completed (in May, 1864), and the church itself was opened and dedicated on April 30th, 1865. †

The congregation thus provided with a home was at first small, but it included men and women of singularly noble Christian character and unusual ability, while the very fact of their small number resulted in increased individual effort, and what was still more important, in a very strong and intimate union of all the members to one another. In a degree rarely known in city churches the people of the Church of the Covenant constituted one household

* From an address by Mr. J. Cleveland Cady, delivered December 16th, 1894, unpublished.

† The cost of the church, chapel, and adjoining parsonage (completed in 1867), including land, organ, and church and chapel furniture, was $160,000.

of faith, bound together by deep personal attachments, and inspired by a common purpose.

What this purpose was is well expressed by their pastor. "I have observed," he says, "that churches, like private Christians, have their peculiar type and individuality of character. It was my earnest desire, from the first, that this church might be marked by a vivid consciousness of the real presence and glory of the risen Christ; by simple whole-hearted devotion to him as a Friend and a Saviour; and by constant growth into his image; as it was my prayer from the first that Christ himself might vouchsafe to dwell in it in all the fulness of his grace and truth." All who knew the church, who attended its services and prayer-meetings, and had opportunity to observe the spirit by which the church life was animated, will bear witness that the prayer of Dr. Prentiss was in no small measure answered. He had warrant for his belief, confidently expressed at a later time, that "Christ Himself has been veritably present with this church, and has wrought in and through it during all these years."

One of the clearest manifestations of the Master's presence was the beginning, almost as soon as the Church of the Covenant was itself started, of a mission work on the East Side of the city. This important step resulted from a young men's prayer-meeting, which met once a month on Sunday afternoons under the leadership of Mr. J. Cleveland Cady, beginning in the fall of 1865. Among those who attended soon grew up "a general desire for a field of labor especially their own," and after earnest debate they decided to start a mission Sunday-school.

When the time came to find a hall or room where the projected school could meet, the best quarters that could be found were over a stable at No. 206 East Fortieth Street. No doubt pleasanter surroundings would have been selected, had they been available, yet the friends of the school have often reflected with pleasure upon the fact that even in the humble place of its origin the Covenant Mission was not unlike its Master, whose cradle was a manger.

At the first meeting * there were twelve teachers ready for classes, but only one scholar could be found, a singular reversal, it has been pointed out, of the text, "The harvest truly is plenteous, but the laborers are few." These twelve modern apostles, however, were not to be discouraged by a small beginning, and soon they saw more ample results of their labors.

A pleasant picture of the school-room has been given us by the man most closely identified with the whole enterprise, Mr. Cady, who, except for the first few months, has been the school's only superintendent, † a record of more than forty years of continuous and devoted service. ‡ Under his guidance, we will take a glimpse at the school as it appeared in its early days. "We pass up a rickety flight of stairs,

---

* On January 28th, 1866. The following were the officers and teachers present: Henry A. Backus, J. Cleveland Cady, Henry A. Crosby, William O. Curtis, John C. Eastman, Edward C. Miles, Miss Isabel N. Miles, Miss Annie L. Prentiss (afterward Mrs. Henry), William Allen Smith, Miss Mallville M. W. Smith (afterward Mrs. McClellan), William R. Sheffield, and Charles Woolsey.

† His predecessor for the brief period named was Mr. Charles Woolsey.

‡ Through practically the whole of this time he has been ably seconded by his friend and fellow-worker in the Covenant Church, Dr. Charles Otis Kimball.

and along a dark, narrow hall until we come to a large low room, seated with settees. This is the home of the Covenant Mission. The wide boards of the bare floor spring under our feet, owing to a too economic construction, but they are scrupulously neat, for the young laborers, however limited their means, will not have filth for an environment. The plastered ceiling is badly cracked and rough with many a rude patching. A piano, a little lectern for the superintendent, a blackboard, and a banner-case, constituted the furniture. This banner-case, of stained pine, with its banners, * was of home manufacture, and a marvel of ingenuity and 'boring,' its chief decoration being a perforated strip, formed by the judicious use of the auger. On the walls are some large, brightly colored scriptural scenes, also of home manufacture. † These alleged water colors have been produced monthly—for the education and edification of the children. Near by is the infant class-room, about fifteen by twenty-five feet (seated with little seats), which three of the male leaders have made a marvellous sensation, by painting in red, white, and blue. They spent several nights in accomplishing the result, and perhaps never completed a more patriotic work."

It is not difficult to see with how much ardor and devotion this enterprise was carried on, nor to believe that work thus heartily done brought its own reward. With a thoroughness that only love could inspire, every detail was faithfully attended to. If the

* Upon the banners the words of the hymns were stencilled by Dr. Kimball, thus obviating the necessity of individual hymn-books.

† Mr. Cady himself painted them and they are still treasured by the school.

task was the preparing and teaching of the lesson, it was undertaken in a spirit of consecration as a most vital service. If it was the guidance of the music, for which the school has ever been famous, no pains were spared in the selection and arrangement. Or if it was only the decoration of the school-room, referred to above, the paint-brush was wielded with enthusiasm.

The outcome was such as might have been expected. "The smile and favor of heaven," said Dr. Prentiss, "have rested upon this school in a wonderful manner. Nor is this any matter of surprise; for it has always been carried on reverently, discreetly, advisedly, and in the fear of God. No false, sensational methods have been followed; no trifling with sacred things has been allowed. The children have been treated as responsible human beings, gathered here, not to be amused, but for the good of their immortal souls; not to keep them out of mischief and teach them to repeat, by rote, verses of Scripture, or even to sing stirring hymns, but to acquaint them with Jesus Christ, their Lord and Saviour, and help to fashion them into honest, dutiful, serious-minded, pious boys and girls. Large numbers have never been one of its chief aims. It has wrought upon the theory that a school of fifty children, instructed and trained in all respects in the right way, will bring forth more and better fruit than a school of five hundred children, conducted upon false, worldly principles. The result is a model Christian school." *

Although, as we are thus told, mere size was never

* "Eleven Years," pp. 23 f.

one of the school's chief aims, the growth was steady and marked, so that after a few years the need of larger and more suitable quarters became urgent. In 1870, the members of the Church of the Covenant took steps to purchase land and erect a building. "It seemed a great venture, considering the large amount which the church had just raised for its fine plant on Park Avenue, but the pastor urged that it would be a shame for them to worship in such comfort and leave their East Side brethren poorly accommodated. . . . This was the first building of its class to consider the matter of beauty and effectiveness. Up to this time it had been thought that accommodation and shelter were all that was needed in such buildings. But this was not the spirit of the Church of the Covenant. It desired that the house of worship which it erected for its East Side branch should be the most attractive place its worshippers should find in all the week." * In spite of the great difficulty of an undertaking so large in itself and so generously conceived, the Covenant people, led by their pastor, accomplished their purpose, and in December, 1871, the "Memorial Chapel," at 310 East Forty-second Street, designed by Mr. Cady and adapted most perfectly to the needs of the work, was dedicated. † Its name referred to a historic event

* From an address by Mr. J. C. Cady, quoted in the "Memorial of Dr. Prentiss," published by Union Seminary, pp. 13 *f.*

† The following "Dedication Hymn" was written for this occasion by **Mrs.** Elizabeth Prentiss:

> Thankfully, O Lord, we come
> To this new and happy home;
> Wilt thou not from heaven descend,
> Here to dwell as friend with friend,
> Granting us the wondrous grace
> To behold thee face to face?

INTERIOR OF THE COVENANT CHAPEL.—THE PRESENT CHURCH OF THE COVENANT

which has already been mentioned in this volume, the reunion of the Old and New School Presbyterians in 1869. * The new chapel of the Church of the Covenant was designed to be a "Memorial" of that reunion.

While the mission Sunday-school was thus prospering, the mother church was quietly and steadily growing in numbers and influence. In 1873, Dr. Prentiss, to whom, in large measure, the church owed its reverent, liberal, and devoted spirit, resigned his charge to accept the Chair of Pastoral Theology, Church Polity, and Missionary Work, in Union Theological Seminary.

He had done a great and lasting work in the Church of the Covenant. His gentle and affectionate nature, his cultured and scholarly mind, and, above all, the wealth of his personal Christian faith, had been used by him to implant a living Christianity in the hearts of his people. "Religion," as has been said of him, "was the great, impelling, controlling

Teach us here to praise and pray,
How to live from day to day;
Teach us who and what thou art,
Write thy name on every heart;
Make us pure, and clean, and white,
Blessed Jesus, in thy sight.

May the weary here find rest
On the tender Shepherd's breast;
May the erring cease to stray,
Learning here the perfect way
And the mourner find that here
Jesus wipes away the tear.

And when life's short day is o'er,
And we hither come no more,
Father, Saviour, loving Friend,
Guide us to our journey's end;
Thankful that we often came
Here to learn thy blessed name.

* See above, p. 316.

force of his life and work," * and under his leadership the Church of the Covenant had, in a marked
degree, acquired a spirit like his own: religion was
not merely its sphere of activity, but the vital force
by which it was moved and directed. Combined with
his unusual spiritual power, Dr. Prentiss possessed
also the vigor and determination by which hard,
practical tasks were carried steadily to their completion. His pastorate was begun by the building of the
church and crowned by the building of the chapel.
To the end of his life, continuing to live and labor in New York, he was the church's faithful and
deeply loved friend, and in his later days he was regarded by his former parishioners with something of
the affection and reverence that must have been felt
for the aged St. John at Ephesus.

The successor of Dr. Prentiss was the Rev. Marvin
R. Vincent, D.D., who was called from the First
Presbyterian Church of Troy, and was installed in
the Church of the Covenant on May 8th, 1873. The
service thus begun was to continue for fifteen years.

A graphic characterization of the church and its
people during this period is provided by Dr. Vincent
himself.† "Dr. Prentiss," he says, "had laid solid
foundations with his Christian culture and his sympathetic personal ministry. The church was distinctly and essentially a family church as distinguished from what is known as a popular church.
Neither its general character, its ministrations, nor
its situation invited the crowd which goes to stare

---

* Funeral Sermon by Dr. Vincent, p. 28.

† In an article in the "Evangelist" quoted by Dr. McIlvaine in the
sermon preached February 11th, 1894, pp. 21–24.

MARVIN R. VINCENT

and to be entertained. But the gospel was faithfully preached, the children were gathered into the fold, and the church was represented strongly by individuals in numerous benevolent and philanthropic enterprises. Its internal harmony was perfect.

"Such a congregation as it was! Representing so many different sides of life! Of ministers there were Dr. Prentiss and Henry B. Smith and Dr. Eastman, Dr. Briggs, Dr. Francis Brown and Dr. Wallace Atterbury. Of doctors, Buck's noble head appeared under the fourth gallery, and his son, Albert, was a little farther down the aisle; Post sat just in front, the light through the colored panes falling on his full white beard, his Greek Testament in his hand. Then there were Noyes and St. John Roosa and McLane and Brayton Ball, Henry Walker, Yale, Stimson, and Streeter. The lawyers, too, were a goodly company: Judge Sutherland was just behind Dr. Post; Charles Butler opposite, John P. Crosby further down; William Walter Phelps over on the left; Daniel Lord not far from the door; on the middle aisle, Charles D. Adams, so early taken away in the freshness of his manhood, with all his sterling worth and graceful culture. Then Theron G. Strong and William G. Choate and William C. Whitney and Hugh J. Jewett and W. W. Hoppin and S. J. Storrs and Walter Howe and Eugene Smith. And the artists, too, Mrs. Candace Wheeler and her daughter Dora, and Oliver Lay and George Yewell and Cleveland Cady.

"There were the two Scribners, John Blair and Charles. There was Charlton T. Lewis and Mrs. Elizabeth Prentiss and Whitelaw Reid and Charles

L. Norton and Edward S. Mead and Stephen Walker. And then the business men, the men of affairs. William E. Dodge and Joseph R. Skidmore sat in adjoining pews. Robert Gordon, with his keen Scotch face; all the artists in New York knew him. Close behind him William H. Osborn, a large man every way; people who had any sham about them generally gave him a wide berth. Thomas Denny's fine, scholarly face looked up from the front pew on the middle aisle. There were Harvey Fisk and Calvin Goddard and Charles H. Rogers. There were William H. H. Moore and Robert H. McCurdy and David McAlpin. There were Enoch Ketcham and Joseph Parsons and Marshall Blake. There were Charles Trumbull White, the chemist, and Mancer M. Backus, the furrier, who would turn from selling a sealskin muff or cloak and discuss Greek roots, or theology, or mathematics with you at your pleasure."

To complete the picture we must place in the pulpit the dignified figure of Dr. Vincent himself, in regard to whose power as a preacher the appreciative words of his successor may be quoted: "No better sermons were preached or published in this city than those delivered in this pulpit during Dr. Vincent's ministry. They were always fresh, thoughtful, suggestive, marked by spiritual insight and wide scholarship, clothed in a vigorous and beautiful style." *

Perhaps the most noteworthy event of Dr. Vincent's pastorate was the appointment of the first chapel pastor, the Rev. Howard A. Talbot. † There had

* Sermon preached February 11th, 1894, p. 20.
† See Appendix R, p. 536.

INTERIOR OF THE OLD CHURCH OF THE COVENANT

before been several missionaries connected with the chapel work, but in 1875, with Mr. Talbot's appointment, the church which we now know as the Church of the Covenant began to take definite shape. A few months later the custom was inaugurated of celebrating the Sacrament of the Lord's Supper at the chapel, a significant step in this instance, as we have already seen it to be in the parallel development of the mission chapel of the Brick Church.

The direction in which things were moving has been well described by Dr. Vincent. * "Before I ceased to be the pastor of the mother church," he says, "the chapel congregation had begun to take steps toward its own maintenance; and, although unable to assume the entire burden, was contributing annually a respectable sum. . . . It has been from the beginning the policy of the workers in this field to encourage and develop the ideal and the fact of self-support. In the early days . . . its work was largely among the poor, and a large amount of poverty and distress appealed to it for relief. But while such appeals were habitually met with a genuine Christian compassion and tenderness, they were also met with a sound common-sense and with an enlightened conception of the nature of true helpfulness. While judiciously assisting the absolutely helpless, it was the constant aim to open the way in each case to self-help; to provide opportunities for honest labor; to train the children so that, in future days, they might command remunerative employment, and thus to put the poorest into a self-respecting attitude. On this

* In the "Thirty-fifth Anniversary Sermon," preached January 27th, 1901, pp. 15 *f.*

line arose the cooking-school, the sewing-school, and the Helping Hand, and along this line were directed the ministrations of the Bible readers and of the pastor, so far as they had to do with the material conditions of the people."

The fuller extension of this ideal of self-support and independence to the organized work of the chapel itself was, however, deferred to a later date. As Dr. Vincent himself has elsewhere said, * there were in the time of his pastorate "many and the best of reasons" why it was inexpedient to transform the Memorial Chapel into an independent church. The accomplishment of that most important undertaking belongs to the history of the next pastorate.

Dr. Vincent resigned his charge in November, 1887, to become Professor of Sacred Literature in Union Seminary; and in December, 1888, his successor was installed, the Rev. James Hall McIlvaine, D.D., who had been called from the Union Church of Providence, R. I.

The new pastor had been on the field but a little over a year when it became necessary to secure a new leader for the chapel work. Mr. Talbot (1875–1881), had been succeeded in turn by the Rev. Henry T. McEwen, (1881–1887), and the Rev. Edwin E. Rogers (1887–1889). When a successor for Mr. Rogers was being sought, it was decided to make his position different from that of the chapel pastor up to this time. "In reviewing the field," says Dr. McIlvaine,† referring to the time of his

* In some unpublished reminiscences written for a memorial service at the present Church of the Covenant on December 16th, 1894.

† In an address (unpublished), delivered on November 8th, 1891.

arrival in New York, "it seemed to me that the pastoral relation [between the chapel minister and the Church of the Covenant] was very unsatisfactory. The pastor was not installed, . . . only hired by a body of men; and I suggested with hesitancy that we should change it all, and that the new pastor should be associate pastor of the Church of the Covenant. To my great delight, the idea was seized with enthusiasm." It was on this basis that the Rev. George Sidney Webster accepted a call to take up the chapel work, and was installed as Dr. McIlvaine's associate in March, 1890.*

The aim of this new arrangement was to assert emphatically that the Covenant Memorial Chapel was not a "mission" in the unworthy sense which that name had acquired, that it was not merely an inferior, dependent institution, maintained by charity, but, on the contrary, an important and highly honored part of the Church of the Covenant itself. As the new associate pastor said a year or so after he had begun his work, "This new relation was rather a proper recognition of [the chapel] than a change in plan or policy of its work. For years a church has existed here in all but the name. Now side by side with our loving mother church, no longer as a daughter, but as a sister beloved, we keep step in our united efforts to advance Christ's kingdom in this part of

---

* He was born at Meredith, Delaware County, N. Y., July 30th, 1853. In 1878 he graduated from Hamilton College, being valedictorian of his class. For a year he was professor of Greek in the Seminary at Whitestone, N. Y., after which he entered Union Theological Seminary, New York City, graduating in 1882. His first ministerial service was as assistant pastor of the First Presbyterian Church, in East Orange, N. J., beginning in 1882, and ending with his call to the Church of the Covenant.

our city. Our interests and our sympathies are interlinked. We rejoice to-day in God's great mercy that has preserved the one Church of the Covenant with its two Sunday-schools, its two church buildings, its two congregations, its two pastors."

The new plan worked well, but not so much, it is evident, because of the excellence of the plan, as because of the spirit in which it was used. The plan indeed, it has been truly said, "was possible only on the basis of the most cordial fraternal feeling between the church and the chapel.* But that feeling existed in a marked degree and was recognized and rejoiced in by all concerned. It is pleasant to read the testimony of the associate pastor, written some years later. "The mutual love that maintained and inspired this work," he says, "was both a revelation and an inspiration to me," to which he makes the special addition: "The two pastors consulted and planned and toiled like brothers, and the fraternal grip upon each other's hearts has never been lost by either of us." † Dr. McIlvaine spoke with equal

---

* "A Decade of Work in the Church of the Covenant," a historical sermon by the pastor, March, 1900, p. 5.

† "A Decade of Work," pp. 5 f. One concrete instance of the good effect upon Mr. Webster's congregation is noted by him in another part of this same sermon, preached, it will be remembered, in 1900. "Recall this room," he says, "as it looked ten years ago. There are no familiar furnishings except the clock and the organ and one tablet on yonder wall. You then had no communion table and no carpet on the floors, except on the pulpit platform and for a little space in front of it. The pews could not be praised for comfort or beauty. Cushions were unknown. The change in ecclesiastical form from a mission chapel to a church suggested the need of a change in the churchliness of this interior. This meant earnest, self-denying work. We were most lovingly assisted, but this congregation raised more than half the $4,000 that was expended here in furnishings and repairs within the first half of this decade."

A more general statement of the success of this "church in a chapel," as

emphasis and enthusiasm of the success of the new pastoral relation. "The result has justified the means," he said, speaking at the chapel in November, 1891, and added, "I want to say that over at the church we are as proud of Mr. Webster as you are." Two years later, after a still further test, he again affirmed that the relation had been "a most helpful and happy one to both congregations." *

When these words were spoken a still further step in the chapel's development had been taken, the step, indeed, by which it ceased altogether to be a chapel and became a church. The story of that event, however, cannot be related in the present chapter, and meantime we must become familiar with the important developments in the life of the mother church by which the chapel's independence was largely brought about.

It may have seemed strange that in narrating the story of the Church of the Covenant so large a propor-

---

Mr. Webster called it, may be quoted from an article by him in the "Evangelist" for April 6th, 1893. "This church," he said, "has one elder and two deacons in its congregation, two pastor's assistants, a flourishing Sunday-school, superintended by an elder of the church, a well sustained church prayer-meeting, Christian Endeavor Society, Ladies' Association, men's meeting, Choral Society, Women's Helping Hand Society, Children's Mission Band, Girls' Sewing-school, Coal Club, and Burial Society. Four of these organizations have been started within the past three years. Through these activities more missionary work is accomplished than was possible under the former conditions. In three years more than five hundred families have felt in some way the sympathetic throb of church life in this chapel, and about ten thousand calls have been made by its pastoral force. . . . Without any revival season there have been accessions to the church at every communion. There have been received at the chapel on confession of their faith 99, and by letter 44; the loss has been, 43 dismissed and 20 died, leaving a net gain in three years of 80 members."

* "The Church of the Covenant: a Historical Sermon," February 11th, 1894, p. 33.

tion of space has been given to the affairs of the chapel, but in doing so we have but fallen in with the strong feeling of the Covenant people, the feeling that of the church the chapel was by far the largest and most important single element. It was, however, by no means the whole. The life of the church had been singularly rich, and fruitful in spiritual and practical results.

Only the briefest sketch of the different departments of the work is here possible. The prayer-meetings, as many who still live heartily testify, were a source of the greatest strength and inspiration, and we may quote without qualification a notice of them printed in the Covenant Year Book for 1891. "The attendance at these services testifies to the benefit derived from them. The spirit and tone of them are such as to leave but little to be desired in the way of improvement. The brief, thoughtful remarks, the earnest, simple prayers, impress all who attend them." *

Of the other most salient features in the church's activity a brief account is given us in a sermon preached by Dr. McIlvaine in February, 1894. He is looking back over the whole history, but refers more particularly to the events and labors of his own pastorate and of that of Dr. Vincent. "In addition to the pew-rents, which have necessarily been high," he says to his congregation, "you have had $5,000 a year to raise for the expenses of the church and $4,000 a year for the chapel. The burden has rested upon a few, and the few have been continually

---

* A choir of young people, which led the singing, added much to the interest and helpfulness of these services.

JAMES H. McILVAINE

becoming fewer, but it has been borne without a murmur. During the thirty-two years of your existence, you have contributed as a church to religious purposes nearly, if not quite, $1,000,000. Fully one-half of this has gone into missionary work; the other half to the building and support of the church. And this represents but a part, perhaps the smaller part, of your gifts. Large contributions have been made directly to the boards of the Church by individuals; many students have been educated for the ministry at private expense; two professorships in Union Seminary have been endowed; Olivet Chapel built, a day nursery purchased and equipped, and many other large gifts have been given by the members of this church. *

"The most efficient agent in the church's work has been the Ladies' Church Work Association. This society was organized November 6th, 1873, by the consolidation of the other missionary and benevolent societies in the church. It has worked for the various boards of the Church and for Covenant Chapel through one organization. It has main-

---

* One other item should be added to this list. It is referred to in the same sermon from which the quotation in the text is made, as follows (pp. 25 ƒ): "The Covenant Church had, from the first, taken an interest in the Bohemian mission, and no cause appealed more successfully to its sympathies. It was after an appeal from the pulpit that the invalid wife of a physician said to me, 'Why cannot those people have a church? Why cannot the ladies build it? Let us call a meeting at my parlor.' The meeting was called. Another meeting followed soon after. The plan was organized and carried out, and though the funds were not all contributed by the Church of the Covenant, its women gave most generously, and one of its trustees personally superintended the work until the day when the new home was dedicated, without a cent of debt, amid the tears of a grateful people. The Bohemian Church owes its church edifice principally to the Church of the Covenant."

tained for twenty years a missionary in Syria, a home missionary in the West and South, a Bible-reader, a sewing-school, and an employment society at the chapel. It has sent fifty boxes of clothing and useful articles to the missionaries in the West; it has cut out and prepared nearly 1,000 garments yearly to be made by poor women, and it has raised and expended upward of $80,000 in its work. Another efficient society has been the Young People's Mission Band. During the fifteen years of its existence about $4,500 has been expended by it in good work in this city and in foreign lands. The Men's Social Organization was formed in 1887, and has met every two months for literary and social purposes. It has been a great help to the church in bringing its members closer together.

"The church Sunday-school was organized a year before the church, in the chapel of the Home of the Friendless, January 20th, 1861. Mr. E. P. Griffin was its first superintendent. He was followed by B. F. Butler, L. N. Lovell, W. H. H. Moore, Wm. Seward, and Alfred E. Marling. It has never been a large school, but it has been a field of most faithful and fruitful activity in training up the children of the church for their Christian privileges and responsibilities. Nearly all of its members have come in due time to the Lord's table. Thirty-five have so come from the Sunday-school during my pastorate." *

It will have been evident from certain allusions in the foregoing review, that, in spite of many elements of very genuine success, the church was working against unequal odds. In the spirit of worship and

* "The Church of the Covenant: A Historical Sermon," pp. 29–32.

service, and in the devotion of its members, many of whom had belonged to the church throughout its entire history, the Church of the Covenant was strong. But its membership was not being proportionately renewed, as the older members dropped out. With the reunion of the Old and New School Presbyterians in 1869, the original reason for the existence of a second Presbyterian Church on Murray Hill had been removed, and with this change of condition certain difficulties, which had already existed, gradually became acute.

Dr. Prentiss, as early as the date of his own resignation in 1873, had observed with great concern the direction in which affairs were tending. In a sermon delivered at that time he said that, in reviewing the history of the church, nothing had struck him more forcibly "than the incessant change that is going on in a New York congregation.

"I do not refer now," he continued, "to the changes wrought by death, for these are peculiar to no time or place, but to those which grow out of the present conditions of society, of business, and of religious life in this city. My impression is, that the changes are more than twice as great and rapid as they were when, nearly a quarter of a century ago, I came to New York. They are, probably, three or four times as great and rapid as they were fifty years ago. Half the people you meet with seem like birds sitting upon a twig, looking in every direction, and ready to fly away on the slightest impulse. In most of our churches, it is a constant coming and going; some of them, in this respect, resemble large hotels or boarding-houses; a few of those who frequent them are permanent; the many never continue in one stay. In ten years a congregation almost loses its personal identity.

"Since the war, and especially within the past four or five years, this feature has become more and more marked, the corrupt state of our municipal affairs having very much accelerated emigration to the country. Our religious interests have suffered exceedingly from the latter cause. A large proportion of the young men and women, who marry and go to housekeeping, leave us; for, unless they are rich, it is extremely difficult for them to remain here. Then the tide of business is rushing in upon the old centres of population and church-life, and driving out all before it. Never in this country, rarely in any country, has there been such an anomalous and revolutionary state of things. In a single generation—yea, in less than a generation—expensive and beautiful sanctuaries are erected and filled, then forsaken and torn down, or else sold, to be converted into theatres, stables, and places of trade. In this whirlpool of change, the strongest religious society is sometimes wrecked. . . .

"The Church of the Covenant, I suppose, would be regarded as composed of more than ordinarily stable elements; and yet last year we lost—mostly by removal to the country—nearly a tenth of our whole congregation and about a sixth of our whole Sunday-school." *

If this was the situation in 1873, we can feel no surprise that after twenty more years, during which the conditions had grown worse rather than better,

* "Eleven Years of the Church of the Covenant," pp. 26–28.

the adoption of some revolutionary change could be no longer deferred. "For a number of years," said Dr. McIlvaine, "the future of this church has been a subject of increasing anxiety to many of you. The situation, beautiful as it is, has never been favorable to the development of a strong and popular church. It is out of the way, and there are forty Protestant churches within a radius of half a mile. The people in this immediate neighborhood are identified with other churches or indifferent to all churches. To the east of us a very small percentage of the population is Protestant, and this is needed by the chapels and churches there. We have had this whole region carefully canvassed and we know it well." *

The way of escape which, to persons confronted by these conditions, would first suggest itself—one that has been used by many other New York churches similarly placed—was to move the whole organization to a more favorable locality. But another and wiser expedient—and an expedient, it must be added, which called for far greater self-sacrifice in achieving its more useful end—presented itself at just this juncture.

It has already been seen that the Covenant's near neighbor, the Brick Church, was at this very time beginning to think seriously of the imperative need of an endowment for the future continuance of her work. The time would almost certainly come, though perhaps not for many years, when the Brick Church would be in exactly the same position as that in which the Church of the Covenant now found itself. Why not meet the problems of both churches, the immediate

* "The Church of the Covenant: A Historical Sermon," p. 34.

need of the one, the approaching need of the other, by uniting forces, the Brick Church thus sharing her present prosperity and opportunity, and the Church of the Covenant providing, by the sale of her valuable property, the needed endowment for the united work?

In the next chapter will be described the steps by which this result was accomplished. Meantime it must be repeated that the act was, on the part of the people and pastor of the Church of the Covenant, singularly high-minded and self-forgetful. One cannot read without deep feeling the words of the last sermon preached in the church on February 11th 1894: but the feeling is not only one of sympathy, it is even more a feeling of great admiration for the high motives by which these men were actuated.

"For nearly a year," said Dr. McIlvaine, "you have had before you the question of union with the Brick Church. You have carefully considered every other alternative, and with wonderful unanimity, without a dissenting voice, you have decided in favor of this union. There is no compulsion upon you. For a long time you could continue as you are, drawing, if necessary, upon your large and valuable property. If you consulted only your own inclinations you would doubtless much prefer to do so. This church is exceedingly dear to you. You have prayed and hoped and struggled and sacrificed for its welfare. It is connected with many of the tenderest and most sacred associations of your life. You love its very stones and walls, its familiar and homelike ways. But you have regarded the question from a higher standpoint than that of personal preference. You have felt that this property was the Lord's property, not yours—that it was a sacred trust committed into your hands. You have asked sincerely, conscientiously, how this trust could be best administered in the interests of Christ's cause. It has seemed to you that, in the reinforcement and permanent endowment of the Brick Church this end would be best accomplished, that amid all the manifold changes of the future, one strong Presbyterian church might be secure for the years to come in the centre of this city.

"It is the highest law of life that you are thus subserving. Self-interest, self-preservation, self-assertion, this is a natural instinct, one of the strong permanent forces which lie at the base of life. But it is not the highest. Nothing moves into fulness of power, nothing attains the highest end of its being, but by the law of self-surrender. Of this law Christ himself is the perfect illustration and fulfilment. 'Except a corn of wheat fall into the ground and die, it abideth alone, but if it die, it bringeth forth much fruit.'" *

* "The Church of the Covenant: A Historical Sermon," pp. 34–36.

CHAPTER XXIII

UNION AND AFFILIATION: 1893–1900

"And they twain shall be one flesh: so then they are no more twain, but one flesh."—*Mark* 10 : 8.

"The union of the Church of the Covenant with the Brick Church has proved to be eminently wise and for the best interests of both, and the results, we believe, will be for the lasting good of the united people, and for the advancement of the cause of Christ in this city."—*Minute of Session*, January 3d, 1896.

EARLY in 1893, the proposal to unite the Church of the Covenant and the Brick Church in the manner described in the last chapter, was broached, and began to be considered by the officers of both churches. The proposed action, it will readily be believed, involved a number of difficult problems. To accommodate to one another the interests of two fully developed organizations, and to bring together two distinct groups of people in a union which should be hearty and happy, required very careful consideration. There were, moreover, certain technical difficulties which must be overcome before the plan would be even possible.

On May 16th, 1893, came a formal communication from the session and trustees of the Church of the Covenant, definitely proposing a union and asking that a committee of the officers of the Brick Church be appointed to confer with the Covenant representatives and to join with them in reporting a plan for adoption by their respective congregations.

This was done, and nearly six months were occupied in this preliminary work.

In the fall, tentative plans were submitted and in general approved. The questions regarding the representation of the Covenant congregation in the official boards of the united church, the disposition of the Covenant property, and the establishment of a double pastorate, were adjusted with satisfaction to both sides. Two other elements in the problem demanded not only agreement, but certain preparatory actions, themselves not free from perplexity.

The first of these was the question regarding the future status of the Covenant Chapel. The chapel of the Brick Church, it will be remembered, had been raised to the dignity of ecclesiastical independence; and it was natural to propose that the Covenant Chapel should now be put on the same footing. On the West Side the experiment had been in the main successful, though certain disadvantages and positive perils had made their appearance in the years that had passed since the organization of the church. With certain precautions, therefore, designed to meet the difficulties which experience had pointed out, it was determined to proceed along these same lines in regard to the chapel on the East Side.

In October, when the question was definitely put to Mr. Webster, the chapel pastor, whether, in his judgment, it was possible to reorganize his congregation as a separate and independent church, he replied, "Yes, if we can have officers that will command the respect and support of the congregation they serve." * Four members of the Church of the

* "A Decade of Work," p. 7.

Covenant were found who were ready to transfer their membership and allegiance to the new church, and to assume a portion of its responsibilities. * At the same time it was made sure that the cordial support formerly given by the members of the old Church of the Covenant, both in money and in personal service, would be continued. These fundamental points having been satisfactorily settled, the new church was organized on November 30th, 1893, and was called "The Church of the Covenant," in order that that dear and familiar name, now to be laid aside by the parent organization, might be continued in the child. Mr. Webster was installed as pastor on January 2d, 1894.

The second perplexing element in the union problem concerned the future standing of the Brick Church. It was agreed by both sides that the name and historic continuity of that church ought to be preserved inviolate, but it was found that under the existing law, this could not be assured in such a union as was desired. The necessity, therefore, of taking preliminary steps to remove this difficulty was clearly perceived, and allowance made for it, when, on January 2d, 1894, the officers of the two churches entered into the following agreement:

"Whereas, at meetings of the congregations of the said † two churches held on December 19th, 1893, resolutions were passed, looking to a union of the two churches in such way as will preserve the name, ecclesiastical organization, and historic continuity of

---

* One of them became the treasurer, while two accepted the office of elder and the fourth the office of deacon.

† The preamble, to which reference is here made, has been omitted.

GEORGE S. WEBSTER

the Brick Church, such resolutions providing that the boards of trustees of the churches be directed and authorized to take such legal steps as might be necessary for the consolidation of the properties of the two churches;

"Now, therefore, in consideration of the premises and of the mutual covenants herein expressed, the parties hereto, by their respective boards of trustees, have mutually covenanted and agreed, and they hereby do mutually covenant and agree, each with the other, as follows:

"First. As soon as the same can be legally accomplished, such proposed union shall, subject to the approval of the Presbytery of New York, take place upon the following basis:

"1. The Brick Church shall preserve its name and ecclesiastical organization and historic continuity, and as such it shall receive into good and regular standing the members of the Church of the Covenant.

"2. The pastor of the Church of the Covenant shall become coördinate pastor of the Brick Church, with the same salary as that received by the present pastor of that church, and the two pastors shall continue to be coördinate pastors until the Brick Church, after the addition of the members of the Church of the Covenant and as thus constituted, shall determine differently.

"3. Six elders from the session of the Church of the Covenant, to wit: Henry D. Noyes, M.D., W. H. H. Moore, William Warner Hoppin, J. C. Cady, Theron G. Strong, and Alfred E. Marling, shall be added to the session of the Brick Church. Six deacons from the Church of the Covenant, to wit, William O. Curtis, William Seward, Charles O. Kimball, Charles W. McAlpin, Gerard Beekman Hoppin, and Henry N. Corwith, shall be added to the board of deacons of the Brick Church. Three trustees from the Church of the Covenant, to wit, Joseph H. Parsons, Arthur M. Dodge, and Eugene Smith, shall become members of the board of trustees of the Brick Church in place of three of the present nine members of the board.

"4. All the property of the Church of the Covenant * shall be transferred to the Brick Church, subject to the encumbrances existing thereon, except that the memorial gifts, tablets, and windows in the Church of the Covenant may be surrendered to the several donors thereof or their legal representatives. † Upon such transfer being made, the then unpaid liabilities of the Church of the Covenant for expenses of its maintenance during the current fiscal year ending May 1st, 1894, shall be assumed by the Brick Church.

"5. Pews in the Brick Church to the number of not less than twenty-five shall be provided for the accommodation of the congregation of the Church of the Covenant, for which pew-rents shall be charged and paid for at the same rate as that applicable to the other pews in the church.

---

* This, of course, included the chapel.

† Two of these memorials were subsequently placed in the new Church of the Covenant. These were the marble bas-relief representing "Faith," originally in the possession of Mr. William Curtis Noyes, and after his death in 1864, given by his family to the church of which he had been one of the founders; and the baptismal font given by Benjamin F. Butler and Robert Gordon in 1876. When the old Church of the Covenant was torn down, its corner-stone was transferred to its namesake, where it is set into the wall of the vestibule.

"6. The work heretofore carried on at the Covenant Chapel in East Forty-second Street is to receive from the Brick Church that cordial sympathy and financial support which it has heretofore had from the Church of the Covenant.

"Second. The two churches covenant and agree, each with the other, that both will coöperate in an effort to obtain from the legislature of the State of New York the transfer of the property of the Church of the Covenant to the Brick Church, the merger of the Church of the Covenant in the Brick Church or the union of the two churches, on the basis hereinbefore stated.

"They also covenant and agree that they will unite in an application to the Presbytery of New York for its approval, and that in all other ways they will coöperate to the accomplishment of the purpose hereinbefore expressed." *

The desired action of the legislature was obtained by an act † passed on March 2d; on the 12th of the same month the consent of the Presbytery was given; and on April 12th, by the final transfer of the property, the union, which had been first formally proposed nearly a year before, became an established fact. The lot on Park Avenue, with the church and parsonage standing upon it, had been sold for $315,000 which, after a small deduction for the pay-

* A third section not here given related to temporary arrangements pending the consummation of the plan of union.

† Providing that the Church of the Covenant, with the approval of Presbytery, might "transfer its property, real and personal, by way of gift, grant, conveyance, or otherwise" to the Brick Church, and that the continued existence of the Corporation of the Brick Church should "not be impaired or affected by such transfer."

ment of outstanding debts, became an endowment fund for the work of the Brick Church. *

The consolidation thus effected proved an unquestionable success. Dr. McIlvaine, for whom, perhaps, it had from the beginning involved the greatest sacrifice, expressed emphatically his satisfaction two years after the event. "The union of the former Church of the Covenant with the Brick Church," he said, "is now confirmed and established, and the united congregation is working smoothly, happily, and efficiently together."

To the Brick Church, on the one hand, the coming of the Covenant people had been a great gain, in spiritual and personal power even more than in financial resources. It was like new blood in the body, and both in the deliberations of the official boards and in the church's practical work, the effect was felt at once. The people of the Covenant, for their part, were happy in the change. They had made their sacrifice and left it behind them; and they

---

* In May, 1897, a tablet commemorating the union of the two churches was placed in the Brick Church vestibule. It is of yellow Sienna marble, and was executed from a design by Mr. J. Cleveland Cady. In the border appear the mottoes of the old and the new Church of the Covenant, quoted as a heading for the preceding chapter of this history (p. 405). The central inscription is as follows:

THE CHURCH OF THE COVENANT
FOUNDED MARCH 21, 1862

PASTORS:

GEORGE L. PRENTISS, D.D.,	1862–1873
MARVIN R. VINCENT, D.D.,	1873–1887
JAMES HALL McILVAINE, D.D.,	1888–1894

UNITED WITH
THE BRICK PRESBYTERIAN CHURCH
APRIL, 1894

were heartily prepared to rejoice in the prosperous and inspiring life of the united church. *

There was, it may be said, but one serious imperfection in the plan of union as it had been carried out, and this was one which had been unavoidable under the conditions by which the union had been governed. It was the duplication of the office of pastor.

The existence in a church of two coequal and coordinate ministers, both of them occupying the same position of leadership and holding identical responsibilities, must always be an arrangement fraught with peculiar difficulty. Something of this sort had been tried by the New York Presbyterians in the eighteenth century and had been at length abandoned as decidedly unsatisfactory. No one, it may be assumed, would have proposed to repeat the experiment for its own sake. At the time of the union it was adopted merely because it was then necessary to the important end in view; and, after the union had been accomplished, the disadvantages which had been foreseen were, of course, only the more apparent. A dual pastorate was clearly not economical, it was cumbersome, and after the success of the union had been assured, it was unnecessary.

No one was more conscious of this fact than were the two pastors, and in January, 1896, they addressed the following joint letter to their people:

* Dr. Richards, the present pastor, speaking in 1904, said, "On both sides the magnanimous spirit of fellowship must have been strong, I think; for the union was so real that, coming to you after a few years' interval, I find it quite impossible to discriminate among you which used to be which. There seems to be no 'which' now; you are all one." "In the Unity of the Faith: A Sermon," p. 9.

"To the Members of the Congregation Worshipping in the Brick Presbyterian Church:

"DEAR BRETHREN:

"The dual pastorate, under which we are at present ministering to you, was entered upon as a condition of the union of the Church of the Covenant with the Brick Church, now happily and successfully accomplished to the satisfaction of all who are concerned. We recognized at the time that this duplicate arrangement of the pastorate was experimental. We are now convinced that it is not calculated to be the best working arrangement for the church, and therefore, that it ought not to be permanent. After earnest and careful consultation, for more than a month, with the session whom you have appointed as your representatives and our advisers, we find them unanimously of the same opinion. Our duty is therefore made perfectly clear and simple. We agreed with each other and with you, at the time of the union, that in the event of the retirement, death or resignation of one of the pastors, the resignation of the other should be immediately presented. We intend to keep this agreement in loyalty to each other and to all the members of the united congregation. With a deep and single desire to promote the best interests of the church, whose servants we are, and with sincere regrets at the thought of the dissolution of relations which have been so pleasant, we come together to place in your hands our resignations from the dual pastorate of the Brick Church. We beg you to unite with us, according to Presbyterian law and usage, in our joint and several application to the Presbytery to dissolve the pastoral relation. And we pray that the Holy Spirit of wisdom may direct you and us in all our actions, and that the Lord Jesus Christ may make us perfect in every good word and deed to obey him and to serve the welfare of his blessed kingdom of peace and love upon earth.

"J. H. McIlvaine,

"Henry van Dyke."

That the church should allow both its pastors to go was manifestly out of the question, and the congregation was brought face to face with the peculiarly embarrassing necessity of making a choice between them.

But here the qualities of Christian generosity and self-forgetfulness in the former members of the old Church of the Covenant, already exhibited by them at the time of the union, once more took control of the situation. They were now members of the Brick Church, and however the fact might be disguised, the choice about to be made was between the pastor whom they had brought with them into the union, and the man who had been pastor of the Brick Church for ten years before the union was so much as thought of.

It was by representatives of the old Covenant Church that the deciding vote was moved and seconded, approving ' the acceptance, in the Christian spirit in which it is proffered of the proposal of Dr. McIlvaine to retire from the copastorate," and recommending "that Dr. van Dyke be requested to withdraw his resignation." No better evidence could be desired of the spirit in which this action was proposed and adopted—for the vote was unanimous in the affirmative—than the words with which Dr. Henry D. Noyes had accompanied his seconding of the motion. "There may, perhaps, never be another time," he said, "when such a word as is in my heart may perhaps be fittingly spoken. It is simply to this effect—it is only the personal confirmation of what has been so abundantly and eloquently said by both the pastors. It is not an easy thing for me to take any step which will eventuate in the removal from the pastoral office of this church of the man whose coming to New York was to no small degree due to my personal efforts. Under his ministrations, I have sat with great comfort and edification and delight, and when the movement to bring the Church of the Covenant into close relations with this one was initiated, it brought with it, not only the earnest purposes of our pastor, but the hearty coöperation of almost all the members—practically all the members—of the Church of the Covenant. Since that consolidation has been effected, I beg to assure all of you that there has been but one heart and one mind on the part of those who have come into this congregation—that our united purpose should be for our mutual good, for our better fitting for the work of Jesus Christ, and that we should here seek together for the prosperity of this old-established and renowned church. And at this moment, when circumstances have pointed to the desirability of a separate arrangement in the pastorate, while I am sure that I voice the sentiment of many that it is with deep regret that this sundering shall be effected, it is at the same time, true that the dominant thought and

feeling in the heart of those who have come here is
that we want the prosperity and the success and the
consolidation in work of this church itself. We are
part of you; we have joined you; we have no purpose to separate from you; we clasp hands with you,
and we will be always with you in the service and
work of our blessed Master."

When the chief action of the meeting had been
taken, another resolution, moved and seconded by
men who represented the older Brick Church of the
days before the union, * and by them supported in
cordial words of a more informal and personal character, was offered in the following terms: "Resolved,
That we cannot allow Dr. McIlvaine to leave us
without putting upon record our high appreciation
of his ability as a preacher and his endearing qualities as a man. To the friends who came with him to
the united church he has added the larger number of
those to whom he has ministered in his new field.
We appreciate the unselfish and self-sacrificing motive which has led him to insist that he shall be permitted to resign, and that Dr. van Dyke shall be
asked to stay. We wish him Godspeed, and shall
pray that he may be safely kept in his journeyings,
and prosper in any new field of labor which he may
select."

When this motion has been heartily and unanimously carried, this trying experience, which had yet
been the means of revealing in a new light the Christian strength of the church, was brought to a close.
A private letter written at the time, said, in describing the meeting, "It was characterized by unusual

* Mr. John E. Parsons and Dr. Albert R. Ledoux.

solemnity and impressiveness, and absolute unanimity as to every resolution offered and proposition made. . . . When the meeting was dismissed and the strain taken off, every face was wreathed in smiles and it looked like the departure of a Christmas party."

In the period between the union of the two churches and the end of the century a large part of the history of the Brick Church was being made in East Forty-second and West Thirty-fifth streets, in the two "affiliated" churches, as the Brick Church loves to call them. It was realized at the time that the experiment then being tried in both of them, of real independence within a real fellowship, was one that had an importance far more than local or temporary.

The new Church of the Covenant had, at its beginning, two adjustments to make, first to the new duties of independence, and second, to the new relation with the Brick Church. Of its success in the first of these something has been already said, * and it need only be added here that both pastor and people used to the full the new privilege of independence, courageously accepting its responsibilities, and that, at the same time, they never showed the slightest sign of forgetting the larger interests of Christ's kingdom which were vitally bound up with the continuance of the plan of affiliation.

The second adjustment, to the Brick Church as successor of the old Church of the Covenant, was made easy by the loyal and thoroughly Christian attitude of the Brick Church itself. When the union

* See above, p. 421,

THE PRESENT CHURCH OF THE COVENANT—FORMERLY
MEMORIAL CHAPEL

was made, "we were assured," said Mr. Webster, in
1900, "of the same interest and sympathy and support that had been given in the past. That pledge
has been fulfilled in the spirit of most fraternal love.
Six years ago we were strangers to most of the members of the Brick Church and to its pastor. Dr. van
Dyke has been, and is to-day, our loyal and loving
friend, and his devoted people have followed him in
this loyalty and friendship. The word 'affiliation,'
which he suggested to characterize our relations, has
love for its root idea. . . . Let us appreciate it more
and more and live up to its opportunities and responsibilities." To this summons his people heartily
responded.

The most interesting and important feature of the
present Church of the Covenant has always been its
strongly marked character as a family church. In
maintaining this characteristic it has made a permanent place for itself in the quarter of the city in which
it is situated, where another church without this distinctive quality might easily have become ineffective
or perhaps failed altogether.

In 1894, at the very time when the Covenant
Church was starting upon its independent career, the
great Protestant Episcopal parish of St. Bartholomew's erected its splendid parish house on East
Forty-second Street, less than a block from the Covenant's modest building. Many prophesied that in
five years' time the church would find its usefulness
gone, that the whole Christian work of the neighborhood would then have been absorbed by its
younger rival. But the Church of the Covenant refused to admit that rivalry had anything to do with

the situation. Coöperation suited them much better. St. Bartholomew's parish house should be welcomed as an ally, supplying in particular all manner of social helps that the people of the district needed, clubs, classes, gymnasium and the like, while the Church of the Covenant would continue to aid in ministering to the distinctly spiritual needs of the population, and with the more concentration of purpose because the other important work was provided for. The result of this enlightened and truly Christian attitude was, for one thing, a most happy relation of cordial fellowship and Christian coöperation between the two neighboring organizations and, for the Church of the Covenant in her individual work, the most cheering and unmistakable success.

Dr. McIlvaine, writing from his parish in Pittsburgh on March 5th, 1900, said to his former colleague, Mr. Webster: "I congratulate you on the completion of ten years of arduous, faithful, hopeful service; and I congratulate the Church of the Covenant on the progress which it has made during these ten years under your charge. From what was virtually a mission chapel, though the name was carefully and wisely avoided, it has passed into the larger duties and dignities of a fully organized church, inheriting the name and traditions, and in part, the affections of a most honored and beloved church. Of all the churches that I have served or may be permitted to serve, the former Church of the Covenant holds the dearest place in my heart and always will. It was so earnest, so united and harmonious, so loyal, so unselfish, so spiritually minded, and so kindly appreciative, that it was a pleasure and a joy to be its pastor. One of the things that I look back upon with the most satisfaction in my ministry was the securing of your services to your present charge."

The happy impression which this letter produces, is deepened by another letter written on the same occasion by Dr. van Dyke. An extract from it will serve to sum up the result of the work of the Church of the Covenant during this period. "My associations, from the beginning, with your church," Dr. van Dyke wrote, "were intimate and cordial. The atmosphere that greeted me, on my first visit to the church as one of the triumvirate of pastors bound together in the affiliation, was warm and friendly. I felt myself at once at home; it seemed to me a 'home church.' The spirit that prevailed there was the quiet, firm, fruitful love that animates the household of our divine Father. The loyalty of the people toward their church and to you, their pastor; the evident sincerity of their worship and their religious work; the temper of gladness and simplicity and order in which all things were done, gave me a deep sense of satisfaction and comfort in your company. All that I heard of your members; of their patient continuance in well-doing, and of their willing sacrifices for the cause of religon, gave me great confidence in them and made me feel sure they were Christians, not in name only, but also in deed and truth. . . . I am sure that the Church of the Covenant is doing good in New York City. It is making a centre of light in the midst of darkness, and the rays from it flow out into many a city home, and beyond that to distant parts of our land. Personal influence, after all, is the thing that counts most in building up the kingdom of Christ. I am sure that you realize this in the Church of the Covenant, and that you are living up to it." *

Christ Church, the affiliated church on the West Side, had six years' start of the church on East Forty-second Street, but it was more slow in "finding itself" than was the younger organization. For a number of years a spirit of disquiet made its appearance from time to time in the congregation and even threatened serious consequences. After the resignation of Dr. Lampe in December, 1895, † great difficulty was found in securing a new pastor and the Rev. Richard R. Wightman was not installed until April, 1897.

When this event had taken place, the session of the Brick Church felt a great sense of relief, and with much thankfulness they received the report that an era of prosperity and good feeling seemed to have set in, that many new members were being added

---

* This picture would be incomplete without a particular reference to one who, from 1882 to the present time has served the Church of the Covenant. "One of the most faithful, devoted and consecrated Christian workers in this or any city," said Mr. Webster, "and most invaluable to the development of the church life here, has been Miss Anna M. Juppe. In addition to the administering of the benevolent work of the parish, she has taught the primary department in the Sunday-school and had charge of an average of three organizations each week. Each summer she manages the fresh-air work, which has brought comfort to thousands of homes and more than 10,000 people in these ten years. . . . She is a tried and trusted assistant to the pastor, as well as a most useful bond between our church and the churches that have furnished her support these years. Her earnest, quiet work in the spirit of prayer and love has entered largely into the life and growth here." "A Decade of Work," p. 11.

† To accept a call to the chair of Old Testament Literature in Omaha Theological Seminary.

under the new pastor's ministry, that the attendance
at the Christ Church services was increasing, and
that, in general, the prospects of the church seemed
bright. It was determined that, if possible, the future
should be made secure. Following the wise plan
which the Church of the Covenant happily adopted
at the beginning, Christ Church now received into
its membership certain chosen members of the Brick
Church, who unselfishly transferred their allegiance
to the organization in which they felt their service
would most contribute to the cause of Christ. These
were Mr. Daniel J. Holden, who had been clerk of
the Brick Church session, Mr. William B. Isham,
Jr., who had been secretary of the board of deacons,
and Mr. Fulton McMahon. The two former were
elected at once to the office of elder and, with Mr. William H. Wilson, also elected at this time, added greatly
to the strength of the Christ Church session. From
that time on the voyage, though often requiring hard
work, of course, on the part of the crew, was, in the
main, smooth sailing.

The Sunday-school had suffered but little from the
church's perplexities. Mr. Holden, who had become
superintendent in 1877, held that office until 1894.
It was a devoted and most successful service, whose
termination was very reluctantly accepted by the
session of the Brick Church. Adding his years as
teacher to those of his superintendency, Mr. Holden
had served the Sunday-school for thirty years, and,
although he felt constrained to retire at this time
from his office in the school, his relation to the work
on West Thirty-fifth Street was very far from being
ended. As has been stated in the preceding para-

graph, he entered two years later, into closer relations with it than ever before. *

Mr. Holden was succeeded in the superintendency by Mr. Fulton McMahon, whose "diligent and faithful attention to the discharge of the duties of that office" was gratefully acknowledged, when he resigned in 1897. Mr. Herbert Parsons, who next held this office, carried forward with great success the work which had been inaugurated by his father.

Reference was made in an earlier chapter to the beginnings of social and industrial work in connection with the Thirty-fifth Street organization. The sewing-school had flourished through all these years and accomplished an incalculable amount of good; and from time to time, other enterprises of a similar nature had been carried on with more or less success. Special mention must be made of the Boys' Club, which "may trace its origin back as far as 1885, when, through the interested activity of Miss Kinnie †

* Mr. Holden's devotion to all the interests connected with the Brick Church is described in the following minute from the session records, passed in November, 1897. "The transfer of his membership to Christ Church by Mr. Daniel J. Holden makes suitable from the session something more than the more formal action which is required. Mr. Holden was brought up in the church: his identification with it has continued during his whole life: his father was a useful and honored member of the session before Mr. Holden's birth. From the time that Mr. Holden's age permitted he has, as teacher and subsequently as superintendent of the branch school, as member of the board of trustees, as an elder and as clerk of session, given to the work of the church an amount of service, the value of which is incalculable. It is because of his belief that he can be of better service by becoming a member of Christ Church, that Mr. Holden makes the sacrifice of breaking up his old associations, of leaving positions which were most congenial to him, and of going among the people who, largely through his instrumentality, have identified themselves with what, for so many years, was the Brick Church Mission." Mr. Holden died on June 21st, 1903.

† Miss Margaret E. Kinnie, who is still one of the faithful workers at Christ Church.

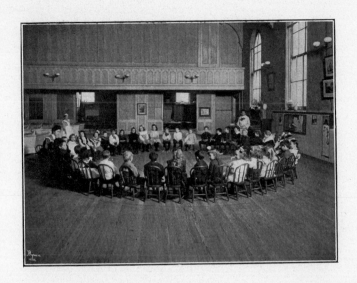

MURRAY KINDERGARTEN AND THE LINCOLN CADETS,
CHRIST CHURCH

a small company of boys was gathered for purposes of amusement and instruction on Thursday and Friday evenings. This group of boys was later organized into the Lincoln Cadets and became the nucleus about which the more extensive activities [of later years] have developed." * It happened that at this juncture, the Brick Church had for the first time called into service an assistant minister, to lighten somewhat the heavy burden which Dr. van Dyke was carrying alone. The Rev. James M. Farr, Jr., had entered upon his duties in January, 1897, and at once he began to interest himself in the work among the boys at Christ Church, a fact distinctly prophetic, as the future proved.

In the fall of 1897, at Mr. Farr's request, a few hundred dollars were secured from Brick Church people for the purpose of providing permanent headquarters for the Boys' Club, and although nothing better could at that time be accomplished than the renting and fitting up of rooms in the basement of No. 262 West Thirty-fifth Street, this may, nevertheless, be regarded as the definite beginning of the larger social and industrial work which grew up so speedily thereafter.

The next steps in the development may be given in Mr. Farr's words: "In the same winter of 1897, the Girls' Club, which had been organized the preceding winter by Miss E. W. Hatfield, secured rooms in the house 222 West Thirty-fifth Street. The following fall, in response to an appeal by Dr. van Dyke for better quarters for the Boys' and Girls' clubs, Mr. D. H. McAlpin presented and remodelled the

* "The Story of the Christ Church Work," pp. 26 f.

house 224 West Thirty-fifth Street, in memory of his son Randolph. The success which attended the opening of the Church House was immediate. Boys' Clubs, Girls' Clubs, McAlpin Society, Van Dyke Club, kitchen garden, cooking classes, were soon crowded to their utmost capacity." * It was evident already that this was but the beginning of a very much greater work, to which God had been leading the people of the Brick Church through many years.

It will have been apparent that the church at the centre, on the brow of Murray Hill, from which had come forth the money and the men necessary for accomplishing the work already described in this chapter, must have been in a most vigorous condition. It would, in truth, be hard to overstate the prosperity which she was enjoying under Dr. van Dyke's remarkable leadership. And best of all, it was not the prosperity of ease, but the prosperity of active and generous enterprise.

In the matter of sharing the wider benevolences of the Church at large, for example, the Brick Church was, in the year 1896–1897, the largest contributor in the denomination to the work of the boards, and a year later Dr. van Dyke was able to report that the total contributions of the church were twice as much as in the year preceding, being "the largest sum given for Christian work by any Presbyterian church in America, and probably in the world."

The attendance at the church services was another indication of success. "On many Sunday mornings,"

* "The Story of the Christ Church Work," pp. 27 f.

HENRY VAN DYKE

'it was reported in 1898, "it has been impossible to accommodate the congregations seeking admittance," and this in spite of the fact that one hundred new sittings had been added in the gallery for the special accommodation of the many young men who regularly attended. One important element in the attractiveness of the Brick Church for young men at this time was the Sunday morning Bible class conducted by Mr. Theron G. Strong, and another was the spirit of work which more and more was taking possession of the membership. The gospel of service was constantly heard from the Brick Church pulpit. "No able-bodied Christian man," said Dr. van Dyke, "has a right to be merely a passenger in the church."*

That Dr. van Dyke should ever go away to any other field was not allowed to be so much as mentioned, though more than once, when his health failed, as it did from time to time, or when his successes in literature proved that there was distinguished service awaiting him in that field also, the fear of his departure was in many hearts.

He could have no doubt that his people were devoted to him. Every opportunity was taken to express the affection with which he was regarded. The celebration of his fifteenth anniversary as pastor was made notable by the dedication of a new organ in the church as well as by a gift to himself. The announcement of his call to the chair of English Literature in Johns Hopkins, in January, 1899, was made the occasion of such strong expressions of the church's gratitude to him and dependence upon him, that he could not mistake their significance.

* Pastoral Letter in "Year Book for 1898–1899," p. 6.

But, although he was persuaded to decline the Johns Hopkins call, there were several different reasons, each in itself weighty, by which he was forced to regard his withdrawal from New York as most advisable, if not imperative, so that when later in 1899, he was called to the newly created Murray chair of English Literature in his own university, Princeton, he felt compelled to accept, and this time his determination was inexorable.

There was, however, one last service which he would render to his church before he said good-bye. He would remain at the helm until his successor had been found and was ready to begin his work. At length, in January, 1900, he could say, "The man whom you have chosen as your pastor has said that he is willing to come to you."

Dr. van Dyke had been pastor of the Brick Church for seventeen years, "the work of a third of a lifetime," as he himself said. He had rendered a remarkable service; he had endeared himself to all his people; he had left the impress of his thought and his faith, not only on the Brick Church, but on the great city in which it stood. "In the succession of pastors of the Brick Church"—with these words the congregation closed their affectionate address of farewell—"there have been noble names, men who were notable in doing the work of the church. To not one does it owe more than to Henry van Dyke." The truth was that the Brick Church of the closing nineteenth century, the church which then held an acknowledged place among the half-dozen leading churches of America, was almost wholly the product of his distinguished ministry.

PRESENT INTERIOR OF THE BRICK CHURCH

Showing choir gallery as enlarged in 1898

CHAPTER XXIV

A GOLDEN YEAR: 1900–1901

"That ye, being rooted and grounded in love, may be able to comprehend with all saints what is the breadth and length and depth and height; and to know the love of Christ, which passeth knowledge."—*Ephesians* 3 : 17–19.

"It seems something of a paradox, but nothing has made me feel so much at home in New York as going away. So many people have written me notes or spoken to me—telling me this or that, of some sermon or letter or little 'confab' that had meant something to them—that I have suddenly felt that I really belonged to you, and found my heart quickening at the thought of coming back home."
—MALTBIE DAVENPORT BABCOCK, "Letters from Egypt and Palestine," p. 1.

"I ACCEPT as from God and for God the call which you have sent me." When these words from the Rev. Dr. Maltbie Davenport Babcock were received in the middle of November, 1899, the people of the Brick Church, with their pastor, who had stood by the ship until a new helmsman should be found, knew that they were accepting a great sacrifice from the man who was coming to them. Yet because of their belief in the unparalleled importance of the work to which they called him, they had not hesitated to urge upon him his removal from the Brown Memorial Presbyterian Church in Baltimore to the Brick Church in New York; and he, on his part, when once the path of duty was clear to him, did not stop because it demanded sacrifice.

One of his intimate friends, to whom he went for counsel,* has shared with us the knowledge of what

* Dr. Charles Cuthbert Hall.

455

the step cost and how nobly it was taken. Dr. Babcock "told me," he says, "how the very roots of his life had taken hold of the Baltimore work and the Baltimore people, and I asked him if that was any reason why, at God's bidding, these roots should not be torn up, that he might come to a place that needed him more. I shall never forget how he took that thought; it seemed to appeal to the heroic elements in his great nature. . . . It was like a veritable tearing asunder of his heart, for him to leave that beloved life in Baltimore, yet so much more did he love Christ than any comfort or luxury of human friendship that he seemed to *rejoice* in his own sufferings, and to be glad that he could test by pain the reality of his devotion to the pure will of God." *

Dr. Babcock's early life had not been marked by unusual events. Born in Syracuse, N. Y., on August 3d, 1858, he "was reared in a home fragrant with Christian influence and in close touch with the life and work of the church. His mother was a woman of unusual strength and beauty of character, whom the son resembled in both face and spirit." †

In 1879 he graduated from Syracuse University, and three years later from Auburn Theological Seminary. Those who knew him during these days of preparation were fond of telling in later years of the place of leadership which was instinctively accorded him by his fellow-students. "He was then regarded," we are told, "as the most brilliant and versatile man of his class—one of those fortunate fellows who can do almost anything equally well, from playing on

* "Brick Church Year Book," 1901–1902, p. 146.
† "Year Book," 1901–1902, p. 149.

a flute to debating a difficult problem of statecraft or gracing a fashionable drawing-room." *

His first pastorate, of five years' duration, was in the First Presbyterian Church of Lockport, N. Y., from which, in 1887, he was called to succeed Dr. Frank W. Gunsaulus in the Brown Memorial Church of Baltimore. Long before the twelve years of his second pastorate were ended, it had been recognized that he was one of the strongest and noblest Christian personalities in the American ministry. Churches in many different cities would have been glad to draw him to them, and Baltimore rejoiced in the possession of him. "His work there," said one of his friends, † "was eminently blessed of God. He followed a line of brilliant preachers, but he equalled them in his hold upon this congregation and the entire community. He attracted to himself more than ordinary affection. He won all hearts by his enthusiasm, his noble manliness, his devotion to his work, his broad sympathies, his fine friendliness. His preaching was intensely earnest, filled with life and spiritual power, practical and modern, vivacious and varied in style, and full of Christ. He gathered around him a large company of men and women to whom he imparted his own warm spirit." ‡

When his departure from Baltimore was determined, the newspapers spoke of it as "a public calamity," and of him as "a man we cannot spare." Not in any formal sense, but literally, his going was felt as a universal personal loss. A street-car con-

* "Brown Memorial Monthly," May, 1900, p. 112.
† Dr. George T. Purves.
‡ "Brown Memorial Monthly," June, 1901, p. 181.

ductor had exclaimed to one of his parishioners when a previous call was pending: "*You* miss him! Why, *I'd* miss him. This whole city would miss him!" *

There could be no doubt that in 1899, when Dr. Babcock was called to the Brick Church, he had a remarkable career behind him; but it was characteristic of him that with this he was very little concerned. We are told that, when asked for an outline of his earlier life for publication in the Brick Church Year Book on the eve of his arrival, he replied, "Do let the sketch go. Let's face the future and see if we can make a little history." The words sound like him. Certainly it was to the future rather than the past that he was looking, as he entered upon his new work. Old victories and regrets for old joys now abandoned were alike left behind him, and he gave himself to his ministry in New York with an enthusiasm, and a fulness of joy in the very effort of it, that could not be mistaken.

His first day in the Brick Church was Sunday, January 14th, 1900. † According to custom it was the day when, in place of the usual sermon, the report of the year from the two affiliated churches was given by the Covenant and Christ Church pastors, preparatory to taking up the usual offering for that double work. Dr. Babcock, therefore, had but to introduce the subject and make the brief application at the close; he was dealing, moreover, with a complex work to which he was still almost a stranger; yet at once every one at the service that morning

* From the "Evangelist," quoted in "Year Book," 1899–1900, p. 12.
† He was not installed until February 27th.

MALTBIE D. BABCOCK

knew that there was a strong hand at the helm, and
that the Brick Church, whose prosperity in recent
years had seemed almost too good to last, might
hope to sail ahead on her course without so much as
slowing down.

Even the strangers who had come to the church
that day out of curiosity, or because deputed to
report the new preacher in the next day's newspapers,
were plainly made aware that they were in the presence of a power. It was not so much what he said
that impressed the congregation, as the man himself,
his personality, whose influence made an instantaneous impression. The "Tribune" thus described
him on Monday morning: "He is a tall, slender, and
well built man, with sharp features that are clean cut
and attractive. . . . He has a habit of throwing his
shoulders back that gives an air of manly frankness
to what he says. . . . Although of youthful appearance"—he was but forty-one years old—"he bore
himself with a natural dignity and confidence that
made him master of the situation at once." This is
manifestly the witness of one who was recording
a first impression, and it deals chiefly with externals,
but even through this crude medium, one is able to
feel the beginning of Dr. Babcock's deep impression
upon the New York public.

A week later the reporter was saying of the new
pastor's second Sunday-morning service in the Brick
Church, "Probably no person who heard the sermon
yesterday could have told afterward without looking
at his watch whether the sermon was long or short";
and his characterization of the preacher's method, if
not altogether adequate, was certainly suggestive:

"Dr. Babcock preached in little whirlwinds," he said. "He took up one thought after another, wound it up in a whirl of apt words, and sent it spinning at the congregation." A letter from a member of the Brick Church recording the impression made by this same sermon, said, "He is a rapid talker— no notes of any kind—full of anecdotes and illustrations, and changes rapidly from wit to seriousness."

It was evident at once, as these informal observations indicate, that Dr. Babcock would not lack for hearers, but it was soon evident, also, that his hold upon his audience was not due to any mere attractiveness of method nor even to the charm of his personality alone. There could be no doubt, as the weeks went by, that people came to hear him because his message satisfied the hunger of their hearts, because he gave them new strength and purpose, because he brought them into real touch with God. This was the final and universal testimony of those to whom he ministered: "Above all," they said, ". . . he was a preacher of the gospel, an ambassador of Christ. This was his only ambition and it satisfied him. . . . What a preacher he was! How his strength and his talents all combined to make him a great and commanding figure in the pulpit! His manner and method were peculiarly his own, but men who crowded * to hear *him* went away with new

---

* Not only at the Sunday-morning service, but in the afternoons as well the church was too small to hold the congregation. The Wednesday evening meetings taxed the capacity of the lecture-room to the utmost. The peculiar charm of the week-day meetings was their more informal and personal character. It was said that Dr. Babcock "believes in making the Wednesday evening prayer-meeting an occasion for exchange of confi-

conceptions of his Master, moved to higher standards of living." *

One is tempted to linger over the reports of those
sermons and services in the spring and fall of 1900;
they came from so many different sources, and are
so cheering in their evidence that the true message of
Jesus Christ will find out and satisfy all that is best
in our common human nature. At least a few fragments from the report of a stranger, who happened
in at a service one Sunday in February, may be
quoted, because they say of Dr. Babcock what every
one was feeling. "If it had not been for the unusual
forcefulness of his sermon," says this visitor, "I
think the dominant impression I should have carried
away would have been that of his remarkable power
in prayer. 'Reality' more than any other word char-
acterizes it." The truth of this judgment will be
confirmed by all who had opportunity to know the
facts; and hardly less significant is this other reference, to his manner of giving the announcements:
"There was an unusual number of notices that morning, but Dr. Babcock was more than equal to them,
injecting a touch of humor into a function which
often is tedious." Nor was it humor only that made
that weekly notice-giving a memorable part of the
Sunday services. There was a note of summons in
Dr. Babcock's way of asking for a gift of money or
for personal service, that stirred and compelled his
hearers like the Master's "Follow me." "The ser-

dences with his congregation." He then shared with his people many of
his pastoral experiences, so far as was possible without revealing the identity of the individuals concerned.
* "Year Book," 1901–1902, p. 140.

mon reached at last," continues the report of this February service, "Dr. Babcock sprang forward with the eagerness of a race horse"; and then follows an outline of what the writer describes as the most tender, logical, and powerful presentation of "the real gospel of Jesus" that he had ever heard.

But perhaps the best expression of the significance of Dr. Babcock's preaching was a single sentence spoken by a member of the Brick Church congregation: "To hear one of his sermons is to assume a great responsibility." *

Back of the preacher was the man. The message had true Christian power because it was spoken by a Christian. No one who knew him had any doubt of that. "His religious life was so real, so positive, so vital, so spiritual, that to be in his presence for only a few minutes was to receive a benediction as from the heavens. His intimacy with Jesus Christ was ever apparent. . . . He walked and talked with God." † And to this testimony of his friends it may be added that the blessing of his own life was imparted freely to others, because he walked and talked with his fellow-men with the same sincerity and simple-heartedness. "Genial and buoyant of temperament, always aglow with sunshine and scintillating with humor, optimistic, sympathetic, appreciative of others' work or efforts, and charitable toward the faults or weaknesses of those less gifted than himself; never patronizing or high-minded, never self-centred or self-conscious—it was an inspiration to be in his company, and one always left

* "Year Book," 1900–1901, p. 4.
† Tribute of "Chi Alpha," "Year Book," 1901–1902, p. 148.

it spiritually regaled and strengthened." * "He had," said one of his friends, "the sprightliness of a boy with the maturity of a man. He was full of humor and fond of healthy play, yet retained the spiritual temper of a servant of God. He had also an artist's soul. Music was a passion with him; song and poetry a delight. . . . His enthusiasm was contagious. . . . His genuineness of character, his sincerity and naturalness, made him peculiarly lovable to those who knew him." † He was, as was said of him at the General Assembly in Philadelphia a few days after the news of his death had been received, "a David for sweet song, a Paul for fiery zeal, an Apollos for eloquence, a Jonathan for friendship, and a John for heavenly spirit." ‡

If it were to be supposed that his preaching was the chief part of his work, a very imperfect conception would be formed of his ministry. The wonder was, when he found time to prepare his sermons, among the thronging duties that filled his days and the demands upon his personal sympathy which he always regarded as having precedence over everything else. How large that personal service was will never be known in this world, but the instances of it that have been told by all sorts and conditions of people, in his church and out of it, friends and strangers, old and young, people in need of almost every conceivable sort of help, of mind, body, and estate, can leave no doubt that his ministry to individuals would alone have provided more than enough work for any ordinary man.

* "Year Book," 1901–1902, p. 148.
† "Brown Memorial Monthly," June, 1901, p. 182.
‡ "Year Book," 1901–1902, p. 139.

A slip of paper, found after his death in an old parish directory of the Brick Church, from which he had apparently been copying, preserves for us, in the form of hasty memoranda, in his own hand-writing, the record of one day's occupations   No doubt it was a day more crowded than was usual, else he would not have thus recorded it, yet with the exception of a few items, it might have been duplicated by many another.   The following is a transcript of this fragment of autobiography:

> Orange—Bible.
> 6.50, Shower bath—exercise.
> 7.30, Quiet time.
> 7.45, Breakfast.
> 8.15, Prayer and music.
>   Call on church work.
> 8.45, Study—30 letters till
> 10.00, Study on sermons.
> 11.00, Funeral.
> 11.30, Photo sitting.
> 12.00, Study—sermon (sitting to artist).
> 1.00, Lunch—company.
> 2.00, Nap.
> 2.30, Six interviews.
> 3.15, Dictation, writing and study on three
>   different themes, shaping for
>   Sunday.
> 4.00, Dress for engagement [?].
> 4.15, Calls.
> 5.00, Wedding.
> 5.30–6.00, Calls.
> 6.00–6.40, Study, prayer-meeting.

6.45, ——* Dinner.
7.30, Study half-hour.
8.00, Prayer-meeting.
9.00, Session meeting.

It has often been regretted that Dr. Babcock never wrote a book, but it is not strange that in a life as full as his, and as exhausting to both mind and spirit, there was no room for that kind of undertaking. "Do not talk to me about such a thing as publication," he is reported to have said to one who urged him to prepare a volume of sermons for the press, "I have no hankering for going down to posterity in half calf. But if I ever do [write a book], it must be some time when I have broken a leg."

The year of Dr. Babcock's ministry in the Brick Church was momentous rather than eventful, yet even in that short time important results had begun to appear. He had in particular seized from the beginning upon the work which had developed in the Christ Church House, as a great opportunity which the Brick Church had only begun to improve. His pastorate was but three months old when he had secured the appointment of a special committee to consider the general subject of the enlargement of the work on the West Side. The Church House, though only a year old when he came, had already proved inadequate to meet the demands of the work, and Dr. Babcock soon determined in his own mind that the first definite task of his ministry along the line of material progress should be the securing of new and larger quarters.

* Here is given the name of his host or guest.

Dr. Babcock's personal participation in the life of the two affiliated churches was one of the wonders of his ministry. He gave to them not only his interest, his counsel, his direction, but personal service. He was known as a friend by the people in the congregation and by the children in the Sunday-school. Large as his own parish was, he found time and strength to carry his welcome ministry into many of the homes of the two other parishes, whenever there was special need of such help as he could give. The Church of the Covenant was glad to remember afterward that some of her young men, who became good servants of the Lord Jesus, were moved to the definite consecration of their lives by Dr. Babcock's personal influence. *

The hopefulness of the Christ Church work was greatly increased when in January, 1901, Mr. Farr, until then assistant minister of the Brick Church, accepted the Christ Church pastorate. † He had himself been one of the prime movers, as we have seen, in the development of the newer activities connected with that church, while his relation to the Brick Church was peculiarly close, and the confidence of the Brick Church officers and people was given to him without reserve. His going, it is true, left Dr. Babcock alone, but Dr. Babcock was one of those who most strongly urged him to take up the larger work, when it appeared that the people of Christ Church had set their hearts upon calling him. With his installation began a new era of prosperity for the whole work on West Thirty-fifth Street, and the question of providing the new buildings seemed to be de-

---

* "Year Book," 1901–1902, p. 152.

† Mr. Wightman had resigned in the preceding November.

JAMES M. FARR

ferred only until Dr. Babcock should feel that the first necessary foundations of his own ministry were laid.

The other most important beginning made during this year in the work of the church concerned particularly the men of the congregation. In November, 1900, "it was decided that the Pastor's Aid Society, which had done such good work for so many years, should be replaced by an entirely new association with similar aims but with broader scope. It was voted that this newly formed society should be called 'The Men's Association of the Brick Church,' and a regular organization was effected." In itself this statement does not seem very significant, but behind it were two facts which indicated that something far more than a new "organization" had been created. First, a man of peculiar ability for this particular work had been found to take the leadership, Mr. Henry L. Smith, who still holds the office of president, and with it the esteem and affection of the many men who have shared in the work of the Men's Association since the time of its origin. And second, Dr. Babcock gave, without stint, his help to make the enterprise a power in the church. He was always the moving spirit of its meetings. To meet him there personally was enough incentive to bring a roomful of men together, and besides that, he always had something unusual, inspiring, characteristic, to say, or to propose in the way of practical Christian work. At these meetings men were made to feel that genuine Christianity ought to be a force in the world, and that they themselves might help to make it so. *

* Dr. Babcock, in the first of the series of letters to be mentioned presently, said of the Men's Association. "I have deeper roots there than you

With such auspicious beginnings as these that have been described, and with an amount of blessing and strength imparted to individual lives which it would be impossible to calculate, the first year of Dr. Babcock's ministry drew to its close—the first year which was also to be the last. We have the record of his own gratitude and hope, as he stood at the end of it, in the pastoral letter, published according to custom in the Year Book, and called by him "A personal message from the pastor." It bore the date January 1st, 1901.

"I cannot realize," he says, "that it has been only a year since I began to work with you, so many changes have come—changes so deep and prophetic —so many new vistas opened, so many friendships begun. It seems in the review like a happy little lifetime. The year's experiences are not among the things behind to be forgotten, but to be held in loving remembrance, to stir us and spur us to reach forth to things that are before, the better things, please God, yet to be. Attainments are for new attempts, and every goal should be a point of departure. Every blessing is a call of God, and every gift, an appeal. New light is to inspire new loyalty, and mountain peaks to give wider horizons. 'A man's reach should exceed his grasp, or what's Heaven for?'

"Oh, let his goodness lead us to repentance! Let a grateful review mean a loving rededication! If the mercies of God have blessedly beset us, let us not

think—for no organization in the church has meant so much to me in the way of friendship, nor made me so hopefully aware of power—patent and latent." "Letters from Egypt and Palestine," p. 2.

build 'Three tabernacles,' and abide, but rather like Paul, thank God at 'Three Taverns,' and take courage, pushing on to fight a better fight, and keep the faith more loyally.

"Thoughts of the New Century may stir us, but such thoughts have short roots. Let us look over the shoulder of Time to the face of the Eternal, past the years to him who is 'the same, yesterday, to-day, and forever,' and for his sake let us make this the best of all our years."

It was already known at this time that a month and a half later Dr. Babcock was going away for the purpose of making a pilgrimage to the Holy Land with a party of old friends connected, like himself, with Auburn Seminary. The plan had been formed before he was called from Baltimore, and it had been arranged that his coming to New York should not interfere with it. Perhaps even then he realized, in some measure, how great the need of rest would be after a year in his new work; and certainly the wisest of his friends, as the time drew near, were glad for his sake that he was going.

On February 24th, 1901, he set sail, and the very next day came back a letter from him, by the pilot, addressed to the Men's Association. It was in fulfilment of a promise which he had made, to send a letter now and then to be read at the meetings, and which he, with characteristic generosity, fulfilled by sending, not "brief, kindly letters of remembrance, as was expected," but a record of his entire journey. Nor did the men of the church receive the only tokens of his remembrance. From Palestine he sent cards of pressed flowers of the Holy Land to the three

Sunday-schools, fourteen hundred of them, one for each scholar and teacher in the schools.

News arrived in due course of the prosperous and delightful sojourn in Egypt and in Palestine, including many an allusion in the letters of Dr. Babcock's companions to the joy of travelling with him, of sharing his love of life and his love of men and his love of God. From Constantinople he himself wrote speaking of his expected return in good health before the end of May. Then, on May 15th came a cable message from Naples telling of his illness there. He had been attacked by gastric fever, that strange, insidious disease, whose effects are sometimes as incalculable as they are disastrous. Three days later came the tragic news of his death.

To the Brick Church the shock of grief and loss was indescribable. But it seemed as though the whole city, almost the whole land, shared the sorrow. Many, like the people of the Brown Memorial Church of Baltimore, had stood as close to him as the Brick Church people had, and thousands who had never stood close to him in any formal relation, but who had found in him comfort or courage, the help of a friend and of a messenger from God, were affected by a truly personal grief. It did not seem possible that he who had given life to so many could be dead.

And he was not. Even in the Brick Church, which seemed bereft indeed without his visible presence, he was a continuing power. It was soon evident that for those whom he had awakened to a new life with God and a new life for men, his going was like a challenge. What they had hoped to do with his help, they must now do alone, that was all.

CLASSES IN BASKET-WEAVING AND CARPENTRY, CHRIST
CHURCH HOUSE

Even the definite undertakings that he had planned or dreamed were not to fall to the ground. In the memorial service, by which at once his people of the Brick Church sought to honor his memory, it was grateful to them to speak of him, to tell and to hear what he had done for many different lives, to read the last of those letters which he had faithfully written from the lands of his travels. But the part of that service which was felt to be really worthy of it was the announcement that some one—no name was given, and none has been given to this day—had contributed $50,000 toward that extension of the Christ Church work which Dr. Babcock had been planning to undertake on his return. *

From January 14th, 1900, till February 24th, 1901, was the length of Dr. Babcock's active ministry in the Brick Church. It hardly seemed possible that a man could have made himself so deeply loved or done so much good in his Master's name in that brief time. The officers of his church, coming together to express as best they could their sense of what he had been to them, were moved by the strangeness of this thought, and by the pity of it, but most of all by the glory of it.

"The active pastorate of Dr. Babcock," they said, "lasted but little over a year. He came to us under circumstances strikingly indicative of the guidance of the good hand of God. He was the unanimous choice of officers and people. There was no second choice, nor was there an instant's hesitation as to his being the man we needed. The Presbytery of New

* The funeral was held in the Brick Church on June 12th. A memorial tablet was erected in January, 1903.

York, too, was so convinced that Dr. Babcock's great heart and devoted service were needed in this city, that they adopted the unusual course of appointing a committee to urge upon him the acceptance of our call. Even then his coming would have been wellnigh impossible, but for the influence of the divine Spirit strengthening him to sever heart-ties stronger than bands of steel; convincing him that sacred duty beckoned him away from all the associations of an ideal home and devoted people and a great work well maintained, to come among strangers; to enter a harder field; to assume heavier responsibilities. . . .

"He came to us—*a man!* 'Greatheart,' in every sense! Tall, strong, full of life, with an eloquence all his own; with that subtle influence we call 'personal magnetism,' for want of a better name. He came trusting us, and holding nothing of himself in reserve—accepting us with all the trust and simplicity of a child. Although he went in and out among us for the brief space of a single year, he has left an indelible mark upon the church, the Presbytery, and the city. His arduous duties were performed with supreme devotion, and, withal, so systematically that it was well said of him he would have been successful as the head of the greatest business organization.

"But it is not our crowded services nor the magnificent successes, with even greater audiences, at the Ecumenical Conference, or People's Institute, that most clearly marked him as a man of God in the highest sense of the term. These count for much, and many have been the souls won for the Master

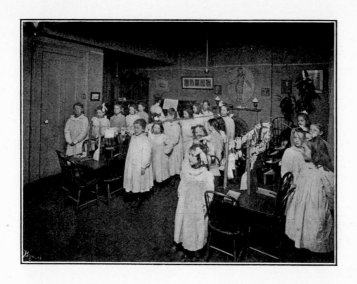

CLASSES IN KITCHEN GARDEN AND COOKING, CHRIST
CHURCH HOUSE

without more personal contact than the divine influence emanating from his pulpit presence; but his
greatest work has been upon individual lives, to whom
he has ministered in season and out of season, by
day and by night, imparting to the feeblest something of his own vitality and faith, demonstrating by
his very look his love of God and assured trust in
him. . . .

"The sense of our loss is too recent, the shock of
the blow too great for measured words. We can
only bow before the insoluble mystery of his death
at forty-two, in the midst of so great a work and the
greater need for such a man as he. But we can at
least turn away in humility from a contemplation of
the Providence which has bereft us, and with one
accord unite in thanks to God that this church was
permitted to have such leadership and we such a
friendship through all too short a year."

CHAPTER XXV

THE CHURCH OF THE PRESENT: 1902–1908

"And there it is unto this day."—1 *Chronicles* 5 : 9.

"A church including just the elements that have been united in this congregation, and standing on the crest of the hill here in the centre of this great city—in the whole western hemisphere where could you find a better site for God's house? . . . There may be sermons in bricks as well as 'sermons in stones,' and our prayer is that the sermon preached here, by our lives, and by every material particle of this structure, may be always the true evangel, so that, of the endless procession moving past our doors, many, when they look upon this house of prayer, may get some clearer sense of the divine goodness and some stronger impulse toward holiness and service."—WILLIAM R. RICHARDS, Pastoral Letter, December, 1902.

D R. VAN DYKE, like a true friend, came back to the church in her time of need. His old parishioners, feeling that for a time it was impossible to think about a new pastor, gratefully accepted his offer, in December, 1901, to serve them as minister-in-charge until such time as they should secure a successor to Dr. Babcock, and to aid them in that undertaking by his counsel and influence. *

Under his guidance, strengthened by his familiar presence, by his example of loyalty to the church, by the inspiration of his preaching, strong as of old, and by the evidence, soon supplied, that the church was in no danger of falling to pieces, the first feeling

* Dr. van Dyke's duties at Princeton made it impossible for him to preach at the second service on Sunday or at the mid-week meetings, or to perform the routine duties of a pastor. He was therefore authorized to employ an assistant. The Rev. Shepherd Knapp served him in that capacity, and continued under the new pastor until 1908.

474

of depression and discouragement was gradually dispersed. * The finding of a new pastor was taken up in earnest, and before long the church came to the assurance that it had found him.

But would he come? It was a repetition of the situation in regard to Dr. Babcock in Baltimore. The Rev. William Rogers Richards, D.D., had been for eighteen years pastor of the Crescent Avenue Presbyterian Church in Plainfield, New Jersey, and rarely have the members of a congregation had such a deep and universal attachment for their pastor as that which bound the Plainfield people to Dr. Richards. They loved him as a man. His preaching satisfied them like bread. He was a true part of their whole life, civic and social as well as philanthropic and religious. † Only in answer to a call of supreme importance would they hear for a moment of his leaving them, and his refusal again and again to consider calls to churches in New York and elsewhere had given his people ground for hope that the im-

* It was during his term of service as minister-in-charge that Dr. van Dyke was elected Moderator of the General Assembly, held in New York in the spring of 1902, and in that capacity contributed largely to the successful revision of the Westminster Confession which was carried at that time.

† In the "Brick Church Year Book" for 1902–1903, was quoted the following estimate of the character of Dr. Richards and his work in Plainfield, by one who had known him for many years: " I consider his chief characteristics to be great intellectual power, stimulated by wide reading and study, and the ability to think clearly and closely, and to express himself in striking and appropriate English. Dr. Richards is by nature modest and retiring, but when intimately known he is found to be warm-hearted, sympathetic, and generous to a fault. He is not only a minister of the gospel, but a good citizen, interested in all questions of a public nature. It was his custom at Plainfield always to attend and take an active part in the primaries of his party. He was for some years a member of the Board of Education of Plainfield, rendering good service, and is now a member of the Board of Foreign Missions of the Presbyterian Church."

perative summons, which both he and they must answer, would not come.

In May, 1902, came the call from the Brick Church, and with it the following personal letter from Dr. van Dyke to Dr. Richards, which was, however, as will be evident, addressed as much to the people as to their minister. "The meeting last night," Dr. van Dyke said, "was large, enthusiastic, and absolutely unanimous in calling you to the Brick Church. There is no doubt in any mind that you are the man for the place, and no hesitation in any heart about asking you to come. We know the value of your present work, the mutual attachment between you and the Plainfield Church, the many ties of love that hold you where you are. The tie by which we would draw you to New York is the tie of duty—clear and strong. The cause of Christ needs you here. The strongest Presbyterian church in America, standing in the great city where its influence is most needed, asks you to come to it and lead it forward. The call is affectionately and respectfully addressed to the Crescent Avenue Presbyterian Church as well as to you. We do not imagine that your people can think of giving you up without great sorrow, but we want you, if it can be so brought about by the Spirit of Wisdom and Love. . . . Our prayer is that the Holy Ghost may guide you in the decision of this matter and my hope is that the appeal of duty may lead you to us."

On the very Sunday when this letter was laid before the Plainfield congregation, Dr. Richards preached a sermon upon Moses' two calls to Hobab. "You see," said he, "Moses first urges Hobab to come with

Israel for Hobab's own sake: 'Come thou with us and we will do thee good'; to which Hobab answers, 'No.' And then Moses urges him to go for Israel's sake: 'Come to us,' he says, 'we need you,' . . . and it appears that he accepted this second invitation." The sermon as it went on, was applied to the call of men into Christian discipleship, but its bearing upon the special problem in practical Christianity, which pastor and people were then together facing, was evident.* On neither side was it at that time determined what the answer to the call of the Brick Church ought to be, but the principle by which the decision was to be reached was here clearly set forth, and it was adopted without hesitation by both Dr. Richards and his parishioners. The call was accepted.

On October 26th, 1902, Dr. Richards was installed. Dr. van Dyke, whose service of the Brick Church might now be said to have been extended to nearly twenty years, handed to the new pastor the keys of the church, and the people thanked God for his mercies in bringing them across the troubled sea of the last year to this desired haven.

In certain interesting particulars, Dr. Richards' preparation had resembled that of two of his predecessors. Like Dr. Spring he was of strong New England ancestry, and was born in Massachusetts.† Like him he had been educated at Yale and Andover, and had then studied for the law. He resembled

---

* The sermon and Dr. van Dyke's letter were both printed in the "Brooklyn Eagle."

† In 1853 in Boston, where his father was pastor of the Central Congregational Church.

him, moreover, in his irenic spirit combined with a strong sense of the historic continuity of the Christian faith. At the same time he was known to be in cordial sympathy with the modern movements of thought. It was evident that he was one who would make for peace and the generous coöperation of different types of men, and therefore for the steady and solid progress which these conditions render possible.* Like Dr. van Dyke, on the other hand, his first pastorate had been in a Congregational church;† and, like him, he had become one of the most popular preachers in the various college pulpits of the Eastern States. The undergraduates looked forward to his coming because he understood them—shared their enthusiasm for athletics, for one thing—and because his sermons were interesting, and perhaps most of all, for the reason that he invariably used his power and his opportunity to speak to them of the things that are most worth while. He was able, not only to hold the attention of college boys, but to exert a real moral and religious influence upon them. To the people of the Brick Church there was a pleasant familiarity in such qualities as these.

But not many Sundays had passed before the congregation made an interesting discovery, by which Dr. Richards' unlikeness to what had gone before began to seem as important as his likeness to it. They discovered that there are at least three ways of preaching great sermons. They had known before

* These qualities were to prove especially valuable in his most arduous and important service as moderator of the New York Presbytery at a critical period of its history.

† In Bath, Maine, where he was minister from October, 1879, to June, 1884.

WILLIAM R. RICHARDS

that there were two ways. They were familiar with
what they would have called "Dr. van Dyke's way"
and "Dr. Babcock's way," and consciously or unconsciously, they had been wondering which of these
two ways Dr. Richards would follow. But he followed neither. He had a way of his own. He had
a singular skill—all the more singular for its quiet
simplicity—in drawing a truth out of the old, familiar words of Scripture, into the light of present
reality, and then unfolding it slowly to the mind of
his hearers as the heat of the sun slowly unfolds a
flower.

The first effect was an absorbing intellectual interest; but before the hearer was well aware, he found
that through the opened door of his mind the truth
had entered in and laid hold upon his will. He had
reached out to grasp it as a truth and found himself
gripped by it as a duty. The applications of the
sermon's principle to the concerns of daily life and to
the vital problems of the time were so varied, so apt,
so unescapable, and withal so simple and direct, and
of such practical significance, that the message of
Sunday became at once the guide of week-day living.
It was found that Dr. Richards, by his quiet, orderly,
and concrete method of exposition, had the rare
power to show that the most spiritual truth is at the
same time the most practical; and this power perhaps was in no way more strikingly evidenced than
by the fact that, though he was recognized as a distinctly intellectual preacher, yet more than once it
happened, as it had in the case of Dr. Babcock, that
families were drawn into permanent relation to the
church because the young people of the household

had expressed unusual interest in Dr. Richards'
sermons. *

In the organization of the church's activities, the
coming of the new pastor was speedily followed by
several interesting and significant developments. It
was felt that conditions then existing in the church
itself would warrant, and the needs of the neighborhood demanded, a larger use of the church as a place
of worship, that therefore its doors should no longer
be closed for the greater part of the time, simply
because no service happened to be in progress, and,
moreover, that the number of the services themselves
should be increased.

The ideal of an ever-open door, Dr. Richards
urged, is one that "any Christian church may well
try to realize—especially a church like this, that is
set on a hill and beside a main thoroughfare of the
city." When these words were written in December,
1903, the plan which it proposed was already in operation. There had also been inaugurated two new
services, and Dr. Richards' comments upon these
ought also to be quoted. "Repeated requests," he
said, "had reached us for the appointment of a service on some week-day afternoon, and the quiet congregations that have assembled for some weeks past
every Friday at twilight give evidence that such a
service meets a spiritual need of the community.

"On the Lord's day especially," Dr. Richards
continued, "we should wish that our room might be
filled as often as possible with successive congregations of different worshippers, thus ministering to

---

* In the report to Presbytery on April 1st, 1906, the membership of
the church for the first time exceeded 1,000.

two or three times as many persons as the walls would hold at a single service. Accordingly, in addition to our usual services of the morning and afternoon, we recently announced another for the evening. Some of our friends, in view of the well-known difficulty of gathering a second Sunday congregation, treated the proposal of a third as somewhat audacious. That was the intention. But we think that the policy of advancing upon the enemy in the hallowing of the Lord's Day, however audacious, may be pleasanter, and in the long run safer, than any policy of continuous retreat." *

One purpose in this freer use of the church had been to reach, not only more people, but more sorts of people. This was, indeed, an ideal that was making its presence increasingly felt in the church, both within the bounds of its own particular work and in its sharing of the labors of the affiliated churches. The open church and the new services were but samples of a more general effort to make the ideal a reality, and it is pleasant to know that some measure of success could soon be recorded. Speaking in April, 1904, Dr. Richards said: "We have been much cheered to learn from a good many friendly testimonies that these efforts are bearing some fruit; that many sorts of tired men and women passing our door, even when no service was going on, seeing the door hospitably open, have ventured in, and have found great comfort in this place of rest and prayer; that at our public services, and especially on Sunday evenings, a good many persons who had long been far from any sort of church connection, happening

* "Year Book," 1903–1904, pp. 5 f.

in here, have felt themselves at home—have felt that
they were made one with the people of God. Oh,
I wish this house might be a house of prayer for all—
all nations, all conditions, all opinions; a true sanctuary of the peace of God; where, if ever, a Greek
Christian and a Roman Christian happened to find
themselves in the same pew, forgetting their age-long
quarrel, they would remember only that they are fel-
low-disciples; where a Jew and a Samaritan might
comfortably look over the same hymn book; or a
Russian and a Japanese; or a bank director and the
president of a labor union; or a college professor
and a socialist; or a shop girl and her customer; or
a master and his servant; or any two neighbors who
for the last dozen years had passed without speaking
on the street—here in this sanctuary all their old
differences and grievances and misunderstandings
forgotten—so completely forgotten that they could
not recall them when they went out."

The helpfulness of these new services, and no less
of those that were not new, was greatly increased by
the character of the music that the church was rejoicing in at this time. It was, in a way, a legacy
from Dr. Babcock, for he had proposed the calling
of Mr. Archer Gibson, then in Baltimore, to the office
of organist and choir-master; but he had already departed on his journey to Palestine when Mr. Gibson
began his work in the Brick Church. Such music as
the new organist produced from his choir of soloists
and chorus had never been heard in the Brick
Church before, music notable for its spirit of worship even more than for its beauty of sound. The
Brick Church organ, remarkable for its quality of

CHOIR REHEARSAL AT THE CHURCH OF THE COVENANT

sweetness and its mellowness of tone, * had never been played as Mr. Gibson played it. No better time could have been chosen for a multiplication of the Brick Church services, or for the exerting through them of a wider Christian influence upon the New York public, than the time when the church could offer this noble ministry of music.

The activities of this period which thus far have been referred to, concerned chiefly the men and women; but the church was far from forgetting the boys and girls. On the contrary, taking the church's work as a whole, the part of it which related to the children was distinctly predominant.

In the first place, the church's own Sunday-school made a distinct advance, under the leadership first of Mr. Alfred E. Marling and then of Dr. William V. V. Hayes. That it should be a large school is not possible, because it is situated in a neighborhood where the number of children is decidedly limited; but by patient and devoted work it has at least been made to cover successfully the restricted field, while in its method of teaching and in its plan of study it has been distinctly improved.

The affiliated Church of the Covenant offers a very much larger field for work among the children, and it has been cultivated with a success proportionately great. The ingenuity of Dr. † Webster and of his helpers, especially Mr. Cady and Dr. Kimball of the Sunday-school, in arousing and holding the children's interest, and the response of the children

---

* It was greatly improved in detail by Mr. Gibson himself.

† He received the degree of Doctor of Divinity from Hamilton College in June, 1902.

both in numbers and in character-development, have together produced as pleasant a chapter of church history as could anywhere be found. There is no danger that the Church of the Covenant will ever die out at the bottom; and the sight of the pews full of children at a Covenant Sunday-morning service, or the sound of their singing, especially at the wonderful festivals at Christmas and at Easter, are not only a promise for the future, when these children shall have grown up and taken their place in the active work of the church; they are also an inspiration for to-day. The men and women in the Church of the Covenant get their sermons from two sources, from the lips of their beloved pastor and from the faces of their own children, who under the church's influence are already unconscious carriers of the sweet gospel of Jesus Christ.

In Christ Church, also, these recent years may be called the age of the children, * the age of clubs for girls and clubs for boys, of sewing-school and kindergarten, of winter sports and summer outings, to say nothing of the great Sunday-school, which in 1907, celebrated its fiftieth anniversary. †

* Among those who have contributed to the enlargement and increased efficiency of this part of the work, one volunteer worker, whose name has not yet been mentioned in this history, must here be gratefully recorded. No one has been a truer friend to the Christ Church children (or to their mothers, either, for that matter) than this resourceful, untiring, modest worker, Miss Mary Stewart.

† Mr. Herbert Parsons, who had become superintendent in 1897, and who held that office till 1905, when his public duties required his presence in Washington during the greater part of the year, brought the school to a very high degree of efficiency. The system of regular examinations which he perfected, introduced a new standard of excellence in Bible study. He was succeeded by Mr. William S. Coffin, under whom the school still advances, meeting with enthusiasm and success the enlarging

CHILDREN'S ROOM AND KITCHEN, CHRIST CHURCH
MEMORIAL HOUSE

Mention has already been made of the movement, begun in the year of Dr. Babcock's ministry, and set a long way forward by the memorial gift of $50,000 at the time of his death, to provide new buildings for all this work which had grown up in connection with Christ Church. To this movement Dr. Richards gave his hearty support. The attainment of the goal toward which it moved 'was to be the chief event of the early years of his pastorate.

At his suggestion, a number of informal conferences were held in the winter of 1902–1903, and the whole subject thoroughly discussed. It so happened that real-estate conditions in the neighborhood of West Thirty-fifth Street had resulted in a large increase in the value of the Christ Church property. In view of the opportunity thus opened, it was deemed advisable to sell, and with the proceeds buy a site more central to the Christ Church congregation, that is, at a point slightly further north and west, where the lower prices would also make it possible to secure a lot of larger size.

At a meeting held at the parsonage on April 23d, so favorable a sentiment was aroused that almost $25,000 was contributed on the spot, and before the season ended, including the original memorial gift, over $100,000 was in hand. With this sum the trustees were enabled to purchase an excellent lot, with a frontage of one hundred and twenty-five feet,

opportunity. The large intermediate department maintains its old record of success under that staunch supporter of the Brick Church, universally beloved, Mr. William D. Barbour, assisted by his brother, Mr. Norman Barbour, among others. Miss Ziesse and Miss Stewart, with admirable skill and patience, take care of the swarms of smallest children, almost babies, in the primary.

on West Thirty-sixth Street between Eighth and Ninth avenues.

In November, 1903, the general scheme for the new buildings was adopted. * Ground was broken in the middle of the following June, and on October 26th, the second anniversary of Dr. Richards' installation, the corner-stone was laid. "The weather was favorable, and a large audience of ticket-holders was admitted to the first floor of the building which had been boarded over for the occasion. A large space at the west end of the building was reserved for the children of Christ Church Sunday-school, who marched in procession six or seven hundred strong from the old building to the new. Not the least interesting part of the audience, however, was composed of those who, having no admission tickets, crowded the windows and even the roofs of the tall tenements on every hand. Every point of vantage was occupied; the workmen sat upon the beams rising for the second story of the parish house in the rear, and the side windows of the adjoining tenements, usually so cheerless of outlook, were upon this occasion much sought for the sake of the view." †
It was an appropriate and auspicious inauguration for a work whose purpose was to bring interest and cheer and every sort of uplift to the whole neighborhood.

Meantime more money for the undertaking was coming in—$30,000, for example, at a single meeting of the men of the church.

In the fall of 1905 the buildings were completed,

---

* The architects being Messrs. Parish & Schroeder.
† "Year Book," 1904–1905, pp. 167f.

CHRIST CHURCH MEMORIAL BUILDINGS

and on October 27th they were formally opened and two days later the church was dedicated. The entire group of buildings was designed to be memorial in its character. The church commemorated "the loving and faithful service of Henry van Dyke." It is a Gothic structure, presenting its side to the street, and forms architecturally the dominant feature of the group of buildings. Within, it is dignified and churchly—all the details being in excellent taste. No church of its size in the city is more attractive.

The church house both perpetuated the gift of its predecessor in memory of Randolph McAlpin and also became a memorial to Dr. Babcock. It was necessarily much larger than the church, but the greater part of it was skilfully placed in the rear of the lot, where the high church roof completely concealed it from the street. It contained everything that Christ Church workers had been longing for and dreaming of for many a year. First of all, of course, there was a great Sunday-school room, where the work, out of which the whole organization had grown, might be continued on a still larger scale. Above, below, and around this central auditorium were placed bowling alleys, pool-room, library, gymnasium, workshop, kitchen, offices, rooms for church work, for kindergarten and for clubs and classes of various sorts, together with living quarters for the janitor and the workers. *

* It may be noted at this point that while this larger enterprise was in hand, the Brick Church had also made some minor improvements in her own building. In the fall of 1903, by a shifting of the stairs and the addition of a mezzanine in the "chapel" in the rear of the church, four new rooms and a large amount of closet-room were added, and the whole arrangement greatly improved. The lecture-room also was redecorated.

Every room in the building meant the meeting of a definite need whose reality had been amply tested by experience in the old quarters. There was nothing theoretical about it from cellar to roof; and no sooner had the transfer been made from the old building to the new, than the enormous benefits of the change began to manifest themselves. * The work commenced to expand at once; the neighborhood responded fully to the opportunity; and during the two and a half years that have passed since the building was opened for use, old enterprises have enlarged their scope and new activities † have sprung up, until every room is occupied for one purpose or another almost the whole week through. There is no busier, cheerier, more inspiring place in the whole city.

And it was entirely paid for in a remarkably short space of time. By the sale of the old site and the continuance of contributions, the whole sum expended had been received, and the last dollar paid, in the early summer of 1907. The total cost of land, buildings, and equipment was $382,097.24.‡

A single event remains to be added to this brief sketch of the activities of the present pastorate. On

---

* With the occupation of the new building a more complete unification of the work at Christ Church, than had heretofore been possible, was achieved, with great gain in economy and efficiency. See "Rules of Government," Appendix Y, page 548.

† Most interesting, perhaps, among the new activities, has been the "Tuberculosis Class," organized in November, 1906, for the purpose of giving to a small group of sufferers the same sort of treatment in their homes that they would receive in special sanitariums. The work has been carried on by the devoted volunteer service of Dr. Walter L. Niles and Miss F. V. Stewart, and its results have already proved the great practical value of the plan.

‡ Of this amount $253,397.24 was met by subscription.

INTERIOR OF THE PRESENT CHRIST CHURCH

January 22d, 1908, the Brick Church lost by death
one of her strongest friends, one of her truest Christians, Mr. Morris K. Jesup. Among the almost incredible number of public interests in which he had
actively shared, and to which he had given generously
in money and personal service, the Brick Church
held a prominent place. He had served on her board
of trustees, and in much of her good work in recent
years he had taken a leading part. When his will
was read, it was found that he had bequeathed to the
Brick Church the sum of $100,000, as an addition to
its endowment fund, with the provision, however,
that if the church should at any time remove from
its present location, the money should revert to his
estate. In his lifetime he had strongly counselled the
turning of a deaf ear to all offers for the Fifth Avenue
property. He believed that the church was needed
where it was, and that it should be anchored there
forever. Even if in the future the residences should
all be driven northward and the Brick Church
stand, as old Trinity does to-day, in a region given
over wholly to business, there she ought still to stand,
he thought; and in this his fellow-officers of the
church heartily agreed with him. One of them said,
on hearing of Mr. Jesup's generous bequest—and
he probably expressed the thought of the whole congregation—"The condition of the gift is as welcome
as the gift itself." If God will, may the Brick
Church stand to serve him on the brow of Murray Hill
as long as New York City occupies Manhattan Island.

Seventeen hundred and sixty-seven to nineteen
hundred and eight—one hundred and forty-one

years: it is, after all, but a short space of time, and what changes have been packed into it! At the beginning we saw the New Church erected on Beekman Street, on the northern edge of the city that then existed. To-day the present Brick Church, more than three miles farther north, is already grappling with the problems of a downtown situation.

These transformations in the outward surroundings are most interesting to observe, but for the purposes of this volume they are far less interesting than the transformation that has gone on within the church itself. If the question be asked—as it sometimes is, and with a tone that seems to call for a negative reply—Is the Church of Christ alive? Is it something more than a venerable monument? Does it maintain a true relation to the needs of successive generations of men, and is it capable of adapting its message and its ministry to the changed, and still changing, conditions of modern life? In particular, is the Church of Christ able so to enlarge its scope as to meet the tremendous social needs of our own day, and to become no longer a mere place of refuge for believers, but a head-quarters for apostles, from which the power of Jesus Christ, incarnated in Christian men and women, shall go out to the relief of every kind of need, the righting of every kind of wrong, the supplying of every kind of good?—if this question be asked, the facts of history related in this volume would seem to have some claim to make an affirmative and encouraging reply.

Less than a century and a half ago there was on Beekman Street a congregation of godly men and women who, in living up to the light of their day, did

GOLDEN WINDOW KINDERGARTEN AT DOOR OF CHRIST CHURCH MEMORIAL HOUSE

produce a church whose interests centred chiefly in itself, in the maintaining of its own worship, the instruction and training of its own membership, in short, the honoring of God and the following of Christ almost entirely within its own boundaries. Worship and preaching, the administering of the sacraments, parish visitation and the supervision of the morals of its members, the taking up of a collection at the Sunday service—"one copper and no more," given alike by each member of the congregation, and used almost exclusively for the church's own poor: such was the work of the church of 1767.

Compare with this the Brick Church of to-day, and see what changes have been wrought by the spirit of Christ in the hearts of its five generations of members, in answer to the changing and increasing needs of the city, the nation, the world. Not so much because of the precise results achieved, the definite ministry rendered, ought this development to be pointed out, but because of the purpose which it reveals, the living power to which it testifies—a promise for the future even more than a record of the past.

The latest report tells us that the people of the Brick Church contributed during the year, for the work of Christ's kingdom among men at home and abroad, something over $155,000. In the Brick Church itself, more numerous services are maintained to-day than were ever regularly maintained on Beekman Street, to which should be added as many more in the two affiliated churches; but to-day these services, and all the more personal work of religious and moral instruction and influence, no longer satisfy the ideal of the people, nor exhaust their energies. On the contrary, this distinctly religious ministry is now regarded as the central and culminating department of a work which reaches out in every direction, to touch and uplift every interest of the neighboring population.

The Brick Church, in union with Christ Church and the Church of the Covenant, that singularly perfect example of true Christian brotherhood, has consciously undertaken the task of ministering to every need that it can discover in an entire district of New York City. It sets no limit to its responsibility. The nursing and doctoring of the sick; the improvement of the homes of the people; the provision of instruction and of the means of culture and of industrial training—books, classes, workshops; the arousing of a sense of civic pride and civic responsibility; the improvement of social and industrial conditions; the promotion of the happiness of individuals, through the ministry of personal friendship, through opportunities for wholesome social intercourse, through the encouragement of sports and other recreations— happiness for people of all ages, from the little children at their nursery games, to the fathers and the mothers, whose need of relaxation and refreshment becomes more and more pressing as the strain of our modern life grows greater—these are some of the activities to which the present church believes itself called by the voice of Jesus Christ.

It is a great change from the conditions of 1767, but it has been accomplished, it should be observed, without the church's losing in the slightest degree its character as a church, without its ceasing for a moment to be still an association of Christian believers,

BOWLING ALLEYS AND LIBRARY, CHRIST CHURCH MEMORIAL HOUSE

of Christian worshippers, of teachers of Christian truth, of trainers in Christian character. But the old ideals and the old work have been transformed, regenerated, by a new baptism of the essential Christian spirit of service.

There is no intention to assert that the Brick Church has yet done its full duty, or that the service it has rendered has been adequate to existing needs. The aim is not at all to declare that the goal has been reached or even that it is within sight, but only to point out that the Church of Christ, as the typical history of the Brick Church makes evident, moves toward that goal with a certainty and a genuineness of purpose which cannot be mistaken. The Christian Church is a living church. It lives in the present world, and hears the cries for help and shares the suffering and trouble, and knows that its commission from the Master is to spend itself in ministry.

If the history of this volume is a fair assurance that the Brick Church has made an inspiring advance in the century and a half already completed, and, if it is a true prophecy of the direction of her development and of the distance that she will travel in the century and a half now lying before us, there is reason why the members of that church should thank God and press on with confidence and courage.

BIBLIOGRAPHY

BIBLIOGRAPHY *

I. KEY

TO ABBREVIATIONS OF TITLES USED IN THE NOTES OF THIS VOLUME

Assembly Digest . . . . See below, No.   3
Br. Ch. Mem. . . . . "   "   " 56
Church of the Covenant (The) . . . . "   "   " 90
Common Council . . . . "   "   " 20
Cutler's Life, etc. . . . . "   "   "   8
Decade of Work (A) . . . . "   "   " 190
Disosway . . . . "   "   "   9
Document No. 37 . . . . "   "   " 82
Eleven Years . . . . "   "   " 111
Historic Church (An) . . . . "   "   " 179
Jones N. Y. in Rev. . . . . "   "   " 13
Life and Times . . . . "   "   " 58
Manuscript Hist. . . . . "   "   " 191
Mem. Hist. of N. Y. . . . . "   "   " 19
Memorial Discourse . . . . "   "   " 110
N. Y. in 1789 . . . . "   "   " 15
Rodgers Mem. . . . . "   "   " 34
Sprague's Annals . . . . "   "   " 16
State Thanksgiving, etc. . . . . "   "   " 166

II. GENERAL AUTHORITIES

CONSULTED IN THE PREPARATION OF THIS HISTORY

ADAMS, JOHN, 2d President of the U. S.—
    1. Works of. (1850.)

ALEXANDER, S. D.—
    2. The Presbytery of New York, 1738 to 1888. (N. Y. 1887.)

BAIRD, SAMUEL J., Editor—
    3. * A Collection of the Acts, Deliverances and Testimonies of the
        Supreme Judicatory of the Presbyterian Church. (2d edi-
        tion, Phil., 1858.)

* Throughout the following lists an asterisk means that the work to
whose name it is prefixed is contained in the Brick Church Library.

BANCROFT, GEORGE—
    4. History of the United States.

BEECHER, REV. LYMAN—
    5. Autobiography of, ed. by C. Beecher. (N. Y., 1865.)

BOURNE, W. O.—
    6. History of the Public School Society of New York. (1870.)

CARTER, R.—
    7. Familiar Conversations on the History of the Evangelical Churches of New York. (N. Y., 1839.)

CUTLER, REV. MANASSEH, LL.D.—
    8. Life, Journals and Correspondence of, by his grandchildren. (1888.)

DISOSWAY, GABRIEL P.—
    9. The Earliest Churches of New York and Its Vicinity. (N. Y., 1865.)

FERRIS, ISAAC F.—
    10. Semi-Centennial Memorial Discourse of the Sunday-school Union. (1866.)

GREENLEAF, J.—
    11. A History of the Churches of all Denominations in New York. (N. Y., 1850.)

IRVING, WASHINGTON—
    12. Life and Times of, by P. M. Irving. (N. Y., 1883.)

JONES, THOMAS—
    13. History of New York during the Revolutionary War. Edited by Edward de Lancy. (N. Y., 1879.)

REED, NEWTON—
    14. Early History of Amenia, N. Y. (Amenia, 1875.)

SMITH, T. E. V.—
    15. The City of New York in 1789. (N. Y., 1889.)

SPRAGUE, REV. WILLIAM B., D.D.—
    16. Annals of the American Pulpit. (N. Y., 1858.)

VAN PELT, DANIEL—
    17. Leslie's History of Greater New York. (N. Y., 1899.)

WASHINGTON, GEORGE—
18. Writings of, ed. with Life, by J. Sparks. (Boston, 1837.)

WILSON, JAMES GRANT, Editor—
19. Memorial History of the City of New York. (N. Y., 1892.)

MISCELLANEOUS—
20. Common Council of the City of New York, Printed Minutes of. (N. Y., 1905.)
21. New York City in the American Revolution. (N. Y., 1861.)
22. * Presbyterian Reunion, The. (N. Y., 1870.)
23. * Presbytery of New York, Hand-book of, for 1903–1904.
24. Westervelt Manuscripts, Lenox Library.

III. BOOKS

RELATING TO THE BRICK CHURCH AND ITS OFFICERS AND MEMBERS, IN-
CLUDING WORKS BY ITS MINISTERS

ALLEN, MOSES—
25. * Memorial of, containing the funeral sermon by Dr. L. D. Bevan. (N. Y., 1878.)

BABCOCK, REV. MALTBIE DAVENPORT, D.D.—
26. Thoughts for Every-day Living. (N. Y., 1901.)
27. Letters from Egypt and Palestine. (N. Y., 1902.)
28. Hymns and Carols. (N. Y., 1903.)
28a. A Reminiscent Sketch of, by Charles E. Robinson, D.D. (N. Y., 1904.)

BEVAN, REV. LLEWELYN D., D.D., see Allen Memorial, No. 25.

CADY, J. CLEVELAND, LL.D., see Forty Years, etc., No. 75.

ELY, ABNER L.—
29. * A Memorial of, containing the funeral sermon by Dr. James O. Murray. (N. Y., 1873.)

HOGE, REV. W. J., D.D., see Brick Church Memorial, No. 56.

HOLDEN, HORACE, see Brick Church Memorial, No. 56.

LORD, DANIEL—
30. * Memorial of, including addresses by Dr. James O. Murray, Dr. Spring, and others. (N. Y., 1869.)
See also Brick Church Memorial, No. 56.

MILLER, REV. SAMUEL, D.D., LL.D.—
31. A Brief Retrospect of the Eighteenth Century. (1803.)
32. Letters Concerning the Constitution and Order of the Christian Ministry. (1807.)
33. A continuation of the same. (1809.)
34. *Memoirs of John Rodgers. (1813.)
35. Letters on Clerical Manners and Habits. (1827.)
    (The rest of Dr. Miller's published volumes, written after his departure from New York, need not be listed here. They are given in Sprague's Annals, Vol. III, p. 605.)
36. Life of, by Samuel Miller. (Phil., 1869.)

MORGAN, GOV. EDWIN DENISON—
37. *Memorial of, including an address by Dr. Murray and a sermon by Mr. van Dyke. Also Memorials of Dr. and Mrs. E. D. Morgan, Jr., (N. Y., 1883.)

MURRAY, REV. JAMES ORMSBEE, D.D., See Ely Memorial No. 29; Lord Memorial, No. 30; and Morgan Memorial No. 37.

RICHARDS, REV. WILLIAM R., D.D.—
38. *The Ways of Wisdom and other sermons. (N. Y., 1886.)
39. An Extraordinary Saint, a sermon in the volume, The Culture of Christian Manhood, a collection of sermons preached in Battell Chapel, Yale University. (1897.)
40. *Victory, An Easter Sermon. (Plainfield, 1902.)
41. *For Whom Christ Died. (Phila., 1902.)
42. *Sermon Commemorating the Two-Hundredth Anniversary of the Birth of Jonathan Edwards, preached at Andover Theological Seminary, October 4th, 1903. Printed with the other proceedings. (Andover, 1903.)
43. God's Choice of Men; a Study of Scripture. (N. Y., 1905.)
44. The Apostles' Creed in Modern Worship. (N. Y., 1906.)
    See also Forty Years, etc., No. 75.

ROBINSON, C. E., see No. 28a.

SPRING, REV. GARDINER, D.D., LL.D.—
45. *Essays on the Distinguishing Traits of Christian Character. (N. Y., 1813.)
46. *Memoirs of the Rev. Samuel J. Mills. (N. Y., 1820).
47. *Christian Confidence, illustrated by the Death of Rev. Edward D. Griffen, D.D. (N. Y., 1838.)
48. *Fragments from the Study of a Pastor. (N. Y., 1838.)
49. The Obligations of the World to the Bible. (N. Y., 1839.)
50. *The Attraction of the Cross. (N. Y., 1845.)

51. *The Power of the Pulpit. (N. Y., 1848.)
52. The Mercy Seat. (N. Y., 1850.)
53. *First Things. (N. Y., 1851.)
54. *The Glory of Christ. (N. Y., 1852.)
55. *The Contrast. (N. Y., 1855.)
56. *The Brick Church Memorial, including also addresses by Horace Holden, Daniel Lord, and Dr. Hoge. (N. Y., 1861.)
57. Pulpit Ministrations. (N. Y., 1864.)
58. *Personal Reminiscences of the Life and Times of. (N. Y. 1866.)
   See also Lord Memorial, No. 30.

VAN DYKE, REV. HENRY, D.D., LL.D.—
   59. The Reality of Religion. (N. Y., 1884.)
   60. *The Story of the Psalms. (N. Y., 1887.)
   61. Straight Sermons, (1893.) A new and enlarged edition under the title * Sermons to Young Men, was published in 1898.
   62. *The Christ-Child in Art. (N. Y., 1894.)
   63. *The Story of the Other Wise Man. (N. Y., 1896.)
   64. *The Gospel for an Age of Doubt. (N. Y., 1896.)
   64a. The Meaning of Manhood, a Sermon in the volume, The Culture of Christian Manhood, a collection of sermons preached in Battell Chapel, Yale University. (1897.)
   65. The First Christmas Tree. (N. Y., 1897.)
   66. *Ships and Havens. (N. Y., 1897.)
   67. The Lost Word. (N. Y., 1898.)
   68. *The Gospel for a World of Sin. (N. Y., 1899.)
   69. *The Poetry of the Psalms. (N. Y., 1900.)
   70. *The Toiling of Felix, and Other Poems. (N. Y., 1900.)
   71. The Friendly Year, edited by Rev. George S. Webster. (N. Y., 1900.)
   72. *Joy and Power. (N. Y., 1903.)
   73. *The Open Door. (N. Y., 1903.)
   74. The Spirit of Christmas. (N. Y., 1905.)
      See also Morgan Memorial, No. 37.
   74a. *Biographical Sketch of, by his daughter, Brooke van Dyke, see The van Dyke Book. (N. Y., 1905.)
      (Dr. Van Dyke has edited the Church Psalter, and also the Book of Responsive Readings used in the Chapel of Harvard University. He also composed a large part of the Presbyterian Book of Common Worship. His many volumes of a less distinctively religious character are not included in the above list. Nos. 63, 65, 67, 70, 74, and also the poems "Vera"and "The Legend of Service," were first used at Christmas services in the Brick Church.)

WEBSTER, REV. GEORGE S., D.D.—

75. *Forty Years of Covenant Mercies, a Description of the Historic Memorials in the Church of the Covenant, including addresses delivered January 28th, 1906, by Rev. William R. Richards, D.D., and J. Cleveland Cady, LL.D.
(N. Y. 1906.)
See also The Friendly Year, No. 71.

MISCELLANEOUS—

76. *Brick Church Hymns (The), for Prayer-meetings, etc.
(N. Y., 1823.)

76a. *Sacrifice of Praise (The). Psalms, Hymns and Spiritual
Songs, published by the session of the Brick Church.
(N. Y., 1869; with tunes, 1872.)

77. Year Books of the Brick Church for *1828, *1832, *1833,
*1866, *1869 (two editions), 1885 and annually thereafter.
(* from 1887–1888 to present except 1891–1892 and
1896–1897.)

IV. PAMPHLETS

RELATING TO THE BRICK CHURCH, ITS AFFILIATED CHURCHES, AND THE
OLD CHURCH OF THE COVENANT, OR WRITTEN BY THEIR PASTORS

78. "Announcements" of the Brick Church, published weekly
October to May of each year from 1890 to the present.
(* All except 1901–1902 and 1902–1903.)

BABCOCK, REV. MALTBIE DAVENPORT, D.D.—

79. *The Success of Defeat, delivered at the Fourth Annual Convention of the Maryland Christian Endeavor Union, December, 1893.   (Baltimore.)

80. *A Day of Testing, What Shall it Bring Out of Us? Addresses
delivered at the Memorial Service for the Martyred Missionaries in China, October 28th, 1900.

BEVAN, REV. LLEWELYN D., D.D.—

81. *Service and Rest, a Sermon in Memory of Frederick Denison
Maurice, M.A., preached at Tottenham Court Road
Chapel.   (London, 1872.)

BOARD OF ALDERMEN—

82. Document No. 37, relating to sale of property of Brick
Church, 1854.

DEWITT, JOHN—

83. *James Ormsbee Murray, D.D., LL.D., A Memorial Sermon.
(Princeton, 1899.)

DODGE, HOSEA, see No. 167.

"EVANGELICUS PACIFICUS," see Nos. 170 and 172.

FARR, REV. JAMES M.—
84. *The Story of the Christ Church Work: an Historical Sermon,
including also an address by Mr. John E. Parsons, and a
letter from Rev. Joseph J. Lampe, D.D.   (N. Y., 1906.)
85. *Fiftieth Anniversary of the Founding of the Christ Church
Work.   (1907.)

FISHER, REV. SAMUEL, A.M.—
86. *A Sermon preached May, 1821, in the Brick Church, New
York, before the Presbyterian Education Society.   (Newark, 1821.)

GRIFFEN, REV. EDWARD D., D.D.—
87. *Living to God, a sermon preached June 16, 1816, at the
Brick Presbyterian Church in the City of New York.
(N. Y., 1816.)

HOGE, REV. WILLIAM J., D.D—
88. Installation Services of.   (1859.)
89. *A Discourse delivered on the resignation of his charge (collegiate pastorate of the Brick Church), July 21st, 1861.
(N. Y., 1861.)

LAMPE, REV. JOSEPH J., D.D., see Story of Christ Church
Work, No. 84.

McILVAINE, REV. JAMES HALL, D.D.—
90. *The Church of the Covenant, a Historical Sermon at the last
service held in the church, February 11th, 1894.

McKNIGHT, REV. JOHN, D.D.—
91. Six Sermons on Faith (recommended by Drs. Rodgers and
Witherspoon).   (1790.)
92. A Thanksgiving Sermon.   (1795.)
93. A Sermon before the New York Missionary Society.   (1799.)
94. A Sermon on the Present State of the Political and Religious
World.   (1802.)
95. A Sermon on the death of the Rev. John King.   (1811.)

MILLEDOLER, REV. P.—
95a. A Sermon preached in the Presbyterian Church in Beekman
Street, 1810, at the ordination and installation of the Rev.
Gardiner Spring as pastor of said church.   (N. Y., 1810.)

MILLER, REV. SAMUEL, D.D.—

96. A Sermon preached in New York at the request of the Tammany Society and the Columbian Order, on the Anniversary of American Independence. (1793.)

97. A Discourse delivered in the New Presbyterian Church before the Grand Lodge of the State of New York. (1795.)

98. A Discourse Commemorative of the Discovery of New York by Henry Hudson. (N. Y. Historical Collection.) (1795.)

99. A Sermon delivered in the New Presbyterian Church, New York, July Fourth, 1795, being the Nineteenth Anniversary of the Independence of America, at the request of and before, the Mechanic, Tammany, and Democratic Societies, and the Military officers. (N. Y., 1795.)

100. *A Discourse delivered April 12th, 1797, at the request of and before, the New York Society for the Promoting of the Manumission of Slaves and protecting such of them as have been or may be liberated. (N. Y., 1797.)

101. A Sermon delivered in New York, May 9th, 1798, recommended by the President as a day of General Humiliation, etc. (1798.)

102. *A Sermon delivered February 5th, 1799. Recommended by the clergy of the City of New York to be observed as a day of Thanksgiving, Humiliation, and Prayer, on account of the Removal of a malignant and mortal disease which had prevailed in the city some time before. (N. Y., 1799.)

103. A Sermon delivered December 29th, 1799, occasioned by the death of General Washington. (1799.)

104. A Sermon before the New York Missionary Society, April 6th, 1802. (1802.)

105. *The Guilt, Folly, and Sources of Suicide: two Discourses preached in the City of New York, February, 1805. (N. Y., 1805.)

106. A Sermon preached March 13th, 1808, for the benefit of a society in New York for the relief of poor widows with small children. (1808.)

107. *The Divine Appointment, the Duties and the Qualification of Ruling Elders: a Sermon, preached in the First Presbyterian Church in the City of New York, May 28th, 1809. (N. Y., 1811.)

108. Address of Introduction at the ordination of Gardiner Spring, August, 1810.
(Other pamphlets of Dr. Miller, published after his departure from New York, were very numerous, but need not be listed here. See Sprague's Annals, Vol. III, pp. 605 *f.*)

MURRAY, REV. JAMES ORMSBEE, D.D.—

109. *Christian Hymnology: a Sermon preached in the Brick Church, New York, December 12th, 1869. (N. Y., 1870.)

110. *A Discourse Commemorating the Ministerial Character and Services of Gardiner Spring, D.D., LL.D., with an Appendix containing the addresses made at the funeral, August 22d, 1873. (N. Y.)

For biographical sketch see No. 83.

PARSONS, JOHN E. See the Story of the Christ Church Work, No. 84.

PRENTISS, REV. GEORGE L., D.D.—

111. *Eleven Years of the Church of the Covenant: a Sermon preached April 27th, 1873. (N. Y., 1873.)

112. *Memorial of, prepared at the request of the Directors and Faculty of Union Theological Seminary, including the funeral address by Dr. M. R. Vincent.

RICHARDS, REV. WILLIAM R., D.D.—

112a. Revision of the Confession of Faith: two sermons preached in the Crescent Avenue Presbyterian Church, Plainfield, N. J., September 22d, 1889.

112b. Sermon preached on Sunday evening, January 25th, 1891, at the Crescent Avenue Presbyterian Church, Plainfield, N. J.

113. *The Ten Commandments Filled Full by Christ: a Sermon preached in the Crescent Avenue Presbyterian Church, Plainfield, N. J., July 10th, 1892.

114. *A Talk on Sunday Observance, published by the Woman's National Sabbath Alliance.

115. *The City and Its Church: annual Address before the Alumni [of Hartford Seminary] and Pastoral Union, June 2d, 1896. Reprinted from the Hartford Seminary Record for June and August, 1896.

116. *Sermon delivered in the Crescent Avenue Presbyterian Church, Plainfield, N. J., May 20th, 1900.

117. *Honor to Whom Honor is Due: sermon preached in the Brick Church, February 22d, 1903. (Sons of the Revolution.)

118. *Desiring a Better Country: the Fourth Annual Sermon preached before the New England Society, on Forefathers' Day, December 20th, 1903.

119. *In the Unity of the Faith: a Sermon preached April 10th, 1904, on the Tenth Anniversary of the Consolidation of the Brick Church and the Church of the Covenant. (N. Y., 1904.)

120. *The Ministry of Quiet Work: a Sermon.
121. *National Prosperity: a Sermon in the interests of Home Missions, preached March 13th, 1904.
122. *Angel or Man? a Sermon preached April 17th, 1904.
123. *Two Sermons, "Privilege" and "To Follow is to Believe." (N. Y., 1907.)

RODGERS, REV. JOHN, D.D.—
124. *The Divine Goodness Displayed in the American Revolution: a Sermon. (N. Y., 1784.)

RUGGLES, S. B.—
125. An Examination of the Law of Burial.

SPRING, REV. GARDINER, D.D., LL.D.—
126. Sermon on Faith and Works, preached April 21st, 1811, for the benefit of a Society of Ladies instituted for the Relief of Poor Widows with Small Children. (1811.)
127. *Something Must Be Done: Sermon preached on the last day of the old year. (Newburyport, 1816.)
128. *The Doctrine of Election: a Sermon. (Cooperstown, 1817).
129. An Oration: February 5th, 1817, before the Alumni of Yale College, rendered in the City of New York in Commemoration of their Late President, Timothy Dwight, D.D., LL.D. (N. Y., 1817.)
130. A Brief Review of Facts in relation to the Formation of the New York Missionary Society of Young Men. (1817.)
131. Remarks on the Charges made against the Religion and Morals of the People of Boston and Vicinity, with a Sermon preached at New York before the New England Society, December 22d, 1820. (1821.) The sermon was printed separately under the title,* "A Tribute to New England," (N. Y., 1821.)
132. A sermon before the American Home Missionary Society. (1823.)
133. *An Appeal to the Citizens of New York in behalf of the Christian Sabbath. (N. Y., 1823.) Reprinted * in modern Greek, 1829, and in Italian.
134. *The Discriminating Preacher: a Sermon at the ordination of the Rev. Carlos Wilcox. (Hartford, 1825.)
135. The Excellence and Influence of the Female Character: a Sermon. (1825.)
136. An Address of the Executive Committee of the American Tract Society. (1825.)
137. The Internal Evidences of Inspiration. (1826.)

138. Funeral Sermon, occasioned by the death of the Rev. Philip Melancthon Whepley. (N. Y., 1826.)

139. A Dissertation on the Means of Regeneration. (1827.)

140. Moses on Nebo, or Death a Duty: Sermon on the death of Rev. Joseph S. Christmas. (N. Y., 1830.)

141. *A Tribute to the Memory of the Late Jeremiah Evarts. (N. Y., 1831.)

142. *A Sermon Preached August 3d, 1832, a Day Set Apart for Public Fasting, etc., on account of the Malignant Cholera. (N. Y., 1832.)

143. Address to the Theological Students at Princeton Seminary. (1832.)

144. *Hints to Parents. (N. Y., 1833.)

145. A Dissertation on Native Depravity. (N. Y., 1833.)

146. The Extent of Missionary Enterprise: Sermon at the annual meeting of the Congregational Union of England and Wales. (London, 1835.)

147. *The Will of God Performed on Earth: a Sermon preached at Utica, N. Y., October 8th, 1834, before the American Board of Commissioners for Foreign Missions. (Boston, 1835.)

148. The Power of Sin: a Sermon. (1837.)

149. Christian Knowledge: a Sermon introductory to the Murray Street Lectures. (1837.)

150. *An Address before the Mercantile Library Association of the City of New York. (N. Y., 1837.)

151. *Death and Heaven: a Sermon preached at Newark at the interment of Rev. Edward D. Griffen. (N. Y., 1838.) Published in book form under the title, Christian Confidence, see No. 47.

152. The New Sepulchre, Discourse on the Death of William Henry Harrison, April 11th, 1841. (1841.)

153. Supremacy of God over the Nations, discourse preached May 14th, 1841, a day of National Fast on the occasion of the Death of William Henry Harrison. (1841.)

154. *The Danger and Hope of the American People, a discourse on the day of the annual Thanksigving in the State of New York. (N. Y., 1843.)

155. The Saviour's Presence with His Ministers, delivered at the opening of the General Assembly at Louisville. (1844.)

156. A Dissertation on the Rule of Faith, delivered at Cincinnati, Ohio, at the semi-annual meeting of the American Bible Society. (N. Y., 1844.)

157. The Bible Not of Man, or the Argument for the Divine Origin of the Scriptures, drawn from the Scriptures Themselves. (N. Y., 1847.)

158. The Bethel Flag: short Sermons to seamen. (1848.)
159. Strictures on the Princeton Review. (1848.)
160. *Influence: a Quarter-Century Sermon, preached in behalf of the American Tract Society. (1850.)
161. Address before the New York Female Bible Society. (1853.)
162. Triumph in Suffering: Sermon preached at the funeral of the Rev. Dr. Spencer. (1855.)
163. Sermon at the Installation of the Rev. Dr. Hoge. (1859.)
164. Sermon on the Death of Horace Holden, Esq. (1862.)
165. The Mission of Sorrow. (1862.)
166. *State Thanksgiving during the Rebellion: a Sermon preached November 28th, 1861. (N. Y., 1862.)
    For Memorial of, see above, No. 110.

SPRING, DR., Pamphlets called forth by publications of:
167. *A Review of a Sermon entitled The Doctrine of Election, etc., by G. Spring, A.M., by Hosea Dodge. (N. Y., 1817.)
168. Strictures on the Rev. Dr. Spring's Dissertation on the Means of Regeneration, by Bennet Tyler. Reprinted from the " Christian Spectator " for 1829. (Portland, 1829.)
169. Review of Dr. Tyler's Strictures (probably by Dr. Taylor of New Haven.) Reprinted from the " Christian Spectator " March, 1830. (New Haven, 1830.)
170. An Evangelical View of the Nature and Means of Man's Regeneration, comprising a review of Dr. Tyler's Strictures, by Evangelicus Pacificus. (Boston, 1830.)
171. A Vindication of the Strictures on Rev. Dr. Spring's Dissertation on the Means of Regeneration, in reply to Evangelicus Pacificus, by Bennet Tyler. (Portland, 1830.)
172. An examination of Dr. Tyler's vindication of his Strictures in the "Christian Spectator," by Evangelicus Pacificus. (Boston, 1830.)
173. Review of Dr. Spring's Dissertation on Natural Depravity. Reprinted from the "Quarterly Christian Spectator." (New Haven, 1833.)

TAYLOR, DR. N. W., see No. 169.

TYLER, BENNET., see Nos. 168 and 171.

VAN DYKE, REV. HENRY, D.D., LL.D.
174. *The Joy of the Christian when He is Invited to enter the Lord's House: Sermon preached at the reopening of the Brick Presbyterian Church, October 28th, 1883.
175. *Holy Days and Holidays: a Humane View of the Sunday Question. Reprinted from the "Christian at Work," of February 11th, 1886.

176. *The National Sin of Literary Piracy. Extracts from a Sermon. (1888.)

177. *A Brief for Foreign Missions: a Sermon preached March 15th, 1891.

178. *The True Presbyterian Doctrine of the Church. (N. Y., 1893.)

179. *An Historic Church: a Sermon preached on the 125th Anniversary of the Brick Presbyterian Church, January 1st, 1893. (N. Y., 1893.)

180. *The Bible as It Is: a Sermon on the present trouble and the way of peace in the Presbyterian Church. (N. Y., 1893.)

181. *The People Responsible for the Character of Their Rulers: a Sermon delivered before the Sons of the Revolution in the State of New York. (N. Y., 1895.)

182. *The Cross of War: a Sermon preached May 1st, 1898.

183. *The Sea, the Men upon It, and the God above It: a discourse before the American Seaman's Friend Society. (N. Y., 1898.)

184. *Salt: Baccalaureate Sermon at Columbia University. (N. Y., 1898.)

185. *The American Birthright and the Philippine Pottage: a Sermon preached on Thanksgiving Day, 1898.

VINCENT, REV. MARVIN R., D.D.—

186. *Thirty-fifth Anniversary Sermon, preached January 27th, 1901, in the Church of the Covenant.
See also Prentiss Memorial, No. 112.

WEBSTER, REV. GEORGE S., D.D.—

187. *Quarter-Century Anniversary of Covenant Chapel: a Sermon delivered November 8th, 1891.

188. *Souvenir of the Quarter-Century Anniversary of the Dedication of the Church Building: historical sketch, dated January 1st, 1897.

189. *Our Church God's Home. A review of four years' work as an independent church, delivered January 2d, 1898.

190. *A Decade of Work in the Church of the Covenant. (1900.)

V. MANUSCRIPT SOURCES

191. History of the Presbyterian Church in New York City till 1795. Anonymous. Preserved in the back of the volume next mentioned.

192. Session Minutes of the First Presbyterian Church, 1765–1808 (in the custody of the Old First Church).

193. *Session Minutes of the Brick Church, 1809 to the present time, 7 Vols.

194. *Trustees' Minutes of the Brick Church, 1809 to the present, 2 Vols.
195. *Minutes of the Brick Church Sunday-school, 1832–1850 (with considerable gaps).
196. *Sunday-school Record Books from 1839 (many years missing).
197. *Minutes of the Employment Society, 1869 to the present.
198. *Treasurer's Accounts of the Female Auxiliary Tract Association of the Brick Church, 1837–1861.

APPENDICES

APPENDICES

APPENDIX A

CHRONOLOGY

NOTE: EVENTS IN THE HISTORY OF THE OLD CHURCH OF THE COVE-
NANT ARE ENCLOSED IN BRACKETS

1706. First Presbyterian Worship in New York.
1716. James Anderson, first minister.
1727. Ebenezer Pemberton, second minister.
1750. Alexander Cummings, colleague of Mr. Pemberton.
1755. David Bostwick becomes minister.
1755. Joseph Treat, associate minister.
1765. John Rodgers succeeds Mr. Bostwick, September 4th.
1766. The "Vineyard Lot" obtained, February 25th.
1767. New Church built.
1768. New Church opened, January 1st.
1783. Thanksgiving after the Revolution, December 11th.
1784. New Church reopened, June 27th.
1785. James Wilson, colleague of Dr. Rodgers.
1789. John McKnight, colleague of Dr. Rodgers.
1790. Charity School opened, May 1st.
1793. Samuel Miller colleague of Dr. Rodgers and Mr. McKnight.
1809. End of the collegiate system, April 12th.
1810. Installation of Gardiner Spring, August 8th.
1810. Lecture-room built.
1811. Death of Dr. Rodgers, May 7th.
1815–16. Revival.
1816. Sunday-schools started.
1822. Beginning of choir.
1832. Chapel replaces lecture-room.
1856. Beekman Street property sold.

513

1856. Last service on Beekman Street, May 25th.
1857. Mission School started, October.
1858. Present Brick Church dedicated, October 31st.
1859. William J. Hoge, colleague of Dr. Spring.
[1860. Beginning of Church of the Covenant, November 25th.]
1862. W. G. T. Shedd, colleague of Dr. Spring.
[1862. Church of the Covenant organized, March 21st.]
[1862. George L. Prentiss installed, May 11th.]
1865. James O. Murray, colleague of Dr. Spring.
[1865. Church of the Covenant dedicated, April 30th.]
[1866. Covenant Mission Sunday-school organized, January 28th.]
1867. Joseph J. Lampe, pastor of Brick Church Mission.
1867. Brick Church Mission Chapel dedicated, October 20th.
1869. Last Old School and New School Assemblies meet in Brick
       Church and Church of the Covenant.
1869. "The Sacrifice of Praise" published.
[1871. Covenant Chapel dedicated, December 24th.]
1873. Death of Dr. Spring, August 18th: Dr. Murray becomes sole
       pastor.
[1873. Marvin R. Vincent succeeds Dr. Prentiss at Covenant, May
       8th.]
1876. Parsonage purchased.
1877. Llewelyn D. Bevan succeeds Dr. Murray, January 16th.
1883. Henry van Dyke succeeds Dr. Bevan, January 16th.
1883. Church interior renovated: reopened, October 28th.
1888. Mission becomes Christ Church, June 6th.
[1888. James H. McIlvaine succeeds Dr. Vincent at Covenant, De-
       cember 17th.]
[1890. George S. Webster, associate of Dr. McIlvaine, March 19th.]
[1893. Covenant Chapel becomes new Church of the Covenant, No-
       vember 30th.]
[1894. George S. Webster installed pastor of new Covenant.]
1894. Union of old Church of the Covenant and Brick Church, Dr.
       McIlvaine becoming co-pastor with Dr. van Dyke, April
       12th.
1896. Dr. McIlvaine resigns.
1897. Richard R. Wightman succeeds Dr. Lampe at Christ Church.
1898. Christ Church House given.
1900. Maltbie D. Babcock succeeds Dr. van Dyke, February 27th.
1901. James M. Farr succeeds Mr. Wightman at Christ Church,
       January 24th.
1901. Death of Dr. Babcock, May 18th.
1901. Dr. van Dyke becomes minister-in-charge, December.
1902. William R. Richards installed pastor, October 26th.
1905. Christ Church Memorial Buildings dedicated, October 27th.
1908. Morris K. Jesup bequest.

TO THIS CHRONOLOGY MAY BE APPENDED A LIST OF THE

RED LETTER DAYS

IN THE BRICK CHURCH CALENDAR

January 1st.	Church on Beekman Street dedicated, 1768.
" 28th.	Covenant Mission Sunday-school organized, 1866.
February 25th.	The "Vineyard Lot" obtained, 1766.
March 21st.	Church of the Covenant organized, 1862.
April 12th.	End of collegiate arrangement: the Brick Church becomes a separate organization, 1809.
" "	Union of Brick Church and the Church of the Covenant, 1896.
" 30th.	Church of the Covenant dedicated, 1865.
June 6th.	Christ Church organized, 1888.
" 27th.	Beekman Street Church reopened after the Revolution, 1784.
October 20th.	The Thirty-fifth Street Mission Chapel dedicated 1867.
" 27th.	Christ Church Memorial Buildings opened, 1905.
" 28th.	Reopening of Brick Church after decoration, 1883.
" 31st.	Brick Church on Murray Hill dedicated, 1858.
November 30th.	Present Church of the Covenant organized, 1893.
December 24th	Covenant Memorial Chapel dedicated, 1871.

APPENDIX B

MINISTERS OF THE BRICK CHURCH

(1) AS A COÖRDINATE PART OF THE FIRST PRESBYTERIAN CHURCH

JOHN RODGERS	1767–1811*
JOSEPH TREAT (Colleague)	1767–1775†
JAMES WILSON (Colleague)	1785–1788†
JOHN McKNIGHT (Colleague)	1789–1809†
SAMUEL MILLER (Colleague)	1793–1809†

(2) AS A SEPARATE ECCLESIASTICAL ORGANIZATION

GARDINER SPRING	1810–1873*
WILLIAM J. HOGE (Colleague)	1859–1861†
WILLIAM G. T. SHEDD (Colleague) . . .	1862–1863†
JAMES O. MURRAY (Colleague)	1865–1873
" " " (Sole Pastor)	1873–1875†
LLEWELYN D. BEVAN	1877–1882†
HENRY VAN DYKE	1883–1900†
JAMES H. McILVAINE (Co-pastor) . . .	1894–1896†
JAMES M. FARR, JR. (Assistant) . . .	1897–1901†
MALTBIE D. BABCOCK	1900–1901*
HENRY VAN DYKE (Minister-in-Charge) . .	1901–1902
SHEPHERD KNAPP (Assistant)	1901–1908†
WILLIAM R. RICHARDS	1902–

* Died.   † Resigned.

APPENDIX C

ELDERS OF THE BRICK CHURCH

ABRAHAM VAN GELDER	⎫	1809–1814†
JOHN THOMPSON		1809–1816†
THOMAS OGILVIE		1809–1815†
BENJAMIN EGBERT	Original Session	1809–1818†
WILLIAM FRAZER		1809–1813†
JOHN BINGHAM		1809–1833†
JOHN MILLS	⎭	1809–1815†
SAMUEL OSGOOD		1809–1813†
WILLIAM WHITLOCK		1809–1836†
RICHARD CUNNINGHAM		1815–1830*
RENSSELAER HAVENS		1815–1846*
JOHN ADAMS		1815–1855†
STEPHEN LOCKWOOD		1817–1827†
ALFRED DE FOREST		1817–1835*
ORANGE WEBB		1817†
HORACE W. BULKLEY		1817–1832*
WILLIAM WILLIAMS, JR.		1817–1826*
PETER HAWES		1823–1829†
ABIJAH FISHER		1823–1832*
HORACE HOLDEN		1823–1862†
GEORGE DOUGLASS		1828–1831*
FISHER HOW		1828–1831*
ERASTUS ELLSWORTH		1828–1833*
MOSES ALLEN		1828–1877†
SILAS HOLMES		1832–1856*
JASPER CORNING		1832–1834*
ABNER L. ELY		1832–1871†
DANIEL LORD		1834–1868†
WILLIAM COUCH		1834–1868†
JOHN C. HALSEY		1834–1837†
SHEPHERD KNAPP		1834–1875†
JAMES McCALL		1834–1844*
THOMAS EGLESTON		1834–1838*
PETER NAYLOR		1856–1872†
THOMAS EGLESTON		1856–1861†

RICHARD S. McCulloh . . . . 1856–1860‡
JAMES DARRACH 1856–1865*
LEVI P. STONE 1856–1862*
WINTHROP S. GILMAN . . . . 1863–1884†
WILLIAM FAXON 1863–1879*
IRA BLISS . . . . 1863–1878†
SAMUEL A. CHURCH . . . . 1863–1879†
BENJAMIN F. DUNNING . . . . 1863–1895†
GEORGE A. BENNETT 1863–1881*
CHARLES SCRIBNER . . . . 1870–1871†
JOHN E. PARSONS 1870–
GEORGE DE FOREST LORD . . . . . . 1870–1892†
THOMAS C. M. PATON 1870–1878*
HAMILTON ODELL 1870–
JOHN C. TUCKER . . . . 1881–1892†
EZRA M. KINGSLEY 1881–1882*
CHARLES G. HARMER . . . . 1881–1891†
WILLIAM N. BLAKEMAN . . . . 1886–1890†
DANIEL J. HOLDEN 1886–1897*
ALBERT R. LEDOUX 1886–
WILLIAM D. BARBOUR 1892–
HECTOR M. HITCHINGS 1892–
ADAM CAMPBELL 1892–
HENRY L. BUTLER . . . . 1892–1895†
HENRY D. NOYES . . . . 1894–1900†
W. H. H. MOORE 1894–
WILLIAM W. HOPPIN 1894–
J. CLEVELAND CADY 1894–
THERON G. STRONG 1894–
ALFRED E. MARLING 1894–
HENRY L. SMITH 1904–
CHARLES O. KIMBALL 1904–
EDWARD C. VAN GLAHN 1904–
THOMAS E. GREACEN 1904–
WILLIAM VAN VALZAH HAYES 1904–

* Transferred to other churches.   † Died.   ‡ Resigned from the Eldership.

APPENDIX D

CLERKS OF SESSION OF THE BRICK CHURCH

SAMUEL OSGOOD	1809–1813
DR. SPRING [?]	1813–1821
HORACE W. BULKLEY	1821–1829
HORACE HOLDEN	1829–1862
ABNER L. ELY	1863–1871
HAMILTON ODELL	1871–1894
DANIEL J. HOLDEN	1894–1897
HAMILTON ODELL	1897–

APPENDIX E

DEACONS OF THE BRICK CHURCH

NOTE: WHEN THE SECOND DATE IS PLACED IN BRACKETS, THE MEAN-
ING IS THAT THE PERSON DIED OR WAS DISMISSED TO ANOTHER
CHURCH AT THAT TIME, BUT WHETHER HE HAD CONTINUED TO
SERVE AS DEACON TILL THEN IS NOT CERTAIN.

RICHARD CUNNINGHAM	1809–1815*
MR. HUTCHINS	1809–?
WILLIAM MILLER	1809–?
JOHN STEPHENS	1815–?
WILLIAM AL-BURTIS	1817–[1822 or 1823‡]
JOHN C. SMITH	1817–?
WILLIAM LUYSTER	1823–?
WILLIAM COUCH	1823–1834*
JOHN McCOMB	1827–[1853†]
ERASTUS ELLSWORTH	1827–1828*
DANIEL OAKLEY	1828–[1840‡]
JOHN C. HALSEY	1828–1834*
NICOLL H. DERING	1832–?
SHEPHERD KNAPP	1832–1834*
ELIJAH MEAD	1832–[1841‡]
RICHARD HARDING	1834–?
ABRAHAM BOKEE	1834–[1851†]
JOHN R. DAVISON	1834–[1837‡]
SAMUEL BROWN	1834–[1844‡]
PETER NAYLOR	1841–1856*
IRA BLISS	1841–1863*
JACOB L. BALDWIN	1841–[1886†]
LEVI P. STONE	1841–1856*
OLIVER E. WOOD	1841–[1846‡]
JOHN C. TUCKER	1860–1881*
ROBERT STEWART	1860–?
SAMUEL A. CHURCH	1860–1863*
THOMAS PATON	1860–[1870‡]
JOHN WILMARTH	1863–[1882‡]
GEORGE DE FOREST LORD	1863–1870*

George W. Comstock	1863–1889†
William N. Blakeman	1870–1886*
Theodore Gilman	1870–[1879‡]
Arthur W. Parsons, Jr.	1870–[1884†]
William D. Barbour	1874–1892*
Daniel J. Holden	1874–1886*
Jacob B. T. Hatfield	1874–?
Daniel Parish, Jr.	1874–
Lucius D. Bulkley	1886–1896§
William Burhans Isham	1890–1897‡
William W. Van Valzah	1890–
Adam Campbell	1890–1892*
Edward W. Davis	1890–1892†
Caldwell R. Blakeman	1892–
William F. Dunning	1892–1907†
Edward W. Davis	1892–
William O. Curtis	1894–
William Seward	1894–1895§
Charles O. Kimball	1894–1904*
Charles W. McAlpin	1894–
Henry N. Corwith	1894–
Gerard Beekman Hoppin	1894–
Guy Richards McLane	1907–
E. D. Murphy	1907–
William H. Wheelock	1907–

* Transferred to the Eldership.   † Died.   ‡ Transferred to other churches.
§ Resigned.

APPENDIX F

TRUSTEES OF THE BRICK CHURCH

DRAKE MILLS . . . . 1836–1848‡
HORACE HOLDEN . . . . 1836–1862†
JAMES MCCALL 1837–1843
PAUL SPOFFORD 1837–1864
THOMAS EGLESTON . . . . 1841–1861†
AUGUSTUS WHITLOCK 1843–1864
IRA BLISS 1846–1864
SHEPHERD KNAPP 1847–1874
RICHARD J. HUTCHINSON 1848–1851
JOHN M. NIXON . . . . 1848–1869†
DRAKE MILLS . . . . 1851–1863†
ABNER L. ELY . . . . 1862–1871†
PETER NAYLOR . . . . 1862–1872†
WINTHROP S. GILMAN 1863–1874
HANSON K. CORNING 1864–1867
JOHN WILMARTH 1864–1867
THOMAS C. M. PATON 1864–1878
HENRY PARISH 1867–1876
FREDERICK W. DOWNER 1867–1882
WILLIAM BLACK . . . . 1868–1874†
EDWIN D. MORGAN . . . . 1869–1883†
JOHN L. LUDLAM 1871–1878
DANIEL JUDSON HOLDEN 1873–1903
THOMAS P. ELDRIDGE . . . . . . 1874†
GEORGE DE FOREST LORD . . . . . . 1874–1892†
WILLIAM B. ISHAM 1874–
ISAAC N. PHELPS . . . . 1875–1888†
DANIEL PARISH, JR. 1876–
JOSIAH G. HOLLAND . . . . 1878–1881†
JOHN E. PARSONS 1878–
FREDERICK BILLINGS . . . . 1882–1891‡
SHEPHERD KNAPP 1882–1892
CHARLES A. MILLER . . . . 1883–1897†
SILAS H. WITHERBEE . . . . 1889†
JOHN A. STEWART 1890–
CORNELIUS B. GOLD 1891–1892
FREDERICK BILLINGS 1892–1894
BENJAMIN H. BRISTOW 1892–1894
ROBERT OLYPHANT 1893–1894
EUGENE SMITH 1894–
ARTHUR M. DODGE 1894–1896
JOSEPH H. PARSONS 1894–1898
D. HUNTER MCALPIN 1896–
WILLIAM D. BARBOUR 1898–
CHARLES E. MERRILL 1898–

† Died in office.   ‡ Reëlected later.

APPENDIX G

PRESIDENTS OF BOARD OF TRUSTEES

APPENDIX H

TREASURERS OF THE BRICK CHURCH

SAMUEL OSGOOD	1809–1813
RENSSELAER HAVENS	1813–1819
JONATHAN THOMPSON	1819–1823
WILLIAM COUCH	1823–1826
BENJAMIN DE FOREST	1826–1829
JOHN C. HALSEY	1829–1836
WILLIAM COUCH	1836–1844
AUGUSTUS WHITLOCK	1844–1862
ABNER L. ELY	1862–1871
JOHN L. LUDLAM	1871–1877
FREDERICK W. DOWNER	1877–1882
SHEPHERD KNAPP	1882–1892
CHARLES A. MILLER	1892–1898
WILLIAM D. BARBOUR	1898–

APPENDIX I

CLERKS OF THE BOARD OF TRUSTEES

JOHN R. MURRAY	1809–1812
JOHN ADAMS	1812–1818
STEPHEN LOCKWOOD	1818–1825
MOSES ALLEN	1825–1827
LOCKWOOD DE FOREST	1827–1828
JOHN C. HALSEY	1828–1829
WILLIAM COUCH	1829–1831
SHEPHERD KNAPP	1831–1833
WILLIAM COUCH	1833–1836
HENRY H. SCHIEFFELIN	1836–1841
THOMAS EGLESTON	1841–1861
IRA BLISS	1861–1862
JOHN M. NIXON	1862–1869
FREDERICK W. DOWNER	1869–1870
HENRY PARISH	1870–1871
FREDERICK W. DOWNER	1871–1876
DANIEL J. HOLDEN	1876–1894
EUGENE SMITH	1894–

APPENDIX J

SUPERINTENDENTS OF THE SUNDAY-SCHOOL

B. J. Seward . . . . 1827–?
Erastus Ellsworth 1832–1833
Albert Woodruff 1833
B. J. Seward 1833–1834
Daniel Lord, Jr. 1834–1837
Horace Holden 1837–1838
Moses Allen 1838–1840
Dr. Spring . . . . 1840–?
Abner L. Ely 1846–1850
Thomas Davenport 1850–1851
Abner L. Ely . . . . 1851–1854 [?]

(School discontinued 1854–Nov., 1856)

Horace Holden 1856–1862
Algernon Sidney Sullivan . . . . . . ?
Hamilton Odell 1869–1876
Arthur W. Parsons . . . . ?
Ezra M. Kingsley . . . . 1880 [?]–1881
Hamilton Odell (ad interim) 1881
Walter Squires (ad interim) 1881
Albert R. Ledoux 1882–1892
L. Duncan Bulkley 1892–1896
Alfred E. Marling 1896–1903
William V. V. Hayes 1903–

APPENDIX K

SEXTONS OF THE BRICK CHURCH

Epenetus Smith	1809–1814
John G. Yonge	1814–1820
Henry Spies	1820–1830
James S. Hull	1831–1873
Nathaniel H. Hodgson	1873–1897
Charles R. Culyer *	1894–

* Mr. Culyer had been sexton of the old Church of the Covenant, 1861–1894.

APPENDIX L

PASTORS OF THE CHURCH OF THE COVENANT

GEORGE L. PRENTISS, ...	1862–1873
MARVIN R. VINCENT, ...	1873–1888
JAMES HALL MCILVAINE, ...	1888–1894
GEORGE S. WEBSTER, Associate Pastor . . .	1890–1894

APPENDIX M

ELDERS OF THE CHURCH OF THE COVENANT

Gurdon Buck	1862–1877†
Hermon Griffin	1862–1865†
Frederick G. Burnham	1862–1865*
Henry D. Noyes	1865–1894
John P. Crosby	1865–1876†
Alfred C. Post	1866–1886†
M. M. Backus	1866–1886*
Wm. E. Dodge	1868–1883†
Thos. Denny	1868–1874†
Benj. F. Butler	1868–1874*
W. H. H. Moore	1868–1894
Chas. T. White	1874–1890†
L. N. Lovell	1875–1880*
J. C. Cady	1876–1894
W. W. Hoppin	1877–1894
S. J. Storrs	1880–1892†
Theron G. Strong	1883–1894
Thos. Greenleaf	1886–1890‡
J. M. Fairchild	1886–1888‡
St. John Roosa	1887–1888‡
Chas. O. Kimball	1890–1894
Alfred E. Marling	1890–1894
D. H. Wiesner	1890–1894‡

* Removed from the city.   † Died.   ‡ Transferred to other churches.

APPENDIX N

DEACONS OF THE CHURCH OF THE COVENANT

J. C. Cady	1866–1876
T. B. Hidden	1866–1874
E. P. Griffin	1866–1870
Chas. O. Kimball	1868–1890
Chas. T. White	1868–1874
L. N. Lovell	1868–1874
W. W. Hoppin	1868–1877
Wm. R. Sheffield	1868–1869
Henry A. Crosby	1868–1882
George B. Bonney	1871–1882
S. J. Storrs	1874–1880
R. G. Bushnell	1876–1882
John Keeler	1881–1894
H. G. Starin	1881–1883
T. G. Strong	1881–1883
W. O. Curtis	1881–1894
Wm. Seward	1882–1894
Lucius Beers	1886–1892
C. S. McKay	1886–1894
D. H. Wiesner	1886–1894
W. D. Moore	1890–1894
Chas. W. McAlpin	1890–1894
G. B. Hoppin	1893–1894
Henry N. Corwith	1894

APPENDIX O

TRUSTEES OF THE CHURCH OF THE COVENANT

532

APPENDIX P

ORIGINAL MEMBERSHIP OF THE CHURCH OF THE COVENANT

ABBOT, REBECCA S.,
APPLETON, MALVINA W.,
ASPINWALL, LOUISA E.,
BUCK, GURDON,
BUCK, HENRIETTA E.,
BUCK, AMELIA H.,
BUCK, SUSAN M.,
BURGER, MARY,
BURGER, SARAH AUGUSTA,
BURGER, SOPHIA,
BUTLER, WILLIAM ALLEN,
BUTLER, MARY R.,
BUTLER, ELIZA OGDEN,
BUTLER, LYDIA ALLEN,
BUTLER, BENJAMIN F.,
BUTLER, ELLEN G.,
BUTLER, CHARLES,
BUTLER, ELIZA A.,
BUTLER, EMILY OGDEN,
BUTLER, ELIZA A.,
BETTS, GEORGE F.,
BETTS, ELLEN P.,
BLEECKER, F. MATILDA,
BRONSON, ANNA E.,
BURNHAM, FREDERICK G.,
CADY, J. CLEVELAND,
CANNON, MARY B.,
CORNING, JANE B.,
CURTIS, EDWIN,
CURTIS, MARY,
CURTIS, REBECCA,
CURTIS, PHEBE ELIZA,
CURTIS, WILLIAM O.,

DE FOREST, MARGARET,
DONAGHE, JAMES,
DONAGHE, ANTOINETTE,
DONAGHE, W. R.,
GRIFFIN, HERMON,
GRIFFIN, LOUISA G.,
GRIFFIN, EDWARD P.,
JUDD, DAVID W.,
KETCHAM, ENOCH,
KETCHAM, E. R. VAN A.,
KIMBALL, HORACE E.,
KIMBALL, HORACE,
KIMBALL, MARY D.,
LEEDS, CATHARINE G.,
LEEDS, MARY ELIZA,
LEONARD, CHARLES H.,
LEONARD, ELIZABETH,
LOCKWOOD, ROE,
LOCKWOOD, JULIA G.,
LOCKWOOD, LOUISA M.,
LOCKWOOD, ELIZABETH R.,
LORD, DANIEL D.,
LORD, MARY H.,
McCURDY, ROBERT H.,
McCURDY, GERTRUDE M.,
McCURDY, ROBERT WOLCOTT,
McCURDY, SARAH LORD,
MERRITT, FRANCES,
NOYES, WILLIAM CURTIS,
NOYES, JULIA F.,
NOYES, EMILY C.,
PRENTISS, ELIZABETH,
QUICK, A. J.,

533

RHINELANDER, FRANCES D.,
SCHERMERHORN, CATHARINE G.,
SCHERMERHORN, LOUISA N.,
SIMS, ELIZABETH,
SKINNER, FRANCES L.,
SKINNER, MARY D.,
SKINNER, HELEN,
SMITH, ELIZABETH L.,
WOOLSEY, ELIZA J.,

WOOLSEY, ABBEY H.,
WOOLSEY, GEORGIANA M.,
WOOLSEY, JANE S.,
WOOLSEY, CHARLES W.,
WOOLSEY, THEODORE B.,
WOOLSEY, CATHARINE CECIL,
WOODWORTH, D. AUSTIN,
WOODWORTH, CAROLINE REED.

APPENDIX Q

PASTORS OF THE BRICK CHURCH MISSION, AND OF ITS SUCCESSOR, CHRIST PRESBYTERIAN CHURCH

JOHN KIMBALL 1859–1862
A. E. RULIFSON 1862–1864
GOVELLO B. BELL 1865–1867
JOSEPH J. LAMPE (installed, 1888*) 1867–1895
RICHARD R. WIGHTMAN 1897–1900
JAMES M. FARR 1901–

* When the chapel became Christ Church. From that time all the pastors were installed.

APPENDIX R

PASTORS OF THE COVENANT CHAPEL, AND OF ITS SUCCESSOR, THE CHURCH OF THE COVENANT

HOWARD A. TALBOT	1875–1881
HENRY T. MCEWEN	1881–1887
EDWIN E. ROGERS	1887–1889
GEORGE S. WEBSTER (installed*)	1890–

* In 1890 as associate of Dr. McIlvaine in the old Church of the Covenant, and again in 1894 as pastor of the present Church of the Covenant.

APPENDIX S

NAMES OF PEW-OWNERS IN 1853,

WHO, AT A CONGREGATIONAL MEETING ON FEBRUARY 1ST OF THAT
YEAR, REQUESTED THE BOARD OF TRUSTEES "TO TAKE THE NECES-
SARY STEPS TO DISPOSE OF THEIR CHURCH PROPERTY IN THE SECOND
WARD, WITH A VIEW TO SECURE A NEW LOCATION BETTER
SUITED TO THE PRESENT WANTS OF THE PEOPLE."

NAMES OF OWNERS	NOS. OF PEWS
Horace Holden	47 and 48
Drake Mills	6
Andrew Whitlock	14 and 40
Wm. H. de Forest	131
Russell Dart	122
Moses Allen	89 and 62
Abner L. Ely	11
T. and J. S. Davenport	65
John C. Tucker	98
Mary Murray	30
William Couch	8 and 54
Peter Naylor	100
Daniel Lord	16 and 19
Paul Spofford	86
S. Robbins	127
Gardiner Spring	134
Wm. H. Bonnett	83
Chas. Mills	64
Mrs. P. Bonnett	55
Mrs. G. E. van Desburgh	84
Robt. Adams	63
Estate of J. C. Halsey, dec'd	81
Moses A. Hoppock	7
Estate of Wm. Adee, dec'd.	37
D. Thompson	44
J. B. Varnum	104
Estate of Lucretia Morrell, dec'd	78
Thos. Egleston	136

NAMES OF OWNERS	NOS. OF PEWS
Dan. Bonnett	23
S. Knapp, by G. Lee Knapp, Atty.	85, 87, 139
Eliza Downer	130
Estate of A. Girard, dec'd.	10
Estate of S. Fulton, dec'd	46
Daniel H. Magee	21
Estate of Ellis Potter, dec'd.	41
George J. Cornell	9
John McComb	95
Sam'l Marsh	56
J. Woodhead	88
Jas. W. Mills, for Mrs. Mills	93
Estate of Mrs. Eliza Archer, dec'd.	68
Maria McElwain	2
G. R. Downing	133
M. Allison	126
John P. Tredwell	59 and 60
R. Cheeseborough	15
Daniel Parish	97
Catherine McCollick	70, gallery
Estate of P. Judson, dec'd.	76
Joseph Bartlett	13, gallery
Estate of P. Hawes, dec'd	50
R. J. Hutchinson	92
Estate of Eli Hart, dec'd	101
E. C. Delavan	52
John R. Davison	106
A. P. Cummings	103
Daniel Oakley	96
Calvin H. Merry	111
Joseph Kernochon	135
John West	141
Geo. Smith	64, gallery
Estate of Jonas Addams	108
Eli Goodwin	45
John Saxton	79
B. K. Hobart	115

APPENDIX T

"FORM OF ADMISSION INTO THE BRICK PRESBYTERIAN CHURCH,"

RECORDED IN THE SESSION MINUTES, APRIL 3D, 1829, AS THE "PROFESSION AND COVENANT," IN USE IN THE CHURCH, BUT NEVER BEFORE ENTERED ON THE MINUTES.

You have presented yourselves in this public manner, before God, to dedicate yourselves to his service, and to incorporate yourselves with his visible people. You are about to profess supreme love to God, sincere contrition for all your sins, and faith unfeigned in the Lord Jesus Christ. [Relying on the strength of divine grace, you are about to enter into a solemn covenant to receive the Father, Son, and Holy Ghost as they are offered in the gospel, and to walk in all the commandments and ordinances of the Lord blameless.] * We trust you have well considered the nature of these professions and engagements. The transaction is solemn, and will be attended with eternal consequences. God and holy angels are witnesses. Your vows will be recorded in heaven, to be exhibited on your trial at the last day.

Yet be not overwhelmed with these reflections. *In the name of Christ* you may come boldly to the God of grace, and if you have sincere desires to be his, may venture thus unalterably to commit yourselves, and trust in him for strength to perform your vows.

Attend now to the Profession and Covenant.

In this public manner you do humbly confess and bewail the original and total depravity of your nature, the past enmity of your heart against God, the unbelief which has led you to reject a Saviour, and the manifold transgressions of your lives:—all which sins you do condemn and in your purpose forever renounce.

And now in the presence of God, his holy angels, and this assembly, you do, so far as you know your own hearts, solemnly avouch the Lord Jehovah to be your God and Portion and the object of your supreme love and delight; the Lord Jesus Christ to be your Saviour from sin and death, your Prophet to instruct you, your Priest to atone and intercede

* All passages in brackets are omitted in a manuscript copy in the hand-writing of Dr. Spring.

for you [your Righteousness to justify you], your King to rule, protect, and enrich you; and the Holy Ghost to be your Sanctifier, Comforter, and Guide, to whom only you look for light, holiness, and peace.

To this Triune God, Father, Son, and Holy Ghost, you do now without reserve give yourselves away in a Covenant never to be revoked, to be his willing servants forever, to observe all his commandments and ordinances, in the sanctuary, in the family, and in the closet. You do also bind yourselves by covenant to this church, to watch over us in the Lord, to seek our peace and edification, and to submit to the government and discipline * of the gospel as here administered. This you severally profess and engage.

(The ordinance of baptism, if not previously received, will here be administered.)

In consequence of these professions and promises, we † affectionately receive you as members of this church and in the name of Christ declare you entitled to all its visible privileges. [We welcome you to this fellowship with us in the blessings of the gospel, and on our part engage to watch over you and seek your edification as long as you shall continue among us. Should you have occasion to remove, it will be your duty to seek, and ours to grant, a recommendation to another church, for hereafter you cannot withdraw from the watch and communion of the saints without a breach of covenant. And now, beloved in the Lord,] ‡ let it be impressed on your minds that you have entered into solemn relations which you can never renounce, and from which you can never escape. Wherever you are, whether continuing among us or seeking the same privileges elsewhere, these vows will remain. § They will follow you to the Bar of God; and in whatever world you may be fixed, will abide on you to eternity. You can never again be as you have been. You have unalterably committed yourselves, and henceforth *must* be the servants of God. Hereafter the eyes of the world will be upon you; and as you conduct yourselves, so religion will be honored or disgraced. If you walk worthy of your profession, you will be a credit and a comfort to us; but if it be otherwise, you will be to us a grief of heart and a vexation.

"But, beloved,|| we are persuaded better things of you, and things

---

* In the MS. of Dr. Spring this reads "government, discipline, and ministrations."

† In the MS. of Dr. Spring this continues, "we thus publicly declare you to be members of this church and entitled to all its visible privileges."

‡ In place of the bracketed words the MS. of Dr. Spring has, "and while we thus welcome you to this fellowship with us in the blessing of the gospel."

§ In the MS. of Dr. Spring the following sentence is here added, "they will bind you in whatsoever part of the earth you dwell."

|| Dr. Spring herein inserts, in the Lord.

that accompany salvation, though we thus speak." May the Lord support and guide you through a transitory life, and after this warfare is accomplished, receive you and us to that blessed Church where our love shall be forever perfect and our joy forever full. Amen.

With slight verbal changes and omissions this form was still in use in 1869.

APPENDIX U

ORDER OF BAPTISM OF CHILDREN, 1866

In presenting this child to God in baptism, you avouch the Lord Jehovah to be your God, the Lord Jesus Christ to be your Redeemer, and the Holy Ghost to be your Sanctifier. You do hereby personally covenant, if God spare the life of this child, to teach it to read his Holy Word, to pray with it, to pray for it, and to teach it to pray; to instruct it in the principles of our holy religion, an excellent summary of which you will find in the catechisms of the Westminster Assembly and the Confession of Faith of the Presbyterian Church; to walk before it in all the ordinances of the gospel; and by the strength of divine grace, to train it up in the nurture and admonition of the Lord. This you severally covenant and promise.

Then follows the prayer and the baptism.

APPENDIX V

ORDER OF THE COMMUNION SERVICE, 1875

1. At the close of the sermon the collection for the poor of the church shall be taken up.

2. After the collection shall have been received, the minister shall announce in substance that, "this church is now about to celebrate the Sacrament of the Lord's Supper, and that a cordial invitation is extended to all persons in good standing in other evangelical churches to remain and take part in this service." And he shall also add that if any communicants are not now provided with seats on the floor of the church, they are requested to find places for themselves at the close of the singing of the following hymn.

3. When the singing shall have commenced, the two elders who are to sit on either side of the minister during the service shall immediately remove the cloth from the table,* folding it carefully and placing it out of sight upon the bench in front of the pews. They shall then resume their former seats.†

4. Before the close of the hymn, the minister shall descend from the pulpit and take his seat at the table: at the same time the two elders who are to sit beside him shall also take their seats.

5. The minister shall make an address, if he shall think proper, and then commence the service by quoting the words of institution: "Our Lord, on that same night in which he was betrayed, took bread, and when he had given thanks he brake it and gave it to his disciples": and he shall add, "Let us, in imitation of his example, give thanks." He shall then offer prayer.

6. Immediately after the close of the prayer those elders and deacons who are to officiate at the table shall take their places, standing in front of it while the minister breaks the bread. ‡

7. When the bread is broken, the minister shall say: "When our Lord had broken the bread, he gave it to his disciples, as I, ministering

---

* Until the service a large table-cloth entirely covered the table with all that stood upon it. This custom continued till 1895.

† It was customary on Communion Sunday for all the elders and deacons to sit together in the "amen" pews.

‡ The bread was in large loaves, so cut that they could be readily broken and placed in the plates.

543

in his name, give this bread to you, a professed disciple of Jesus Christ: 'Take, eat: this is my body which is broken for you; this do in remembrance of me.'" While repeating this passage, he shall first present the bread to the two elders sitting beside him, and shall then distribute the plates among the officiating elders and deacons, who shall forthwith pass the bread to the congregation—the elder or deacon standing at the extreme right of the minister first offering it to him.

8. After the distribution of the bread the minister shall say: "If any communicants have been omitted in the distribution of the bread, they will please signify it by rising." If any shall rise on either side, the bread shall be served to them by the elder sitting on that side of the minister. If none shall rise, the two elders who sit beside the minister shall distribute the bread to the other elders and deacons, and shall then immediately remove the bread from the table * and resume their places.

9. The minister shall then offer a prayer before dispensing the cup, and immediately upon the close of the prayer the officiating elders and deacons shall resume their places before the table, standing while the minister pours out the wine.

10. The minister shall then dispense the cup to the two elders who sit beside him, and then pass the same to the officiating elders and deacons, saying, "After the same manner, also, he took the cup, when he had supped, saying, 'This cup is the New Testament in my blood: this do as oft as ye drink it in remembrance of me. For as often as ye eat this bread and drink this cup, ye do show the Lord's death till he come.'" Upon receiving the cup, the officiating elders and deacons shall pass it to the congregation, the elder or deacon standing on the extreme left of the minister first offering it to him.

11. After the dispensation of the cup, the same forms shall be observed which followed the distribution of the bread.

12. The minister shall then, if he think fit, make another address, and give out the concluding hymn. After the hymn, he shall pronounce the following benediction (Hebrews 13 : 20, 21): "Now the God of peace that brought again from the dead our Lord Jesus, that great Shepherd of the sheep, through the blood of the everlasting covenant, make you perfect in every good work to do his will, working in you that which is well pleasing in his sight, to whom be glory for ever and ever. Amen."

* Both the large platters and the plates were placed on the bench in front of the pews. This custom was discontinued in 1895.

APPENDIX W

CONSTITUTION OF THE BRICK CHURCH SUNDAY-SCHOOL, 1833

PREAMBLE

The Teachers and Conductors of Sunday-school No. 3, in New York, would feel that everything in the revealed purposes of God, everything in his promises, all indications of his providence, invite and urge us on in the work in which we are engaged. The millions that are famishing for want of the Bread of Life in heathen lands, and the urgent demand for intelligent and efficient services in the cause of Christ in our own country, admonish us that there is pressing need of unremitting labor in training the young for the work of the Lord. Be this, then, the teachers' aim: "*To win souls to Jesus Christ; and to prepare them for usefulness in his kingdom.*"

May the Great Head of the Church fit us for the responsible duties we have assumed, and keep us in the observance of the following

CONSTITUTION

I

This school shall consist of

1st. A Superintendent, whose duty it shall be to arrange the classes, preserve order, and to determine all questions that may occur between different teachers, and between teachers and their classes.

2d. An Assistant Superintendent, who shall ordinarily teach a Bible Class, and take the place of the Superintendent when he is absent.

3d. A Female Superintendent, who shall aid in the government of the School.

4th. A Librarian, who shall supply the School from time to time with catalogues of the books in the Library, deliver books to the teachers according to the rules of the school, keep an accurate account of the volumes received and issued from the Library, and hold himself responsible for books not accounted for.

5th. A Secretary, who shall keep full and accurate records of the proceedings of the School, aggregate quarterly returns of which shall be approved in teachers' meeting and read to the School.

6th. Teachers, who shall be punctual in attendance, faithful in the study of the lessons, prompt in visiting absentees, and laborious in endeavors to enlighten the minds and improve the hearts of the youth committed to their care.

7th. Scholars, who shall be punctual, obedient, and studious during school hours, and silent and respectful in the house of God.

II

The officers of this School shall be chosen by ballot once in each year at a teachers' meeting in the month of April, and oftener if need be; and the teachers shall be appointed by the Superintendent upon every election of that officer.

III

Books shall be furnished upon one Sabbath to the male department, and upon the succeeding Sabbath to the female department, alternately; deliverable in the afternoon, upon condition of punctuality and the safe return of the previous volume in the morning. Teachers shall make a list of the books desired for their scholars, and be responsible for them to the School.

IV

This Constitution may be amended by a vote of two-thirds of the members present in teachers' meeting.

The SUPERINTENDENT expects of the TEACHERS,

1st. That they will be in their seats five minutes before the hour of opening, ready to greet their scholars as they appear, approbating punctuality and reproving delinquency, and that they will not unnecessarily leave their seats during school hours.

2d. That they will always accompany their classes to the door of the church, maintaining order among the scholars, and in cases of necessary absence from the school, a teacher will feel it to be his [or her] duty to provide a substitute.

3d. He still further expects that at the ringing of the bell there will always be perfect silence throughout the School, and that this silence will prevail during the opening and closing exercises of the School.

4th. In conclusion, he expects no idleness in any class for a moment, but, on the contrary, that teachers will be prompt, faithful, and punctual in everything relating to their classes, and that they will insist upon the same in every one of their scholars.

APPENDIX X

SUPREME COURT ORDER

At a special term of the Supreme Court, held at the City Hall, of the City of New York, on the fifteenth day of February, one thousand eight hundred and fifty-three.

Present, Henry P. Edwards, Justice.

In the matter of the Petition of the Corporation of the Brick Presbyterian Church, in the City of New York, to sell their church property in the Second Ward.

On reading and filing the petition of the Corporation of the Brick Presbyterian Church, in the City of New York, under the corporate seal, and duly verified by the oath of William Couch, President of the Board of Trustees of said Corporation, and on motion of Mr. Horace Holden, of counsel for said petitioners,

It is ordered, that the said petitioners be, and they are hereby authorized to sell and convey all their church property, lands, and tenements, situate in the Second Ward of the City of New York, bounded by Park Row, Beekman Street, Nassau Street, and Spruce Street, and either at public or private sale, subject to the conditions and restrictions contained in the grant, under which they hold the same, and to execute, to the purchaser or purchasers thereof, good and sufficient conveyances therefor; and to apply the proceeds of such sale to the purchase of other lands in said city, and to the erection of a new church edifice thereon, agreeably to the prayer of the said petition; but the purchaser or purchasers thereof shall not be required, or bound to see to the application of the purchase moneys, to any of the purposes specified in said petition.

RICHARD B. CONNOLLY, *Clerk.*

APPENDIX Y

RULES FOR THE CARE AND MANAGEMENT OF THE CHRIST CHURCH MEMORIAL BUILDINGS AND THE WORK CARRIED ON IN CONNECTION THEREWITH

It is expressly understood that the following plan shall not apply to such of the internal affairs of Christ Church as are legally under the control of its session or trustees nor to the internal affairs of the Sick Children's Aid Society, including its finances, constitution and election of officers.

1.—THE COMMITTEE

ITS PURPOSE AND NAME

The general control and management of Christ Church Memorial Buildings and of all activities carried on in the Church House, shall be in the hands of a Committee to be known as the *Christ Church Memorial Buildings Committee*, but the session of the Brick Church in respect to spiritual matters and the board of trustees in respect to other matters may modify, change or annul the action of the Committee.

2.—CONSTITUTION OF THE COMMITTEE

(a) *Membership.* The Committee shall consist of the following persons: The pastors of the Brick Church and of Christ Church; an elder from the Brick Church and one from Christ Church appointed by their respective sessions; the superintendent of the Christ Church Sunday-school, who shall be appointed by the session of the Brick Church; the presidents of the Christ Church Mens' Club, the Boys' Club, the Babcock Club, the Van Dyke Club, the Junior Department and the Sick Children's Aid Society; the general treasurer (hereinafter provided for) and the treasurer of the Brick Church, and the secretary of the Committee.

(b) *Advisory Members:* The pastor of the Church of the Covenant and the assistant ministers of the Brick Church and of Christ Church shall be entitled to attend the meetings and take part in the discussions of the Committee but without a vote. (This, however, does not exclude them from being members in full of the Committee by virtue of some other office.)

(c) *Occasional Representation:* Representatives of organizations or departments of work in Christ Church House, not directly represented on the Committee, may be present by invitation while business of special concern to them is under discussion. Such delegates shall not, however, have voting power.

(d) *Enlargement of the Committee:* The Committee shall have power from time to time to add to its membership representatives of such organizations or departments of the work in Christ Church House as shall have gained sufficient importance to warrant representation, and to drop from its membership officers of any society which has ceased to be active in the work under the supervision of this Committee.

3.—ORGANIZATION OF THE COMMITTEE

(a) *The officers of the Committee* shall be a Chairman, the General Treasurer, and a Secretary.

The Chairman shall be elected by the Committee. He shall preside at Committee meetings, and shall have general supervision over the whole work of the Church House, acting as the executive officer for the Committee. The first Chairman shall be the pastor of Christ Church.

The General Treasurer shall be appointed by the session of the Brick Church. He shall receive all funds contributed by the Brick Church or coming from other sources for the general work. Appropriations made by the Committee to the several organizations and departments shall be paid by him to the respective treasurers, whose accounts he shall annually audit. He shall, under the direction of the Committee, make the general payments connected with the work, and shall have charge of the internal maintenance of the buildings. No appropriation or expenditure of money shall be made, however, without the approval of the General Treasurer. He shall submit his accounts annually to the session and trustees of the Brick Church.

The Secretary shall be elected by the Committee either from among or from outside of its members. It shall be his duty to preside at meetings in the absence of the chairman, to keep the minutes of all meetings, to send notices of meetings and to perform the duties usual to the office.

(b) *Meetings:* The Committee shall meet regularly once a month from October to May, and at other times upon call of the chairman or of any three members.

(c) *Quorum:* Five regular members shall constitute a quorum.

4.—Duties and Powers

(a) *Management and use of Buildings:* The Committee shall manage the Memorial Buildings and shall determine and prescribe the use of the various parts thereof. The treasurer of the Brick Church and the general treasurer, together with the pastor of Crist Church and the superintendent of Christ Church Sunday-school shall be a Special Sub-Committee on maintenance of the buildings and the employment of house servants, and shall report to the general Committee.

(b) *Control of Activities:* The Committee shall exercise general control over the various activities carried on in the Memorial Buildings. It shall receive reports from the different organizations and departments, shall receive and act upon suggestions regarding the work and shall make such recommendations or regulations as may be necessary. The Committee shall in every way seek to promote the harmony and efficiency of the work as a whole. The Committee shall appoint or approve the appointment of the presidents of the various departments of the work, and shall engage all paid workers connected therewith, except as otherwise provided for herein or by the Committee. All *Constitutions* or rules of management of the different departments and organizations shall be subject to the approval of the Committee. *Details of management* shall be left to the proper officers of the different departments and organizations, but the Committee shall have power to veto any forms of activity and to prescribe such activities as in its judgment are necessary, or advisable.

(c) *Estimates:* Prior to the December meeting in each year there shall be presented to the Committee by the heads of departments and organizations and by the general treasurer estimates of the sums of money needed for the ensuing year. The Committee shall examine these estimates together with such estimate as shall be presented on the part of Christ Church, and on the basis of them prepare a general budget which shall be submitted to the session of the Brick Church.

(d) *Expenditures:* The Committee, from the money received by the general treasurer shall make appropriations to the various departments and organizations, and shall authorize expenditures for the internal maintenance and repair of the buildings and for the salaries of officials and employees except the pastor of Christ Church.

(e) *Reports:* The Committee shall at any time make reports to the session and board of trustees of the Brick Church at their requests respectively.

INDEX

INDEX

A

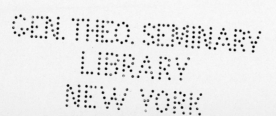

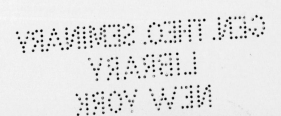